EXPLORING
CORPORATE
STRATEGY
2nd edition

EXPLORING CORPORATE STRATEGY

2nd edition

GERRY JOHNSON

Cranfield School of Management

KEVAN SCHOLES

Sheffield Business School

Prentice Hall

New York   London   Toronto   Sydney   Tokyo

First published 1988 by
Prentice Hall International (UK) Ltd,
66 Wood Lane End, Hemel Hempstead,
Hertfordshire, HP2 4RG
A division of
Simon & Schuster International Group

Printed and bound in Great Britain at the
University Press, Cambridge.

British Library Cataloguing in Publication Data

Johnson, Gerry
Exploring corporate strategy. – 2nd edn.
1. Corporate planning
I. Title   II. Scholes, Kevan
658.4'012   HD30.28

ISBN 0–13–296393–0

2 3 4 5   92 91 90 89 88

ISBN 0-13-296393-0

CONTENTS

ILLUSTRATIONS

FIGURES

TABLES

PREFACE

The four years which have passed since our first edition was published has seen some important and interesting developments which impinge on the subject of Corporate Strategy, and the ways in which it is viewed and practised in both private and public sector organisations. There has been a growing recognition of the importance of the subject in many more educational programmes at undergraduate, postgraduate and professional levels, as well as a major surge of interest in post experience management development in the area. Since we argued in the first edition that a greater strategic awareness was necessary amongst all levels of managers, these are developments which we welcome.

In revising this book we have tried to ensure that we reflect the changing views, attitudes and approaches to Corporate Strategy but that we do this within the framework and style of the first edition, which many of you have kindly complimented us on. We hope we have achieved this and that you continue to find *Exploring Corporate Strategy* a useful and stimulating text. Much of its content has changed – and this is explained more fully below – but the purpose of the book remains the same: to develop a greater capability for strategic thinking amongst managers and potential managers.

We began the first edition by quoting the Group Corporate Planner of one of the UK's biggest companies explaining that the main problem he faced was to get managers to understand that it was their responsibility to formulate strategy:

> This is my biggest difficulty. First, because they seem to think it's someone else's responsibility and, second, because they think there is some set of techniques which is going to create strategy for the company. I try to get them to understand that if the managers of the business aren't responsible for strategy, then no-one is: and that they already have – or can easily get – any techniques that are necessary. The problem is the inability of managers to think strategically.

This book aims to provide readers with an understanding of:

- What corporate strategy is.
- Why strategic decisions are important.
- Approaches to formulating strategy.

It is not a book of corporate planning techniques but rather builds on the practice of good strategic management, as researchers and practitioners in the area understand it. It is a book primarily intended for students of strategy on undergraduate, diploma and masters courses in universities and colleges; students on courses with titles such as Corporate Strategy, Business Policy, Strategic Management, Organisational Policy,

Corporate Policy and so on. However, we know that many such students are already managers anyway who are undertaking part-time study: so this book is written with the manager and the potential manager in mind.

Traditionally the study of corporate strategy in organisations has been taught using intensive case study programmes. There remain teachers who argue that there can be no substitute for such an intensive case programme. At the other extreme there is a growing school of thought which argues that the only reason cases were used was that there was an insufficient research base to the problems of strategy resulting in a lack of theoretical underpinning. They argue that since the 1960s the strides made in research and the development of theory make such intensive case programmes redundant. It seems to us that this is a fruitless division of opinion probably rooted in the academic traditions of those involved, rather than a considered view of the needs of students. The position taken here is that case work, or appropriate experiential learning, is of great benefit in the study of strategy for it allows students both to apply concepts and theories and – just as important – to build their own. However, it is also the case that the growing body of research and theory can be of great help in stimulating a deeper understanding of strategic problems and strategic management. Our approach builds in substantial parts of such research and theory and encourages readers to refer to more: but we also assume that readers will have the opportunity to deal with strategic problems through such means as case study work or projects or, if they are practising managers, through their involvement in their own organisations. Our view in this respect is exactly the same as the writers of a medical or engineering text and we encourage readers to take the same view: it is that good theory helps good practice, but that an understanding of the theory without an understanding of the practice is very dangerous – particularly if you are dealing with a patient, a bridge or, as with this book, organisations.

Strategic management is a responsibility of *all managers*, and what is more, a responsibility that is becoming more and more important. It is not sufficient for a manager to think of management in some operational or functional context, simply to know his piece of the jigsaw well and trust that others know theirs equally as well. Modern organisations exist in a complex environment with an increasing demand for fast and effective strategic responses. The very least that a manager requires is to understand how his bit of the jigsaw fits into the rest in the context of the strategic problems and direction of the organisation. If he does not, then the effectiveness of strategic management, and particularly the implementation of strategy, can be severely impaired.

In preparing this second edition we have tried to bear in mind the needs of the manager in understanding strategic problems in many different organisations. In so doing, we have developed further some of the themes running through the first edition.

The text more explicitly develops the theme, introduced in the first edition, that strategy and the management of strategy can be thought of in at least two rather different ways. First it can be seen as a matter of essentially *economic analysis and planning*. And second it can be seen as a matter of *organisational decision making* within a *social, political, and cultural process*. Both these aspects of strategic management are relevant to the study of strategy and the text incorporates both. For example, one of the themes running through the the book is the importance of a clear analysis of the strategic situation facing the organisation and a rational assessment of the future options available to it. In considering such issues, the book includes, for example, discussion of the value of environmental audits, structural and strategic group analysis of competitive environments, the relevance of experience curve concepts, value chain analysis, life cycle models of strategic analysis and choice, and the findings of those researchers who have tried to understand the relationship between strategic positioning of organisations and financial performance. In short, one of the themes is that the employment of rational models of analysis and choice in organisations is important to strategic management.

There is also a growing expectation that managers will be able to take decisions about change and implement change with a great deal more assurance and skill than hitherto. Yet the evidence is that managers are not good at handling change, particularly of the magnitude involved with strategic change. Strategic management cannot be developed by providing 'a bag of management techniques'; it is also to do with developing in managers a sensitivity to an increasingly turbulent environment, together with an understanding of the culture of the organisation in which they work and the means whereby they can manage change within that culture. Herein lies one of the fundamental problems of strategic management. The environment that organisations face is increasingly turbulent, so the need for management sensitivity to change is growing. Yet the values, expectations and assumptions of members of an organisation working within a particular culture can be a very constraining and conservative influence on the understanding of strategic problems and the development of solutions. The first edition of the book contained within it an explicit recognition that it was important for managers to understand the processes of decision making in organisations within a social and political context. This second edition develops this theme further, it draws on the growing amount of research and literature on decision making processes within a political and cultural context, considers explicitly how such influences can be analysed and also what mechanisms exist for managing strategic change within such systems. There is, therefore, an expectation that readers will seek to reconcile 'scientific management' about the complex issues of strategy with an understanding of the human and social side of management. Whilst this is a demanding task, it is the challenge of the effective management of strategy and a fundamental task of managers in today's organisations.

As in the first edition, the book also recognises that strategic management is as relevant to the public sector and to not-for-profit organisations as it is to the private sector of industry and commerce. We have included sections which discuss this specifically, and also a good many references, examples and illustrations of the application of strategic management concepts to the public sector.

The book, whilst using up-to-date theory and research, is not primarily an academic treatise, but a book for managers and those who intend to be managers: so a few words about its style are in order. The reader will find that throughout the book there are 'Illustrations' which enlarge upon or give case material related to a point in the text. These illustrations are all taken from actual incidents reported in the press, in journals, from case studies, or from the authors' personal experience and, wherever possible, the organisation or individuals involved are named. Most of these illustrations are based in UK organisations.

As far as terminology is concerned, we have tried to avoid some of the pitfalls of jargon that management writers often fall into: if we have failed to do so on occasions then it is not for the want of trying. The word 'organisation' has been used most frequently but there are times when 'company', 'enterprise' or 'firm' is used: these tend to be where commercial operations are being discussed but it does not mean that the discussion only relates to the private sector. We have also chosen not to make dogmatic distinctions between descriptions of the subject of study such as 'corporate strategy', 'business policy', 'strategic management' and so on.

The structure of the book is explained in some detail in Chapter 1. However, it might be useful to explain the basic structure of the book here and also to outline some of the structural changes from the first edition. The book is in four parts. Part I comprises an introduction to corporate strategy, first in terms of its characteristics, and the elements of strategic management, (Chapter 1) and then in terms of how strategic decisions actually come about in organisations (Chapter 2). Since the second edition more fully examines the relationship between organisational strategy and culture, Chapter 2 introduces this theme rather more specifically than in the first edition. Part II of the book is concerned with Strategic Analysis. The main change here from the first edition is that we have combined the old Chapters 5 and 6 into a single Chapter 5, which examines the ways in which the expectations and objectives of stakeholders in organisations can be understood within the context of the political and cultural systems. As previously indicated, this part of the book also contains more explicit coverage of some more recent research and concepts in strategic management; in particular the influential work of Michael Porter, and structural, strategic, group and value chain analyses are discussed. Part III of the book is concerned with Strategic Choice and now consists of three chapters rather than two. Chapter 6 is a review of strategic options which organisations face; Chapter 7 introduces some principles of evaluation and provides general guidelines on the subject; Chapter 8 discusses some techniques of evaluation of specific options. Finally Part IV of the book is about strategy implementation. The main changes here from the first edition are the use of value chain ideas in resource planning (in Chapter 9) and a fuller consideration of cultural mechanisms for strategic change in Chapter 11.

There are those who have been particularly helpful in the development of this second edition and we would like to acknowledge our thanks to them. First, and most important, the current adoptors of the first edition provided us with many useful comments and suggestions over the last four years; it is not possible to list them all but we would like to extend our thanks to everyone who has made such comments. Second, we are working currently on a North American edition of the text in collaboration with Bob Sexty of the Memorial University of Newfoundland; Bob has been especially helpful in reviewing the first edition and suggesting changes for this second edition. We would also like to thank the Strategic Planning Institute for their valuable comments on Chapter 7 and for the many organisations that have given permission for us to use material related to their organisations in the illustrations in the book. We would also like to extend our thanks to John Heath for his help with the text and to Jenny Scholes, Christine Guest, and Manchester Business School's Central Office Services for their help in typing the manuscript.

Gerry Johnson
Kevan Scholes

Part I
INTRODUCTION

Chapter 1

CORPORATE STRATEGY

AN INTRODUCTION

In December 1986 Graham Day, the Chairman of the Rover Group had been in his post just eight months and was preparing to present the group corporate plan of the state owned corporation to the government. He faced a daunting task. Between 1952 and 1968 Austin, Morris, Leyland, Standard Triumph, Rover and Jaguar had been brought together to form the British Leyland Motor Corporation. By 1975 the Company was, effectively, nationalised and losing £75 million on the year. By 1980 and 1981 it was losing over £300 million. Attempts to turn around the situation had included the Ryder plan of 1974 and the rationalisation strategies of Michael Edwardes in the late 1970s and early 1980s. By November, 1986, redesignated the Rover Group, the corporation was registering its lowest ever share of the UK car market – 12.76%. The task Mr Day faced in arriving at a strategy for the business to take it forward profitably and be acceptable to the government provided him with a major challenge. Illustration 1.1 is an outline of some of the problems that Graham Day faced, some of the options he considered and the strategic plan which emerged.

The changes that had taken place for Rover had been dramatic and, it appeared, would continue to be so.[1] They were concerned with the future direction of the business as a whole: they were long term in nature and were bound to have far ranging implications on employment, the financing of the business and the types of product manufactured. They were, in short, major *strategic* decisions that had to be taken. All organisations are faced with the need to formulate strategies; they are not all faced with the problems of the Rover Group, but even the magnitude of Graham Day's problems are not so unusual when it comes to the formulation of strategy. This book deals with why reviews of strategic direction take place in organisations, why they are important, how such decisions are taken and some of the tools and techniques that managers can use to take such decisions. This chapter is an introduction and explanation of this theme and of the structure of the book as a whole. The chapter will draw on the Rover Group illustration for the purposes of discussion, and as the book progresses other such illustrations are used to help develop discussion.

This first chapter deals with the questions of what is meant by 'corporate strategy' and 'strategic management', why they are so important and what distinguishes them from other organisational decisions. In discussing these it will become clearer how the book deals with the subject.

One other point should be made before proceeding. The term 'corporate strategy' is used here for two main reasons. First, the book is concerned with strategy and strategic decisions in all types of organisation – small and large commercial enterprises as well as public services – and the work 'corporate' embraces them all. Second, because, as the term is used in this book (discussed more fully in Section 1.1.2), 'corporate strategy' denotes the most general level of strategy in an organisation and in this sense embraces other levels of strategy. Readers will undoubtedly come across, outside this book, terms such as: 'business policy', 'management policy', 'corporate policy' and 'strategic management', all of which deal with the same general area of study.

1.1 THE NATURE OF CORPORATE STRATEGY

Why are Rover's historical and future changes described as 'strategic' changes? What sorts of decision are strategic decisions, and what distinguishes these from other sorts

---

ILLUSTRATION 1.1

Graham Day, Chairman of the Rover Group for just under a year, entered 1987 with the task of presenting the company's corporate plan to the Secretary of State for Trade and Industry at a time when the Group continued to face financial losses and declining market share.

In December, 1986, the *Financial Times* reported that 'the underlying objective remains the one stated in the April annual report; "The return of all the constituent businesses, either together or separately, to the private sector as soon as practicable".' The Chairman therefore faced not just a problem of returning the corporation to profits, but also fulfilling the political and economic expectations of the government.

The situation faced by the corporation remained unhealthy. Graham Day argued that the problems now related to achieving profitability and customer satisfaction, rather than the industrial relations, productivity, investment and design problems of the past. However, the fact was that financial performance continued to deteriorate with losses in the first half year to June 1986 rising from £42.6 million to £118.9 million and unit sales declining in 1986 to 296,000 from 324,000 in 1985, as overseas manufacturers, particularly the Japanese, continued to take share in the UK and Rover failed to make inroads against Ford and General Motors.

Rover could, however, draw on some positive factors. 1986 had been the best year since 1979 in Europe for sale of Rover cars with the improvement of the dealer network and the availability of new models. The Rover 800, jointly developed with Honda, had been well received, particularly by the 150 dealers in the US. However, other models in the Rover range, particularly the Montego in the saloon market sector, were disappointing, and even the Metro had not lived up to expectations. The past weakness of the pound had helped export markets and put pressure on Ford and General Motors who imported many of their cars from European factories. Also Mr Day had already restructured the Group, dismantling a somewhat cumbersome multidivisional structure to just two divisions which facilitated more control from the centre.

The *Financial Times* reported that 'Mr Day's preferred option ... involves scaling down output while moving the car model range up market. If [he] followed such a route he would stop production of the Mini and run down output of the Metro and Montego. That would concentrate effort on the new Rover 800 series, to give Austin Rover an executive prestige image on the continent as well as in the US. The AR 8, the model being developed jointly with Honda to replace the Maestro and Rover 200 series late in 1989,

of decision that were no doubt taken in the company at that time? Many of the characteristics of strategic decisions can be illustrated by using Rover – and Graham Day's preparation of his corporate plan – as an example.

1.1.1 The characteristics of strategic decisions

The characteristics usually associated with the word strategy and strategic decisions are these:

1. Strategic decisions are likely to be concerned with the *scope of an organisation's activities*: does (and should) the organisation concentrate on one area of activity, or does it have many? For example, should the Rover Group focus on a few ranges of cars or, as

---

The Rover Group: the 1987 Corporate Plan

would be a sporty, high performance car. . . . This policy would inevitably result in closure of a car plant . . . and could pose a threat to Austin Rover's 1400 dealers and the supply industry because the company's annual car production . . . would fall to between 215,000 and 300,000.' The paper went on to report that the Conservative government, conscious of its need for marginal seats in the Midlands where the car plants were located, would probably rule out such an option. It quoted the Secretary of State for Industry as emphasising 'that I expect Mr Day's plan to set out a positive course for the continuation of the company as a major producer and leading exporter of cars made in Britain'. Other industry experts were advocating that the company should follow a niche strategy and seek to add value to every car to make it different enough to be attractive to particular market segments and thus attract premium prices. Others debated the need for a continuation or extension of the joint venture arrangements with the Japanese Honda firm, and still others advocated the wisdom of a full merger with Honda.

The constraints on the choices that Day could make were considerable. It was difficult to see how management could cope with all the key tasks being advocated – the renewal of the model range; the continued rationalisation of production facilities, the expansion of continental markets, and the improvement of quality. There was no sign that Rover had an extensive new model range to launch in the near future; and Honda was divided as to whether it should develop further joint venture arrangements. Against this however, it had to be recognised that Graham Day himself was enthusiastically keen to demonstrate his own ability by turning around the business.

When announced in February 1987 the plan confirmed the aims of returning the company to private ownership and the intent to maintain a full, up-to-date range of models for Austin Rover. It went on to confirm the intent to pursue further joint ventures with Honda and continue the programme of rationalisation by reducing indirect and fixed costs whilst emphasising the need to improve the quality of cars. Go-ahead was also given to the new AR8 medium-sized car in collaboration with Honda and the development of a new engine and gear box for small cars at a cost of £200 million, thus confirming the Group's intent to continue their commitment to this market segment. The plan also clearly laid out that the corporation would focus on the Austin Rover and Land Rover ranges and confirmed the disposals of Unipart, the parts manufacturer, Leyland Bus and Leyland Trucks. The government also agreed to write off rationalisation costs and accumulated debts from the Rover's truck and bus companies.

in the past, have a very diverse range, not only of cars, but of trucks and buses as well as a parts business? To what extent should it be integrated backwards into manufacturing or forwards into distribution? And should it attempt to compete widely in international markets – indeed could it survive without a wider international role?

The issue of scope of activity is fundamental to strategic decisions because it concerns the way in which those responsible for managing the organisation conceive its boundaries. It is to do with what they want the organisation to be like and to be about.

2. Strategy is to do with the *matching of the activities of an organisation to the environment* in which it operates. Until the 1960s and 1970s Austin, Morris, Rover and the other companies that came to make up British Leyland regarded themselves as competing largely in a home market in which they were dominant. However, in the 1960s and, in particular, the 1970s the changes that took place in the car industry were dramatic. Most significant, perhaps, was the growth in market power and technological competence of Japanese producers who, building on a large home market, adopted a strategy of worldwide dominance for their cars. The effect not only on the UK but also on the USA was marked. Home car producers faced a major loss in share: for example, in just one decade British Leyland's share of almost thirty per cent of the UK market was reduced to under fifteen per cent for the re-formed Rover Group.

Foreign competition was not the only environmental change to affect the Rover Group, or indeed the car industry in general. The oil price increases of 1973 changed customer expectations of car performance and running costs; technological advances provided opportunities for car design which accelerated throughout the 1970s and 1980s and provided car manufacturers with opportunities to differentiate their products; changing demographic patterns and household earnings provided opportunities to increase car ownership in the family; pollution control regulations in different countries meant that imported cars had to meet quite rigorous performance standards; and fluctuations in exchange rates provided both constraints and opportunities in an international market.

In short, the car industry in general, and BL/Rover within it, was faced with the problems of an increasingly competitive market in a changing business environment; the need was to match the organisation's activity to this environment in such a way as to take advantages of such opportunities that might be provided and overcome the many threats that arose. Since the environment is continually changing for all organisations, strategic decisions necessarily involve change: in the case of the Rover Group the environmental changes were of a major nature and the changes required were of a fundamental kind. This is not always the case; the extent and speed of environmental change will vary and the pace at which strategy must change will necessarily vary too. However, the BL/Rover Group provides a good example of a business, faced with major environmental changes, which found it immensely difficult to make the sorts of fundamental strategic change necessary; a management problem which is not uncommon.

3. Strategy is also to do with the *matching of the organisation's activities to its resource capability*. Strategy is not just about countering environmental threats and taking advantage of environmental opportunities, it is also about matching organisational resources to these threats and opportunities. There would be little point in trying to take advantage of some new opportunity if the resources needed were not available,

could not be made available or if the strategy was rooted in an inadequate resource base. For example, many of the problems faced in the 1970s and 1980s by BL and later by Rover stemmed from a failure to invest in modern plant and modern technology in the 1950s and 1960s. The result was a corporation that was faced with efficient, low-cost foreign competition when it, itself, had an insufficient base for increasing productivity. Throughout most of the 1970s it therefore faced the problems of major investment at a time of falling market share and attempts to squeeze more and more productivity out of an increasingly demoralised workforce. Increasingly the financing of the business became dependent on government funding which eventually took the corporation into public ownership. The problem that Graham Day faced was to evolve a strategy which would adjust the activities of the business to a level at which it could survive and prosper within a resource capability it could reasonably expect to sustain in the 1990s. He was therefore faced not only with trying to understand how a changing environment would affect his business, but also having to project the availability and requirements of resources such as finance, plant, design and technological capability, workforce skills and so on for the future.

4. Strategic decisions therefore often have *major resource implications* for an organisation. These may be decisions to do with the disposal or acquisition of whole areas of resource. Rover had already witnessed a major rationalisation of its operations and, as Illustration 1.1 shows, one of the options which had to be considered by Day was the further closure of plant. The company had also moved into whole new areas of technology and production including robotised manufacturing operations which were necessary to compete in volume car manufacturing. Over the years, the workforce of the Group had been cut significantly. In other words, the strategic decisions of the last decade had resulted in major changes in the resource base of the business.

5. Strategic decisions are therefore likely to *affect operational decisions*, to 'set off waves of lesser decisions'.[2] In the case of BL/Rover the decisions in the 1970s to rationalise the operation and cut back on manufacturing capacity and the workforce gave rise to a concentration, for much of the decade, on industrial relations problems. And similarly strategic decisions about range rationalisation and planning required, which led to revised product and manufacturing plans, inevitably meant that the sorts of day-to-day problem faced by a production manager, or a sales manager, in the company came to be different. Again, then, it is important to understand that strategic decisions have wide ramifications across the organisation.

6. The strategy of an organisation will be affected not only by environmental forces and resource availability, but also by the *values and expectations* of those who have *power* in the organisation. In some respects, strategy can be thought of as a reflection of the attitudes and beliefs of those who have most influence in the organisation. Whether a company is expansionist or more concerned with consolidation, or where the boundaries are drawn for a company's activities, may say much about the values and attitudes of those who most strongly influence strategy. A word sometimes used to describe attitudes and expectations about scope and posture of an organisation is the *mission* for an organisation. Mission may comprise views about the organisation's standing *vis-à-vis* competition, or in terms of technological advance, in terms of product quality or perhaps in terms of its role in society. It may also be to do with the

ownership of a firm particularly in the case of small companies where the desire to perpetuate family ownership may be a very important influence on strategy. In the case of Rover, the desire to return the corporation to private ownership had come to take on such connotations of 'mission'. Such views are not to do with specific aims so much as conceptions about where the organisation is conceived to be throughout time. In this sense mission is a 'visionary' view of the overall strategic posture of an organisation and is likely to be a persistent and resistant influence on strategic decisions. Certainly in the case of the Rover Group the expectations of government were very influential on the mission of the corporation: as the Industry Secretary had made clear he expected the company to maintain a position as a major producer and leading exporter of cars made in Britain.

7. Strategic decisions are likely to affect the *long term direction* of an organisation. Graham Day must have been aware in 1986 that the decisions he was to make over the next year would be likely to affect the future, even the existence, of the Rover Group. Similarly the decisions taken in the 1960s by the management of the company at that time had had long term repercussions on the health of the business in later decades. Strategic decisions therefore tend to have long time horizons and/or long term implications.

8. Strategic decisions are often *complex in nature*. It can be argued that what distinguishes strategic management from other aspects of management in an organisation is just this complexity. The complexity arises for at least three reasons. First, because strategic decisions usually involve a *high degree of uncertainty*; they may involve taking decisions on the basis of views about the future which it is impossible for managers to be sure about. Second, strategic decisions are likely to demand an *integrated* approach to managing the organisation. Unlike functional problems, there is no one area of expertise, or one perspective that can define or resolve the problems. Managers, therefore, have to cross functional and operational boundaries to deal with strategic problems and come to agreements with other managers who, inevitably, have different interests and perhaps different priorities. This problem of integration exists in all management tasks but is particularly problematic for strategic decisions. Third, as has been noted above, strategic decisions are likely to involve *major change* in organisations. Not only is it problematic in deciding upon and planning those changes, it is even more problematic in actually implementing them. Strategic management is therefore distinguished by a higher order of complexity than operational tasks.[3]

These are the sorts of characteristic associated with the idea of strategy in an organisational context. They are summarised in Figure 1.1.[4]

Strategic decisions are concerned with:
- The scope of an organisation's activities.
- The matching of an organisation's activities to its environment.
- The matching of the activities of an organisation to its resource capability.
- The allocation and reallocation of major resources in an organisation.
- The values, expectations and goals of those influencing strategy.
- The direction an organisation will move in the long term.
- Implications for change throughout the organisation – they are therefore likely to be complex in nature.

Figure 1.1 The characteristics of strategic decisions.

1.1.2 Levels of strategy

Strategies will exist at a number of levels in an organisation. An individual may say he has a strategy – to do with his career, for example. This may be relevant when considering influences on strategies adopted by organisations but it is not what is meant by corporate strategy. Taking Rover as an example, it is possible to distinguish at least three different levels of strategy. There is the *corporate* level: here the strategy is concerned with what types of business the company, as a whole, should be in and is therefore concerned with decisions of scope. As discussed earlier such decisions for Rover were to do with the extent of manufacturing and of vertical integration and with the types of business and market it should be involved in. In the case of Rover the corporation was becoming more narrow in scope. Other corporations might be much more diverse: and here corporate strategy would be concerned with which businesses to acquire or divest, or what resources should be allocated to which businesses by the corporate headquarters. Corporate strategy is therefore also likely to involve questions about the financial structure and organisational structure of the firm as a whole.

The second level can be thought of more in terms of *competitive or business strategy*. Here strategy is about how to compete in a particular market. So, whereas corporate strategy involves decisions about the organisation as a whole, competitive strategy is more likely to be related to a unit within the whole. In the case of Rover the prime concern was how to formulate a strategy to compete in the highly competitive saloon car market which had become dominated by the major multinational car producers. Should Rover try to match the product ranges of Ford or Toyota: or should there be an attempt to focus more on particular market segments with rather more specialised products? And, whatever the strategy, should this be pursued alone or in partnership with some other firm such as Honda? How far should rationalisation and modernisation of plant go? Should Rover aim to lead in technology and invest heavily in automated plant?

The third level of strategy is at the operating end of the organisation. Here there are *operational strategies* which are concerned with how the different functions of the enterprise – marketing, finance, manufacturing and so on – contribute to the other levels of strategy. Such contributions will certainly be important in terms of how an organisation seeks to be competitive. Competitive strategy may depend to a large extent on, for example, decisions about market entry, price, product offer, financing, manpower and investment in plant. In themselve these are decisions of strategic importance but are made, or at least strongly influenced, at operational levels.

The ideas discussed in this book are of relevance to all three levels of strategy but are most specifically concerned with the areas of corporate and competitive strategy – what businesses (or areas of operation) should an organisation be in and how should it compete in each of these.

1.2 STRATEGIC MANAGEMENT

What, then, is 'strategic management'? The easy answer is to say that it is the management of the process of strategic decision making. However, this fails to make a number of points that are important both in the management of an organisation and in the area of study with which this book is concerned.

First it must be pointed out that the nature of strategic management is different from other aspects of management. In most areas the individual manager is required to deal with problems of operational control,[5] such as the efficient production of goods, the management of a salesforce, the monitoring of financial performance or the design of some new system that will improve the efficiency of the operation. These are all very important tasks but they are essentially concerned with effectively managing a limited part of the organisation within the context and guidance of a more overarching strategy. Operational control is what managers are involved in for most of their time. It is vital to the effective implementation of strategy but it is not the same as strategic management.

Strategic management is concerned with deciding on strategy and planning how that strategy is to be put into effect. It can be thought of as having three main elements within it and it is these that provide the framework for the book. There is *strategic analysis* in which the strategist seeks to understand the strategic position of the organisation. There is *strategic choice* which is to do with the formulation of possible courses of action, their evaluation and the choice between them. Finally there is *strategy implementation* which is concerned with planning how the choice of strategy can be put into effect. This three-part approach, summarised in Figure 1.2, is not dissimilar to the ways in which managers often describe their strategies, as Illustration 1.2. shows.

Before discussing these stages in detail it is important to make clear how they relate to each other and, therefore, why Figure 1.2 is shown in the form it is. The figure could have been shown in a linear form – strategic analysis preceding strategic choice, which in turn precedes strategic implementation. Indeed, it might appear that this would be quite logical, and many texts on the subject do just this.[6] However, in practice, the stages do not take this linear form. It is very likely that, far from being separate, the stages are very much involved with each other: it is quite possible that one way of evaluating a strategy would be to begin to implement it, so strategic choice and strategy implementation may be carried out together. It is also very likely that strategic analysis will be an ongoing activity and so will overlap with the implementation of strategy. A linear representation of the process gives the impression that one stage is totally distinct from or precedes or follows another when, in fact, they are part of the same process. The process is examined more fully in the light of research on the subject in Chapter 2 so as to provide readers with a greater 'feel' for the realities of strategic management. It is for structural convenience only that the process has been divided into sections in this book.

1.2.1 Strategic analysis

Strategic analysis is concerned with understanding the strategic position of the organisation. What changes are going on in the environment and how will they affect

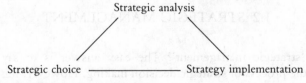

Figure 1.2 A basic model of the strategic management process.

ILLUSTRATION 1.2

IBM and the elements of strategic management

A company's description of its strategy in its annual report is likely to contain within it the elements of strategic management. These quotations are from the annual report of IBM in 1986. They illustrate how its description of its strategy corresponds to the principles of the strategic framework outlined in Chapter 1.

Strategic analysis	Strategic choice	Strategy implementation
IBM ... play[s] a leading role in the information technology industry.	Exploitation of profitable growth opportunities in the UK market place, the introduction of exciting new products from our manufacturing plants and laboratory, the continued drive to reduce expenses, further working capital improvements and selective fixed capital investment ...	We are determined to increase output per head, and, with full co-operation of our workforce, we shall exploit the benefits of our investment in technology.
For some years, we have seen a fall in UK demand.		
Growth in revenue was achieved despite ... the slow-down in capital investment in machinery and equipment in the UK, and increasing competition.	We have now added a goal – to enhance our customer partnerships .... to forge stronger partnerships with our customers.	We are having to reduce our workforce and we are also closing some uneconomic factories.
		We have increased expenditure on research and development by £10m to £55m.
Our market research shows that many companies still use little or no information technology and that ... there are many opportunities for improving efficiency and effectiveness through increased use of IT.	We intend to continue our present high commitment to research and development.	We can introduce a new regional organisation that brings decision-making closer to customers and their specific needs.
	We intend to demonstrate quite clearly that IBM offers a complete solution to business needs.	We are increasing resources available in the field by offering new marketing careers to hundreds of people previously engaged in administration.
The weakness of the pound inevitably put pressure on our margins.	The three general purpose architectures – system/370, systems/36/38 and the PC – provide one of our key strengths ... we are committed to enhancing consistency across the three architectures.	Training and retraining of our employees has been given added emphasis.
The group's balance sheet remains strong, as a result of the continued focus on the control of working capital.		A great deal of time was spent on ensuring that all our employees understand our quality programme.
	We have increased considerably our overseas business and opened up worldwide markets for our exports ... In this way we have mitigated some of the effects of the decline of our UK operations.	We made great efforts to contain costs and expenses whilst continuing to reward and motivate our high-calibre employees.

Source: IBM Annual Report, 1986.

the organisation and its activities? What is the resource strength of the organisation in the context of these changes? What is it that those people and groups associated with the organisations – managers, shareholders or owners, unions and so on – aspire to and how do these affect the present position and what could happen in the future?

Certainly Michael Edwardes,[7] on taking over the Chairmanship of British Leyland in the 1970s, undertook such analysis and arrived at the conclusion that the corporation was uncompetitive in most of its markets, burdened with out-of-date plant, low productivity and high costs. Graham Day would have needed to reassess the situation and concluded that these issues had given way, in the main, to ones of the need for greater customer satisfaction in a deteriorating financial situation, in which loss of share was not being stemmed. He would also have concluded that such strengths as he could draw upon were mainly from some of the more successful product launches (such as the new Rover 800 designed in collaboration with Honda) though others, less successful, were major weaknesses in the product range. He would also have seen potential in the possibility of enhanced export markets (whilst being acutely aware of the extent to which this was dependent on the value of the pound), and the increasingly sophisticated expectations of customers.

However, Rover also illustrates that, in order to appreciate fully the strategic position of the firm it is necessary to understand how other *stakeholders* – the government, unions, distributors and the local community, for example – view the situation that the business faces, and where it is going. Further, it illustrates that it is important to understand the less explicit, but nonetheless powerful, influence of organisational culture; by culture is meant the types of belief and assumption current in the organisation and its ways of doing things very often inherited over many years of operating. Understanding the values, expectations, objectives, and the less precise but nonetheless key influence of culture is therefore also a vital part of strategic analysis.

Thus the aim of *strategic analysis* is to form a view of the key influences on the present and future well-being of the organisation and therefore on the choice of strategy. These influences will be from many sources but they are summarised in Figure 1.3 and discussed briefly below.

1. The *environment*. The organisation exists in the context of a complex commercial, economic, political, technological, ethical and social world. This environment changes

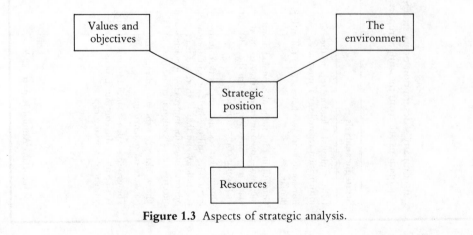

Figure 1.3 Aspects of strategic analysis.

and is more complex for some firms than for others. Since strategy is concerned with the position a business takes in relation to its environment, an understanding of the environment's effects on a business is of central importance to strategic analysis. The historical and environmental effects on the business must be considered, as well as the present effects and the expected changes in environmental variables. This is a major task because the range of environmental variables is so very great. Many of those variables will give rise to *opportunities* of some sort and many will exert *threats* upon the firm. The two main problems that have to be faced are, first, to distil out of this complexity an analytically based view of the main or overall environmental impacts for the purpose of strategic choice; and second, the fact that the range of variables is so great that it may not be possible or realistic to identify and analyse each one. Chapter 3 of this book addresses itself to these types of problem.

2. The *resources* of the organisation. Just as there are outside influences on the firm and its choice of strategies, so there are internal influences. A straightforward way of thinking about the internal strategic position of a firm is to consider its *strengths* and *weaknesses* (what it is good or not so good at doing or where it is at a competitive advantage or disadvantage, for example). These strengths and weaknesses may be identified by considering the resource areas of a business such as its physical plant, its management, its financial structure, and its products. Again, the aim is to form a view of the internal influences – and constraints – on strategic choice. Chapter 4 examines resource analysis in detail.

3. The *expectations* and objectives of different stakeholder groups are clearly important because they will directly affect what will be seen as acceptable in terms of the strategies advanced by management. However, the beliefs and assumptions that make up the *culture* of an organisation, though less explicit, will also have an important influence. The environmental and resource influences on an organisation will be interpreted through these beliefs and assumptions; so two groups of managers, perhaps working in different divisions of an organisation, may come to entirely different conclusions about strategy, although they are faced with similar environmental and resource implications. Which influence prevails is likely to depend on which group has the greatest *power*, and understanding this can be of great importance in recognising why an organisation has followed, or is likely to follow, the strategy it does. Chapter 2 discusses the important influence of beliefs and organisational culture on the formulation of strategy and this is followed through in Chapter 5 with a discussion of how the culture, expectations and power structures in an organisation can be analysed and the ways in which such beliefs and expectations are likely to affect organisational objectives.

Together a consideration of the *environment*, the *resources*, the *expectations* and *objectives* within the *cultural* and *political* framework of the organisation provides the basis of the strategic analysis of an organisation. However, to understand the strategic position an organisation is in, it is also necessary to examine the extent to which the direction and implications of the current strategy and objectives being followed by the organisation are in line with and can cope with the implications yielded by the strategic analysis. Is the current strategy capable of dealing with the changes taking place in the organisation's environment or not? If so, in what respects and, if not, why not? It is unlikely that there will be a complete match between current strategy and the picture which emerges from the strategic analysis. The extent to which there is a mismatch here is the extent of the strategic problem facing the strategist. It may be that the adjustment that is required is marginal or it may be that there is a need for a fundamental realignment of strategy. For example, the extent to which British Leyland had come to be out of line in its competitive environment in the 1970s posed Michael Edwardes, and later Graham Day, with the problems of fundamental strategic repositioning.

1.2.2 Strategic choice

Strategic analysis provides a basis for strategic choice. This aspect of strategic management can be conceived of as having three parts to it.

1. *Generation of strategic options*. There may be many possible courses of action. Graham Day, for example, had to decide the basis of competing in a worldwide industry: Could Rover compete on a cost-leadership basis? Would it need to differentiate itself from competitors, or perhaps select particular market segments or products to focus on? Within these broad choices, what *strategic directions* were likely to be most sensible: Should further rationalisation take place? Should the company seek to increase its market share in the UK, or perhaps grow internationally? What product development should be pursued? Furthermore, should the company attempt to follow its strategies by internal development, joint ventures – perhaps with Honda – or by acquisition? All of these considerations are important and needed careful consideration: indeed, in developing strategies, a potential danger is that managers do not consider any but the most obvious courses of action – and the most obvious is not necessarily the best. So an important step in *strategic choice* is to generate strategic options.

2. *Evaluation of strategic options*. The strategic options can be examined in the context of the strategic analysis to assess their relative merits.

An organisation may seek for strategies which build upon strengths, overcome weaknesses and take advantage of the opportunities, whilst minimising or circumventing the threats it faces – in this book this is called the search for 'strategic fit' or *suitability* of a strategy. Many commentators on the Rover Group argued that, given inherited resource weaknesses, low share (particularly internationally) and the strength of the mass market competitors, Rover's most suitable strategy had to involve a much more focused approach to particular market segments in which they might justify some added value and price precision and avoid a head-on clash with the volume car producers. This, they argued, would have a much greater chance of being workable. It would not require such high capital investment; it would find more support in the financial institutions; it would not necessarily require a global presence in the car market; it would avoid an over-reliance on low-cost production; and so on. In other words, they argued that a vital consideration in deciding on strategy was whether or not it could pass the test of *feasibility*. However, the proponents of such views might also acknowledge that, following such a strategy might involve further slimming down the corporation and reducing its overall presence in the car market; and this might simply not be *acceptable* to some of the stakeholders – most notably the government. This is a third criteria to be used in evaluation.

3. *Selection of strategy*. This is the task of selecting those options that the management is going to pursue. There could be just one strategy chosen or, as in the case of Rover, several. There is unlikely to be a clear-cut 'right' or 'wrong' strategy because any strategy must inevitably have some dangers or disadvantages so, in the end, it is likely to be a matter of management judgement. It is important to understand that a selection of strategy cannot always be viewed or understood as a purely objective, 'rational' act. It is strongly influenced by the values of managers and other groups with interest in the organisation and, in the end, may very much reflect the power structure in the organisation.

Strategic choice is dealt with in Part III of the book. In Chapter 6 there is a discussion of the various strategic options that organisations most typically consider. Chapter 7 discusses the criteria of evaluation in more detail and discusses several approaches to assessing the suitability of different types of strategies. Chapter 8 goes on to consider some techniques for evaluating specific options and the ways in which strategy selection might occur.

1.2.3 Strategy implementation

Strategy implementation is concerned with translation of strategy into action. A strategy might be the rationalisation of Rover which might take shape in terms of how many factories there should be, what sort of plant should be used and what the size of the workforce should be. This problem of translating strategy into action is certainly part of strategic management, and at least as problematic as strategic analysis or choice. Implementation can be thought of as having several parts.

Implementation is likely to involve *resource planning* in which the logistics of implementation are examined: What are the key tasks needing to be carried out? What changes need to be made in the resource mix of the operation? By when? And who is to be responsible for them? It is also likely that there will be changes in *organisational structure* needed to carry through the strategy. For example, Graham Day took over a corporation with many business activities organised in many divisions. If further rationalisation were to take place and some business activities sold off, how would this affect the divisional structure? And if a greater emphasis were to be placed on international activity, how best should this be organised?

There is also likely to be a need to adapt the *systems* used to manage the organisation. What will different departments be held responsible for? What sorts of information system are needed to monitor the progress of the strategy? Is there a need for retraining of the workforce? What of the cultural systems of the organisation? If strategy is to change it will be necessary to find ways of getting the people in the organisation to change the way they perceive their 'organisational world'. How might this be done?

Part IV of the book deals with strategy implementation. Problems of planning resource allocation are discussed in Chapter 9, issues of organisational structure are dealt with in Chapter 10 and the problems of managing the people and systems for strategic change are discussed in Chapter 11.

1.2.4 A summary of the strategic management process

It was stated earlier that there is a danger in thinking of the process of strategic management as a specific, orderly sequence of steps; the danger is that readers may not find the same stages described here as existing in reality and therefore argue that strategic management in their organisation does not take place. It is important to stress that the model used in this book, and summarised in this chapter, is a useful device for the structuring of the book and a means by which managers and students of strategy can think through complex strategic problems. It is not, however, an attempt to describe how the processes of strategic management necessarily take place in the political and cultural arenas of organisations. Chapter 2 deals with how strategic decisions are made in practice and shows that a study of the process of strategic management yields somewhat different descriptive models.

It is therefore with some trepidation that a summary model of the influences on, and elements of, strategic management is given in Figure 1.4. It is not intended as a prescription of what strategic management should be but as a framework which readers can use to think through strategic problems. It also forms the structure of the remainder of the book.

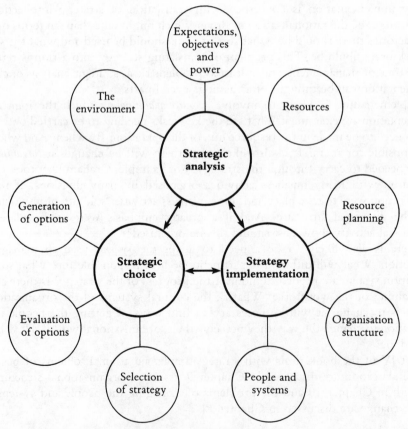

Figure 1.4 A summary model of the elements of strategic management.

It was stated earlier that the process cannot be regarded as linear and it should now be clear why this is so. In practice, so many elements of the model are expressions of the same thing. For example, a consideration of culture and expectations is not simply to do with strategic analysis. It is also directly relevant to an assessment of the acceptability of a given strategy. Similarly, in considering the planning of resources for the purposes of strategic implementation, a study of feasibility is in fact being undertaken and so too is a reassessment of existing resources, which might also be described as strategic analysis. The point to emphasise is that the elements of strategic management are relevant one to another.

1.3 THE CHALLENGE OF STRATEGIC MANAGEMENT

It should be clear by now that the breadth of concern of strategic management is much greater than that of any one area of functional management. The concern is with organisation-wide issues in the context of a whole range of environment influences. This gives rise to some problems for those who seek to develop their skills in this area.

1.3.1 Developing a strategic perspective

One obvious problem is that managers have to be able to cope with overall consider-ations of their organisation and its environment. This is not easy to do, as managers who move from functional responsibilities to general management responsibilities often find. The accountant finds that he still tends to see problems in financial terms, the marketing manager in marketing terms and so on. Each aspect in itself is most worthy, of course, but none is adequate alone. The manager has to learn to take an overview, to conceive of the whole rather than the parts.

It is necessary to develop a facility to take an holistic view of the situation and conceive of major, overall problems rather than dwell on difficulties which, real as they may be, do not help develop a strategic perspective. Implicit in the arguments put forward in this book is the view that managers need to be competent both as operators in a functional sense and as strategists: that it is not enough for managers to simply maintain what the organisation has always done, but that he or she must be capable of contributing to a debate about where the organisation is going, and become involved in the practical tasks of making strategies work.

1.3.2 Coping with change

To cope with the vast variety and range of environmental inputs in the strategic decision process, managers have to operate within some simplified model of that environment. Essentially managers reduce the 'infinite' to a personally manageable model of reality. More precisely, there is evidence to show that to some extent this 'model of reality' is inherited by the manager in the sense that there exists 'recipes', or perceived wisdom, about the key factors for business success in a particular business environment.[8] The idea of recipes is discussed more fully in Chapter 2: suffice it to say at this stage that their influence can be a significant constraint on change.[9] For example, it was difficult for those in British Leyland – managers, staff or shopfloor workers – to accept change. They had years of experience in a company broken up in business units closely identified with car models inherited from once-independent family firms, and with an emphasis on engineering rather than marketing. It was not a simple matter to accept the strategic implications of the competitive environment of the 1970s and 1980s. For years prior to the appointment of Michael Edwardes the company's profits had declined but management could not see their way out of the decline because they were constrained in the way they saw the business and the influences on it. It took a steadily worsening position and a new chairman to break through such constraints and to enter business areas which would not have been considered in previous years. It is important for those who wish to understand, or develop, skills in strategic management to consider the problems of achieving changes in strategy. To achieve such changes effectively, what is being asked of managers may well be a change in the way they and their colleagues perceive their organisational world. How such changes came about, indeed whether they can be brought about at all, underlies the study of strategic management and is considered in more detail in Chapters 2, 5 and 11.

1.3.3 Strategy in the public sector and not-for-profit organisations[10]

The development of concepts and techniques of corporate strategy have, in the past, mainly occurred in the area of commercial enterprises. Are they applicable to public sector and not-for-profit organisations? The answer is most certainly 'yes'. There are of course differences in such organisations, and, arguably what matters most is that managers can identify what those differences are and therefore what the focus of attention should be in considering strategic developments in the organisation. For example, consider the difference between a commercial operation and a government agency. 'A business company has a sales market in which it sells its products or services for money, a labour market from which it gets people to whom it pays money, a purchase market from which it gets its supplies for money, the money market from which it gets money and interest, loans or equity and to which it pays interests and dividends. The *raison d'être* of a business company lies in its sales market. It also gets there direct feedback for success or failure'.[11] However, although a government agency is in some respects similar – it too has a labour market, a money market of sorts; it too has suppliers and users or customers – the fundamental difference is that at its heart lies a 'political market which approves budgets, and provides subsidies'. It is the explicit nature of this political dimension which managers – or officers – have to cope with which particularly distinguishes government bodies, be they national or local, from commercial enterprises. This may in turn change the time horizons of decisions, since they may be heavily influenced by political considerations and may mean that analysis of strategies requires the norms of political dogma to be explicitly considered. However, although the magnitude of the political dimension is greater, the model of strategic management posed here nonetheless holds. What is different is that the emphasis placed upon certain aspects of strategic analysis and choice, notably those to do with the political dimensions, are the more important.

Similarly, there will be differences in not-for-profit organisations such as charities, churches, private schools, foundations and so on.[12] Here the differences may be both to do with the different expectations of influencing bodies and also the special nature of revenue generation in terms of resources. The likelihood is that funding bodies may be diverse and, quite likely, not direct beneficiaries of the services offered. Moreover, they may well provide funds in advance of the services being offered in the form of grants for example. The implications here are several. The influence from the funding bodies is likely to be high in terms of the formulation of organisational strategies; indeed the organisations may well develop strategies as much to do with and influenced by the funding bodies as by their clients. Moreover, since they are heavily dependent on funds which emanate not from clients but from sponsors, a danger is that the organisation becomes more concerned with resource efficiency then service effectiveness. It is also likely that there will be multiple sources of funding and this, linked to the different objectives and expectations of the funding bodies, might lead to a high incidence of political lobbying, difficulties in clear strategic planning, and a requirement to hold decision making and responsibility at the centre where it is answerable to external influences rather than delegate it within the organisation. These characteristics and difficulties of strategic management in not-for-profit organisations are summarised in Figure 1.5. However, it must be pointed out that it is still necessary for such organisations to make surpluses if they are to carry out their work and, whether the focus is on the clients who use the services, or the sponsors who provide the revenue, strategies for achieving such surpluses are nonetheless necessary.

Other public sector operations may be commercial enterprises anyway. They may be nationalised companies for example. Here the differences are likely to be associated with the nature of ownership and control. A commercial enterprise that is state controlled may well have differences in planning horizons, different bases of financing, and require that top management more centrally control their organisation for reporting purposes, for example to government ministers. Nonetheless, it is likely that

CHARACTERISTICS	LIKELY EFFECTS
Objectives and expectations	
• May be multiple service objectives and expectations.	• Complicates strategic planning.
• May be multiple influences on policy.	• High incidence of political lobbying.
• Expectations of funding bodies very influential.	• Difficulties in delegating/decentralising responsibilities and decision making.
Market and users	
• Beneficiaries of service not necessarily contributors of revenue/resources.	• Service satisfaction not measured readily in financial terms.
Resources	
• High proportion from government, or sponsors.	• Influence from funding bodies may be high.
• Received in advance of services.	• May be emphasis on financial or resource efficiency rather than service effectiveness.
• May be multiple sources of funding.	• Strategies may be addressed to sponsors as much as clients.

Figure 1.5 Some characteristics of strategic management in not-for-profit organisations.

ILLUSTRATION 1.3

In its 1983 report on securing economy, efficiency and effectiveness in local government, the Audit Commission emphasised that the 'effectiveness of an organisation stems from the interaction of several factors which must be managed in such a way as to reinforce each other'. In their report they included a questionnaire to enable local authorities to assess their standing in these different areas. Some of the questions they asked are shown below, using the Audit Commission's own terminology.

Vision

- Is there any statement of the most significant changes (in services or the way the authority is managed) that the council expects over the next few years?
- Is there a summary statement of the aims of the council's major services?

Strategy

- Is there a strategic planning process for implementing the vision, covering more than two years? If so, does it cover:
- An analysis of the area – physical, economic and social?
- Planned changes in client, service and management priorities?
- Planned allocation of resources (principally staff) by service, with an analysis of the reasons for change from status quo?
- Planned capital expenditure by project, identifying committed and new approvals?
- Are there agreed contingency plans to cope with the main risks to the council's plans?

Structure

- Is the committee structure aligned with the management organisation and council policies and services?
- Is there a review system to keep the organisation structure under regular scrutiny?
- Is responsibility for each service and cost clearly assigned to individual officers, with minimal duplication of responsibilities?

the same competitive pressures will be exerted on these businesses as on private organisations.

Overall what matters is that there is a need to recognise that different parts of the model of strategic management presented in this chapter and developed throughout the book will be relevant to varying degrees according to the differences between such organisations. There is no one right way of approaching the problems of strategic management and the consideration of public sector and not-for-profit organisations makes this point well. Illustration 1.3 provides an example of how strategic management in the public sector is seen to be important.

Strategic management and the Audit Commission

Systems

Policy Review

- Is there a systematic, long term policy review process for all significant services? If so, does it cover:
    - (i)   The continued relevance of services, the assumptions underlying service standards and alternative methods of delivery?
    - (ii) Comparisons with other similar authorities, within the authority and with the private sector as appropriate?

Planning, budgeting

- Is there an annual action plan, related to the overall strategy, summarising the steps to be taken and performance milestones within each service or function?
- Is there an annual budget identifying responsibility for income and expenditure for recognisable costs centres, i.e. does it relate to the organisation?

Style

- Do the Leader and Chief Executive regularly discuss the style of the organisation and how (if at all) it needs to be changed?
- Does the Leader meet staff members regularly to discuss his or her priorities and concerns? Does the Chief Executive routinely spend time within individual departments understanding problems at first hand?

Skills and staffing

- Are the individual responsibilities of the top three levels of management defined in terms of the results to be achieved?
- Is there any system for rewarding managers who consistently achieve more than their planned results?
- Is there a significant investment in training for members and officers in relation to their policy and general management responsibilities?

1.4 SUMMARY

This chapter has set out to explain the focus, concept and scope of the study and to propose a framework by which to approach the subject. The aim is that by this stage readers will have some idea about the types of problem with which the study is concerned. The remainder of the book sets out to amplify the different elements of strategic management identified and outlined in this chapter.

However, before this, the next chapter looks at how strategy formulation occurs in practice so that readers can place the ensuing discussion in the context of managerial practice.

REFERENCES

1. For an interesting historical case study of the BL/Rover Group, together with a discussion of the reasons for the difficulties it faced, see K. Williams, J. Williams and D. Thomas, *Why Are the British Bad at Manufacturing?*, Routledge & Kegan Paul, 1983.

2. From D. J. Hickson, R. J. Butler, D. Cray, G. R. Mallory, and D. C. Wilson, *Top Decisions: Strategic decision making in organisations'*, p. 28, Basil Blackwell, 1986.

3. These reasons for the complexity of strategic management are based on the explanations given by Gerry Johnson in *Strategic Change in the Management Process*, pp. 5–6, Basil Blackwell, 1987.

4. We have chosen not to provide a definition as such of what is meant by strategy, preferring to discuss the characteristics of strategic decisions as a means of explanation. A useful analysis of alternative definitions can be found in C.W. Hofer and D. Schendel, *Strategy Formulation: Analytical concepts*, pp. 16–20, West, 1978.

5. A useful distinction is made by R. N. Anthony and J. Dearden, *Management Control Systems* (Irwin, 1976) between operational levels of management and strategic levels. They identify three levels of management activity:

    (i) Strategic planning [which] is the process of deciding on the goals of the organisation, on changes in these goals, on the resources used to attain these goals and on the policies that are to govern the acquisition, use and disposition of these resources.
    (ii) Management control [which] is the process by which managers assure that resources are obtained and used effectively and efficiently in the accomplishment of the organisation's goals.
    (iii) And operational control [which] is the process of assuring that specific tasks are carried out effectively and efficiently.

    Whilst we recognise that the majority of managers are engaged in the third level of activity for most of their time, the first two levels are clearly of great importance and it is with these levels that this book is mainly concerned.

6. See for example, W. F. Glueck, *Business Policy and Strategic Management*, McGraw-Hill, 1980; or Y.N. Chang and F. Campo-Flores, *Business Policy and Strategy*, Goodyear, 1980.

7. Michael Edwardes has written a book on his experiences with BL entitled *Back from the Brink* (William Collins, 1983).

8. For a detailed discussion see J-C. Spender, 'Strategy making in business' which is a PhD thesis from the Manchester Business School (1980). Spender's views are also summarised in P. Grinyer and J-C. Spender, *Turnaround: Managerial recipes for strategic success*, Associated Business Press, 1978. Also see P. Grinyer and J-C. Spender, 'Recipes, crises and adaptation in mature businesses', *Int. Studies of Management and Organisation*, **IX**: 113, 1979.

9. One of the most stimulating papers which addresses itself to the problems arising from an over-constrained view of the scope of a business is that by Theodore Levitt called 'Marketing myopia' (*Harvard Business Review*, July/Aug., 1960).

10. Chapter 18 in G. Steiner and J. Miner, *Management Policy and Strategy*, Collier Macmillan, 1977, discusses aspects of strategy in 'not-for-profit' organisations. An interesting and brief discussion of the problems and differences in the non-commercial sector can also be found in an article by M. L. Hatten called 'Strategic management in not-for-profit organisations', *Strategic Management Journal*, Apr./June, 1982.

11. An interesting discussion of strategy in government departments can be found in 'Strategic management in a government agency' by H. Tendam in *Long Range Planning*, **19**: 78–86, 1986.

12. This discussion on strategy in not-for-profit organisations is based on Chapter 11 of *Strategic Management* (2nd edn) by T. L. Wheelan and J. D. Hunger, Addison-Wesley, 1987.

Recommended key readings

• For a discussion of the concept of strategy which incorporates definitions by a number of writers see Chapter 2 of C. W. Hofer and D. Schendel, *Strategy Formulation: Analytical concepts*, West, 1978.

• An interesting discussion of different concepts of strategy can also be found in chapters 1 and 5 of *Strategies for Change: Logical incrementalism* by J.B. Quinn (Irwin, 1980).

• For a review of the role and relevance of strategic management to the public sector see 'Applying private sector strategic planning in the public sector' by J. M. Bryson and W. D. Roering in the *Journal of the American Planning Association*, Winter, 1987.

Chapter 2
STRATEGIC DECISION MAKING IN PRACTICE

2.1 INTRODUCTION

In Chapter 1 the idea of corporate strategy was introduced, as were the elements of strategic management – strategic analysis, strategic choice and strategy implementation. It is important to emphasise that these elements are parts of a model, the purpose of which is to help readers think about strategic problems and formulate strategy. It is also important, however, to understand that the model does not necessarily describe how strategies followed by organisations *actually* come about. There now exists a good deal of evidence about just how this does occur, so before going on to examine the elements of the model in more detail in Parts II, III and IV, it is important to have a clearer understanding of the process of strategic decision making in practice. This chapter sets out to provide a basis for that understanding and its content will be developed further in Chapters 5 and 11 in particular.

The first part of the chapter is concerned with the *nature of strategic change*, i.e. the ways in which strategic changes are observed to come about in organisations. The conclusion reached is that strategic changes may take different forms but that, typically, they do not occur as major, one-off changes in direction but as more gradual, 'incremental developments', with only occasional more 'global' change.

The second part of the chapter is concerned with *how managers make strategic decisions*. Here the focus is on the process of decision making: how a strategic problem is recognised and defined; how a decision to take a course of action is actually made. It emerges that a neat and rational process is not necessarily employed by managers and that some of the aspects of the strategic management model outlined in Chapter 1 may not be apparent in the processes actually employed. Rather, strategy needs to be understood as an outcome of the social, political and cultural processes of management in organisations. In this sense planning processes may more sensibly be seen as contributions to, rather than accounting for, strategic decisions.

In the final part of the chapter there is a discussion of what can be learned from the practice of strategic decision making in terms of *implications for the study of strategy*. It is, however, important to sound something of a warning: just because managers behave in particular ways does not mean these are the 'right' ways or the most sensible ways. It is important to assess what is 'good practice' and build on that. The approach taken in this book is that readers will be able to assess a good deal better for themselves which of the techniques and concepts in the rest of the book are most useful if they have an understanding of strategic decision making as it happens.

2.2 THE NATURE OF STRATEGIC CHANGE

Strategic changes are often conceived as one-off major changes. However, there is increasing evidence to show that the strategic development of organisations is better described in terms of continuity. There is a tendency towards 'momentum' of strategy;[1] once an organisation has adopted a particular strategy then it tends to develop from that strategy and within it rather than changing its direction. The result is that fundamental changes in strategy in organisations are relatively rare. Henry Mintzberg's historical studies of organisations[2] over many decades showed that 'global' change did take place but was infrequent. Rather, typically, organisations changed *incrementally*, during which times strategies formed gradually; or through *piecemeal* change during which some strategies changed and others remained constant; there were periods of *continuity* during which established strategy remained unchanged; and also period of *flux* in which strategies did change but in no very clear direction. Figure 2.1 illustrates these patterns.

On the whole, then, organisations' strategies tend not to change dramatically from year to year, perhaps even for very many years. One strategic move may well grow out of the existing mainstream strategy which, in itself, gradually changes. Over time, then, the organisation may develop a quite significant shift in strategy, but gradually. Illustration 2.1 shows how this might occur. In many respects, from a management point of view, such gradual, incremental change makes a lot of sense. No organisation could function efficiently if it were to undergo major revisions of strategy frequently; and, in any case, it is unlikely that the environment will change so rapidly that this would be necessary. Incremental change, might, therefore be seen as an adaptive process to a continually changing environment; indeed, this is the view held by some writers on the management of strategy and by many managers themselves. There are, however, dangers here. Environmental change may not always be gradual enough for incremental change to keep pace: if such incremental strategic change lags behind environmental change then the organisation may get out of line with its environment and, in time, need more fundamental, or global, strategic change to occur. Mintzberg's

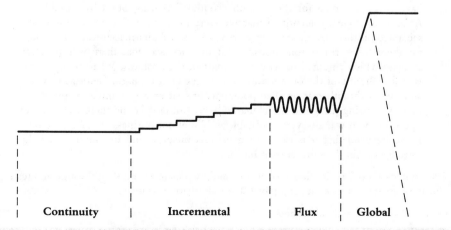

Continuity   **Incremental**   **Flux**   **Global**

Figure 2.1 Patterns of strategic change.

ILLUSTRATION 2.1

Incremental strategy development in Glaxo

The strategy followed by Glaxo has changed markedly in the last decade, not by huge strategic leaps, but incrementally.

In 1986 Glaxo announced a growth in profits before tax of over 50% to £612 million. Paul Girolami, Glaxo's Chairman stated that, 'Our concentration on prescription medicines, together with a commitment to generate growth from internal sources has enabled us to devote resources and management effort to the development of our mainstream business not only of a high quality but also with a potential for high growth'. This deliberate strategy of concentration on prescription medicines was the result of top management answering its core question, 'What is our business?' Answering this question in Glaxo took seven years. Mr Girolami described the way in which the issue was resolved.

In the 1970s Glaxo was in milk foods, over-the-counter medicines, surgical goods, horticultural products, laboratory chemicals and pharmaceutical wholesaling, as well as the manufacture of ethical pharmaceuticals. The decision we reached to concentrate on the manufacture of ethical pharmaceuticals was both protracted and difficult. The process started with the view that we were in the health business; and anything in that area went: we tended to extend our business boundaries by adding on to those areas. It seemed logical. All the initiatives we took were carefully studied but we realised over time that it was deforming the group. The top management spent years studying the problem and the changes we made gradually emerged. One of the things that influenced me was that the ethical pharmaceutical business was growing fast and taking up a lot of time of top management. So the other activities were being neglected and I thought they shouldn't be. Also there was no synergy at all between the prescription medicine business and other areas. The time scales of developments are different, the markets are different and the marketing was different. At one stage we came up with the idea that we should 'copy Beechams'. We should have an over-the-counter business and an ethical pharmaceuticals business and we should separate the two. But then we asked what resources do we have. We shall have to get them in for the over-the-counter business; but why should we? At another stage we identified that we were in seven different businesses. We separated off those businesses that were not in ethical pharmaceuticals and looked for them to be run autonomously. But the fact was that there was no clear strategy which emerged for that other part of the business. What became clear was that the life of the organisation was in the ethical pharmaceuticals business and not in the other areas. The potential for that area was huge, many of the medicines being produced in the market were not perfect and there was a world opportunity. It was also very profitable and I'm in the business of making money. I also believed that it is easier to manage a business and its culture if all the activities are in the same sort of business.

The strategy therefore developed over time and by managers thinking through and testing out the possibilities, benefits and pay-offs of alternative strategies.

Source: Correspondence with authors.

work seems to suggest that this is so; global change tends to occur at times of crisis in organisations, typically when performance has declined significantly.

Conceiving of organisations' strategies in terms of such patterns of change means it is important to be careful about just what is meant by 'strategy'. Typically, strategy is written about as though it is developed by managers in an *intended*, planned fashion. This may be so but it should be recognised that strategies may also come about in other ways. There may be *emergent* strategies that come about, are 'realised', without the explicit intention of managers but which result from the flow of more operational, day to day decision making.[3] It may also be that the strategies which managers do advocate explicitly are not put into effect: these are *unrealised* strategies.

These distinctions raise the point as to whether or not strategy should be thought of as that which managers say they are following (or think they should be following), or that which is actually being implemented by the business over time. They may well be the same, but it is also possible that they may not. It is an issue which is discussed further at the end of the chapter.

2.2.1 Incremental strategic management

In the late 1950s Lindblom[4] suggested that rational, planning models of strategic choice were unrealistic. He argued that, given the complexity of organisations and the environments in which they operate, managers cannot consider all possible strategic options in terms of all possible futures and evaluate these against pre-set, unambiguous objectives. This is particularly so in an organisational context in which there are likely to be conflicting views, values and power bases. Rather, choice of strategy is made by comparing options against each other and considering which would seem to give the best outcome and would be possible to implement. Lindblom called this strategy building through 'successive limited comparisons'. The implication is that those options most approximating to past decisions are likely to be those looked upon most favourably because they build on the experience of the organisation and its managers. The decision will then be put into operation and, in effect, tested in action before being developed further.

It is a position in many respects similar to that argued by Quinn.[5] His study of nine major multinational businesses concluded that the management process could best be described as *logical incrementalism*. By this he meant the following:

1. Managers have a view of where they want the organisation to be in years to come but try to move towards this position in an evolutionary way. They do this by attempting to ensure the success and development of a strong, secure but flexible core business, but also by continually experimenting with 'side bet' ventures.
2. Effective managers accept the uncertainty of their environment because they realise that they cannot do away with this uncertainty by trying to 'know' factually about how the environment will change: rather they seek to become highly sensitive to environmental signals through constant environmental scanning. They also manage uncertainty by testing changes in strategy in small-scale steps.
3. They also try to encourage experimentation in the organisation: moreover, there is a reluctance to specify precise objectives too early as this might stifle ideas and prevent the sort of experimentation which is desired. In addition, there is a recognition that

such experiments cannot be expected to be the sole responsibility of top management – that they should be encouraged to emerge from lower levels, or 'subsystems' in the organisation.

4. Such a process is seen by managers to have significant benefits. Continual testing and gradual strategy implementation provides improved quality of information for decision making and enables the better sequencing of the elements of major decisions. There is also a stimulation of managerial flexibility and creativity and, since change is always likely to be gradual, it is more likely to be possible to create and develop a commitment to change throughout the organisation. Such processes also take account of the political nature of organisational life since smaller changes are less likely to face the same extent of resistance as major changes. It is also more

---

ILLUSTRATION 2.2

A logical incrementalist view of strategic management

Managers often see their jobs as managing adaptively; continually changing strategy to keep in line with the environment, whilst maintaining efficiency and keeping stakeholders happy. Some quotes from managers illustrate this.

1 We tend to test a number of different approaches on a small scale with only limited or local company identification. If one approach works, we'll test it further and amplify its use; if another bombs, we try to keep it from being used again. ... then along comes another issue and we start all over again. Gradually the successful approaches merge into a pattern of actions that becomes our strategy.

2 I begin wide-ranging discussions with people inside and outside the corporation. From these a pattern eventually emerges. It's like fitting together a jigsaw puzzle. At first the vague outline of an approach appears like the sail of a ship in a puzzle. Then suddenly the rest of the puzzle becomes quite clear. You wonder why you didn't see it all along.

3 We had no particularly entrenched ideas as to where we were ... so there was an infinite amount of flexibility. One thing we decided was that we wanted to keep this appeal – it might not bring us an enormous leap forward, but as long as we can keep adjusting our merchandise mix and image satisfactorily, we can keep a fair share of the market.

4 The real strength of the company is to be able to follow these peripheral excursions into whatever ... one has to keep thrusting in these directions; they are little tentacles going out, testing the water.

5 We haven't stood still in the past and I can't see with our present set up that we shall stand still in the future; but what I really mean is that it is a path of evolution rather than revolution. Some companies get a successful formula and stick to that rigidly because that is what they know – for example [company x] did not really adapt to change, so they had to take what was a revolution. We hopefully have changed gradually and that's what I think we should do. We are always looking for fresh openings without going off at a tangent.

Sources: Extracts 1 and 2 from J. B. Quinn, *Strategies for Change*, Irwin, 1980; extracts 3, 4 and 5 from G. Johnson, *Strategic Change and the Management Process*, Basil Blackwell, 1987.

possible to accommodate the variety of resource demands and political ambitions of different groupings – or coalitions – in the organisation (see Chapter 5).

One implication of this is that the idea of a neat sequential model of strategy has to be questioned. The idea that the implementation of strategy somehow follows a choice, which in turn has followed analysis, does not hold. Rather strategy is here seen to be worked through in action. In a sense the implementation of strategy is the continual testing of the suitability of a strategy to the circumstances of that organisation.[6]

This view of strategy making as a process bears similarity to the descriptions managers themselves often give to how strategies come about in their organisations. Illustration 2.2 provides some examples of managers talking about the strategic decision making process in their organisation. It is essentially a 'logical incremental' view. They see their job as 'strategists' as continually adapting to their environment whilst not 'rocking the boat' too much so as to maintain efficiency and performance, and keeping the various stakeholders in the organisation – shareholders, other management departments and the employers, for example – content. Quinn himself argues that:[7]

> Good managers are aware of this process, and they consciously intervene in it. They use it to improve the information available for decisions and to build the psychological identification essential to successful strategies ... properly managed, it is a conscious, purposeful, proactive, executive practice.

He also suggests that the various decisions in the incremental process should not be seen as entirely separate. Because the subsystems of the organisation are in a continual state of interplay, the managers of each will know what the others are doing and can interpret each other's actions and requirements. They are, in effect, learning from each other about the feasibility of a course of action in terms of resource management and its internal political acceptability. Moreover, the formulation of strategy in this way means that the implications of the strategy are continually being tested out. This continual

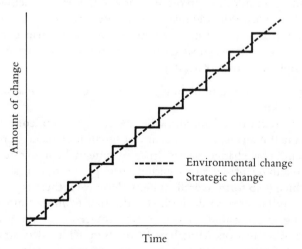

Figure 2.2 Notional incremental change – the environment changes gradually and organisation strategy develops incrementally in line with it. (From G. Johnson, *Strategic Change and the Management Process*, Basil Blackwell, 1987.)

readjustment does, of course, make a lot of sense if the environment is considered as a continually changing influence on the organisation. It is a process through which the organisation keeps itself in line with such change, as shown notionally in Figure 2.2.

2.2.2 Planning and strategic management

Where within all this, then, is the relevance and role of planning processes? The words 'strategy' and 'planning' have become so inextricably associated that it becomes necessary to define the role and forms of planning more clearly. This necessity stems from a common confusion between planning as a formalised activity, often known as corporate planning within an organisation, and planning as a more generalised term for what managers do when making strategic decisions.[8]

Planning, in the sense of analysing situations, considering the outcomes of proposals and thinking through the sequence of actions required to put change into effect, is part of the job of managers anyway: so, as far as strategic decisions are concerned, planning is not just the task of the corporate planner. Indeed, given an incremental process of strategic change, planning at the managerial level may be a more significant influence than planning at a corporate level.

It is also important to be clear as to the role of corporate planning in an organisation. There is little evidence to support the idea that corporate planning as an activity or corporate planners as managers in organisations are actually responsible for strategic decisions being taken.[9] Rather, the role of corporate planning appears to be to contribute to the strategic management process in three main ways:[10]

1. Assisting in the adaptation of the organisation to its environment by means of monitoring changes in the environment, formulating environmental and strategic scenarios and acting in a consultancy capacity to parts of the organisation that wish to examine the implications of environmental change. In this sense corporate planning is carrying out a strategic analysis function.
2. Providing an integration role in an organisation in the sense of acting as a communication channel between, for example, a corporate head office and its divisions.
3. Providing a control mechanism to monitor the performance of parts of the organisation (e.g. divisions) against strategic priorities. Here corporate planning has a role in the implementation of strategy.

The picture emerges of corporate planning as an aid to, rather than as the means of, strategic decision making.

It should also be clear that planning, whether in the form of corporate planning or as a task of individual managers, may occur within an incremental process of change just as it may when global change occurs. In an incremental context planning may take the form of the planning of decisions within parts of the organisation dealing with strategic issues which help form overall strategy. However, there is some evidence that formal planning may be more to do with contributing to more fundamental shifts in strategy originating at a corporate level. For example, in his study of the different patterns of strategy formulation, Mintzberg[11] found that 'intended' strategy (by which he meant the sort of formalised planning of change of strategy traditionally associated with strategic planning) tended to occur most often where there was global change.

Planning, then, is the responsibility of managers and is an important aspect of strategic management: and strategic management is not the property of a corporate planning department but the responsibility of managers and just as much part of managing incremental change as it is of more global change.[12]

2.3 HOW STRATEGIC DECISIONS ARE MADE

'Logical incrementalism' can be thought of as a rational, but action oriented, process of strategic management. However, it does retain the notion that managers consciously and logically seek to manage strategy, and that strategy comes about through such management logic. There is, however, other research which emphasises the 'organisational action' dimensions of strategic management a good deal more. This research[13] has sought to understand more fully the processes which actually occur in organisations and give rise to strategic decisions. There are four stages which can be used to describe such decision processes:

1. *Problem awareness*. The recognition that 'something is amiss', that a state of affairs exists which needs remedying.
2. *Problem diagnosis*. The collection of information about, and examination of the circumstances of the problem and the definition of the problem.
3. The *development of solutions*. The generation of possible solutions to the problem.
4. The *selection of a solution*. The means by which a decision about what is to be done is reached.

These stages are amplified in the discussion that follows, represented in Figure 2.3 and illustrated in Illustration 2.3.

2.3.1 Problem awareness

The awareness of a strategic problem typically occurs at an individual level. It is individuals who are likely to get a 'gut feeling' that something is wrong: and these may not be managers of course; they might well be salespeople, office staff or machine operators. This awareness is likely to develop through a period of what Lyles[14] calls 'incubation' in which managers sense various stimuli that confirm and define a developing picture of the problem. These stimuli are what Norburn[15] calls 'signals' or 'ear twitchers' and appear to be primarily of three sorts. First, there are internal performance measurements such as levels of turnover or profit performance. Second, there is customer reaction particularly to the quality and price of services or products. And third, there are changes in the environment, particularly in terms of competitive action, technological change and economic conditions. Together they create a picture of the extent to which an organisation's circumstances deviate from what is normally to be expected. This deviation may not be from a specified set of performance criteria such as profit measures, but could well be a perceived divergence from a normal trading pattern or a change from a typical customer response for example.

This accumulation of stimuli eventually reaches a point where the amount of

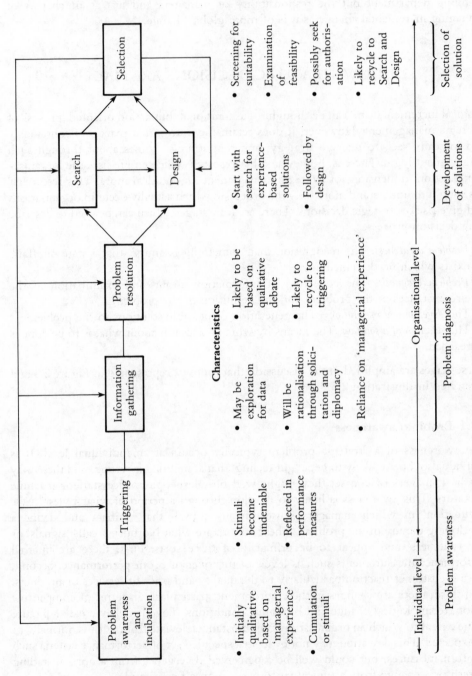

Figure 2.3 A model of the strategic decision process.

evidence is such that the presence of a problem cannot be ignored at an organisational level. This 'triggering point' is likely to be reached when the formal information systems of the organisation begin to highlight the problem; perhaps the variance against budget becomes undeniable or a number of sales areas consistently report dropping sales. It is at this point that more organised activity takes over from individual consideration of the problem.

The importance of this first stage of the individual's role in problem recognition needs to be emphasised. There is evidence to suggest that successful business performance is associated with management's capability in sensing its environment.[16] This does not necessarily mean that the company needs to have complex or sophisticated means of achieving this sensitivity but rather that managers respond to or take into account a wide range of influences and have an internally consistent view of these influences.

2.3.2 Problem diagnosis

At the organisational level problem diagnosis may involve information gathering and problem resolution (or definition).

Information gathering is likely to take the form of:

1. Exploration for information to determine more clearly the facts about the problem. Such information is likely to be sought and gathered on a verbal and informal basis[17] and this appears to be the more so the more senior the management. What these managers are in effect doing is building up a picture of the strategic position of their organisation through environmental sensing. There is little evidence of extensive formalised systematic environmental analysis.
2. The rationalisation of information and stimuli relevant to the problem so as to clarify the situation. This is a process which is likely to draw heavily on existing managerial experience. It appears that the role of information generated from more formalised environmental analysis in this process is likely to be to post-rationalise or justify managers' emerging views of the situation.
3. A process of 'diplomacy' to establish what peer groups or those with power in the organisation think about the problem and to gather political support for individuals' views of the problem.

The resolution (or definition) of what constitutes the nature of the problem may prove difficult. There is likely to be an attempt, through debate and discussion, to get some sort of organisational view or consensus on the problem that is to be tackled. In effect the resolution of the nature of the problem is, then, also through a process of diplomacy and is likely to take shape in terms of both collective managerial experience and the political processes in the organisation. Some organisations may also find difficulty in proceeding beyond this stage and find that the process reverts to information gathering or the triggering of a different problem.

Overall, it needs to be emphasised that, in practice, formal analysis tends to play much less of a role than might be suggested in some management texts. Rather, problem diagnosis tends to be rooted in managerial experience and different views resolved through social and political processes.

ILLUSTRATION 2.3

Toxicem's decision to reduce energy costs

Toxicem (a pseudonym), a chemical company facing rising energy costs, decided to generate in-plant electricity to reduce costs. The decision illustrates the iterative nature of the decision process, and the role of triggering and diplomacy.

PROBLEM/OPPORTUNITY AWARENESS	PROBLEM DIAGNOSIS	DEVELOPMENT OF SOLUTIONS	SELECTION OF SOLUTION
Rising costs of energy increase company costs	Production Director (A) considers if in-plant excess steam pressure could be utilised to reduce energy costs	Could excess steam be used to generate in-plant electricity?	
	Fuel Efficiency Service advises it is possible with use of higher pressure boiler		
Production expanded raising question of need for new boiler. Also National Coal Board offered lower quality, lower priced coal to companies with boilers to burn it.	A aware that required extra capital not available: also Purchasing Director (B) in opposition to idea because of lack of supporting evidence and personal opposition to A	Proposed purchase of new boiler	Purchase of new boiler agreed
	B recognised possibility of negotiating beneficial boiler contract for use of low-price coal and with potential benefit of in-plant electricity.		
Limits of new boiler reached unless operated at higher pressures (giving capabilities of electricity production)		A proposes to MD purchase of turbo-alternator for generation of electricity	Proposal put to Capital Control Committee. Opposed by B and Development Director (C).

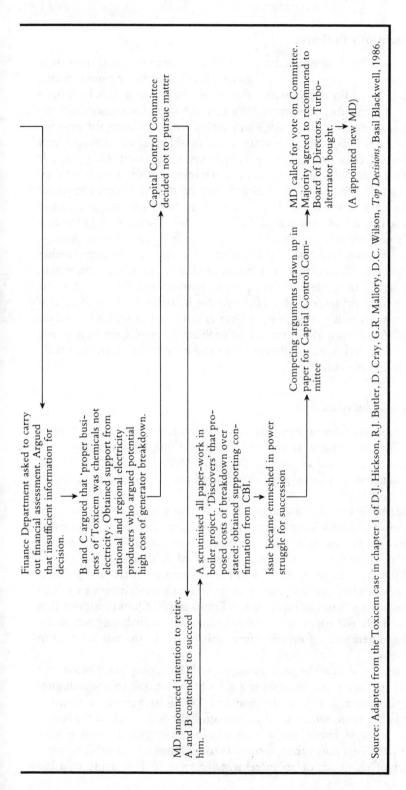

Finance Department asked to carry out financial assessment. Argued that insufficient information for decision.

B and C argued that 'proper business' of Toxicem was chemicals not electricity. Obtained support from national and regional electricity producers who argued potential high cost of generator breakdown.

Capital Control Committee decided not to pursue matter

MD announced intention to retire. A and B contenders to succeed him.

A scrutinised all paper-work in boiler project. 'Discovers' that proposed costs of breakdown over stated: obtained supporting confirmation from CBI.

Issue became enmeshed in power struggle for succession

Competing arguments drawn up in paper for Capital Control Committee

MD called for vote on Committee. Majority agreed to recommend to Board of Directors. Turbo-alternator bought.

(A appointed new MD)

Source: Adapted from the Toxicem case in chapter 1 of D.J. Hickson, R.J. Butler, D. Cray, G.R. Mallory, D.C. Wilson, *Top Decisions*, Basil Blackwell, 1986.

2.3.3 The development of solutions

Mintzberg[18] shows how the choice of solution is likely to have two stages: the first is the development of possible solutions, and the second is the selection between them.

Managers will first search for ready-made solutions to the problems that have been triggered. This will first occur through *memory search*, in which the manager seeks for known, existing or tried solutions, or *passive search* which entails waiting for possible solutions to be thrown up. It is only if these are unsuccessful that the manager will move on to more active searches, calling upon personal experience as a starting point. It is likely there will be a number of these searches in which managers draw on what they have experienced and tried in the past before there is any attempt to design a solution. By *design* is meant the custom-made building of a strategy to handle the problem at hand. In either case the process of choice tends to be iterative. Managers begin with a rather vague idea of a possible solution and gradually refine it by recycling it through selection routines (see below) back into problem identification or through further search routines. The process is developmental, based on debate and discussion within the organisation and, again, the collective management wisdom and experience in the organisation. There is little evidence that such a process is highly structured or that there is a clear set of options neatly set down, or clear criteria against which to analyse the choices available.[19] Again, as with the process of problem diagnosis, the importance of what might loosely be called managerial experience and its role within an essentially social and political process is evident.

2.3.4 The selection of a solution

As has been seen, the process of developing solutions may overlap with the processes of selecting solutions. They are somewhat arbitary categorisations for the purposes of description and might be regarded as part of the same process in which a limited number of potential solutions gradually get reduced until one or more emerges. This may occur in a number of ways.

First through 'screening' in which managers eliminate that which they consider not to be feasible. However, the predominant criterion for assessing feasibility is not formal analysis but managerial judgement followed by political bargaining. Formal analysis is the least observed of these three approaches. The use of analytical techniques in organisations should therefore be seen, again, within an essentially social and political process. It should also be realised that analysis, in itself, is not the only means by which insights into problems or solutions can be obtained. For example, Quinn suggests that successful managers actively use bargaining processes in order to challenge prevailing strategic inclinations and generate information from other parts of the organisation to help in making decisions.

It should be remembered that the process might well be taking place below the most senior levels of management, so referring possible solutions to some higher hierarchical level may be required, and another way of selecting between possibilities is to refer the choice to this more senior level of management – to seek *authorisation*. Typically, though not always, authorisation is sought for a completed solution after screening has taken place. This raises the question as to whether it is sensible to view this referral as a sort of checking of an incrementally generated strategic solution against some overall strategy. It would certainly be in line with Mintzberg's view that whilst most strategic decisions emanate from decisions from within management subsystems, it is the role of leadership to maintain some sort of general direction. If this view is taken then the process of authorisation can be thought of as the matching of one strategic decision against an overall, more generalised, strategy or mission of the organisation.

These findings about decision processes are, in general, borne out by David Hickson and his colleagues[20] in a study of 150 major decisions in thirty different public and private sector organisations in the UK. They identified three broad types of decision making process:

1. *Sporadic* processes characterised by many delays and impediments, many sources of influence and information on decisions and, therefore, protracted personal inter-action and informal negotiation.
2. *Fluid* processes in which there are fewer delays and sources of influence, and more formal channels of communication which take rather less time.
3. *Constricted* processes in which information sources are more readily available and decisions can be taken within groups who or by individuals without extensive reference to others in the organisation. This might be the case in a business with a dominant chief executive, or where there is an issue which relates primarily to one part of an organisation.

Over time all three types of process are likely to be found in most organisations. However, there seems to be some bias towards sporadic decision making in manufac-turing industries, in which decision making tends to be more decentralised and subject to many conflicting interests, compared with service industries, which are rather more characterised by fluid processes and face rather less complexity. Public sector organisa-tions tend to be characterised by more sporadic decision processes largely because of committee procedures, external intervention and the need to arrive at politically acceptable consensus.

2.4 STRATEGY FORMULATION AS A CULTURAL PROCESS

Traditionally, strategy has been viewed as the response of an organisation to its environment. The environment changes and management rethinks and adjusts strategy as necessary. However, the organisation has severe limitations on making such readjustments. The constraints that have received most attention from writers have been constraints in the environment itself that hinder change (competitive action, government legislation, economic forces and so on), and internal organisational resource constraints (a lack of finance or competent management, for example).

This view omits a major influence on strategy formulation to do with the strategy makers themselves. It is too simple to think of strategy as a response to the environment for it is evident that, faced with similar environments, organisations will respond differently: as has been seen, the response is likely to be influenced by the past experience of the managers and by the wider social and political processes in the organisation. It is these social processes of strategy formulation that have received so much attention in the work of those writers and researchers[21] who have sought to understand how some businesses seem to perform consistently so much better than others – the so-called excellent companies. And the general conclusion that these writers come to is that processes of strategic management need to be understood as an essentially cultural process.

In this book 'organisational culture' is taken to mean 'the deeper level of basic *assumptions and beliefs* that are shared by members of an organisation, that operate unconsciously and define in a basic 'taken for granted' fashion an organisation's view of itself and its environment';[22] and also the ways that members of the organisation behave towards each other, the rituals and routines of organisational life, the stories that are told of organisational history, the type of language and expression commonly used, and the organisational 'symbols' such as logos, organisation charts, status symbols policies on rewards and incentives, and so on:[23] in short, 'the way we do things around here'.[24]

2.4.1 Culture and strategy

There is now a growing understanding that the strategy of an enterprise, its structure, the sorts of people who hold power, its control systems and the way it operates, tend to reflect the culture of that organisation. The work of Miles and Snow[25] which will be referred to on several occasions, illustrates this. They point out that there are organisations in which the prevailing beliefs are essentially conservative, where low-risk strategies, secure markets and well-tried potential solutions are valued: they call these types of organisation 'defenders'. In contrast, there are organisations in which the dominant beliefs are more to do with innovation and breaking new ground. Here management tends to go for higher risk strategies and new opportunities. Miles and Snow call these 'prospector'-type organisations. The different beliefs and assumptions within these two different types of operation are also reflected more widely.[26] For example, organisational stories in defenders are typically to do with historical stability and consensus whereas in prospector organisations they are about growth and change with tales of dissension rather than consensus. The routines in the types of organisation are also different; prospector organisations tend to have less rigid approaches to decision taking and planning, for example, with less of an emphasis on formal relationships between people and groups.

The point is that prospectors and defenders do not behave in the same way even within similar environments. The strategies that such organisations follow are better accounted for by their prevailing beliefs than by the environmental stimuli. For example, faced with a declining market demand, the defender is likely to follow a strategy of concentration on the market niche in which it specialises and a tighter control of costs, whilst the prospector searches for opportunities to obtain new markets or increase market share. In turn, in defender-type organisations, conservative approaches and an emphasis on efficiency tend to be institutionalised by a dominance over time of managers with personally conservative ideologies, often from managerial functions which emphasis control and efficiency – notably accountants and production management.

2.4.2 The recipe and the cultural web

The set of beliefs and assumptions which form part of the culture of an organisation have variously been called interpretative schemes,[27] paradigms[28] and recipes.[29] Here the word recipe[30] is used. The recipe is the set of beliefs and assumptions held relatively

---

ILLUSTRATION 2.4

Recipes

The recipe for success in an industry takes the form of managers' views of 'how to succeed' in their business environment.

A fashion retailer

To run a successful fashion retailing operation, managers believe that they should:

- Look for growth.
- Continually experiment with new merchandise or ventures.
- Provide promotion opportunities.
- Continually adapt to changes in customer shopping habits.
- Closely monitor variable costs.
- Centralise control of merchandise, distribution, marketing decisions and shop appearance.

A milk processor and distributor

To operate a successful milk processing and distribution business, managers believe they should:

- Pursue greater volume of sales.
- Expand territory serviced.
- Monitor other distribution operations with a view to takeover.
- Optimise length and sales volume of delivery rounds.
- Increase sales per customer.
- Sell additional products and not just milk.
- Concentrate throughput into larger processing plants.

Managers in these two different businesses therefore conceive of the recipe for success in their businesses quite differently.

The fashion retailer faces a business environment that is dependent on consumer tastes. The emphasis in coping with this uncertainty is to continually test the consumers' reaction to change. Growth is seen as a motivator for staff and a means of attracting new talent, both of which are thought necessary to generate new ideas. Centralisation of decision making is seen as beneficial in providing speedy decisions and controlling the merchandise and store image.

The business environment faced by the milk processor and distributor is, by contrast, very stable. They operate within a 'set margin', fixed on the one hand by the Milk Marketing Board which sets the price at which the company buys, and on the other by the government which fixes the price at which the company sells to the consumer. The method of coping with this situation is more 'internalised', geared towards the efficiency of operations. They seek to concentrate milk processing into larger plants to achieve greater economies of scale. However, to be in a position to build these large processing plants, the company must increase the throughput of milk; therefore pursuing greater sales volume by expanding the territory serviced and increasing sales per customer become important criteria for success.

Source: Authors and J-C. Spender, 'Strategy-making in Business', PhD thesis from the Manchester Business School.

commonly throughout the organisation, taken for granted in that organisation, but discernible to the outside observer in the stories of organisational history and explanations of events. The recipe makes sense of the situation managers find themselves in and provides a basis for formulating strategy. Illustration 2.4 gives examples of such recipes.

It is not suggested that the beliefs and assumptions which make up the recipe are necessarily identical for everyone in the organisation – although there is evidence to suggest that in some organisations it is particularly uniform.[31] Nor is it suggested that it is a static set of beliefs – although it is quite likely that it will evolve gradually rather than change suddenly. What it does represent, however, is the collective managerial experience that is seen to be so important in the formulation of strategy. Managers cannot 'reinvent their world' afresh for all circumstances they face or decisions they take: the recipe allows the experience gathered over years to be applied to a given situation so as to decide upon relevant information by which to assess the need for change, a likely course of action, and the likelihood of success of that course of action.

The relationship and distinction between the recipe and organisational strategy need to be made clear. Figure 2.4 helps to do this. Environmental forces and organisational capabilities do not in themselves create organisational strategy: it is people who create strategy. The mechanism by which this is done is through the recipe. The forces at work in the environment, and the organisation's capabilities in coping with these, are made sense of through the assumptions and beliefs called the recipe and in this way strategy is formulated. The strategies that managers advocate and those that emerge through the social and political processes previously described are, then, typically configured within the bounds of this recipe. However, environmental forces and organisational capabilities, whilst having this indirect influence on strategy formulation, nonetheless do impact on organisational performance much more directly. For example, in the menswear clothing company cited in Illustration 2.3, it was certainly the case in the late 1970s that the competitive environment for the company was changing dramatically. Large companies such as Burtons and Marks & Spencer,

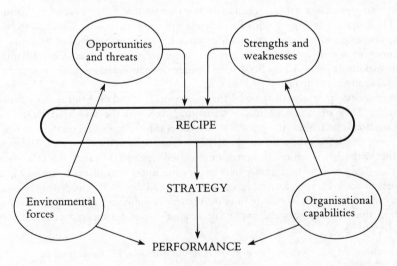

Figure 2.4 The role of the recipe in strategy formulation.

not previously direct competitors, were now becoming so. Until the early 1980s, however, the managers of the company felt themselves 'insulated' from such changes largely by their traditional market positioning and their buying expertise. The strategy of the business therefore developed little by little – incrementally – within the dominant recipe. However, the actual impact of the competitive activity of Burtons and Marks and Spencer did, of course, have a major impact on the performance of the company and, eventually, forced a reappraisal of strategy.[32] This potential difference between the actual influences and managerial perceptions of the influences on the organisation can give rise to significant problems – and is an issue returned to later.

The recipe may, then, be a very conservative influence on strategy. This is the more so since, as has been seen, the links between the recipe itself and 'the way we do things around here' is likely to be close. This is shown in Figure 2.5. For example, the links between the power structure in the organisation and the core set of beliefs held by managers in that organisation are likely to be strong. The recipe represents the 'formula for success' which is taken for granted in the business and likely to have grown up over years; the most powerful groupings within the business are likely to have derived their very power from association with this set of beliefs and their ability to put them into operation.[33] In the menswear retailer discussed above the buyers had always had a good deal of power for example. One implication of this is that it is likely that a purely analytical questioning of the recipe not only will be taken as evidence of the analyst's lack of understanding of the problems of the business but may actually be perceived as a political threat, rather than objective analysis, for it will very likely be perceived as an attack on those most associated with those core beliefs, and an attempt to 'rock the boat'. Even if managers 'intellectually' accept such analysis they may be more influenced by the recipe and its cultural underpinnings in formulating, persisting with, or adjusting strategy. The recipe is also likely to be associated with the control systems, routines and rituals of the organisation which will tend to preserve the status quo: and

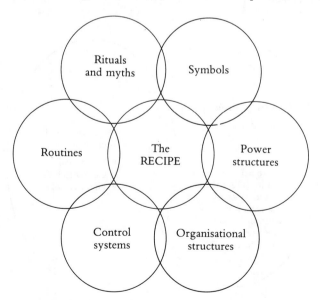

Figure 2.5 The cultural web of an organisation.

ILLUSTRATION 2.5

The cultural web of the Barshire Building Society*

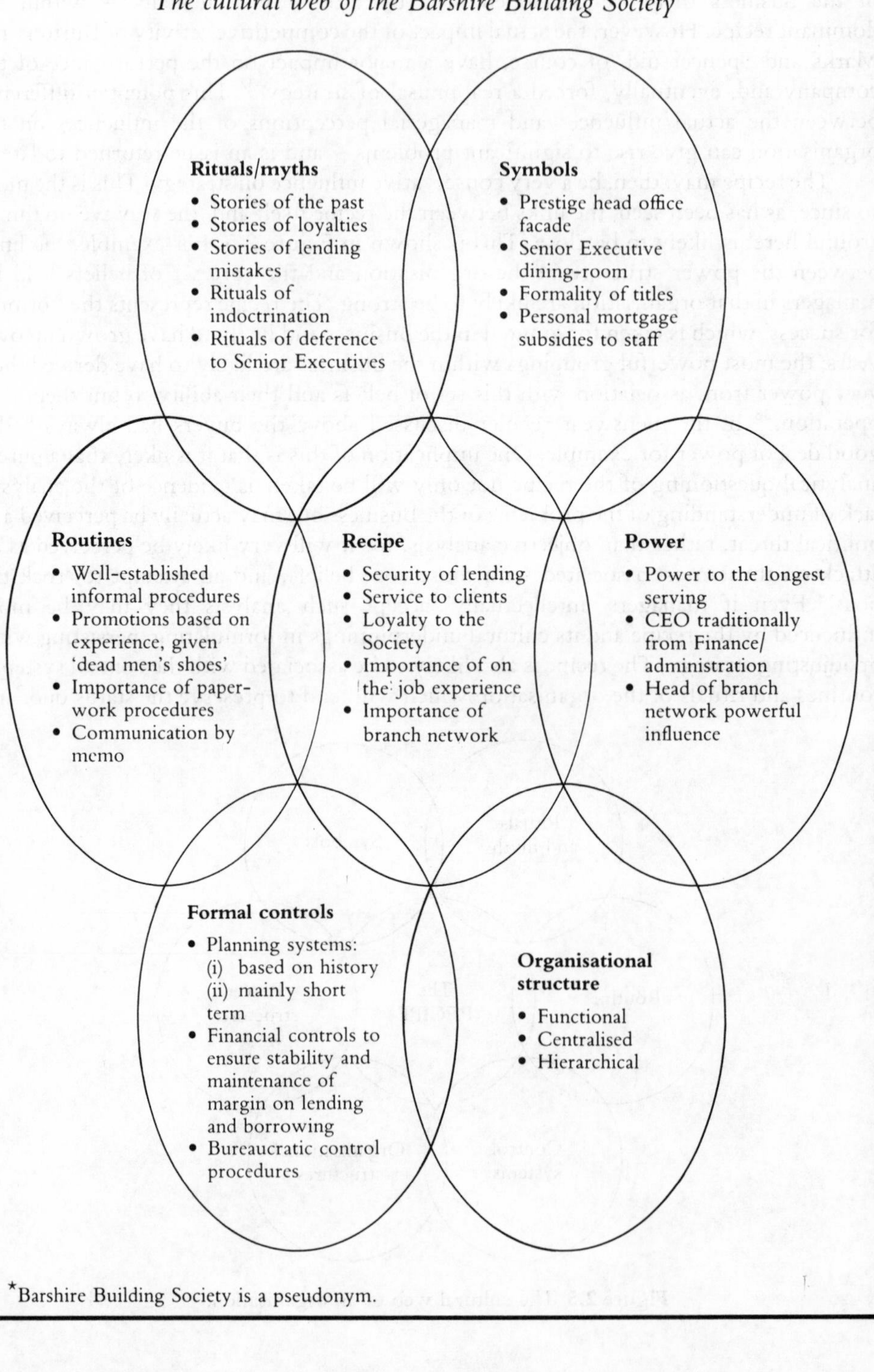

Rituals/myths
- Stories of the past
- Stories of loyalties
- Stories of lending mistakes
- Rituals of indoctrination
- Rituals of deference to Senior Executives

Symbols
- Prestige head office facade
- Senior Executive dining-room
- Formality of titles
- Personal mortgage subsidies to staff

Routines
- Well-established informal procedures
- Promotions based on experience, given 'dead men's shoes'
- Importance of paper-work procedures
- Communication by memo

Recipe
- Security of lending
- Service to clients
- Loyalty to the Society
- Importance of on the job experience
- Importance of branch network

Power
- Power to the longest serving
- CEO traditionally from Finance/administration
- Head of branch network powerful influence

Formal controls
- Planning systems:
  (i) based on history
  (ii) mainly short term
- Financial controls to ensure stability and maintenance of margin on lending and borrowing
- Bureaucratic control procedures

Organisational structure
- Functional
- Centralised
- Hierarchical

*Barshire Building Society is a pseudonym.

here the sorts of myths and stories and the types of language used will tend to reflect and support the core beliefs that exist. The point is that the recipe is not just a set of beliefs and assumptions; rather it is embedded in a set of organisational-specific cultural web which legitimises and preserves the assumptions and beliefs in the organisation. This is shown in Illustration 2.5.

2.4.3 A cultural view of patterns of strategic change

Faced with pressures for change, managers will be likely to deal with the situation in ways which protect the recipe from challenge. This raises difficulties when managing strategic change for it may be that the action required is outside the scope of the recipe and the constraints of the cultural web – that members of the organisation would be required to change substantially their core beliefs or 'the way we do things around here'. Desirable as this may be, the evidence is that it does not occur easily.[34] Managers are much more likely to attempt to deal with the situation by searching for what they can understand and cope with in terms of existing recipe. In other words, they will attempt to minimise the extent to which they are faced with ambiguity and uncertainty by looking for that which is familiar. Figure 2.6 illustrates how this might occur. Faced with a stimulus for action, in this case declining performance, managers first seek for means of improving the implementation of existing strategy: this could be through the tightening of controls. In effect, they will tighten up their accepted way of operating. If this is not effective, then a change of strategy may occur, but still a change which is in

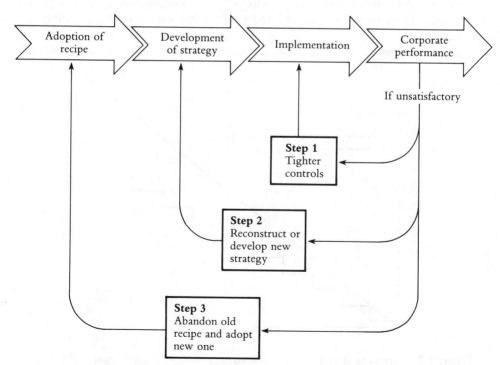

Figure 2.6 Dynamics of recipe change. (From P. Grinyer and J-C. Spender, *Turnabout: Managerial recipes for strategic success*, p.203, Associated Business Press, 1979.)

line with the existing recipe. For example, managers may seek to extend the market for their product but retain the same views about the range of products they produce, the main virtues of the products, the nature of what remains as the main markets, and how they should go about operating in those markets. There has been no change to the recipe itself and there is not likely to be until this attempt to reconstruct strategy in the image of the existing recipe also fails. What is occurring is the predominant application of the familiar and the attempt to avoid or reduce uncertainty or ambiguity.

This is, of course, an alternative explanation of the observed phenomenon of incrementalism; and some writers have accounted for incrementalism not as a logical phenomenon but as a phenomenon rooted in the belief systems of organisations.[35] However, the outcome of processes of decision making of this kind is not likely to be the careful, logical, adaptive strategy making which keeps in line with environmental change as shown in Figure 2.2. Rather it is likely to be an adaptation in line with the perceived management wisdom as enshrined in the recipe. Nonetheless the forces in the environment will have an effect on performance. Over time this may well give rise to the sort of drift shown in Figure 2.7 in which the organisation's strategy gradually, if imperceptibly, moves away from the environmental forces at work. This pattern of drift is made more difficult to detect and reverse because not only are changes being made in strategy – albeit within the parameters of the recipe – but, since such changes are the application of the familiar, they may achieve some short term improvement in performance, thus tending to legitimise the action taken. The recipe is then, a virtually inevitable feature of organisational life which, at best, can be thought of as encapsulating the distinctive competences of organisation[36] or, more dangerously, as a conservative influence likely to prevent change and result in the sort of strategic momentum noted earlier.

As will be argued later in the book, the important conclusions would appear to be

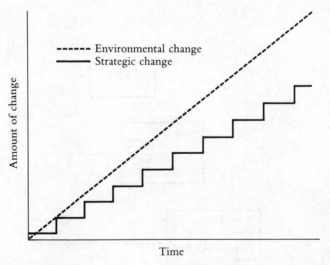

Figure 2.7 Incremental strategic change and strategic drift – the environment changes but organisation strategy fails to develop in line with it. Strategy moves imperceptibly away from environmental 'reality'.

that there is a need for the strategist to understand what beliefs and assumptions comprise the recipe, what mechanisms in the cultural web preserve it, and how the recipe can be challenged sufficiently to prevent an inability to achieve strategic change.

2.5 A SUMMARY OF IMPLICATIONS FOR THE STUDY OF STRATEGY

This chapter has dealt with the processes of strategic management as they are to be found in organisations. The chapter is therefore descriptive not prescriptive. There is no suggestion here that, because such processes exist, this is how strategy *should* be managed. However, it is important to understand the reality of strategy making in organisations not least because those who seek to influence the strategy of organisations must do so within that reality. There is little point in formulating strategies which may be elegant analytically without having an understanding of the processes which are actually at work. Moreover it is this book's intention that the subject should be approached in such a way that it builds upon this understanding of reality and, wherever possible, relates an essentially analytical approach to the real world of managers.

In this concluding section of the chapter, the basic lessons of this chapter are briefly summarised and related to what follows in the rest of the book.

2.5.1 A summary of the key points

1. It is important to distinguish between the *intended* strategy of managers – that which they say the organisation will follow – and the *realised* strategy of an organisation – that which it is actually following. This is particularly important when considering how relevant current strategy is to a changing environment: it may be more useful to consider the relevance of realised strategy than intended strategy.
2. Strategy, usually evolves incrementally: strategic change tends to occur as a continual process of relatively small adjustments to existing strategy through activity within the subsystems of an organisation.
3. However, there is likely to be an overall strategic direction, a strategic momentum, a change of which is often associated with an organisation getting out of line with a changing environment (strategic drift) and eventually reaching a point of crisis.
4. Formal planning (e.g. in the sense of corporate planning) is important as an aid to analysing strategic positions and thinking through options, but is not normally a vehicle for the formulation of strategy.
5. The way in which managers assess the need for strategic change is through an essentially qualitative assessment of signals which accumulate from inside and outside the organisation.
6. The definition of strategic problems and choice of strategies by managers are not so much reliant upon dispassionate analysis of data but (a) on perceptions of what powerful individuals in the organisation see as the problems, and (b) upon the manager's reconciliation of the circumstances of the situation with past experience

and the received wisdom encapsulated in the core assumptions and beliefs of the organisation, known as the recipe.

7. The 'cultural web' of an organisation — its political structures, routines, and rituals and symbols are likely to exert a preserving and legitimising influence on the core beliefs and assumptions that comprise the recipe and hence make strategic change the more difficult to achieve.

2.5.2 The implications for exploring corporate strategy

There is no reason to discard the more traditional frameworks for considering strategic issues. For the strategist, building up a clear picture of the strategic position of the organisation through some sort of analysis is vital; deciding what strategies are more or less sensible can also be aided greatly through techniques of analysis and evaluation; and the logical planning of implementation is also important. However, all of this has to take place in such a way as to address the reality of strategic management as a social, political and cultural phenomenon. The approach in this book has been influenced strongly by this dual need of the strategist: some of the ways in which this is done can usefully be spelled out at this stage.

First, as has been said in Chapter 1, the idea of a purely sequential model of strategic management has been rejected. The headings of strategic analysis, choice and implementation are a useful structure for the book, and for thinking about the problems of strategy, but readers are urged to regard these aspects of strategic management as interdependent and an influence on one another.

This chapter has highlighted the substantial influence of the beliefs and assumptions of managers within a cultural setting. If the strategist is to have an influence on the formulation of strategy and is to consider sensibly the ability of the organisation to implement that strategy, it is important that these cultural aspects of the organisation are explicitly understood. Without such an understanding, strategy making is of little relevance to organisational reality. For this reason emphasis is placed in this book on the importance of understanding the nature of the beliefs and assumptions of managers and the cultural and political context in which they exist. This is regarded as an integral part of the process of strategic analysis, and in Chapter 5 there are sections on how an analysis of such systems may be usefully undertaken. It is also regarded as a factor to be considered in strategy evaluation and is therefore considered again in Chapter 7 when the notion of 'cultural fit' is discussed.

Moreover, it is recognised that it is the political and cultural barriers to change that may well provide the major stumbling blocks to the implementation of strategic change. Chapter 11, therefore, comes back to the processes of strategic management with a view to examining how strategy and strategic change can be implemented within the cultural context of the organisation. In Chapter 11 it is argued that whilst the formulation of strategy may well benefit from the sort of rational, analytical approach that is traditional in the subject, and it is necessary to plan logically the allocation of resources, managing the acceptance of a strategic change is essentially a cultural process and needs to be considered as such and implemented as a culture change process. Chapter 11 considers how this might be achieved. It is also argued in Chapter 11 that leadership in organisations needs to be seen quite clearly as a task which requires both rational, analytical aspects of management and cultural aspects to be harnessed in order to implement strategic change.

Whilst the reality of judgement and the prevalence of bargaining processes in organisations are accepted, the book also contains examples of and references to many techniques of quantitative and qualitative analysis. The value of such analytical approaches is not to be diminished. Not only do they provide an essential tool for managers to conceive of strategic problems and analyse possible solutions, they also provide means whereby the 'taken for granted' wisdom of the organisation and assumed courses of action can be challenged.

The overall aim is, then, to provide a framework for strategy and strategic management which usefully combines the rigour of analysis with the reality of the processes of management.

REFERENCES

1. The idea of strategy 'momentum' is discussed fully in 'Momentum and revolution in organisational adaptation' by D. Miller and P. Friesen in the *Academy of Management Journal*, **23**: 591–614, 1980.

2. These generalised patterns of strategy development are based on those discussed by Henry Mintzberg in 'Patterns of strategy formation', in *Management Science*, May 1978, pp. 934–48, although his own categorisation is a good deal more complex than the one used in this book.

3. Terms such as 'deliberate', 'realised' and so on, are again those used by Henry Mintzberg (reference 2).

4. Lindblom's paper 'The science of muddling through' (*Public Administration Review*, **19**: 79–88, Spring 1959) is one of the earliest which criticises an over-rational view of strategy formation and argues for an incremental perspective within a social and political context.

5. J. B. Quinn's research involved the examination of strategic change in companies and has been published in *Strategies for Change*, Irwin, 1980.

6. The term 'unfolding rationality' is used by Lou Pondy in explaining incrementalism in a paper entitled 'The union of rationality and intuition in management action' published in *The Executive Mind*, S. Srivastava (ed.), Jossey Bass, 1983.

7. See *Strategies for Change* (reference 5), p. 58.

8. In 'What is planning anyway?' (*Strategic Management Journal*, **2**: 139–324, 1981) Henry Mintzberg suggests that planning has taken on different meanings for managers. Planning may mean any of the following: future thinking, integrated decision making, formalised procedures of planning (which is what Mintzberg suggests is assumed in most of the literature), and planning as programming (for example, budgeting). He makes the point that all of these different meanings are relevant to the management task and it is often not entirely clear what is being referred to when the word 'planning' is used.

9. This is borne out in much of the research into strategic decision making and corporate planning. For example, see Quinn (reference 5); H. Mintzberg, O. Raisinghani and A. Theoret, 'The structure of unstructured decision processes', *Administrative Science Quarterly*, **21**: 246–75, 1976; W.K. Hall, 'Strategic planning models: are top managers really finding them useful?', *Journal of Business Policy*, **3** (2), 1973.

10. The role of corporate planning is based on the research findings in the PhD dissertation of H. Bahrami entitled 'Design of corporate planning systems' (University of Aston, October 1981). This research was conducted in fourteen large, mainly multinational, UK-based firms.

11. Again, see reference 2.

12. Writers who advocate a step-by-step, formalised planning approach as a basis for thinking about strategic management, recognise the importance of the less formalised management aspect. For example, G. Steiner and J. Miner in *Management Policy and Strategy* (p. 92, Collier Macmillan, 1977) say: 'The formal system (of planning) should help managers to sharpen their intuitive anticipatory inputs into the planning process. At the very least, the formal system should give managers more time for reflective thinking ... But formal planning cannot be really effective unless managers at all levels inject their judgements and intuition into the planning process'.

13. For a summary of 'organisational action' explanations of strategic management see Chapter 2 of *Strategic Change and the Management Process* by Gerry Johnson (Basil Blackwell, 1987).

14. For a thorough discussion of the problem awareness and diagnosis stages of the decision making process, see M. A. Lyles, 'Formulating strategic problems: empirical analysis and model development', *Strategic Management Journal*, **2**: 61–75, 1981.

15. The presence and nature of these signals are confirmed and discussed in D. Norburn and P. Grinyer, 'Directors without direction', *General Management*, **1**(2) 1973/4.

16. This proposition is supported by the research of P. Grinyer and D. Norburn (reference 15), J. B. Quinn (reference 5), and D. Miller and P. Friesen, 'Archetypes of strategy formulation', *Management Science*, **24**(9) 1978.

17. Researchers who have examined environmental influences on strategy would broadly agree with this. See, for example, P. Grinyer and D. Norburn, 'Directors without direction' (reference 15); F. Aguilar, *Scanning the Business Environment*, Macmillan, 1967; H. Mintzberg *et al.* (reference 9).

18. This discussion is based on the findings detailed in Mintzberg *et al.*'s research (reference 9).

19. Fahey confirms the absence of the establishment of clear options or clear criteria of evaluation in his study 'On strategic management decision processes' (*Strategic Management Journal*, **2**: 43–60, 1981).

20. The discussion on sporadic, fluid and constricted processes of decision making is based on work by David Hickson and his colleagues at Bradford Management Centre published in *Top Decisions: Strategic decision making in organisations*, Basil Blackwell, 1986.

21. There has now been a number of writers who have attempted to study 'excellence' in organisations. This began early in the 1980s with Peters and Waterman's book *In Search of Excellence* (Harper & Row, 1982), but has also included such studies as *The Change Masters* by Rosabath Moss Kanter (published in the UK by Unwin/Counterpoint, 1985), and has included replications of such studies in different parts of the world. For example, see D. Clutterbuck and W. Goldsmith *The Winning Streak* (Weidenfeld and Nicolson, 1984) for a UK study, and *Theory K: The key to excellence in New Zealand management* by K. Inkson, B. Henshall, N. Marsh, and G. Ellis (David Bateman Ltd, 1986).

22. Edgar Schein, *Organisational Culture and Leadership*, p. 6, Jossey Bass, 1985.

23. The approach in this book, in common with some other writers, is that culture can be

understood not just as sets of beliefs and assumptions, but also as the behaviour patterns, language, and social devices such as rituals and control systems. This view is generally known as 'cultural adaptationist' and is expressed more fully by Roger Keesing in 'Theories of culture', *Annual Review of Anthropology*, **3**: 73–9, 1974.

24. The expression 'the way we do things around here' as an explanation of culture was coined by Deal and Kennedy in their book *Corporate Cultures: The rites and rituals of corporate life*, Addison-Wesley, 1982.

25. This section is based on the work of R. Miles and C. Snow, which can be found in *Organisational Strategy, Structure and Process*, McGraw-Hill, 1978.

26. A. D. Meyer, worked with Miles and Snow on their research and separately published findings on the different cultures of defenders and prospectors. This can be found in 'How ideologies supplement formal structures and shape response to environments', *Journal of Management Studies*, **19**: 45–61, 1982.

27. The term 'interpretative schemes' is used by J. M. Bartunek in 'Changing interpretative schemes and organisational restructuring the examples of a religious order', *Administrative Science Quarterly*, **29**: 355–72, 1984.

28. The term 'paradigms' is used by Jeffrey Pfeffer in 'Management as symbolic action: the creation and maintenance of organisation paradigms', in L. L. Cummings and B. M. Staw (eds), *Research in Organisational Behaviour*, Vol. 3, pp. 1–15, J.A.I. Press, 1981. It is also a term used by A. Sheldon in 'Organisational paradigms, a theory of organisational change' (*Organisational Dynamics*, **8** (3): 61–71, 1980) and by Gerry Johnson in *Strategic Change and the Management Process*, Basil Blackwell, 1987).

29. The term 'recipes' is used by J-C. Spender in his PhD thesis 'Strategy making in business', School of Business, University of Management, 1980. It was also a term used by Peter Grinyer and J-C. Spender in 'Recipes, crises and adaptation in mature businesses', *International Studies of Management and Organisation*, **9**: 113–23, 1979) and in *Turnaround: Managerial Recipes for Strategic Success; The fall and rise of the Newton Chambers Group*, Associated Business Press, 1979. Both Grinyer and Spender used the term to signify those beliefs and assumptions held at an industry rather than organisational level.

30. Although we use the term 'recipe' in this edition it is used in an organisation-specific sense. We have chosen to retain the use of the word 'recipe' rather than 'paradigm', largely for purposes of continuity, since it was used in the first edition.

31. The word 'clans' was used by W. G. Ouchi (see 'Markets, bureaucracies and plans', *Administrative Science Quarterly*, **25**: 129–41, 1980) to refer to organisations with particularly homogeneous sets of beliefs and assumptions.

32. In *Strategic Change and the Management Process* (reference 13) Johnson gives a detailed account of strategic change in Foster Brothers, the menswear clothing retailer in the UK, which shows the way in which managerial perceptions and environmental influences affected strategy formulation over time and the performance of the business.

33. A number of writers and researchers have pointed to the links between the locus of power in organisations and the perceived ability of such powerful individuals or groups to 'reduce uncertainty' (see D. J. Hickson *et al.*, 'A strategic contingencies theory of intra-organisational power', *Administrative Science Quarterly*, **16**: 216–29, 1971; D. C. Hambrick, 'Environment, strategy and power within top management teams', *Administrative Science Quarterly*, **26**: 253–76, 1981). Since the recipe is, in effect, the 'perceived wisdom' of how to operate successfully in the organisation, it is likely that those most associated with the recipe will be

the most powerful in the organisation; although he uses the term 'paradigm', Johnson makes this point (reference 13).

34. Certainly Chris Argyris vividly illustrates the extent to which 'theories-in-use', as a code of behaviour, are very resistant to change and challenge (see *Organisational Learning: A theory of action perspective*, Addison-Wesley, 1978).

35. See Miller and Friesen (reference 1) and Johnson (reference 13, particularly Chapter 8).

36. Both S. A. Lippman and R. P. Rumelt ('Uncertain imitability: an analysis of inter-firm differences in efficiency under competition', *Bell Journal of Economics*, **13**: 418–38, 1982), and R. R. Nelson and S. G. Winter (*An Evolutionary Theory of Economic Change*, Harvard University Press, 1982) point out that the routines of organisations can provide distinctive competences upon which organisations can build in order to achieve competitive advantage.

Recommended key readings

- For an examination of how strategic decisions are made in private and public sector organisations: D. J. Hickson, R. J. Butler, D. Cray, G. R. Mallory and D. C. Wilson, *Top Decisions*, Basil Blackwell, 1986.

- On incremental strategic change: J. B. Quinn, *Strategies for Change: Logical incrementalism*, Irwin, 1980.

- On cultural influences on strategy: R. E. Miles and C. C. Snow, *Organisational Strategy, Structure and Process*, McGraw-Hill, 1978.

- For a detailed historical examination of strategic change processes in organisations see Gerry Johnson, *Strategic Change and the Management Process*, Basil Blackwell, 1987. Some general conclusions from this are discussed in 'Rethinking incrementalism' by Gerry Johnson in the *Strategic Management Journal*, **9**: 75–91, 1988.

Part II

STRATEGIC ANALYSIS

The first part of this book has shown that organisations need to adjust strategy as circumstances within and around it change. To effect these changes successfully, managers need to form a view of the key influences on their choice of strategy. Strategic analysis is concerned with providing an understanding of the strategic situation which an organisation faces. Such an analysis provides the background against which sensible future choices may be made and also provides some useful insights into the difficulties of implementing strategic change. Readers should remember, however, that this relationship between analysis, choice and implementation is not a simple one in practice and, therefore, strategic analysis should not be viewed as a one-off exercise which precedes choice and implementation. Strategic analysis should be a process of becoming better informed about an organisation's situation, and in some circumstances this can only be gained by implementing changes (perhaps on a limited scale). Indeed, the process of strategic choice and strategic implementation described in Parts III and IV will constantly challenge the validity of the strategic analysis as well as building upon the analysis.

Analysing an organisation's situation can be a very complex task and, for convenience, it is helpful to divide the analysis into the different types of influence on strategy as described in Chapter 1. The structure of this part of the book follows this division:

- Chapter 3 is concerned with the influence of the environment on an organisation. The challenge is to make sense of this complexity so as to understand the key variables affecting the performance of the organisation and how well the organisation is positioned in terms of such influences.
- Chapter 4 looks at the resources which an organisation possesses in an attempt to understand the organisation's strategic capability. These resources will include plant, people and their skills, finance, and systems. The need is to understand how the configuration of such resources (its value chain) influences strategic capability.
- Chapter 5 shows how the culture of an organisation might be understood as an influence on strategy. It also examines how individuals and groups can influence the development of strategy in terms of their own interests or expectations. The importance of assessing the bases and configurations of power is also discussed. The objectives of organisations are seen as an outcome of political and cultural processes rather than as preordained targets.

Although this part of the book is divided into three chapters it should be remembered that there are very strong links between these various influences on strategy. For example, environmental pressures for change may be constrained by the resources available to make changes, or by the organisational culture which may lead to resistance to change. The relative importance of the various influences will change over time and show marked differences from one organisation to another. A good strategic analysis must provide an understanding of all these issues.

Chapter 3

ANALYSING THE ENVIRONMENT

3.1 INTRODUCTION

Strategists, faced with the need to understand the effects of the environment, are dealing with a difficult problem. The formulation of strategy is concerned with matching the capabilities of an organisation with its environment. But the notion of the environment encapsulates very many different influences, and the difficulty is understanding this diversity in a way which can contribute to strategic decision making. The danger is the adoption of a 'balance sheet' approach which consists of listing all conceivable environmental influences in an attempt to identify opportunities and threats. It is relatively easy to see that an organisation might have a whole range of things going for it and a range going against it: long lists can be generated for most organisations. However, if environmental analysis consists of this alone the limitations are significant. No overall picture emerges of what are really important influences on the organisation. What is more, there is the danger that attempts will be made to deal with environmental influences in a piecemeal way rather than make more fundamental strategic responses.

In practice, managers cope with the range of influences by evolving, over time, accepted wisdom about their industry, its environment and what are sensible responses to different situations. This was discussed in Chapter 2. This chapter, however, takes a rather more analytical approach and provides a series of steps which enable an assessment of the environment to take place. It is necessary to see the role of each step in relation to the other so they are briefly introduced here and summarised in Figure 3.1.

1. A first step might involve some sort of *auditing of environmental influences*. Here the aim is to identify which of the many different sorts of environmental influences have influenced the organisation's development or performance in the past and to take an initial view as to which will in the future.
2. Second, it is useful to take an initial view of the *nature of the organisation's environment* in terms of how uncertain it is. Is it relatively static or does it show signs of change, and in what ways? This helps in deciding what focus the rest of the analysis is to take. If the organisation is in a fairly simple/static environment then detailed, systematic historical analysis may be very helpful. If the environment is in a dynamic state or shows signs of becoming so, then a more future orientated perspective is more sensible. This approach may also highlight some environmental considerations to be examined in more detail later. For example, it may become clear

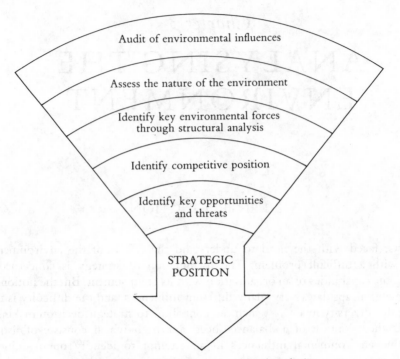

Figure 3.1 Steps in environmental analysis.

that there are particular aspects of the environment which are changing: it will be necessary to consider if these changes are strategically significant.

3. The third step moves the focus much more towards an explicit consideration of individual environmental influences. The general understanding already begun can be enhanced by a *structural analysis* which aims to identify the key forces at work in the competitive environment and why they are significant.

From these steps should emerge a view of the really important developments taking place around the organisation. It may be that there are relatively few of outstanding significance: or it could be that there are many interconnected developments. What matters is that there should be an attempt to understand why these are of strategic significance.

4. The fourth step is to analyse the organisation's *competitive position*; that is how it stands in relation to those other organisations competing for the same resources, or the same customers as itself. This may be done in a number of ways but this chapter concentrates on: (a) strategic group analysis which seeks to map competitors in terms of similarities and dissimilarities of the strategies they follow, and (b) market share analysis, which seeks to map out the relative power of an organisation within its market.

5. The final step is to relate this understanding of the environment more specifically to the organisation. Here there is a need to ask to what extent the forces identified are *opportunities or threats* (or indeed both). This can be done by considering the extent to which the organisation's strategy and structure are matched or mismatched to

developments in the environment. What this analysis seeks to provide is a picture of environmental influences which is clear enough to provide an understanding of opportunities which can be built upon and threats which have to be overcome or circumvented. Such a picture is important when it comes to strategy evaluation.

3.2 AUDITING ENVIRONMENTAL INFLUENCES ON ORGANISATIONS

Illustration 3.1 shows some of the environmental influences important to organisations. The illustration is not intended to provide an exhaustive list but does serve to give examples of ways in which strategies of organisations are affected by the environment and also indicates some of the ways in which organisations seek to handle aspects of their environment.

It would be possible to devote the whole of this chapter – indeed of the book – to a discussion of the ways in which different sorts of environmental influence affect organisations.[1] This is not done here because the chapter is primarily concerned with how to understand the strategic importance of the influences rather than provide a catalogue of them. It is also important to appreciate that over time different environmental forces will be more, or less, important. For example, the concern with oil prices of the mid 1970s, and of accelerating inflation which followed, gave way in the UK at the end of the decade to the effects of recession and of the cost of capital. It is also the case that what are key environmental issues for one organisation may not be the same for another. A multinational corporation might be primarily concerned with government relations, since it may be operating plants or subsidiaries within very many different companies with quite different systems of government and governmental attitudes. A local authority is likely to be especially concerned with the politics of national government too, and the officers running that authority with the political complexion of the elected members. A retailer, on the other hand, may be primarily concerned with customer tastes and behaviour. A computer manufacturer is likely to be concerned with the technical environment which leads to innovation and perhaps obsolescence of his own equipment. The point is that there is unlikely to be any definitive set of environmental issues which are especially important for all organisations over time.

Whilst it is not possible to identify such a definitive list, it is useful to consider as a starting point just what influences in the wider environment have been particularly important in the past and the extent to which there are changes occurring which may make any of these more or less significant in the future for the organisation and its competitors. Figure 3.2 is designed to help with such an audit by providing a summary of some of the questions to ask about likely key forces at work in the wider environment.[2] Later in the chapter there is a consideration of how the more specific competitive forces at work in the environment are likely to affect the organisation.

The ability to sense changes in the environment is important because perceived changes in environmental influence signal the possible need for changes in strategy: they throw up opportunities and warn of threats. The evidence is that organisations which are better at sensing the environment perform better than those which are weak at it.[3] The problem of coping with environmental influences affecting the organisation is twofold. The first is understanding the extent to which environmental changes will affect strategy: this is a matter of analysis and will be dealt with in this chapter. The second is relating these changes to the capability of the organisation to cope with such changes. This will be introduced at the end of this chapter and taken up again in the following chapter. However, it is important to stress that techniques of analysis are, in

ILLUSTRATION 3.1

The following are examples of ways in which

Economic environment

Changes in exchange rates have a major impact on operators in the global automobile industry.

    For example, Fiestas are manufactured in parts in Germany, Spain and the UK, making integration of costs of finished goods, problematic. The majority of Jaguar sales are in the USA where price competitiveness against German and local luxury cars is influenced heavily by exchange rates.

Capital markets

In 1986 Screen Entertainments Ltd, the management buy-out team negotiating to buy Thorn/EMI's Screen Entertainments business, agreed a financing deal for capital funds and working capital with a consortium of US banks. When the banks decided, after all, not to provide the funds for working capital, the Bond Corporation of Australia stepped in to acquire the business.

Demographics

- A declining baby population in the 1980s led Johnson and Johnson to advertise the use of their baby powder for adults.
- An increase in the proportion of two income households helped persuade banks to develop budget accounts, cash dispensing and Saturday opening.

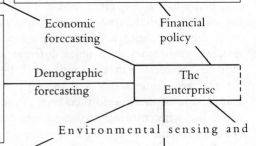

Economic forecasting

Financial policy

Demographic forecasting

The Enterprise

Environmental sensing and

Socio-cultural

The increasing health lobby of the 1980s resulted in:
- Sainsburys developing new grocery ranges of health foods.
- Tesco providing clear on-pack explanations of food values.
- Firms traditionally involved in manufacturing sweet products launching 'healthy' cereal bars, reduced-sugar jams, diet drinks etc.

Technology

In 1986 the Virgin Group joined a consortium to launch a broadcasting satellite. Awarded the contract in 1987, this gave them the opportunity to provide three new television channels to homes from Christmas 1989. For a company mainly involved in record production and retailing this posed the question of how to develop a commercial service from the facility to provide high definition television communications to millions of homes.

themselves, no guarantee that organisations will be able to respond to change. The extent to which an organisation will be successful in sensing and adapting to change will depend largely on its flexibility and sensitivity which, in turn, depend on the quality of its management, its organisational culture and its structure. These aspects of change will be dealt with in Chapters 10 and 11.

Examples of environmental influences

organisations interact with aspects of the environment.

Labour markets

The work-to-rule and selective strike system by teachers in 1986 affected curriculum design in schools, prompted local authorities to review staffing policies and hastened central government's review of its education strategy.

Competitors

As building societies were relieved of some of the constraints on their activities in the mid 1980s they began to develop interests in personal financing, insurance, house sales, and even legal advice. They thus provided new competition for banks, insurance companies, estate agents and solicitors.

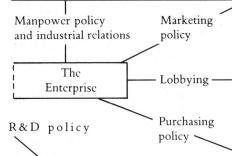

Manpower policy and industrial relations

Marketing policy

The Enterprise

Lobbying

R&D policy

Purchasing policy

Government

The lifting of Government restrictions on the provision and advertising of spectacles in 1984 and 1985 resulted in a 12% increase in retail outlets in a static market, consequent increases on marketing expenditure and reduced prices to retain market share, the introduction of franchising and the transformation of retail practices.

Ecology

The growing demands and legislation in West Germany for pollution control at power stations, particularly to lower sulphur dioxide and nitrogen oxide emissions, meant that RWE, the main electricity utility, expected to see increases of 20% on production costs. However, companies such as Thyssen and Deutsche Babcock experienced a boost in demand for pollution control equipment.

Supplies

The drop in cocoa prices in mid 1987 resulted in:
- Support buying by the International Cocoa Organisation in an attempt to hold prices.
- A reluctance of producers to sell at deflated prices.
- Short term surpluses of cocoa offered to users by dealers.
- Uncertainty for dealers and users on longer term price movements.
- The Ivory Coast, world's biggest producer, informing creditors it could not service its external debt.

---

1. What general environmental factors are affecting the organisation?

2. Which of these are the most important at the present time? In the next few years?

Economic factors

Business cycles • GNP trends • Interest rates • Money supply • Inflation • Unemployment • Disposable income • Energy availability and cost

Socio-cultural factors

Population demographics • Income distribution • Social mobility • Lifestyle changes • Attitudes to work and leisure • Consumerism • Levels of education

Technological

Government spending on research • Government and industry focus of technological effort • New discoveries/developments • Speed of technology transfer • Rates of obsolescence

Political/legal

Monopolies legislation • Environmental protection laws • Taxation policy • Foreign trade regulations • Employment law • Government stability

---

Figure 3.2 An audit of environmental influences.

3.3 UNDERSTANDING THE NATURE OF THE ENVIRONMENT

Strategic decisions are, by their very nature, made in situations of uncertainty. Uncertainty is a problem for managers and in practice managers cope with it through the mechanism of the recipe, the employment of organisational routines and the reliance on organisational culture discussed in Chapter 2. However, it is also possible to make sense of uncertain conditions through analysis. Strategic analysis is an attempt to reduce the many environmental influences to a pattern which is capable of being understood and acted upon. To do this it makes sense to begin by asking: (a) Just how uncertain is the environment? (b) What are the reasons for that uncertainty? (c) How should the uncertainty be dealt with?

Environmental uncertainty increases the more environmental conditions are dynamic or the more they are complex.[4] The degree of dynamism in the environment is to do with the rate and frequency of change, and many organisations are finding themselves in a more dynamic environment than they have previously experienced. The idea of complexity perhaps needs a little more explanation. Complexity may result in different ways, for example:

● Complexity may result from the sheer *diversity* of environmental influences faced by an organisation. A multinational company operating in many different countries is an example of this. Whilst it could be that few of the influences are in themselves changing rapidly, the number of influences the organisation has to cope with increases uncertainty.

● Complexity may also arise because of the amount of *knowledge* required to handle environmental influences. An extreme example of this would be a space agency like NASA. The environmental variables it is having to deal with are enormously complex just in terms of gaining knowledge about them.

● A third way in which complexity may increase is if the different environmental influences are, in themselves, interconnected.[5] Suppose influences such as raw material supplies, exchange rates, political changes and consumer spending, are not independent of each other but related one to another: then it is much more difficult to understand influence patterns than if they are unconnected.

Lowest uncertainty exists where conditions are static and simple. An extreme example would be a post office in a sleepy English village. There is little change (low dynamism) and relatively few and fairly straightforward influences (low complexity) to cope with. It is as environmental influences become more dynamic or more complex that uncertainty increases. Figure 3.3 summarises this. The significance as far as the chapter is concerned is that differences in the nature of the environment call for different approaches to understanding and responding to the environment.

3.3.1 Understanding simple/static conditions

In simple/static conditions an organisation is faced with an environment which is not too difficult to understand and is not undergoing significant change. Raw material suppliers and some mass manufacturing companies are, perhaps, examples. Here technical processes are relatively straightforward, competition and markets may be fixed over time and there may well be few of them. If change does occur it is likely to be fairly predictable. Solicitors in the UK certainly used to consider themselves in this situation, hedged around with legislation which minimised competition, within a profession which was regularised, with no lack of demand and capable of commanding high earnings. In such circumstances it makes sense to analyse the environment on an historical basis: an historical pattern, once identified, might well be expected to continue over time, or at least be sensibly refined systematically. In fact, there is evidence that in static conditions, environmental scanning is likely to be a more continuous, systematic exercise than in dynamic situations where it is more intermittent:[6] since there is more likelihood of being able to use the past as a predictor of the future it is worth investing management time in systematic auditing of environmental influences over time.

In situations of relatively low complexity it may also be possible to identify some

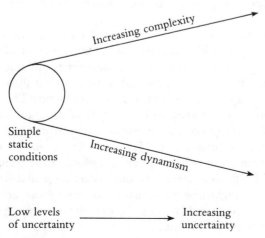

Figure 3.3 Growing uncertainty according to the nature of the environment.

predictors of key environmental influences. For example, in public services demographic data such as birth rates might be used as lead indicators to determine the required provision of schooling. Another example of such a predictor might be the way in which sales of consumer durables were thought to be dependent on real income in the UK. Since, historically, sales seemed to be related to movements in real income, it was thought possible to predict a rise or decline in market demand according to changes in real income. The danger is that the influence of real income may not always be independent of other influences: and a company that relied on real income as a predictor in the consumer durables industry would have been taken by surprise in 1976, when increasing inflation persuaded customers to offset future decline in purchasing power of savings by bringing forward purchases of consumer durables.

3.3.2 Understanding dynamic conditions

In dynamic conditions the environment shows signs of major change. For example, organisations faced with technological advances, more sophisticated consumers and an internationalisation of markets, find that they can no longer make decisions based on an assumption that what has happened in the past will continue.

There is evidence that as dynamic conditions increase the interpretation of these conditions becomes more 'inspirational'.[7] Managers sensibly address themselves to considering the environment of the future, not just of the past. There are, however, more 'structured' ways of trying to understand and deal with the future: some form of scenario planning approach might be taken, for example. This could involve identifying possible major future changes by a method such as the Delphi technique[8] and based on these projections, building alternative scenarios[9] of the future. In effect, the analyst would construct possible 'alternative futures'. These scenarios might then be considered in terms of the likely behaviour of suppliers, competitors and consumers so that an overall state of possible competitive environments is built up. It is then possible to carry out strategic analysis based on each of the different scenarios, evolve different strategies for different possible futures, and monitor environmental change to see which of the scenarios – and hence which of the contingency strategies – is likely to be most appropriate. (Scenario planning is also discussed in Chapter 8 in considering the evaluation of strategic options.)

There are dangers of course. Both a reliance on individuals' sensitivity to trends and the more formal approach of scenario and contingency planning suffer from the risk of myopic perception and response. It is sometimes difficult to get managers to conceive of markedly different scenarios and responses than those already familiar to them – a problem of recipes again. Another danger is that possible scenarios cease to be thought of as possibilities and start to be thought of as 'real'. There is a, no doubt apocryphal, story of a very senior cabinet minister of a British government attending a presentation of future scenarios by the Treasury. At the end of the presentation he thanked the civil servants and remarked that 'we should have scenario number three'! Managers may build inflexible strategies and organisational structures around mere possibilities rather than regarding the scenarios as conceptions around which to consider future strategic options and creating the flexibility in strategy and structure that would allow speedy responses to environmental change as it actually occurs.

3.3.3 Understanding complex conditions

Organisations in complex situations are faced with environmental influences difficult in themselves to comprehend. They may, of course, also face dynamic conditions. With the growth and application of more and more sophisticated technology, in particular, there is an increasing move to this condition of greatest uncertainty. The computer industry, airlines, the electronics industry are all in, or moving into, this dynamic/complex situation. Furthermore, a multinational may, as a corporate body, be in a complex condition because of its diversity but find that different operating companies face varying degrees of complexity and dynamism.

How, then, do organisations facing such complexity cope with their conditions? There are organisational and information processing approaches. Complexity as a result of diversity might be dealt with by ensuring that different parts of the organisation responsible for different aspects of diversity are separate and given the resources and authority to handle their own part of the environment.[10] Where high knowledge requirements are important it may also be that those with specialist knowledge in the organisation become very powerful because they are relied upon, not only to make operational decisions, but are trusted to present information in such a way that a sensible strategic decision can be made: or indeed they themselves become responsible for the strategic decisions. As an information processing approach there may be an attempt to model the complexity. This may be done through a financial model, for example, which seeks to simulate the effects on an organisation of different environmental conditions (see also Chapter 8). In its extreme form there may be an attempt to model the environment itself. The Treasury Office draws on a model of the UK economy for example. However, for most organisations facing complexity, organisational responses are probably more common than extensive model building.

3.3.4 The nature of the environment: the use of the perspective

Table 3.1 summarises the discussion on understanding the nature of the environment: the approach has both conceptual and practical uses. The key points are:

- If the organisation's environmental situation is fairly static and simple, then a detailed analysis of past environmental influences may be very sensible.
- The more the situation becomes dynamic then the more a focus on the future is essential, perhaps through some exercise such as scenario building.
- The more complex the environment becomes then, in terms of information processing, the more it may be necessary to move towards more sophisticated techniques such as model-building and simulation.
- In both dynamic and complex conditions there are organisational responses to coping with environmental conditions. It is therefore important to remember the significance of examining the suitability of the organisation structure (discussed in Chapter 10) and management systems (Chapter 11) as part of the strategic analysis. It may be that many of the organisations' problems arise from a structure or control system not suited to its environment.

Table 3.1 Handling different environmental conditions.

	CONDITIONS		
	Simple/static	*Dynamic*	*Complex*
Aims	• Achieve thorough historical understanding of the environment	• Understand the future rather than rely on the past	• Reduce complexity
Methods	• Analysis of past influences and their effect on organisational performance • Forecasting based on past trends/influences	• Managers' sensitivity to change • Techniques such as scenario planning, contingency planning, sensitivity testing	• Specialist attention to elements of complexity • Model building
Dangers	• The advent of unexpected or unpredicted change	• Management myopia • Inflexible organisational structures	• Unsuitable organisational structure or control systems

3.4 STRUCTURAL ANALYSIS OF THE COMPETITIVE ENVIRONMENT

Whichever approach to analysis outlined above is taken, the aim is to gain a 'picture' of the environment which provides a useful basis for constructing strategy. The difficulty, of course, is that the number of influences and the degree of their relevance for any given organisation is, potentially, very great. There is a need for some framework of analysis which provides a structure for conceiving of environmental influences.

A useful guide on the necessary sort of considerations for this is provided by Porter.[11] The section that follows draws on the approach he proposes and is summarised in Figure 3.4. It is essentially a structured means of examining the competitive environment of an organisation so as to provide a clear understanding of the forces at work. Although designed primarily with commercial organisations in mind, it is of value to most organisations which face strategic problems. Illustration 3.2 is a summary of a structural analysis of the UK confectionery industry which highlights the competitive significance of market share and the growing power of supermarkets in a highly competitive market. It might usefully be referred to in conjunction with this section of the chapter.

Porter argues that, 'competition in an industry is rooted in its underlying economics, and competitive forces exist that go well beyond the established combatants in a particular industry'.[12] The task of the strategist is to determine which of these forces are of greatest importance to the organisation and which can be influenced by the strategic decisions of management. There are four key forces to be considered.

3.4.1 The threat of entry

Threat of entry will depend on the extent to which there are *barriers to entry* which most typically are:

● *Economies of scale*. These will differ by industry. The really important question is not what the optimum scale of operation is, but how damaging it is to operate below that level. For example, in the machine tool industry the optimum scale of production is theoretically very high but the cost of producing at half that level is relatively low: for producers of nylon, on the other hand, it has been shown that the optimum scale of production is much lower but the cost of producing at half that level is high. [13] The problem in analysing the significance of this is that economies of scale are difficult to assess precisely, as indeed are the costs of producing below optimum levels of scale. However, some sensible and quite basic questions can be asked. For example, how large is the market and how many competitors are already there? If the market opportunity is small then it is likely to be more difficult to achieve adequate levels of scale than if it is large. In a given market is there any indication that profitability is linked to scale? For example is there a major producer who is profitable and smaller competitors who are not?

- The *capital requirement* of entry. This is linked to economies of scale. For the building societies to compete fully with banks in the handling of day-to-day personal financing, they would have to create the facility to process cheques, involving enormous capital expenditure to set up a clearing system.
- *Access to distribution channels.* Whilst little capital is required to enter the soft drinks market – indeed there are many contract bottlers and canners – one of the major barriers to entry is the availability of profitable channels of distribution. Many of the large soft drinks companies have extensive and exclusive distribution channels

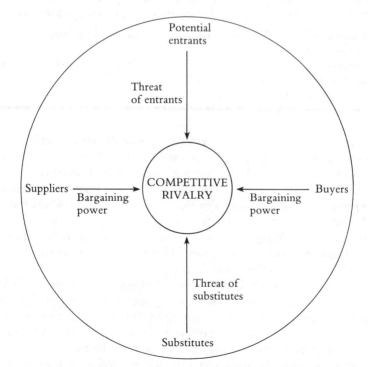

Figure 3.4 A model for structural analysis. (Adapted from M.E. Porter, *Competitive Strategy*, p.4, Free Press, 1980. Copyright by the Free Press, a division of Macmillan Publishing Co., Inc. Used with permission.)

ILLUSTRATION 3.2

A structural analysis can provide a basis for understanding the key competitive forces at work in an industry.

The value of the UK confectionery market in 1985 was £2.86 billion, or almost £1 per consumer per week. Dominated by three major producers, Rowntree, Mars and Cadbury, the market nonetheless also included many smaller companies operating within the chocolate confectionery and sugar confectionery sectors.

Threats of entry

The main barriers to entry into the industry were:

● The minimum efficient scales of production, particularly in the chocolate sector, necessary to compete effectively with the industry leaders.
● Advertising expenditure necessary to achieve brand awareness in competition with the big three manufacturers who spent between them £63 million in 1984.
● The necessity to obtain entry into an increasingly concentrated retail supermarket sector to obtain volume distribution.
● The experience in production and distribution of the major operators.

Threat of substitutes.

The growth of confectionery sales was part of an overall growth in the sale of light snacks. But this in itself introduced the possibility of substitute products; in particular:

● The blurring of the distinction between chocolate countlines and traditional confectionery products.
● The introduction of healthier snacks such as cereal bars and non-sugar products as a response to healthier eating lobbies.
● The growth of savoury snacks.

---

because they are part of diversified groups sharing the same distribution network. For example, in the UK, Britvic Corona is owned by Pepsi and the brewers, Bass, Allied Lyons and Whitbread; the company's soft drinks are therefore distributed through the pubs owned by those brewers. It is a major reason why, in the industry, two companies each have twenty-five per cent of the market whilst more than two hundred other companies compete for the remaining fifty per cent.

● *Cost advantages independent of size.* To a large extent these are to do with early entries into market and the experience so gained. This phenomenon is usually known as the 'experience curve' and is dealt with in the next chapter.

● *Legislation or government action.* Until the early 1980s public services in the UK such as the telephone service or postal system were operated as monopolies, and private companies were prevented from competing by law. Deregulation and privatisation in the UK in the 1980s meant that many managers in such hitherto protected operations, found themselves facing competition for the first time.

● *Differentiation.* By differentiation is meant the provision of a product or service regarded by the user as meaningfully different from competition; its importance will be discussed more fully in Chapter 6 in particular. However, here it is important to

A structural analysis of the UK confectionery industry

The power of suppliers.
Milk and sugar prices are both subject to the European Community Agricultural Policy which keeps prices relatively inflated but fairly stable and common to competitors. Cocoa, however, is more subject to price fluctuations giving opportunities for larger manufacturers to make use of futures markets to hedge against price variations.

Power of buyers
There has been the concentration of market share in the hands of the six largest retailers which account for around 60% of total UK food sales. The effect has been the forcing down of margins and prices on branded goods, a demand for own-label products, and the need to achieve high market share and brand awareness to maintain shelf space.

However, unlike other food products, only 30% of confectionery (by volume) is sold through supermarkets – the remainder is sold through a variety of retail channels such as tobacconists, petrol stations, off licences and vending machines – so that the effect of retail concentration can be offset somewhat.

Competitive rivalry
Rivalry in the confectionery market is high due to:

- The roughly equal shares of major competitors; the big three each control about 25% of the market and have done so for ten years.
- The major spending on advertising by the major manufacturers to preserve market share and maintain brand awareness.
- The relatively mature nature of the market – about 2% growth per annum since 1980 before when it was relatively flat.
- The centralised and increasingly capital intensive nature of production requiring a concentration on capital utilisation.

point out that organisations able to achieve strategies of differentiation provide for themselves very real barriers to competitive entry. For example, Marks and Spencer is perceived by customers as a unique retailer with an image for reliability and quality which it seeks to ensure through a carefully co-ordinated mix of staff training, product and quality specification and control at supplier level, high levels of technical competence within the firm and strong corporate values supportive of the quality image. Nor is the idea of differentiation peculiar to the private sector. For example, universities and polytechnics in the UK have sought to differentiate courses and qualifications that they offer; and museums, art galleries or exhibition centres have sought to differentiate themselves from competitors through the services they offer, the architecture of buildings or featured special exhibitions.

These barriers to entry differ by industry so it is impossible to generalise about which are more important than others. What is important is that the analyst should establish: (a) which barriers, if any, exist; (b) to what extent they are likely to prevent entry in the particular environment concerned; and (c) the organisation's position in all this – is it trying to prevent entrants or is it attempting to gain entry.

3.4.2 The power of buyers and suppliers

The next two forces can be considered together because they have similar effects on the competitive environment. Buyers and suppliers influence margins: the greater their power the more likely it is that margins will be low: so it is important to assess the power of buyers and suppliers and any likely changes. There are useful indicators of the extent of this power which can be used by the analyst.

Supplier power is likely to be high when:

- There is a concentration of suppliers rather than a fragmented source of supply.
- The 'switching costs' from one supplier to another in the industry are high; perhaps because a manufacturer's processes are dependent on the specialist products of a supplier, or a product is clearly differentiated.
- There is the possibility of the supplier integrating forward if they do not obtain the prices, and hence the margins, they seek.
- The supplier's customers are of little importance to the supplier, in which case the supplier is not likely to regard the long term future of the customers as of particular importance.

Buyer power is likely to be high:

- When there is a concentration of buyers, particularly if the volume purchases of the buyers is high.
- When there are alternative sources of supply, perhaps because the product required is undifferentiated between suppliers or, as for many public sector operations in the 1980s when the deregulation of markets spawned new competitors.
- If the component or material cost is a high percentage of their total cost, buyers will be likely to 'shop around' to get the best price and therefore 'squeeze' the suppliers.
- Where there is a threat of backward integration by the buyer if satisfactory prices or suppliers cannot be obtained.

A good example of this is in the grocery market. The power of multiple retailers has grown enormously since the 1970s. At that time grocery manufacturers could expect to exert strong marketing power over retail channels. By 1986, however, around fifty-five per cent of grocery sales were accounted for by just five retail chains. Any one supplier was relatively unimportant to these major companies. In the largest of the retailers – Sainsbury – over seventy per cent of total sales was accounted for by own-label or own-packed products: here Sainsbury themselves exercised control over product quality and, to a large extent, specification of prices. For the grocery supplier the balance of power had changed entirely within a period of less than fifteen years.

   The problem of constructing strategies which will maintain or provide power along the supplier–buyer channel can therefore be critical for competitive success or efficiency. For example, local authorities, having realised that their historically frag- mented mode of buying reduced buying power, sought to increase this by forming buying groups. The converse is also the case of course; it might also be possible for a supplier to seek out market segments with less powerful buyers, or differentiate products so that buyers become more dependent on that product.

3.4.3 The threat of substitutes

The next force which Porter identifies is the threat of substitutes. The question here is to what extent an organisation can legitimately regard itself as operating in a discrete market with a limited number of like competitors, as opposed to having as potential competitors a wider range of substitute products. The threat may take different forms. There could be substitution of one product for another – the calculator for the slide rule is an extreme example, or sugar substitutes for sugar. A substitute may hold down or depress margins: for example, the producers of natural fabrics found that the advent of man-made fibres depressed prices and margins. It may be that competitors need to be thought of as those competing for discretionary expenditure: for example, furniture manufactures or retailers need to understand that they compete for available household expenditure with suppliers of televisions, videos, cookers, cars and holidays.

The issues that arise are to what extent is there a danger that substitutes may encroach upon an organisation's activities? What steps can be taken to minimise the risk of such substitution, perhaps through differentiation or low-cost profiles? And, more positively, is there the possibility that one's own products could find new markets as substitutes for some other product?

3.4.4 The extent of competitive rivalry

Competitors will also be concerned with the degree of rivalry between themselves in their own industry. How intense is this competition? What is it based upon? Is it likely to increase or decrease in intensity? How can it be reduced? All these are questions which need to be thought about in the process of strategic analysis. The degree of rivalry is likely to be based on the following:

- The extent to which competitors in the industry are *in balance*. Whatever their number, where competitors are of roughly equal size there is the danger of intense competition as one competitor attempts to gain dominance over another. Conversely, the most stable markets tend to be those with dominant organisations within them.
- A market in *slow growth* – particularly one which is entering its maturity stage and where competitors are keen to establish themselves as market leaders – is likely to be highly competitive.
- *High fixed costs* in an industry, perhaps through high capital intensity [14] or high costs of storage, are likely to result in competitors cutting prices to obtain the turnover required. This can result in price wars and very low margin operations.
- If the addition of *extra capacity is in large increments* then the competitor making such an addition is likely to create at least short term over-capacity and increased competition.
- Again the importance of *differentiation* is clear. If a product or service is not differentiated then there is little to stop customers switching between competitors, which in turn raises the degree of rivalry between them. This is sometimes referred to as a 'commodity market' situation.
- Where there are *high exit barriers* to an industry, there is again likely to be the

persistence of excess capacity and consequently increased competition. Exit barriers might be high for a variety of reasons: they may vary from a high investment in non-transferable fixed assets such as specialist plant, to the cost of redundancy, to the reliance on one product to be credible within a market sector even if the product itself makes heavy losses.

Illustration 3.3 shows why the market for private hospitals in the UK became more competitive in the 1980s.

ILLUSTRATION 3.3

Increasing competitiveness for UK independent hospitals

From a buoyant base in the 1960s and 1970s independent hospital operators faced increasing competitive rivalry in the 1980s.

The independent hospital sector includes both charitable and 'for profit' organisations. In the 1980s there was a decline in charitable hospital representation in the sector from 58% to 45%. However, the 'for profit' sector which includes both British and American chains, whilst experiencing sector growth also found increasing competitive rivalry. The reasons for this were several:

● The traditional private hospital of the 1960s and 1970s, usually with about fifty beds, was superseded by the expansion in the late 1970s and early 1980s of commercial hospitals in particular run by American companies, attracted by projected rates of return on capital employed of 30% and the relative ease of funding of new projects in the UK. The market therefore witnessed considerable entry of new competitors.

● By 1986 there was an over-capacity of beds and hospitals with companies keen to maintain utilisation and market share, particularly since the large investment under-taken during 1979–1985 made recovery of investment costs crucial for the hospital groups.

● There was also a contraction in the growth rate of private health insurance due to increased subscription rates caused by accelerating medical costs; this resulted in a plateauing of demand and a fall in the fees that hospitals can charge for treatment, resulting in declining margins.

● Low differentiation of the hospitals and low switching costs for insurance firms meant that the bargaining power of the buyers (mainly the insurance companies) was great; they tend to negotiate large volume deals with hospital groups.

● Exit barriers are high within the industry both for emotional reasons in the case of, for example, Nuffield, and also for financial reasons; for example MAR UK have invested £150 million since its formation and investments in technology can be high – one ilthotripter (kidney stone remover) can cost £1 million.

● There was increasing competition from the National Health Service as the provision of pay beds rose over 1980–1985 from 2,543 to 3,220.

● On top of all this the market was fragmented; the largest operator provided only 13% of the total beds available.

Source: Authors.

3.5 IDENTIFYING THE ORGANISATION'S COMPETITIVE POSITION

All organisations – public or private – are in a competitive position. That is, they are competing either for customers or, perhaps in the case of public services, for resources. It is therefore important that they understand the nature of their competitive position. This may be achieved in a number of ways. First, the sort of audit of environmental influences outlined in Section 3.2 is likely to provide indications of key factors which will affect competitors in an industry. These can be used to examine the extent to which such competitors are likely to be able to respond effectively to such influences: Illustration 3.4 provides an example of just such a competitive assessment of retail stores in terms of changes occurring in demographic patterns in the UK.

Whilst such an approach can be used to build up a picture of competitors, it is also useful to be able to consider competitive positions in terms of more general frameworks of analysis. This section explains three such frameworks: lifecycle models, the notion of strategic groups and the importance of market power in considering market structures.

3.5.1 Lifecycle models and the nature of markets

Perhaps the most common basis for conceiving of the way in which forces in the environment affect an organisation in competitive terms is the idea of the lifecycle.[15] The notion here is that conditions in the market place, primarily as between growth stages and maturity of markets, will fundamentally affect market conditions and competitive behaviour. For example, in situations of market growth an organisation might expect to achieve its own growth through the growth in the market place; this is clearly different from situations where markets are mature and where market growth has plateaued. Here growth for an organisation has to be achieved by taking market share from competitors. This is an altogether different task and will be likely to require quite different strategies.

A comparable situation exists in public sector services: if government funding increases, as it did in the UK on defence expenditure in the 1980s, then strategies in government departments or research institutions will need to be reviewed accordingly. If expenditure is reduced, as it was on education during the same period, similar, if less palatable, reviews need to take place.

Whether it be private sector industry or public services, understanding the extent to which the market (for sales or resources) is growing is therefore important in formulating strategy. Moreover, competitors face similar circumstances, and the strategies being adopted by those competitors will also differ according to the nature of the market. The lifecycle model provides one useful basis for conceiving of such competitive influences. Figure 3.5 summarises some of the conditions that can be expected at different stages in the lifecycle. (The idea of the lifecycle is also useful in the evaluation of strategies and will be discussed again in Chapter 7.)

3.5.2 Strategic group analysis[16]

A problem that the strategic analyst will face is conceiving of the nature of competition that the organisation faces. In particular who are the most direct competitors and on

ILLUSTRATION 3.4

Quilter Goodison, the stockbrokers and analysts, undertook a study of the demographic influences on six

Store group	*Ageing population*	*Household structures (increasing)*	*Working women*
GUS	+ Slight advantage as GUS consumer profile is over 30	0 Neutral	+ + + Strong advantage through shortage of time and increased
Marks & Spencer	+ + Strong advantage as consumer profile is over 30	0 Neutral	+ + Slight advantage through increase in the number of dual income and shortage of time
Next	+ + Strong advantage as consumer profile is over 25	0 Neutral	+ + Merchandise offer is specificially targeted at 'working women'. Good for Grattan and Next home shopping
Sears	+ + Most subsidiaries' largest customers are over 30	+ Slight advantage for Wallis and to dept store division	+ Mildly favourable to womenswear subsidiaries
W.H. Smith	0 Neutral. The main retail chain has heavy exposure to under 25s but this is offset by other divisions	+ + Do it All (DIY) is a major beneficiary as are electronics goods departments	+ Slight advantage through increase in dual incomes
Woolworth	+ + Consumer profile is over 30	+ + Beneficial to B&Q and Comet	+ Slight advantage through increase in dual incomes

Reprinted with kind permission of Yazgan Musanif of Quilter Goodison Company.

Impact on stores of shifts in consumer profiles

competitive standing of retail stores. An example of their assessment in terms of major store groups is shown below.

'Two nations'	Decaying inner cities	Home ownership	Car ownership	Overall impact
– – Disadvantages as mail order is more popular in the	0 Neutral	0 Neutral	– Increased consumer mobility is a potential disadvantage	– Poor
+ Widespread geographical location provides a cushion	+ All the outlets are in City centres but prime locations provide cushion. Future expansion will be out of town	+ Household and furniture division is a major beneficiary	0 Neutral now but a beneficiary in the future	+ + Good
0 Largely neutral but Grattan has wide exposure in the North	+ All the stores are located in high street but cushioned by prime locations	+ Next Interiors is a major beneficiary	0 Neutral – but unfavourable to Gratton	+ Fair
0 5,500 neutral outlets even out regional differences	+ Most outlets are in central locations but cushioned by prime positions	+ Slightly favourable to dept stores division	0 Neutral	+ + Good
+ + Strong in the SE and London	+ + Do It All out of town based	+ + Highly beneficial to Do It All	+ + Good for Do It All	+ + + Excellent
+ Largely neutral but demand for DIY and durable goods are less weak in the north	+ + Woolworth's central locations are offset by Comet and B&Q	+ + Beneficial to B&Q and Comet	+ + Beneficial to B&Q and Comet	+ + + Excellent

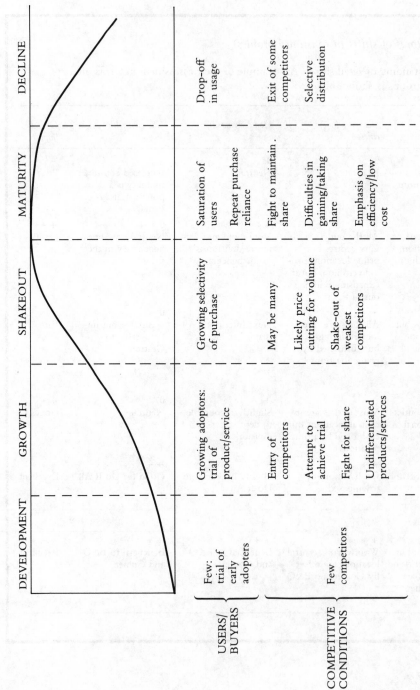

Figure 3.5 The lifecycle model.

what basis is competition likely to take place. Given this understanding it is then possible to gauge the extent to which strategy is appropriate in the competitive circumstances. One problem here is that the idea of the 'industry' is not particularly helpful because the boundaries of an industry can be very unclear and are not likely to provide any precise delineation of competition. In a given industry there may be many companies each of which has different interests and competes on different bases. There is a need for some intermediate mapping of the bases of competition between the individual firm and the industry level.

Strategic group analysis is one means of providing this intermediate level of analysis. The idea is to identify more finely-defined groupings of organisations so that each grouping represents those with similar strategic characteristics, following similar strategies or competing on similar bases. Porter argues that such groups can usually be identified using two, or perhaps three, sets of key characteristics as a basis of competition. For example, in the UK brewing industry (see Illustration 3.4) it becomes clear that firms tend to differ in terms of the extent to which they are national or local and the extent to which they have diversified from purely brewing activities. It also becomes clear that both these measures are linked to size: the companies that are largest tend to be those that are national and more highly diversified. So the diagram in Illustration 3.5 shows a two by two map of companies on the basis of these key characteristics: a device which can be very useful[17] in clarifying bases and groupings of competition.

However, these characteristics, whilst appropriate in brewing, are not likely to be appropriate in other industries. A number of writers have provided checklists by which analysts can look at company characteristics to establish the extent to which such characteristics differentiate between the companies and help identify strategic group-ings. These characteristics are summarised in Figure 3.6.[18] Which of these characteris-tics are particularly relevant in terms of a given organisation or industry is a matter for identification according to the history and development of that industry, and identifica-tion of the forces at work in the environment (see Sections 3.2 and 3.4), the sort of competitive activities of the firms being studied and so on. What the analyst is looking for is to establish which characteristics most differentiate firms or groupings of firms from one another.

This sort of analysis is useful for all organisations which seek to understand competition: its use is not restricted to commercial operations only. For example, universities, or local schools and medical practitioners might sensibly identify nearest and furthest competition in such a way. Moreover, it is likely to yield a better understanding of the competitive characteristics of competitors. It also allows the analyst to ask how likely or possible it is for the organisation to move from one strategic group to another – a debate which, for example, directors of polytechnics in the UK have been having for many years as they consider their competitive position with regard to universities on the one hand and Colleges of Further Education on the other. Mobility between groups is of course a matter of considering the extent to which there are real barriers to entry between one group and another in terms of how they compete (see Section 3.4.1). For example, in the UK brewing industry, whilst it is difficult for the local and regional brewer to make the move to a national operator, not least because of the capital investment required, it is also difficult for the national

ILLUSTRATION 3.5

Strategic groups in the brewing industry

The structure of the UK brewing industry in 1985 can be understood in terms of strategic groupings of firms with similar strategic characteristics.

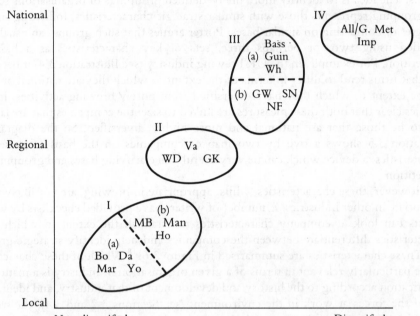

Key:
All:	Allied Lyons	GW:	Greenall Whitley	SN:	Scottish & Newcastle
Bass:	Bass	Ho:	Home	VA:	Vaux
Bo:	Boddingtons	Imp:	Imperial Foods	WD:	Wolverhampton &
Da:	Davenports	Man:	Mansfield		Dudley
GK:	Greene King	Mar:	Marstons	Wh:	Whitbread
G. Met:	Grand Metropolitan	MB:	Matthew Brown	Yo:	Youngs
Guin:	Guinness	NF:	Northern Foods		

Group I: Local brewers concentrating on single business brewing. However, (b) are rather more diversified, particularly in terms of soft drinks production and distribution.

Group II: More geographically extended Regional brewers.

Group III: National (a) or semi-national (b) brewers who have grown and diversified from a brewing base.

Group IV: Diversified conglomerates with interest in brewing.

Source: G. Johnson and H. Thomas, research in the brewing industry.

It is useful to consider the extent to which organisations *differ* in terms of **characteristics** such as:

- Extent of **product (or service) diversity**
- Extent of **geographic coverage**
- Number of **market segments served**
- **Distribution channels** used
- Extent (number) of **branding**
- **Marketing effort** (e.g. advertising spread, size of salesforce etc.)
- Extent of **vertical integration**
- Product or service **quality**
- **Technological leadership** (a leader or follower)
- **R&D capability** (extent of innovation in product or process)
- **Cost position** (e.g. extent of investment in cost reduction)
- Utilisation of capacity
- **Pricing policy**
- Level of **gearing**
- **Ownership structure** (separate company or relationship with parent)
- Relationship to **influence groups** (e.g. government, the City)
- **Size** of organisation

Figure 3.6 Some characteristics for identifying strategic groups. (Adapted from M.E. Porter, *Competitive Strategy*, Free Press, 1980, and J. McGee and H. Thomas, 'Strategic groups: theory, research and taxonomy', *Strategic Management Journal*, **7**: 141–60, 1986.)

operator, concerned to maintain national brands, to compete with the local brewer with well established and often preferred local brands.

3.5.3 Market structures and market power

As will be seen in the next chapter, the extent to which one competitor has a greater market share than another is an important aspect of the capability of that competitor. Market share is, in effect, a measure of market power[19] and it is important to gain an understanding of both the structure of a market and the relative power of competitors within that structure. One way of doing this is to break down the market according to its segments and to examine market shares within those segments.

The extent to which an organisation has located and exploited a clear market segment is likely to affect its vulnerability to substitutes, its bargaining power with regard to suppliers and buyers, the threat of entry into its market area and the degree of rivalry it faces. Moreover, it will be seen in Chapter 6, segmentation has important implications in considering strategic options and thus warrants some attention.

It may be possible to identify how a market may be segmented and which competitors are concentrating on which segments in a quantitative way by establishing the values of market segment and competitor shares by segment; or a more qualitative approach may be sensible. In either case what is needed is a breakdown of the market into the segments which are important from a strategic point of view. The importance could arise for a number of reasons: for example, because certain segments are more competitive than others; or because by segmenting the market in a particular way new opportunities for product differentiation emerge; or because some segments are growing and others are not; or some segments are much bigger than others.

It is also important to remember that a market can be segmented in various ways: and each different basis of segmentation could give rise to a different assessment of environmental opportunities. Suppose that Table 3.2 represents the structure of a

Table 3.2 Competitor analysis by market segment.

Segment	Size £m	Competitor positions			
		A	*B*	*C*	*D*
I	40	Dominant	Weak		No. 2
II	25	No. 2	Dominant		Weak
III	15	Weak		Weak	Weak
IV	10			Dominant specialist	
V	10 (growing)	No-one specialising (all weak)			
Total market	100				

market worth £100 million, and suppose that all the companies involved are manufacturing much the same sort of basic product. If company C thinks of its markets in overall terms, then it would consider itself to be fairly weak. But suppose the segments shown in the table are based on different customer types: then it is clear that company C is strong in one part of the market – segment IV – and this could substantially affect the strategic opportunities open to it depending on the opportunities and threats in that segment.

Again by looking at the market segmentation in Table 3.2 other implications about the competitive environment emerge. Segments I and II are the largest where the competitive battle is at its most fierce. Companies A and B are concentrating on these segments with company D running behind. Company C specialises in Segment IV which it dominates. But what of Segments III and V which are growing? They account for £25 million and no-one is really concentrating on them. Even as simple a model as this raises questions about the strategic positions of the various firms and the possible limitations and opportunities they have. Company D with, say, a twenty-five per cent share of I (£10 million), a ten per cent share of II (£2.5 million) and a ten per cent share of III (£1.5 million) has a turnover of £14 million and is probably having to operate at low margins to try to compete in I and II. Is there an opportunity to concentrate on dominating III and V, achieving perhaps a forty per cent share of each and sales of £10 million at higher margins? Companies A and B, of course, are probably more concerned with retaining their dominance of I and II respectively. Again, this simple segmentation exercise might point out an opportunity in V that A and B had not previously considered.

The relationship between market share (and power) and strategic choice will be taken up again in Chapters 6 and 7.

3.6 SWOT ANALYSIS

If the forces at work in the environment and likely future changes in that environment are identified, then there are bases for considering the opportunities and threats that might exist for the organisation. However, a word of warning is needed here.

Opportunities and threats cannot be 'absolute'. As was said in Chapter 1, considering a strategic situation is an iterative problem: what might at first appear to be an opportunity may not be so when considered against the resources of the organisation (Chapter 4), its culture or expectations of stakeholders (Chapter 5), the strategies available (Chapters 6 and 7) or the feasibility of implementing the strategy (Part IV). However, at the risk of oversimplification, the idea of strategy formulation is to construct a strategy which will take advantage of the opportunities and overcome or circumvent the threats. Given that it is not always clear which environmental changes constitute opportunities and which constitute threats, how can the problem be considered? And how can potentially dangerous preconceptions be challenged?

The analysis outlined here is one approach. The aim is to identify the extent to which the current strategy of an organisation and its more specific strengths and weaknesses are relevant to, and capable of, dealing with the changes taking place in the business environment. Moreover, the aim is to do this in such a way as to isolate the key opportunities and threats whilst at the same time identifying key aspects of organisational capability that provide strengths or indicate weaknesses in dealing with those environmental changes. SWOT, therefore, stands for strengths, weaknesses, opportunities and threats, but rather than just listing these in terms of managers' perceptions, the idea is to undertake a more structured analysis so as to yield findings which can contribute to the formulation of strategy. Although what follows is somewhat crude as an analytical device it has proved in practical application to be a helpful means of achieving these aims.

The procedure can be undertaken in a number of steps, and for the purposes of this description it is assumed that a group of managers is working on the problem of strategic analysis.

1. The managers would first identify the current or prevailing strategy or strategies that the organisation is following. This would not necessarily be the strategy as advocated or published, but the realised strategy (see Chapter 2) of the organisation. This in itself might be problematic; managers do not always agree on the strategy they are following: so this debate is often very important.
2. Managers should then identify the key changes in the organisation's environment following the procedures outlined in this chapter. It is helpful, first to do this individually, and then to pool individual views and attempt to reach a group view on this. The aim should be to arrive at a list of key changes or influences on the organisation. Whilst there is no fixed number which should be agreed upon, it is helpful if the list does not exceed seven or eight key points.
3. The managers then do the same in terms of the resource profile of the organisation. Following the procedures that will be outlined in Chapter 4, they try to identify the key capabilities (strengths) and key limitations (weaknesses) of the organisation. They might do this individually first and then pool their views to provide a consolidated list. It is useful to keep the total list to no more than ten points. Also, the managers should attempt to avoid over-generalising their views and keep to quite specific points: so a statement such as 'poor management' means very little and could be interpreted in any number of ways; if they really mean that senior managers have, historically, not been good at motivating change in the organisation, then that is a more specific and more useful point.

4. The group then has a list of key environmental issues against which it can establish the relevance and significance of the current strategy or strategies and the strengths and weaknesses of the organisation. Illustration 3.6 gives an example of the types of lists drawn up by one company undertaking this exercise.
5. The managers then need to examine the statements one against another. They can do this by taking each statement in the left-hand column in turn, examining it in terms

---

ILLUSTRATION 3.6

A *SWOT* analysis

Examining environmental influence in terms of current strategies and organisational strengths and weaknesses can yield useful insights into key environmental impacts and key issues of current strategy.

The results below represent the outcome of such an exercise undertaken by a manufacturer of chocolate confectionary products.

Key issues in the environment	Over-capacity in industry	Growing retail concentration	Health lobby/healthier eating	Increased 'casual' eating	Low growth in market	Ageing population	Competitors' market power	+	−
Current Strategies									
Rationalisation	+	−	0	0	+	0	+	2	1
Gain market share	−/+	+	−	+/−	−/+	0	−	4	5
Main strengths									
Availability of funds	+	+	+	+	+	+	+	8	0
R&D/technology/ innovation	+	0	−	+	+	−	−	3	3
Known brands	0	−	−	+	+	+	−	3	3
Extensive distribution	+	+	0	+	+	0	+	5	0
Good labour relations	+	+	0	0	+	0	+	4	0
Main weaknesses									
Subsid. B. low share	−	−	−	+	−	−	−	1	6
Few brand leaders	−	−/+	0	0	−	0	−	1	4
Too traditional	−	−	−	−	−	0	−	−	6
Over-wide product range	+	−	−	+	−	+	−	3	4
Information systems	−	−	0	0	−	0	−	0	5
+	7	5	2	7	7	3	4		
−	5	8	5	1	6	2	8		

Source: Authors.

of the key environmental issues and 'scoring' either a + (or a weighted + +) or a – (or a – –), as follows:

(a) Mark + if there would be a benefit to the organisation, i.e.:
   ● A strength would enable the organisation to take advantage of or counteract a problem from an environmental change.
   ● A weakness would be offset by the environmental change.

(b) Mark – if there would be an adverse effect on the organisation, i.e.:
   ● A strength would be reduced by the environmental change.
   ● A weakness would prevent the organisation from overcoming the problems associated with an environmental change or would be accentuated by that change.

When this procedure is completed the analysis will look something like the completed Illustration 3.6. What this yields is a much clearer view of the extent to which the environmental changes and influences provide opportunities or threats given current strategies and organisational capabilities. For example, Illustration 3.6 shows that the major opportunities for the organisation are the increasing 'casual' eating habits of customers. The managers also found that they were reasonably well placed to deal with an industry-wide problem of over-capacity. However, other environmental issues seem to be rather limited in opportunity and there are major threats in terms of the growing concentration of retailers, the trend to 'healthier eating' and competitors' market power. The maturation of the market could be an opportunity or threat as could other issues, depending on the extent to which the organisation can utilise and develop the strengths in funds availability and its distribution network, and overcome the main weaknesses it has.

Illustration 3.6 also shows that some of what the managers originally conceived as strengths seem to be more neutral when examined against the key environmental issues; they may be strengths as far as the history of the organisation is concerned, but do not seem to be so relevant (indeed some are actually scored negatively) in terms of the way the organisation's environment is developing. Similarly an analysis of perceived weaknesses shows that their importance varies. The analysis also shows the extent to which the current strategies address the issue of a changing environment and comes to the conclusion that they do so only partially, raising important questions in particular about the pursuit of market share in current, main line confectionery products.

A SWOT analysis, therefore, provides a mechanism for systematically thinking through the extent to which the organisation can cope with its environment. However, the analysis requires both an understanding of the environment and the resource capabilities of that organisation. It is this which is the subject of the next chapter.

3.7 SUMMARY

This chapter has provided a step-by-step approach to analysing the complexity and uncertainty of the organisation's environment and its effect on the organisation. It started with identifying a problem that the analyst faces: that the influences of the environment are so many and so varied that trying to understand their effects can reduce the strategist to a rather unhelpful listing exercise. The approach proposed here starts with an identification of the many different forces at work in the environment but seeks to analyse these in terms of their impact on the organisation and its competitive position. The aim of such analyses is to move towards an explicit understanding of:

1. The environmental influences which have most affected the organisation and its performance.
2. The extent to which competitors are similarly or differently affected by the environmental forces; and therefore the organisation's competitive position.
3. The specific opportunities and threats for the future development of strategy.

REFERENCES

1. There are books which do review environmental influences on organisations. For example, M. Glew, M. Watts and R. Wells,. *The Business Organisation and Its Environment* (Books 1 and 2), Heinemann Educational, 1979; and *Macroenvironmental Analyses for Strategic Management*, L. Fahey and V. K. Narayanan, West Publishing, 1986.

2. For an example of a more detailed and more systematic approach to environmental auditing for strategic purposes see George Steiner, *Strategic Planning: What every manager must know*, Free Press/Collier Macmillan, 1979.

3. D. Norburn's work supports this and is summarised in 'Directors without direction'. *Journal of General Management*, **1**(2), 1973/74. D. Miller and P. Friesen, in 'Strategy making in context: ten empirical archetypes', *Journal of Management Studies*, **14**(3), 1977, also support this assertion.

4. R. Duncan's research on which this classification is based can be found in 'Characteristics of organisational environments and perceived environmental uncertainty', *Administrative Science Quarterly*, pp. 313–27, 1972.

5. This notion of interconnectedness was put forward by F. E. Emery and E. L. Trist in 'The causal texture of organisational environments', *Human Relations*, **18**, 1965. The idea has been developed in the context of the implications on uncertainty by R. H. Miles in *Macro-organizational Behavior*, pp. 200–209, Goodyear, 1980.

6. L. Fahey and W. King summarise a survey carried out in twelve large business organisations in the USA which shows that it is firms in stable environments that tend to have regular and continuous scanning mechanisms. Firms in less stable conditions tend to have more irregular (ad hoc, reactive, crisis initiated, etc.) scanning mechanisms. This survey is outlined in 'Environmental scanning for corporate planning'. *Business Horizons*, August, 1977.

7. The term 'inspirational' is used by J. D. Thompson and A. Tuden in 'Strategies, structures and processes of organisation decision' in J. D. Thompson (ed.), *Comparative Studies in Administration*, University of Pittsburgh Press, 1958. They argue that as dynamic conditions increase, managers cease to be as reliant on understanding what has gone before and become more concerned with sensing what they expect will happen.

8. For a useful guide on the Delphi method see 'Delphi inquiry systems' by F. J. Parente and J. K. Anderson-Parente in G. Wright and P. Ayton (eds), 'Judgemental Forecasting', John Wiley, 1987.

9. For an example of method and an illustration of the use of scenarios in global economic forecasting see D. Norse, 'Scenario analysis in interfutures', *Futures*, **11**(5), 1979. For a brief discussion of the role of scenario analysis see R. D. Zentner, 'Scenarios, past, present and future', *Long Range Planning*, **15**(3), 1982.

10. Breaking up the organisation into different parts to cope with such diversity is sometimes called 'differentiation', a term coined by P. Lawrence and J. Lorsch in *Organisation and Environment*, Irwin, 1969, to describe this aspect of organisational design. It is an aspect of organisational structure that will be returned to in Chapter 10.

11. See M. E. Porter, *Competitive Strategy: Techniques for analysing industries and competitors*, Free Press, 1980.

12. This quotation is taken from M. E. Porter, 'How competitive forces shape strategy', *Harvard Business Review*, Mar./Apr. 1979, which is a useful summary of his approach.

13. For a discussion of these differences in economies of scale by industry see C. Pratten, 'Economies of scale in manufacturing industries', Department of Applied Economics Occasional Papers, No. 28, Cambridge University Press, 1971.

14. High capital intensity has been shown to be a major cause of rivalry since, to maintain utilisation of plant, competitors will reduce prices (and margins) to achieve volume. This is discussed more fully in Chapter 7 of this book and in S. Schoeffler, 'Capital-intensive technology vs ROI: a strategic assessment', *Management Review*, September, 1978.

15. A good discussion of the relevance of the idea of lifecycle is to be found in Peter Doyle, 'The realities of the product life cycle', *Quarterly Review of Marketing*, Summer, 1976.

16. The term 'strategic groups' was used initially by Michael S. Hunt in his doctoral dissertation, 'Competition in the major home appliance industry, 1960–70' (Harvard University, 1972), and is now commonly used in writings on competitive strategy.

17. Porter discusses the value of strategic maps as an analytical tool on pages 152–5 of his book (reference 11).

18 The characteristics listed in Figure 3.6 are based on those discussed by Porter (reference 11) and by J. McGee and H. Thomas, 'Strategic groups: theory, research and taxonomy', *Strategic Management Journal*, **7**: 141–60, 1986. The latter paper, in particular, provides a very useful review of the sorts of strategic group analysis that have been undertaken and a good many other references that readers can follow up.

19. The relationship between market share and the strategic position in organisations is taken up again in Chapter 4 when the idea of the experience curve is discussed (see P. Conley, *Experience Curves as a Planning Tool*, available from the Boston Consulting Group as a pamphlet, and B. Hedley, 'Strategy and the business portfolio', *Long Range Planning*, **10**, Feb., 1977). In Chapter 7 the importance of market share is discussed in terms of the PIMS data, the basic findings of which are available in *PIMS Letters* available from the Strategic Planning Institute, Haymarket, London.

Recommended key readings

- M. E. Porter, *Competitive Strategy: Techniques for analysing industries and competitors*, Free Press, 1980. Essential reading for those who are faced with the structural analysis of an organisational environment.

- L. Fahey and V. K. Narayanan, *Macroenvironmental Analyses for Strategic Management*, West

Publishing, 1986, is a sound structured approach to analysing the strategic effects of environmental influences on organisations.

For more thorough treatment of techniques of forecasting for management purposes the following are useful:

- S. Makridakis and S. Wheelwright, *The Handbook of Forecasting*: *A manager's guide*, John Wiley, 1987, or *Forecasting Methods for Management*, John Wiley, 1985.

Chapter 4
ANALYSING RESOURCES

4.1 INTRODUCTION

The previous chapter has emphasised the importance of matching the organisation's strategies to the environment within which the organisation is operating. However, any individual organisation must pursue strategies which it is capable of sustaining. This chapter is concerned with understanding an organisation's *strategic capability* and ways in which resource analysis can contribute to this understanding.

In the private sector strategic capability is crucially linked to the competitive position of an organisation and its ability to sustain competitive advantage. In public services, strategic capability is concerned with the extent to which the organisation is able to fulfil its expected role within acceptable financial limits and without undue overlap with other providers.

In order to understand strategic capability it will be necessary to consider organisations at various levels of detail. Certainly there are broad issues of resource capability which are relevant to the organisation as a whole. It will be seen that these are largely concerned with the overall *balance* of resources. However, the capability of any organisation is fundamentally determined by the separate activities which it undertakes in designing, producing, marketing, delivering and supporting its products or services. It is an understanding of these various activities and the *linkages* between them which is crucial when assessing strategic capability.

This concern about an organisation's resource profile is not confined to strategic analysis. It will be a key determinant during strategic choice, helping to identify directions which best match the organisation's strategic capabilities (where possible). The need for detailed resource planning and deployment is also a key ingredient of successful implementation of new strategies. These two further aspects of resources will be discussed in Chapters 8 and 9 respectively. Illustration 4.1. shows the importance of various resources on company performance. This chapter will be concerned with the analysis of an organisation's strategic capability.

An organisation's resources are not confined to those which it 'owns'. Strategic capability is strongly influenced by resources outside the organisation which are an integral part of the chain between the product or service design, through production and marketing to the use of the product or service by consumers. Section 4.2 will introduce this important concept of the *value chain* and the way in which it affects the capability and competitive performance of an organisation. The most successful organisations have a consistent resource 'theme' running through the value chain. For example, if an organisation chooses to compete largely through cost leadership – this should be found in many aspects from procurement, to targeting markets and customer support. Importantly, this cost competition will also be sustained by the special *linkages* which are developed within the value chain or with suppliers, channels or customers.

Before reviewing methods which can be used to analyse an organisation's resource position, it is necessary to understand how the various analyses will contribute to the overall assessment of *strategic capability*. These analytical methods can be grouped under four headings, as summarised in Figure 4.1.

ILLUSTRATION 4.1

The quality of resources

Employers perceive different sorts of resource strengths as a basis for their strategic development.

Traffic rights constitute British Airway's international scheduled route network. It is the basis of BA's business and the Directors will continue to safeguard these rights.

British Airways
Annual Report 1986/87

The **calibre of people** who work for us is second to none and these (financial) figures confirm that fact.

John Laing plc
Annual Report 1986

The **names** of Royal Worcester and Spode stand, as for centuries past, at the apex of renown and approbation wherever the highest qualities of workmanship are admired and sought.

Lyn T. Davies, Chairman
Royal Worcester & Spode, 1981

As a result (of acquisitions) our **share** of the national liquid milk **market** has increased from 8% to 13.5% and a strong regional base for the future has been established.

Northern Foods plc
Annual Report 1981

As always we continue to devote major resources to improving the quality and consistency of our **products**.

Tioxide Group plc
Annual Report 1986

The company's **ability to interpret lifestyle changes** in international markets accounts for much of its success.

Report on Royal Doulton in
Pearson plc Annual Report, 1985

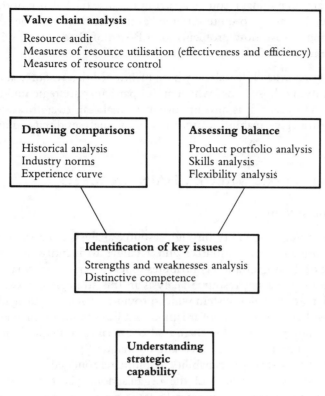

Figure 4.1 Methods of analysing resources.

1. A resource analysis needs to build on a bank of data, much of which will be in quantitative form (the data base). If the strategic capability of an organisation is to be understood then this analysis must go beyond a simple listing of resources. It must assess resources in relation to the organisation's strategic purpose and, in addition to a *resource audit*, data will be needed on how resources have been *utilised* and *controlled*. The concept of the *value chain* will be used here as a way of relating resources to strategic capability and providing this data base. It should be remembered that in terms of understanding the strategic capability of an organisation these data are of little value unless subjected to further analysis. This is an important observation, particularly in relation to the use of financial data in resource analysis. Many managers are capable of producing a wide variety of financial ratios and performance indicators but fail to extract any strategic significance from them.

2. *Comparison.* The strategic capability of an organisation is better understood in relation to how the resource base has changed historically and the relationship of this to company performance. The concept of the value chain emphasises the importance of competitor comparisons when assessing capability. Additionally, the concept of the experience curve can be helpful in understanding the relative standing of an organisation's products in their markets *vis-à-vis* competition.

3. *Balance.* Very often an organisation's strategic capability is impaired, not because of

problems with any individual resource area, but because the balance of these resources is inappropriate. To take two quite different examples, there may be too many new products resulting in cash flow problems, or a Board of Directors all with experience which is too similar.

4. *Identification of key issues*. It has already been mentioned that resource analysis must be capable of identifying those issues which are of particular strategic importance in any given situation. However, it is also important to make an overall assessment of key issues affecting strategic capabilities after the various analyses discussed in this chapter.

4.2 VALUE CHAIN ANALYSIS

4.2.1 The value system

Understanding strategic capability through resource analysis can easily degenerate into a listing of an organisation's resources and a failure to identify how the particular resource profile of the organisation contributes to its strategic performance. *Value chain analysis*[1] is helpful in placing resource analysis in this strategic context. This section introduces readers to the value system which provides a background against which the later discussions should be set. There are important links to future chapters of the book since an understanding of the value chain is also crucial to strategic choice (Chapter 7) and resource planning during implementation (Chapter 9).

An organisation's strategic capability is ultimately judged by the consumers or users of the products or services of the organisation. The extent to which these products/services are valued by consumers/users is determined by the way the various activities required to design, produce, market, deliver and support the 'product' are performed. It is these strategically important *value activities* which need to be analysed and understood when assessing an organisation's strategic capability. The analysis must pay attention to some important issues:

- The concept of value relates to how the ultimate consumer/user views the organisation's product/service in relation to competitive offerings. An analysis of resources must be undertaken in a way which establishes how such competitive differences are achieved throughout the value chain.
- Many of the value activities will be performed outside the organisation (e.g. by suppliers, channels or customers). It is essential that the organisation's own *value chain* is seen in this wider context (Figure 4.2).
- The *linkages* and relationships between the various value activities are often the basis on which competitive advantage is achieved. This also applies to linkages between the value chain of an organisation and those of its suppliers, channels and customers.

4.2.2 Value chain activities

Figure 4.3 is a schematic representation of the value chain showing its constituent parts. The *primary activities* of the organisation are grouped into five main areas; inbound logistics, operations, outbound logistics, marketing and sales, and service.

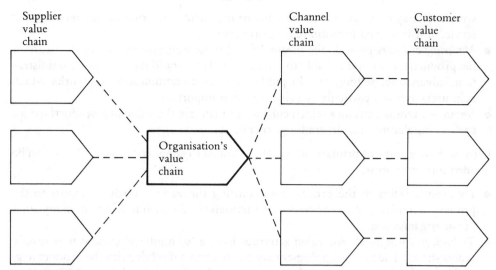

Figure 4.2 The value system. (Adapted from M.E. Porter, *Competitive Advantage: Creating and sustaining superior performance*, Free Press, 1985. Used with permission of The Free Press, a Division of Macmillan, Inc. Copyright 1985 Michael E. Porter.)

- *Inbound logistics* are the activities concerned with receiving, storing and distributing the inputs to the product/service. This includes materials handling, stock control, transport, etc.
- *Operations* transform these various inputs into the final product or service. For example, machining, packaging, assembly, testing, etc.
- *Outbound logistics* collect, store and distribute the product to customers. For tangible products this could be warehousing, materials handling, transport, etc. in the case of

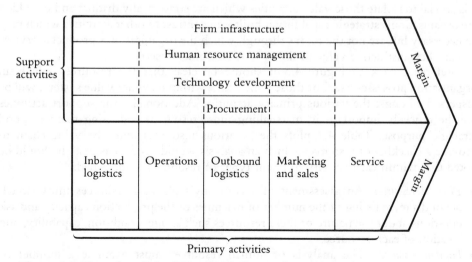

Figure 4.3 The value chain. (From M.E. Porter, *Competitive Advantage: Creating and sustaining superior performance*, Free Press, 1985. Used with permission of The Free Press, a Division of Macmillan, Inc. Copyright 1985 Michael E. Porter.)

services it may be more concerned with arrangements for bringing customers *to* the service if it is a fixed location (e.g. sports events).

- *Marketing and sales* provide the means whereby consumers/users are made aware of the product/service and are able to purchase it. This would include sales administration, advertising, selling, etc. In public services communication networks which help users access a particular service are often important.
- *Service* – all those activities which enhance or maintain the value of a product/service such as installation, repair, training, spares, etc.

Each of these groups of primary activities are linked to support activities. These can be divided into four areas:

- *Procurement* refers to the process for acquiring the various resource inputs to the primary activities (not to the resources themselves). As such it occurs in many parts of the organisation.
- *Technology development*. All value activities have a 'technology' even if it is simply 'know-how'. The key technologies may be concerned directly with the product (e.g. R&D, product design) or with processes (e.g. process development) or with a particular resource (e.g. raw materials improvements).
- *Human resource management*. This is a particularly important area which transcends all primary activities. It is concerned with those activities involved in recruiting, training, developing and rewarding people within the organisation.
- *Management systems*. The systems of planning, finance, quality control, etc. are crucially important to an organisation's strategic capability in all primary activities.

4.2.3 The resource audit[2]

Simply listing all the activities performed by an organisation is not an adequate basis on which to analyse the value chain. Although the analysis does need to be comprehensive it is crucial to isolate those value activities which are strategically distinct and on which the organisation's strategic capability is built – in contrast to other activities which may be necessary but are not the means through which the organisation's products/services sustain their distinctive value in the eyes of consumers/users.

Referring back to Figure 4.3 it should be clear that the resources which an organisation possesses itself, or those which exist within its wider value system, will be dispersed amongst the various primary activities. Additionally, the support activities will be crucially important in marshalling those resources and using them to good strategic purpose. Table 4.1 plots these various resources onto the value chain to provide a checklist of resources which an analysis would need to assess.[3] It should be noted that within each activity different types of resource are identified:

- *Physical resources*. An assessment of a company's physical resources must stretch beyond a mere listing of the number of machines or the production capacity and ask questions about the nature of these resources such as age, condition, capability, and location of each resource.
- *Human resources*. The analysis of human resources must examine a number of questions. An assessment of the number and types of different skills within an organisation is clearly important, but other factors such as the adaptability of human resources must not be overlooked. For example, if a company is likely to face a

Table 4.1 A checklist for resource auditing.

Support activities	Primary activities				
	Inbound logistics	Operations	Outbound logistics	Marketing and sales	Service
Procurement	Transport Warehousing Capital	Machines Consumables	Transport Warehousing	Product/service Patents/licences Brand names Market research	Franchisees Credit facilities
Technology development	Know-how Design Technology transfer (in)	Process development	Shipments	Network of contacts Information systems	Fault diagnosis
Human resource management	Recruitment Supplier vetting Shareholders Creditor relations Image in City	Team spirit Job satisfaction Subcontractors	Subcontractors	Agents Salesforce Distributors Merchandisers Goodwill	After-sales staff Reputation Maintenance staff
Management systems	Purchasing systems Vehicle scheduling Materials handling	Production planning Quality control Cash management Stock control Facilities layout	Delivery scheduling	Order processing Debtor control	Customer service system

period of difficulty or retrenchment then it is important to know how able the people are to cope with a situation where some of the traditional boundaries and demarcation lines will have to change to ensure economic survival. As with physical resources the location of key human resources could be important. A multinational company may be concerned that all its skilled operatives are in high-wage countries making it difficult to compete on world markets.

● *Financial resources.* This would include the sources and uses of money within the value chain such as obtaining capital, managing cash, the control of debtors and creditors, and the management of relationships with suppliers of money (shareholders, bankers, etc.).

● *Intangibles.* One mistake which can be made in a resource analysis is to overlook the importance of intangible resources. There should be no doubt that these intangibles have a value since when businesses are sold part of their value is 'goodwill'. Illustration 4.2 makes this point. In some businesses, particularly services such as solicitors, retail shops, and the catering industry, goodwill could represent the major asset of the company and may result from brand names, good contacts, company image or many other sources.

4.2.4 Resource utilisation

One of the key aspects of value chain analysis is the recognition that organisations are much more than a random collection of machines, money and people. These resources are of no value unless organised into *systems* which ensure that good products or services are produced in a way which ensures that they are valued by the final consumer/user. In other words, it is *value activities* and linkages between them which are more important than resources *per se*. A resource analysis must therefore proceed beyond a simple audit of resources to an assessment of how those resources have been utilised. This is related to the decisions which have been made about the *linkages* between value activities and also with the value chains of suppliers, channels or customers. The measures of resource utilisation discussed below would need to be applied in that broader context. It is the planning of these linkages which can provide either distinctive cost advantages or become the basis on which the organisation's

---

ILLUSTRATION 4.2

The Thomas Cook reputation

Thomas Cook is such a well established name the world over that it proved to be an invaluable resource when the company was sold to the private sector in 1972.

In 1986 Thomas Cook was part of the Midland Bank Group of companies: however, from the end of World War II up until 1972, it was owned by the British government. Throughout that time, it had stayed rigidly in the two activities in which it had operated over its 130 years history, namely *travel* (commission on sales of rail and air tickets, and its own somewhat up-market but old-fashioned tours) and *banking* (sales of foreign currency and travellers cheques). Although this formula had been successful in establishing the Thomas Cook name across the globe from the Victorian era right up to World War II, what it had failed to cater for was the huge demand generated by growing affluence from the late 1950s onwards. The pioneers in this market were newcomers such as Horizon, Clarksons and Thomson. In a similar vein, Cook's dominance of the travellers cheques market had also been long overtaken by American Express who had built their reputation on the strength of the dollar and also on the presence of US forces around the world. When the Conservative government issued a prospectus for the sale of Cook's at the end of 1971, it showed how profits had fallen from over £2 million in 1965 to around £200,000 for that year end. Indeed, Cook's management systems, accounting practices and planning processes were so ossified that no-one could say with any certainty where the profit had come from, or therefore, how it could be protected in the future, let alone increased.

Despite the overwhelming presence of this downward spiral, when the bidding opened the two interested consortia: Barclays, Grand Met, the State Airlines, and the Midlands Bank or Trust Houses Forte, and the Automobile Association, pushed the bidding up first from £6 m to £8 m, £15 m and finally £22 m. The banks naturally had an interest in the foreign exchange and travellers cheques business as well as the prepayments on holidays and travel, but the undoubted prop behind all this was the Thomas Cook name. Stronger abroad than at home, the name of Thomas Cook had achieved worldwide recognition and was of inestimable value in an industry like travel where so much depends on good faith and their acceptability of travellers cheques around the world.

With a core resource as stable as this, Thomas Cook was given a new lease of life to demonstrate how good direction of existing resources might exploit the potential of the growing travel industry.

Source: *Management Today*, October 1978 .

products/services are differentiated from competitive offerings. Whereas competitors can often imitate the separate activities of an organisation it is more difficult to copy linkages within and between value chains. Illustration 4.3 shows one example of this. Any of the following types of linkage may help sustain competitive advantage:

1. It has already been mentioned that the primary activities within the value chain will be linked to support activities (Figure 4.3). Any one of these linkages could provide advantage. For example, an organisation may have a unique system for procuring materials, or sales order processing.

2. There will be important links between the primary activities. In particular, important choices will have been made about these relationships and how they influence overall value and strategic capability. For example, a decision to hold high levels of finished stock might ease production scheduling problems and provide for a faster response time to the customer. However, it will probably add to the overall cost of operations. An assessment needs to be made as to whether the added value of stocking is greater than the added cost.

3. In many organisations there are possibilities that the same strategic outcome can be achieved in different ways. For example, the quality image of a cinema may be sustained through its careful selection of films or the technical excellence of its equipment, or its customer booking system or the general ambience of the cinema. It is important to understand which of these activities is actually valued by consumers/users and plan the utilisation of resources accordingly.

Linkages to the value activities undertaken in supplier organisation can be a key source of competitive advantage. For example, a publisher may be able to persuade (or help) its authors to provide manuscripts on computer discs which are compatible with the typesetting facilities, hence reducing the work needed in book production.

4. An analysis also needs to assess the extent to which *suboptimisation* is occurring within the overall value system. For example, the organisation may reduce its own in-house costs of storage and find that distribution channels are carrying unduly high stocks which is then reflected in their mark-up and hence the relative competitiveness of the products in the shops.

There are often circumstances where the overall cost can be reduced (or value increased) by collaborative arrangements between different organisations in the value system. So, for example, within the UK Higher Education system from the mid 1980s there were serious attempts to institute and approve 'credit transfer' arrangements between institutions and even between industry-based training establishments.

5. It will be seen in Chapters 7 and 8 that one of the crucial strategic decisions for organisations is the extent to which an organisation should specialise or diversify its activities. Within its own industry this means deciding which value activities should be entirely within the organisation's own value chain; which should be undertaken on a 'tied basis' (e.g. subcontracting, sole agencies) and which should be entirely within another organisation's value chain (i.e. deciding demarcation lines). During strategic analysis it is important to establish the organisation's current position in relation to this issue and the impact on its strategic capability.

Overall, it needs to be emphasised that the greater the number of linkages within

ILLUSTRATION 4.3

Kwik Save Discount

Kwik Save's ability to compete with the major grocery multiples depended on a cost based competitive strategy which was sustained throughout the value chain.

Linkages throughout the value chain – Kwik Save Discount Stores

	IL	O	OL	M/S	S
FI	Minimum corporate HQ				
TD	Computerised warehousing		Checkouts simple		
HRD		De-skilled store-ops	Dismissal for checkout error		
P	Branded only purchases Big discounts	Low cost sites			Use of concessions
	Bulk warehousing	1,000 lines only Price points Basic store design		Low price promotion Local focus	Nil

Kwik Save's strategy was based on ability to provide low-priced goods supported by a low-cost operation. The whole of the operation was designed for this purpose. The corporate headquarters was simple with few staff; bulk, computerised central warehousing fed stores with a limited number of branded only lines. Because the policy was branded goods only, Kwik Save were able to obtain maximum discounts from manufacturers. Stores themselves were basic in design and the approach to merchandising simple; time and cost was saved by not price-marking goods but keeping the number of price points to a minimum and requiring checkout staff to remember all price points; indeed checkout staff could be dismissed if they failed to recall prices accurately. Store managers were required to keep to a simple and relatively deskilled operation with branded goods only; more complex areas of greengrocery and butchery were dealt with on the basis of concessions. Overall, the marketing approach of the store group was to promote a discount image to the local community.

Source: 'Kwik Save Discount', case study by Derek Channon, Manchester Business School.

the organisation's value chain or between the value chain of an organisation and its suppliers, distributors or customers, the more difficult it will be for competitors to imitate their activities.

In assessing how resource utilisation influences this strategic capability it is helpful to distinguish between two separate measures of utilisation – *efficiency* and *effectiveness*. These relate directly to discussion in later chapters on how organisations choose strategies which will ensure competitive advantage. *Efficiency* is a critically important measure for those organisations which either choose or are required to compete on the basis of cost competitiveness. This applies, for example, to many public services. In contrast, *effectiveness* is a key measure for organisations who choose to differentiate themselves from competitors by sustaining products/services which are valued for their uniqueness. These measures will now be considered in a little more detail.

EFFICIENCY

Efficiency is concerned with how 'well' resources have been utilised irrespective of the purpose for which they were deployed. Efficiency can be assessed by analysing the current configuration of the organisation's value chain and applying a number of different measures (Table 4.2).

1. *Profitability* is a broad measure of efficiency for commercial organisations, particularly if it is related to the amount of capital being used to run the business.[4] Other financial measures are concerned with the utilisation of specific resources contributing to this overall picture (e.g. stock turnover, debtors' turnover).

Table 4.2 Some measures of resource utilisation.

Resource	Efficiency	Effectiveness
Physical resources		
Buildings	Capacity fill	Match between production/ marketing resources and nature of work
Plant and machinery	Capacity fill, unit costs Job design, layout, materials flow	
Financial	Profitability, use of working capital	Capital structure
Materials	Yield	Suitability of materials
Products	Damage (e.g. in transit)	Match between product and market need
Marketing and distribution	Sales per area Sales per outlet	Choice of channels Choice of advertising method
Human resources	Labour productivity Relative size of departments	Allocation of jobs to people Duplication of effort
Intangibles	N/A	Exploitation of image, brand name, market information, research knowledge, etc. Consumer complaints level

2. *Labour productivity* is a measure of how efficiently the human resources are being used. To some extent it combines an assessment of both efficiency and effectiveness since poor allocation of people to jobs (effectiveness) would also result in low productivity. Often productivity can be improved by attention to linkages within the value system. For example, the salesforce of an organisation may be used on an agency basis to sell a complementary range of product. In other cases productivity improvements may have occurred due to the rationalisation of certain activities between the organisation and a supplier (e.g. where manufacturers package items ready for display, removing the need for unpacking and repackaging).

3. *Yield* can be a very important measure of efficiency in industries where raw materials or energy are a major element of cost. The efficiency of the cutting department in a clothes manufacturing company will be assessed in this way and could determine the cost competitiveness of the company. Again improvements may be achieved by proper planning through the value chain. For example, wastage through handling damage or deterioration of perishable goods may well be reduced by attention to transport and storing arrangements with suppliers and channels.

4. *Capacity fill* is often a prime measure of efficiency for organisations whose major cost is overheads. This is particularly important in many service industries where there is often no extra cost attached to satisfying additional customers such as a theatre or British Rail.

   During the 1980s the need to sustain high levels of capacity fill became so critical to cost-structure and competitiveness for many organisations they decided to subcontract certain of their activities. This occurred in public services too as budgets tightened.

5. *Working capital* utilisation can reveal much about the way in which the financial resources are used strategically. An assessment needs to be made of how well the company has managed to achieve an appropriate balance between the risk it runs from operating at low levels of working capital and the inefficiency of having too much capital. Some organisations choose to change the balance of their working capital by factoring out certain aspects such as debtors in return for cash. In other words, they redefine the boundaries of the organisation's value chain in order to maintain efficiency.

6. *Production systems.* Understanding the various aspects of a company's production system such as job design, layout and materials flow are important when assessing a company's efficiency in production terms. It may be found, for example, that excessive costs have been incurred through unnecessary handling and transportation of materials during manufacture, or that the company could take advantage of new operational methods. A good example here was the growth of the 'fast food' industry in the UK during the 1980s, led by American-based franchising companies like MacDonalds. Many public services have found that efficiency can be improved if emphasis is switched from one value activity to another. So, for example, in a library an up-to-date 'self-help' computer system can avoid the need for a high level of personal back-up in helping readers locate books.

EFFECTIVENESS

A full understanding of a company's use of resources also requires an analysis of the *effectiveness* with which resources have been used. The effectiveness of an organisation can be critically influenced by the ability to get all parts of the value chain working in harmony – including those key activities which are within the value chains of suppliers, channels or customers. This is a key task of management and is largely concerned with developing and sustaining common attitudes and values amongst all of those in the value chain so that people see the purpose of the products/services in similar ways and 'agree' on which activities are critical to success. Many of the misunderstandings between suppliers and buyers stems from differences in attitudes and perceptions on these issues. There are a number of different measures of effectiveness (Table 4.2).

1. *Use of people.* There are many situations where people may be used ineffectively. For example, an engineering design team may be designing for lowest cost whilst the organisation is actually competing on uniqueness of product.

2. *Use of capital.* An analysis of changes in a company's long term funding (capital structure) may give useful insights. A company may be foregoing the opportunity of additional long term funds (loans or share issues) and, as a result, finding difficulty in carrying out necessary investment programmes. Sometimes the opposite is true, where a company may be too highly geared[5] for the realities of the markets in which it is operating. Many companies have found that when general levels of profitability are low and interest rates high, the conventional wisdom of using gearing to improve profitability is impossible to achieve. Organisations which have grown by a series of mergers and takeovers (e.g. Hanson Trust) are particularly astute at putting together packages of finance (money and share options) which are regarded as attractive by the shareholders of the organisations being taken over.

Table 4.3 Aspects of resource control.

Resource area	Typical controls to investigate
Physical resources	
Buildings	Security, maintenance
Plant, machinery	Production control Maintenance system
Financial	Costing system Budgets Investment appraisal
Materials	Supplier control (quantity, quality and cost) Control of stock
Products	Stock control Quality control Losses (e.g. theft)
Human resources	Control of key personnel Leadership Working agreements Control of outlets (e.g. distributors)
Intangibles	Control of image (e.g. public relations) Industrial relations climate Control of vital information

3. *Use of marketing and distribution resources*. The effectiveness with which a salesforce is being used might be judged by assessing the volume of sales which each salesperson produces. However, expenditure on other items like advertising or distribution may be more difficult to assess. Companies often use rules of thumb, like percentage of turnover spent on advertising, or might attempt more rigorous and expensive analysis such as advertising effectiveness research. A crucial judgement when analysing the value chain is whether the marketing effort could have been delivered more effectively in a different way. For example, would agents have been better than an in-house salesforce.

4. *Use of research knowledge*. The assessment of how effectively research knowledge is used is equally problematic. Tangible measures are available, such as the number of product and process changes developed internally or the competitive advantage which has been gained from technical improvements resulting in better quality or lower cost. Companies are increasingly trying to cope with their worries about their underutilisation of the R&D resource by providing better links with the commercial function and improving monitoring and control arrangements. During the 1980s many UK organisations started to look more seriously at the possibilities of *technology transfer*[6] rather than producing new developments themselves. The motor industry saw several developments of this kind as seen in the Rover Group illustration (Chapter 1).

5. *Use of production systems*. Poor utilisation of resources may result from the choice of an inappropriate system of production. For example, a hotel may have designed its production systems to cope with the normal summer trade where individual families stay at the hotel. However, these systems are most ineffective in coping with large conferences used as 'fill-in' during the winter months.

   The use of a production system needs to be geared to the basis on which the organisation competes. Where cost competitiveness is crucial highly integrated production systems may be essential. However, more flexible systems will be required if quality of service (e.g. delivery time) is the main competitive weapon.

6. *Exploitation of intangible assets* such as image, brand name, or market information is another measure of effectiveness. The extent to which the image of celebrities such as television personalities have been exploited is an example of the effective use of an intangible asset.

4.2.5 Control of resources

The last criterion against which a company's resource capability needs to be assessed is the extent to which the resources have been properly controlled. Table 4.3 identifies some controls which should be investigated. There could be situations where good quality resources have been deployed in the right way and used efficiently, but still performance is poor as the resources are poorly controlled.

   The way in which linkages within the value chain and with the value chains of suppliers, channels or customers is controlled can also be important. Often the financial control systems of an organisation tend to discourage such linkages because they do not fit the compartmentalised systems of resource control. The following illustrates some important aspects of resource control.

1. *Control of key personnel.* Sometimes certain individuals or departments operate in ways which are not conducive to the smooth functioning of the company as a whole. This can be a particular problem with creative and professional people within organisations who often have their own views on what their jobs should entail. It may be desirable for creative people to be outside the organisation (e.g. freelance broadcasters in radio and television) whilst continuing to be a key resource within the value chain.

2. *Costing.* This is an area where small, fast-growing, organisations often fall down. The management know what resources are needed to establish the company in the market and how to deploy those resources to good effect. However, they are often unaware of how their method of operating will influence costs and revenue and hence the profitability of the company. In other words, they do not understand how they should exert control over their resources. In many large organisations, and particularly the public sector, there is a confusion between cost effectiveness and cost minimisation. As a result the organisation becomes obsessed with cost-pruning whilst failing to realise that this creates a downward spiral, leading to a product/service which is valued less by consumers/users, creating a worsening cost structure as demand falls and so on.

3. *Quality of materials.* In certain industries the quality of the finished product is highly dependent on the quality of certain materials or components which are bought-in. A car will not function properly if its tyres, or battery, or carburettor are defective and all these items will normally be bought in their finished form from suppliers. Any difficulties which the car manufacturer experiences with customer complaints are traced back to the way in which control is exerted over these important supplies. In the context of the value chain there are different ways in which this might be achieved. For example, by establishing rigid quality specification; by inspecting the suppliers quality control *systems* or *inspection* of incoming supplies. The relative cost and effectiveness of these alternatives is an important consideration. In many cases it is absolutely essential to 'roll-back' the control of quality into the suppliers as seen in Illustration 4.4 (IBM) and at Marks & Spencer.

4. *Marketing outlets.* Many manufacturers fail to exert sufficient control over the way in which their outlets present and sell their goods. Retail outlets may sell 5,000 to 10,000 different products including many products which are directly competitive with each other. Monitoring and controlling the marketing efforts of outlets is important, but often difficult. Again, different approaches are possible ranging from the ownership of own outlets (i.e. bringing distribution into the organisation's own value chain); appointment of approved dealers; the provision of customer training and the use of merchandising teams.

5. *Stock and production control.* On occasions a company's poor performance can be traced to poor control of stock or the system of production. A poor delivery record often results from ill-developed production control systems relying on high 'buffer' stocks between the various steps in production.

6. *Control of losses.* Most companies face the problem of losses due, for example, to theft. Retailers are particularly vulnerable in this respect and euphemistically refer to those losses as 'shrinkage'. Poor company performance may be attributable to lack of control in this area. However, organisations face a real dilemma since the introduction of more stringent controls and checks could be counterproductive in reducing the

'value' of the service in the eyes of consumers. This is a problem shared by shops, and many public services such as libraries and sports centres.

7. *Control of intangibles.* The company's ability to control its image through its public relations activities is one example. The industrial relations' record can indicate how well 'team spirit' or 'organisational culture' are controlled. In some cases the control of vital information which may be of commercial benefit to competitors would be particularly important to monitor.

The importance of control during the implementation of strategy will be given further consideration in Chapter 11. At this stage it is hoped that readers have recognised that in order to understand the strategic importance of a company's resources it is necessary

---

ILLUSTRATION 4.4

Quality drive at IBM

If an organisation embarks on a new strategy, such as improved quality, this requires changes through the value chain of the organisation.

Long-term quality improvement cannot normally be achieved by *adding-on* a better quality control system to an otherwise unchanged operation. At IBM, Havant, they decided that quality improvement meant changes in most parts of their operation. The decision to start the quality drive came in 1980, not because of worries about declining quality but through the knowledge that competitors (particularly Japanese) were setting and achieving higher standards which gave them real competitive advantage.

One particular electromechanical product illustrated this process of quality improvement very well. Too many products were reaching the testing stage with major defects from the subassembly and final assembly processes. This was leading to overall poor quality and delivery performance. The immediate problem appeared to be variable performance between individual operators – but this problem was soon solved by discussion and some training. It was then apparent that problems were often due to inadequacies in the manufacturing or support services rather than assembly. Representatives from engineering and other support services were progressively drawn into the improvement process. These service groups started to focus on defining more realistic parameters for their own quality performance. The next 'knock-on' effect was that buyers and procurement engineers improved the quality of purchased parts. This drew external suppliers into the improvement chain.

Major improvements in quality were due to the combined effect of raising the quality issue to the front of everyone's mind as a key strategic goal and two other powerful forces. First, was what they called 'service pressure', i.e. when one part of the organisation made a specific request for the removal of service problems which were preventing quality improvement. Second, peer pressure, or the embarrassment factor, where some groups were visibly achieving better results than others.

The results were impressive – the output quality of the plant (measured by failures at installation or within warranty) was improved fivefold in a four year period through this 'rolling-back' of quality improvement within the organisation and its supply chain.

Source: *Management Today*, April 1986.

to look at how resources are utilised and controlled as well as the intrinsic nature of those resources.

4.2.6 Financial analysis

Financial analysis is useful at all stages of resource analysis, and not only as part of value chain analysis. It will be seen later in the chapter, for example, that the forecasting of the cash requirements of different activities will be an important measure of how well an organisation's resources are balanced (portfolio analysis). Equally, financial measures such as profitability, gearing or liquidity will be used to compare the performance of a company with its competitors as a means of analysing that company's resource position.

Financial analysis is included as a separate section here because many managers are unclear about the contribution that financial analyses can make to understanding an organisation's strategic capability. Financial ratio analysis can be very useful but is also potentially very misleading if not interpreted in the context of the overall resource analysis.[7] When using financial analyses[8] as part of resource analysis the following issues need to be borne in mind.

1. Financial ratios (such as stock turnover, sales margins, gearing, etc.) are of no

FINANCIAL RATIO	USED TO ASSESS
1. **Return on capital**	Overall measure of performance
2. **Cost structure**	
Sales profitability	Sales performance
Gross margin	Direct costs
Sales expenses ⎫ Overheads ⎭	1. Indirect cost 2. Value of expenditure
Labour	1. Labour productivity 2. Relation to 'value'
Materials	1. Purchasing policies 2. Quality of materials 3. Relation to 'value'
Dividends	Power of shareholders
Interest	Capital structure (see below)
3. **Asset turnover**	
Fixed assets	Capital intensity
Stock	1. Cash tied up 2. Delivery performance 3. Risk of write-offs
Debtors	1. Cash tied up 2. Use of credit 3. Risk of bad debts
(Creditors)	Choice of suppliers
4. **Liquidity**	Short term risk
5. **Capital structure** (gearing)	1. Long term risk 2. Using available resources

Figure 4.4 Financial ratios and resource analysis.

importance in themselves. It is the implications of these ratios which are critical. This may not emerge until some sensible basis of comparison is established (see below). Even then a word of warning is necessary. It may be that an organisation is successfully differentiating itself from its competitors by extra spending in selected areas (e.g. advertising). Provided this results in value (possibly through price or market share) this may well be a defensible spending pattern.

2. Only certain *value activities* will be of critical strategic importance to an organisation. The financial analyses which relate to those activities will be particularly useful. For example, rate of stock-turnover may be important to a high street store, unit profit margins to a market stallholder, or sales volume to a capital intensive manufacturer.

3. The key value activities will change over time and so should the key financial measures to monitor. For example, during the introduction of a new product the key factor may be establishing *sales volume*; once established *profit/unit* might be most important, whilst during decline *cash flow* may be essential to support the introduction of the next generation of products. In addition to published financial data, the management would normally have access to additional financial information (such as cost data) which would help provide a fairly comprehensive analysis of many of the resource *utilisation* and *control* issues raised above. Figure 4.4 summarises some ways in which financial ratios can be helpful in understanding an organisation's resources from the point of view of strategic capability.

4.3 COMPARATIVE ANALYSIS

The preceding two sections have paid considerable attention to the concept of the value chain and the ways in which it might be used to assess strategic capability. Value chain analysis encourages managers to take a critical look at their organisation's resources with the purpose of understanding how particular value activities and the linkages between activities help the organisation sustain its competitive advantage within its 'industry'. However, it is also valuable to assess how the value chain has changed and developed historically, since this gives insights into how (and perhaps why) the organisation has chosen, or been forced, to shift its resource base.

In addition, the work of the Boston Consulting Group (BCG) on the *experience curve* of organisations is valuable in understanding how cost structure and competitiveness might be related to the nature of an organisation's markets and its relative position within them.

This section discusses these different bases of comparison, the historical, the industry norm and the experience curve as valuable means of improving the understanding of an organisation's strategic capability.

4.3.1 Historical analysis

An historical analysis looks at the deployment of the resources of a business in comparison with previous years in order to identify any significant changes in the overall levels of resources. Typically, measures like sales/capital ratio, sales/employees will be used (as discussed earlier) as well as identifying any significant variations in the proportions of resources devoted to different activities. Although this seems like a fairly straightforward analysis to perform, it can reveal trends which might not otherwise be apparent. For example, a manufacturing company which owns it own retail outlets may find that because of the relatively favourable climate for retailing there has been a slow drift of the business away from the traditional base of manufacturing. It is only when a comparison of the deployment of resources is made with the situation five years before that the significance of this slow drift becomes apparent. In some cases it has prompted companies to reassess where the major thrust of their business should be in the future. In other words, they have redefined the boundaries of their value chain slowly over time.

4.3.2 Comparison with industry norms

An historical analysis can normally be improved significantly by the additional comparison with similar factors analysed for the industry as a whole: it helps to put the company's resources and performance into perspective and reflects the fact that it is the relative position of a company which matters in determining its performance. The danger of industry norm analysis is that the company may overlook the fact that the whole industry is performing badly and is losing out competitively to other countries with better resources or even other industries which can satisfy customers' needs in different ways.

If an industry comparison is performed therefore, it is wise to make some assessment of how the company's resources compare with those in other countries and industries. This can often be done by looking at a few of the more important measures of resource utilisation such as stock-turnover, or yield from raw materials, etc. Illustration 4.5 shows one example of comparisons within local government. However, readers are reminded of the preceding discussion concerning the importance of establishing and maintaining a distinctive *value chain* for an organisation. A comparison of similar *value activities* between organisations can be valuable if the strategic context is not forgotten. For example, a straight comparison of resource deployment between two competitive companies (say in terms of an analysis of cost structures) may reveal quite different situations in the labour cost as percentage of total cost. The conclusions drawn from this, however, depend upon circumstances. If the firms are competing head-on largely on the basis of price, then differentials in labour costs will be of crucial importance. In contrast, the additional use of staff by one organisation may be an essential support for the special services provided which differentiate that organisation from its competitors. For this reason some authors[9] have given more emphasis to undertaking a parallel resource analysis of major competitors rather than trying to establish the 'norm' within the industry. Although in principle this approach is of considerable value – keeping detailed profiles of competitors' resources may prove very difficult and expensive.

4.3.3 The experience curve

The idea of the experience curve results from the work of the Boston Consulting Group (BCG) – a worldwide business consultancy operation which has conducted

ILLUSTRATION 4.5

Extremes in local government spending

Comparisons with 'industry norms' can be used in the public services when assessing an organisation's resources.

Local authorities in England and Wales receive their income from two main sources: from central government through the annual *rate support grant*, and from locally levied income through domestic and commercial *rates* (property tax). The provision of public services varies considerably from one geographical area to another for two main reasons. First, the characteristics and needs of the population, and second, the political priorities of ruling parties. These variations in financing and levels of service can be illustrated by the extreme cases in each of the five different local authority types (in 1985–86).

Extremes in net expenditure 1985–86

	Net rate and grant borne expenditure per head of population	Average domestic rates bill	Proportion of expenditure met from central government grants
Inner London:			
Camden	£694	£745	15%
Wandsworth	£287	£372	84%
Outer London:			
Haringey	£792	£748	36%
Bromley	£352	£418	48%
Metropolitan districts:			
Manchester	£620	£427	45%
Dudley	£342	£371	43%
English districts:			
Blackburn	£146	£231	73%
Vale of White Horse	£26	£339	25%
Welsh districts:			
Rhondda	£169	£130	89%
Montgomery	£71	£168	77%

Whereas these data can be valuable in terms of comparing spending between local authorities there are some obvious dangers to be avoided:

- Expenditure levels do not measure value for money as they do not assess the level of service provided.
- Rural authorities (such as the Vale of White Horse) will not have the burden of *housing* management and maintenance which partially explains their low levels of spending (and low percentage of government grant).
- Some services in urban areas (e.g. parks, leisure, roads) are clearly used by non-residents.

Nevertheless these data can be a useful starting point for interauthority comparisons.

Source: *Local Government Chronicle*, 16 May 1986.

studies of company performance showing a direct and consistent relationship between the aggregate growth in volume of production and declining cost of production.[10] It should also be pointed out, however, that they claim that their findings are as relevant to service organisations as they are to manufacturing businesses. The concept is useful both in strategic analysis and choice. For convenience, the underlying principles behind the experience curve will be introduced here though much of this is relevant to later discussions – particularly in Chapter 7. The premise of the BCG findings is that in any market segment of an industry, price levels tend to be very similar for similar products. Therefore what makes one company more profitable than the next must be the levels of its costs. Hence it is a particularly relevant analysis for organisations competing on the basis of cost leadership.

It is the key determinants of low levels of cost that the BCG attempted to unearth. Their arguments can be summarised as follows.

1. The relationship between unit costs and total units produced over time resembles that shown in Figure 4.5. It is this curve that the BCG calls the experience curve.
2. Some of the reasons for this suggested by the BCG are:
   (a) *The learning function.* Anyone doing a job learns to do it better over time and given increased experience: labour costs should in fact decline by about ten to fifteen per cent each time cumulative experience doubles.
   (b) *Specialisation.* As scale of production increases so it becomes possible to split jobs into more and more specialist jobs. 'Doing half as much but twice as often' equals the same amount of effort but twice the experience with the task.
   (c) *Scale.* The capital costs required to finance additional capacity diminish as that capacity grows.
3. Since cost is, in general, a function of experience then cost is also a function of market share. If this is true then the importance of gaining and holding market share becomes very important indeed. This is what was referred to as 'market power' in Chapter 3.
4. Market share does not necessarily relate to the overall market. If a product is competing in a definable, relevant market segment, then it is the market share of that segment that is important.

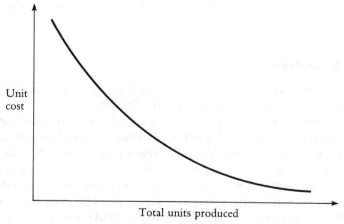

Figure 4.5 The experience curve.

The overall implication of the BCG's findings is that successful companies make their profits from products or services in which they dominate their market segment. This view has become a very strong influence on many companies' choices of strategy.

However, it should also be noted that there have been some significant reservations voiced about the value of the experience curve ideas: (a) because some of the key variables such as market growth and share are not always easy to be precise about; and (b) because there is a risk that managers interpret the conclusions too simplistically, e.g. by failing to recognise the opportunities afforded by market segmentation or product differentiation. [11]

The use of experience curve analysis is confined to a qualitative comparison of an organisation resource situation *vis-à-vis* its competitors particularly in relation to cost efficiency but can prove very valuable for that purpose, in particular in clarifying the key determinants of competitiveness in conjunction with a more detailed assessment of the value chain for each business unit.

4.4 ASSESSING THE BALANCE OF RESOURCES

Value chain analysis, which has been the continuing theme of the previous sections, is a powerful analytical approach when applied at the level of individual business or service units. It helps to identify the key value activities and important linkages between these activities and with the value chains of suppliers, channels and customers.

However, in many organisations there is an additional resource issue which is of equal, and complementary, importance, namely the extent to which the organisation's resources are balanced as a whole. Three important aspects of such an analysis are:

- The extent to which the various activities and resources of the organisation complement each other. *Portfolio analysis* is particularly useful in analysing this issue.
- The degree of balance of the *people* within the organisation in terms of both individual skills and personality types.
- Whether the *degree of flexibility* in the organisation's resources is appropriate for the level of uncertainty in the environment and the degree of risk the company is prepared to take.

4.4.1 Portfolio analysis

The concept of the experience curve (discussed above) underlines the important relationship between market dominance and profitability.

In order to dominate a market, a company must normally gain that dominance when the market is in the growth stage of the product lifecycle. In a state of maturity, a market is likely to be stable with customer loyalties fairly fixed. It is therefore more difficult to gain share. But if all competitors in the growth stage are trying to gain market share competition will be very fierce: therefore only those companies prepared to invest in order to gain share will gain dominance. This might well mean that a company following the principles suggested by the BCG will need to price low and spend high amounts on advertising and selling. Such a strategy is one of high risk unless such low margin activity is financed by higher profit earning products. This leads to the idea of a balanced product mix. The BCG has suggested the model of the product portfolio or the growth share matrix as a tool by which to consider product strategy. This product portfolio is shown as Figure 4.6.

The matrix combines market growth rate and market share and thus directly relates to the idea of the experience curve.

- A *star* is a product (or business) which has a high market share in a growing market. As such the company may be spending heavily to gain that share but the experience curve effect will mean that costs are reducing over time and hopefully at a faster rate than competition. The product (or business) could, then, be self–financing.
- The *question mark* (or problem child) is also in a growing market but does not have a high market share. Its parent company may be spending heavily to increase market share but, if they are, it is unlikely that they are getting sufficient cost reductions to offset such investment because the experience gained is less than for a star and costs will be reducing less quickly.
- The *cash cow* is a product (or business) with high market share in a mature market. Because growth is low and market conditions more stable the need for heavy marketing investment is less. But high market share means that experience in relation to low share competition continues to grow and relative costs reduce. The cash cow is thus a cash provider.
- *Dogs* have low share in static or declining markets and are thus the worst of all combinations. They are often a cash drain and may use up a disproportionate amount of company time and resources.

Portfolio analysis can also contribute to strategic evaluation as will be seen in Chapter 7. In the context of resource analysis it is particularly useful in as much as it raises some important questions about resources. For example:

- Whether the mix of products, services or businesses is balanced across the organisation. The idea of a portfolio of interests emphasises the importance of

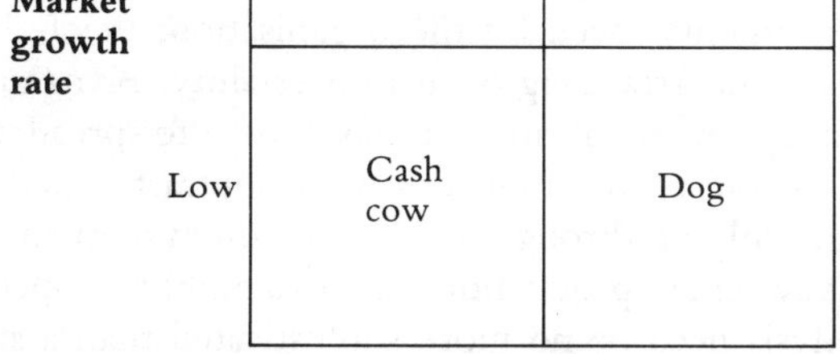

Figure 4.6 The product portfolio.

having areas of activity which provide security and funds (cash cows) and others which provide for the future of the business (stars and question marks).

- Drucker[12] has long emphasised the importance of reviewing activities to ensure that the appropriate amount of management, physical and financial resource is being allocated to the activities: that management is not providing excessive resources to dogs whilst starving question marks and thus reducing the chance of turning them into stars.
- Whether the balance of a company's products/markets matches resources available to the company. If a company is particularly good at development and design this may not match the analysis of product/market position which indicates a pre-dominance of mature products in static markets. This may suggest the need to move funds from the development area into a greater emphasis on promotion or market development.

Although portfolio analysis was developed in the context of private sector business, the resource lessons are similar in public services. For example, the funding of new ventures/services is often achieved informally by using resources from well established areas (particularly staff time). There are some classic 'dogs' in the portfolios of most public service departments – the question is whether there is the political will to kill some of them off, releasing resources for other purposes.

4.4.2 Skills analysis

Organisations must possess the necessary balance of skills needed to run a business successfully. Companies need the capability to manage their production and marketing systems as well as controlling the financial and personnel aspects properly. Belbin[13] has looked at another aspect of the balance of human resources, namely the extent to which management teams contain an adequate balance of personality types to operate effectively. Some of the more common personality types needed within an effective team are identified in Figure 4.7.

For example, it is often argued that one of the strengths of the British government services is the complementary nature of the team within departments – particularly the relationship which ministers, as the political leaders, share with the senior civil servants and, in turn, their relationship with the analysts within their departments.

4.4.3 Flexibility analysis

Another issue which needs to be assessed is the extent to which an organisation's resources are flexible and adaptable. It is important to assess how far flexibility is balanced with the uncertainty faced by the organisation; flexibility has no strategic significance without an understanding of this uncertainty. A manufacturing company facing a highly volatile raw materials market may choose to spread its sources of supply despite the fact that this could prove more costly. In contrast, it may be happy to have a highly inflexible, high volume throughput production system since it is trading in a stable market and this system of production ensures a highly competitive cost structure.

A flexibility analysis need be no more sophisticated than a simple listing of the major areas of uncertainty and the extent to which the company's resources are geared

Chairman/team leader	**Company worker**
Stable, dominant, extrovert	Stable, controlled
Concentrates on objectives	Practical organiser
Does not originate ideas	Can be inflexible but likely to adapt to
Focuses people on what they do best	established systems
	Not an innovator
Plant	**Monitor evaluator**
Dominant, high IQ, introvert	High IQ, stable, introvert
A 'scatterer of seeds', originates ideas	Measured analyses not innovation
Misses out on detail	Unambitious and lacking enthusiasm
Thrustful but easily offended	Solid, dependable
Resource investigator	**Team worker**
Stable, dominant, extrovert	Stable, extrovert, low dominance
Sociable	Concerned with individual's needs
Contacts with outside world	Builds on others' ideas
Salesperson//diplomat/liaison officer	Cools things down
Not original thinker	
Shaper	**Finisher**
Anxious, dominant, extrovert	Anxious, introvert
Emotional, impulsive	Worries over what will go wrong
Quick to challenge and respond to challenge	Permanent sense of urgency
Unites ideas, objectives and possibilities	Preoccupied with order
Competitive	Concerned with 'following through'
Intolerant of woolliness and vagueness	

Figure 4.7 Personality types for the effective team. (Source: R.M. Belbin, *Management Teams: Why they succeed or fail*, Heinemann, 1981, and R.M. Belbin *et al.*, 'Building effective management teams', *Journal of General Management*, **3**(3), 1976.)

Table 4.4 Flexibility analysis – an example.

Major areas of uncertainty	*Flexibility* Required	*Actual (at present)*	*Comments*
1. Demand for product A	Capacity (possibility +20%) or Stocks	Overtime could cover Low	Probably OK
2. Price of raw materials from present supplier	New suppliers New materials	None known at present Production system cannot cope	Problem area Seek information on new suppliers
3. Major customer may go bankrupt	Replacement customer	No leads	Sound out potential customers
4. Long term loan may not be renewed next year	Other sources of capital	Good image on stock market	New share issue looks favourable
5. Chief design engineer may retire	Design capability for products presently in development	Deputy not suitable Chief may agree to part-time 'consultancy' arrangement	Training and/or recruitment needs urgent attention

to cope with each of these. Table 4.4 sets out such an analysis which seeks to compare the major areas of uncertainty faced by a company with the degree of flexibility in the related resource areas.

4.5 IDENTIFICATION OF KEY ISSUES

The last major aspect of resource analysis is the identification of the key issues arising from previous analyses. It is only at this stage of the analysis that a sensible assessment can be made of the major *strengths and weaknesses* of an organisation and the strategic importance of these (see Illustration 4.6). The resource analysis starts to be useful as a basis against which to judge future courses of action. There are several assessments which can be made.

ILLUSTRATION 4.6

Strengths and weaknesses of Cadbury/Schweppes plc

The threat of takeover bids in 1986 brought into sharp focus the strengths and weaknesses of the company as perceived by potential predators.

STRENGTHS		WEAKNESSES
Company/brand names Both Cadbury and Schweppes were synonymous with quality. Other strong brands were *Kenco* (coffee), *Typhoo* (tea), *Chivers–Hartley* (jam)	**New product** The *Wispa* bar was a major success	**Saturated markets** Leading to highly competitive trading, high promotion costs, squeezed margins (a particular problem in Food division)
Market share 28% share of UK chocolate market 25% of soft drinks	**Technology** A leader in confectionery technology	**Losses in USA** 1985 was disastrous in USA, largely due to small size of operation making marketing costs high
Effective advertising A reputation for stylish advertising	**Saleable divisions** Household products division had been sold Food division could be diminished to raise cash	**Credibility in City** Traditionally a strength but shaken by US results
Financial management Financial management was regarded as strong	**Industrial relations** Generally good	**Plant location** Concentrated in UK (saturated market), products shelf life fairly low too

Source: *Management Today*, March 1986.

1. SWOT analysis[14] has already been referred to in Chapter 3. This can be a very useful way of summarising many of the previous analyses and combining them with the key issues from the environmental analysis. One of the benefits of using *value chain* analysis is that it should have helped avoid some of the common pitfalls of SWOT analysis. In particular the analysis must be clear on:

 (i) The reasons why particular activities or resources are identified as strengths or weaknesses.

 (ii) That value activities are more important than resources *per se*. In other words, it is the use to which resources are being put which is critical.

 (iii) That it is the *linkages* between various value activities which are likely to be the key strengths (or weaknesses) of the organisation. This would include linkages with the value chains of suppliers, channels and customers.

2. A strengths and weaknesses analysis can be particularly powerful if it incorporates a comparison with competitors. This can be done using the concept of distinctive competence. *Distinctive competence*[15] is concerned with identifying those particular strengths which give the company an edge over its competitors and those areas of particular weakness which are to be avoided. This may require a parallel analysis of competitors' resources as previously mentioned. Illustration 4.7 shows how one company developed 'competitiveness achievement plans' as a means of addressing this issue. A supermarket's distinctive strength might be found in its layout, display and control systems which allow for high volume trading at minimal cost. Its particular weakness would be its inability to provide advice to customers. This analysis would help in assessing how viable a move into new product areas might be, such as DIY or furniture.

This is, of course, the main reason why there has been so much emphasis on value analysis in this chapter. It is a valuable way of understanding the distinctive competence of an organisation, particularly where a comparison is made of the value chains of major competitors.

 It should be noted that some authors have argued that it is more useful to develop resource analyses specifically designed to detect the onset of important strategic phases in a company's development. In particular, Argenti[16] has concentrated on the identification of companies which are likely to go bankrupt. Although others[17] have not given the same degree of emphasis to resources, there is general recognition that poor resources, badly managed, can be a significant contributing factor to company failure.

4.6 SUMMARY

Resource analysis is an important means of assessing an organisation's *strategic capability* which in turn is necessary if sensible choices of future strategy are to be made. Traditionally, much of the discussion of resource analysis has centred around the idea of strengths and weaknesses.

 The concept of the *value chain* is particularly useful in understanding an organisation's strategic capability since it concentrates on value activities and the linkages

ILLUSTRATION 4.7

Competitiveness Achievement Plans (CAPs) at Lucas

Resource analysis is particularly valuable when it improves the understanding of
the competitive position of an organisation.

Like many UK engineering companies, component manufacturers Lucas Industries
suffered badly in the early 1980s. They woke up to the fact that they were operating in a
single world market and they must judge their resource strengths (and weaknesses)
accordingly. They simply had to be competitive with the best in the world to survive, and
the unpalatable truth at the beginning of the 1980s, according to chairman Sir Godfrey
Messervy, was that, 'the performance in most markets was fundamentally uncompetitive'.
    What emerged from a period of soul-searching were the company's Competitiveness
Achievement Plans (CAPs). These were action plans which measured up, in every detail, to
each company's or division's particular (international) competitor. These CAPs became a
way of cracking the inward-looking mould and forcing managers to judge their
performance against an international backcloth. What they revealed was that the company's major deficiency was in manufacturing methods rather than product technology.
Although Lucas did not look too bad by UK standards, a comparison against the best
Japanese practice was very revealing in measuring the extent of 'drift' – particularly on
resource utilisation. Specific measures were:

● The ratio of indirect support staff to labour was 1.2 compared to Japanese 0.5.
● Stock turnover at four times per annum compared with ten to twenty times per annum
  in Japan.
● Development lead times were double in the UK.
● Sales per employee in the UK were about one-third of those in Japan.

As a result, Japanese product costs were some 60% to 80% of UK equivalents. The crucial
difference was that the Japanese had long recognised that with 70% of their capital tied up
in their production assets, manufacturing methods were as much a part of company
strategy as marketing or research.

Source: *Management Today*, June 1986.

between activities rather than simply resources *per se*. This underlines the fact that
capability is strongly related to the way in which resources are deployed and
controlled. It has also been emphasised that a resource analysis must not be confined to
those resources which an organisation *owns*. Often it is the linkages with the value
chains of suppliers, channels and customers which are the cornerstones of an
organisation's capability, and which prevent imitation by competitors.
    Perhaps the most crucial issue has been the contention that strategic capability is
best understood in relation to other (competitive) organisations. It is the *distinctive
competence* of the organisation *vis-à-vis* competitors or other providers which is so
important to unearth in a resource analysis.
    Equally it should be remembered that resource capability is only one piece of the
jigsaw. The strategic importance of the environment has been discussed in Chapter 3.
The next chapter considers the third ingredient, namely the extent to which an
organisation's culture and power structure can influence strategy.

REFERENCES

1. An extensive discussion of the value chain concept and its application can be found in Michael Porter's book *Competitive Advantage* (Free Press, 1985): The concept is introduced in Chapter 2 of the book.

2. There are a number of papers and standard texts which include traditional resource audits, for example, C. W. Hofer and D. Schendel, *Strategy Formulation: Analytical concepts*, p. 149, West, 1978, and R. B. Buchelle, 'How to evaluate a firm', *California Management Review*, Fall, 1962, look at resource analysis within functional areas. The latter, provides extensive checklists. T. G. Whelan and J. D. Hunger, *SAM Advanced Management Journal*, Winter, 1987, extend the audit to management processes too.

3. Chapters 4 and 8 in R. G. Murdick, R. H Eckhouse, R. C. Moor and T. N. Zimmerer., *Business Policy: A framework for analysis* (2nd edn), Grid, 1976, look at strategic analysis from a functional viewpoint and, as such, provide some useful guidelines and checklists for functional resource analysis. However, readers who are unfamiliar with the details of resources in any functional area might consult one of the following:
   - P. Kotler, *Marketing Management: Analysis, planning and control* (4th edn), pp. 652–7, Prentice Hall, 1980, for a systematic marketing audit. Kotler's 'audit' also reviews the market and competitive situation together with marketing objectives. He also tries to assess aspects of resource utilisation and control.
   - A. G. Cowling and C. J. B. Mailer, *Managing Human Resources*, Arnold, 1981. Chapter 11 is concerned with manpower planning and illustrates how an analysis of the manpower resources of a company can be undertaken.
   - R. Wild, *Production and Operations Management* (3rd edn), Holt, Rinehart & Winston, 1984. Chapter 1 is concerned with the nature of operating systems and the role of operations management. Although the text does not specifically list an 'operating audit' the discussion gives an understanding of how to analyse and assess a company's operating system.
   - J. M. Samuels and F. M Wilkes, *Management of Company Finance* (3rd edn), Nelson, 1980. Chapters 5, 7, 8 and 14 give a full picture of the sources and applications of companies' financial resources.

4. J. Sizer, *An Insight into Management Accounting* (2nd edn), Pitman, 1979, is a good source for readers who wish to improve their understanding of profitability measurement.

5. For an explanation of the importance of gearing see chapter 5 of *An Insight into Management Accounting* (reference 4 above).

6. For discussions of technology transfer on an international dimension, see W. H. Davidson, 'Structure and performance in international technology transfer', *Journal of Management Studies*, **120**, 1983; and M. G. Harvey, 'The application of technology life cycles to technology transfers', *Journal of Business Strategy*, **5**(2), 1984.

7. D. Beaven, 'What the ratios saw', *Management Today*, July, 1982, points out some pitfalls of using ratio analysis too blindly.

8. Chapter 4 in *An Insight into Management Accounting* (see reference 4 above) deals in detail with the value of financial ratio analysis and how such an analysis can be done (with examples). Some authors suggest analyses which can help detect important aspects of strategy. For example, E. I. Altman, *Corporate Bankruptcy in America*, Heath Lexington, 1971, explains how his 'Z-factor' can be used to predict the failure of companies. C. J. Sutton, *Economics and*

Corporate Strategy, chapter 7, Cambridge University Press, 1980, relates analyses to mergers and takeovers.

9. For example, M. E. Porter, *Competitive Advantage*, Free Press, 1985, argues that strategic capability can only be properly understood by assessing the competitive advantage of individual organisations.

10. Further reading on the BCG models are:
    - P. Conley, *Experience Curves as a Planning Tool*, available from the Boston Consulting Group as a pamphlet.
    - B. Hedley, 'Strategy and the business portfolio', *Long Range Planning*, **10**(2), 1977.
    - J. H. Grant and W. R. King, 'Strategic formulation: analytical and normative models', in D. Schendel and C. Hofer (eds), *Strategic Management: A new view of business policy and planning*, Little Brown, 1979.

11. Readers may refer to the following:
    - S.P. Slatter, 'Common pitfalls in using the BCG product portfolio matrix', *London Business School Journal*, Winter, 1980.
    - R. Wensley, 'PIMS and BCG: new horizons or false dawn', *Strategic Management Journal*, **3**(2), 1982.
    - John Thackeray, 'The corporate strategy problem', *Management Today*, Oct., 1979.

12. P. Drucker, in *Managing for Results* (Pan, 1973), shows how resources can be mismatched with opportunities and how this might be remedied.

13. R. M. Belbin, B. R. Aston and R. D. Mottram, 'Building effective management teams', *Journal of General Management*, **3**(3), 1976.

14. The idea of SWOT as a commonsense checklist for use in strategic analyses and evaluation has been used by writers on strategy for many years: for example S. Tilles in 'Making strategy explicit' which was written in 1966 and is reproduced in *Business Strategy*, I. Ansoff (ed.), Penguin, 1968.

15. An interesting discussion of distinctive competence can be found in M. A. Hitt and R. D. Ireland, Corporate Distinctive Competence, Strategy Industry and Performance, *Strategic Management Journal*, Vol 6, 1985.

16. J. Argenti, *Corporate Collapse: Causes and symptoms*, McGraw-Hill, 1976, is based on research into a number of major British companies (most notably Rolls Royce prior to the 1971 collapse).

17. See, for example, Chapter 2 in S. Slatter, *Corporate Recovery*, Penguin, 1984.

Recommended key readings

- M.E. Porter, *Competitive Advantage*, Free Press, 1985, is the seminal text on value chain analysis. Readers should, in particular, refer to Chapters 2 and 3 in the context of this chapter.

- An approach to carrying out a resource audit is given by T. L. Wheelan and J. D. Hunger in 'Using the strategic audit', *SAM Advanced Management Journal*, **52**(1), 1987. Also see chapter 8 of *Strategic Planning* (Free Press/Collier Macmillan, 1979) by G. A. Steiner.

- To understand the value of financial analysis readers should refer to texts such as J. Sizer, *An Insight into Management Accounting* (2nd edn), chapter 6, Pitman, 1979. This should be read in conjunction with the cautionary words in 'What the ratios saw' by D. Beaven in *Management Today*, July, 1982.

Chapter 5

EXPECTATIONS, OBJECTIVES AND POWER

5.1 INTRODUCTION

There is a temptation to look for a neat and tidy way of formulating strategy. Such a method might, apparently, be achieved through the analysis of the organisation's environment (Chapter 3) and the extent to which the company's resources, or strategic capability (Chapter 4) are matched with the environment. However, this 'economic' analysis of strategy fails to recognise the complex role which people play in the evolution of strategy as discussed in Chapter 2. This chapter looks at how the cultural and political systems of an organisation can be analysed and understood as part of a strategic analysis. This is a recognition that strategy is also a product of what people *want* an organisation to do or what they feel the organisation should be like. There has been a growing awareness of the central importance of these issues in understanding strategy formulation and implementation since the early 1980s.

It should be clear from earlier discussions (Chapter 2) that strategies tend to evolve in organisations within a cultural and political system and the concept of an objective, value-free, analysis of an organisation's strategies (either past or future) is misplaced. Although the analysis of an organisation's environment and resource position provides an important background to the strategic choices which the organisation faces, any changes need to take place within the cultural and political realities of the organisation. A strategic analysis must provide a proper understanding of how the social and political situation might affect the viability of different strategies and Figure 5.1 provides a framework for such an analysis. The figure identifies different 'layers' of cultural/political influences on strategy, ranging from broad issues such as the values of society to very specific influences on strategy such as organisational objectives. Of crucial importance too is the need to assess the power structure within and around any organisation. It should be remembered that there are multiple connections between these various influences and the figure is a simplification of reality. It is these complex interconnections which need to be understood. An analysis needs to assess the influence of the following factors on company strategies (Figure 5.1):

- There are a number of cultural factors in an organisation's *environment* which will influence the internal situation. In particular the values of society at large and the influence of organised groups need to be understood.
- The *nature of the business,* such as the market situation and the types of product and technology are important influences not only in the direct sense discussed in Chapter 3 but in the way they affect the expectations of individuals and groups.

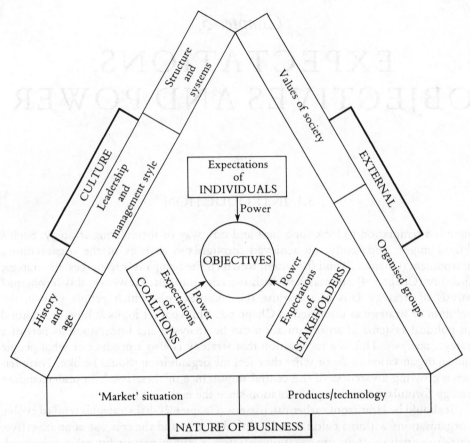

Figure 5.1 Expectations, objectives and power.

- Most pervasive of all these general influences is the organisational *culture* itself. The meaning and importance of culture has already been discussed in Chapter 2, which has also shown why culture is a key driving force behind an organisation's strategies.
- At a more specific level, individuals will normally have shared expectations with one or more groups of people within the organisation. These shared expectations may be concerned with undertaking the company's tasks and reflect the formal structure of the organisation (e.g. departmental expectations). However, *coalitions* also arise as a result of specific events and can transcend the formal structure.
- Internal groups and individuals are also influenced by their contacts with *external stakeholders* – groups who have an interest in the operation of the company such as customers, shareholders, suppliers or unions. For example, sales staff may be pressurised by customers to represent their interests within the company.
- Individuals or groups, whether internal or external cannot influence an organisation's strategies unless they have an influencing mechanism. This mechanism is called *power* which can be derived in a variety of ways which will be discussed.
- Organisational *objectives* traditionally have been afforded a central/dominant role in influencing strategy. (i.e. strategy is seen as the means of achieving preordained and

unchangeable objectives). That is not the view taken in this book. Whereas organisations do have objectives which are often valuable in strategy formulation they should not be regarded as an unchangeable set of expectations. They should be viewed as an important part of the strategic equation, and open to amendment and change as strategies develop.

- Objectives tend to emerge as the wishes of the most dominant coalition; usually the management of the organisation although there are notable exceptions. However, in pursuing these objectives the dominant group is very strongly influenced by their reading of the political situation (i.e. their perception of the power structure). For example, they are likely to set aside some of their expectations in order to improve the chance of achieving others.

This chapter is concerned with providing some approaches to analysing these issues as part of a strategic analysis.

5.2 GENERAL INFLUENCES ON INDIVIDUALS AND GROUPS

There is a wide variety of factors which influence the expectations that individuals and groups are likely to have of an organisation. For convenience these general influences can be grouped into three categories as shown in Figure 5.2.

When analysing the significance of these factors on the strategic development of any organisation it is useful to ask the following questions:

1. Which factors inside and outside the organisation have most influence on the expectations of groups and individuals within the organisation?
2. To what extent do current strategies reflect the influence of any one or combination of these factors?

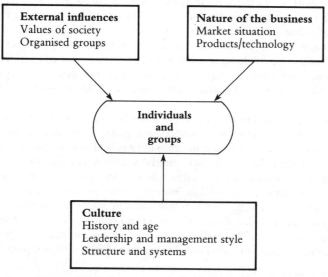

Figure 5.2 Influences on individuals and groups.

3. How far would these factors help or hinder the changes which would be needed to pursue new strategies.

Readers are encouraged to bear these questions in mind whilst reading this section.

5.2.1 External influences

VALUES OF SOCIETY

Attitudes to work, authority, equality and a whole range of other important issues are constantly shaped and changed by society at large. From the point of view of corporate

---

ILLUSTRATION 5.1

Sport and the values of society

The popularity and viability of individual sports changes markedly over time.
One key ingredient in this has been the way in which sport reflects the changing
values of society.

Sport in both the public and private sectors has been a major industry for many years in the UK. Indeed, its importance in a commercial sense has been felt by the vast array of other businesses/organisations which have developed to support the sports industry. So manufacture, import and distribution of sports equipment and clothes had grown immensely since the 1960s. More recently supporting services such as sports injury clinics, specialist magazines and advisory/coaching services had blossomed on the back of the sports boom. However, all of these were vulnerable to the changing 'tastes' within sport and needed to keep their eye on these trends – the decline of football spectators and the jogging phenomenon of the 1980s were well-documented examples.

One factor which had been cited in influencing 'consumer choice' in sport was the way in which sport tended to mirror the changing values of society. So in the early part of the twentieth century the dominant values in a mass-production manufacturing society were those of industrial work, division of labour and social uniformity. This led to the most popular sports being those with rigid and formal rules, comprising team work and differentiated roles. The underlying ethic was one of intergroup competition. As leisure time was limited and worktime highly programmed, games also tended to take place in fixed short blocks at fixed locations. Organised team sports such as football were extremely popular in that era.

In sharp contrast, in the 1970s and 1980s the dominant culture of society started to shift to one of a greater emphasis on services, the quality of life and personal autonomy. The nature of work – particularly for the growing bands of middle classes – also started to emphasise these values. As a result, new interest started to emerge within sport towards more flexible, individualistic sports – often where 'rules' were less important. Teamwork and interteam competition became less important than pitting oneself against personal targets or the elements at large. Sports which could be pursued at widely different times and locations became popular. Running, jogging and outdoor pursuits – climbing, hang-gliding all boomed in the 1980s and with them the fortunes of those companies that saw these trends. Public authorities too needed to readjust their sports provision considerably.

Source: *Leisure Management*, August 1986.

strategy it is important to understand this process for two reasons. Firstly, values of society change and adjust over time and, therefore, policies which were acceptable twenty years ago may not be so today. Illustration 5.1 shows one example. There has been an increasing trend within the UK for the activities of companies to be constrained by legislation, public opinion, and the media. Secondly, companies which operate internationally have the added problem of coping with the very different standards and expectations of the various countries in which they operate.

Hofstede[1] has undertaken extensive research into how national culture influences employee motivation, management styles and organisational structures. He concludes that individual countries are markedly different from each other. For example, British culture appears to be far more tolerant of uncertainty than many other societies – notable European examples being France, Spain and West Germany. Terry[2] has undertaken an interesting study of how British culture affects the performance of British managers. He concludes that the biggest single advantage of the British is that they do not panic when things get rough. However, against this he identifies insularity, chauvinism and a low regard for professionalism in business as significant problems.

ORGANISED GROUPS

Individuals often have allegiances to other groups which are very influential on their attitudes. These allegiances may be highly institutionalised and directly related to their working situation (such as membership of trade unions), or may be more informal and unrelated (such as membership of churches or political groups). The membership of professional bodies or institutions can be particularly important in organisations with a high proportion of professional staff. Engineering companies, R&D departments, accountancy sections, and many public service departments are all dominated by people who very often have a strong 'professional' view of their role which may not be in accord with the managerial view on how these people can be best used as a resource. At the corporate level, the whole organisational ethos of the company may be influenced by its membership of a trade association or similar body. These bodies may exert influence informally but often seek to impose norms of behaviour on member companies through the development of 'codes of conduct'. There are many examples in UK industries such as the Association of British Travel Agents (ABTA), the National House Builders Registration Council (NHBRC) and the British Insurance Brokers Association (BIBA). This process also occurs on an international scale, a well known example being the Organisation of Petroleum Exporting Countries (OPEC).

5.2.2 Nature of the business

There are a number of issues concerning the nature of a business which will also influence attitudes to company policy. These are much more specific to the particular circumstances of a company but are often concerned with the market situation and the nature of the products/technology within the company.

MARKET SITUATION

Different companies face quite different market conditions and any one company will face different conditions as time goes on. As a result of this, the attitudes of people within the company will also change, often quite markedly, as external conditions change. Policy decisions which can be made in companies facing a highly competitive and depressed market would meet considerable resistance in other companies which face less stringent conditions. During the 1980s in the UK, companies, and even whole industries, were subjected to massive changes in scale, working practices, and product/market strategy. Both the steel and motor car industries were reshaped in this way whilst attempts to follow similar changes in the coal mining industry were initially halted by strong union opposition, but later were implemented too.

People are also influenced by the position of the company in relation to the lifecycle of its products and/or markets. People who have only known a company during a period of rapid growth may have developed expectations which are inappropriate when its products enter the stage of maturity.

PRODUCTS/TECHNOLOGY

Technology influences attitudes in two main ways. First, technology may put a constraint on the way in which the company is able to operate and survive in a competitive environment and therefore dictate methods of operating and the tasks which people perform. For example, the impact of production line working in the motor car industry on the attitudes and antagonisms which had built up within the motor companies has received much discussion.[3] Second, technology changes the mix of skills required by companies which, in turn, may change company culture. If a company has developed for a long time with little outside influence, individuals and groups may become very introspective. A change in technology may necessitate the company 'buying-in' outside help and, as a result, introducing new attitudes to the company which can have a profound influence on the way people view future policy.

5.2.3 Organisational culture

It should be clear from the discussions in Chapter 2 that an understanding of the processes of policy making in organisations cannot be achieved without paying attention to the issue of *organisational culture*. It is equally important when analysing the strategic position of an organisation to assess how this culture has influenced the development of the organisation and the strategies which it has pursued. Chapter 2 suggested that a useful analysis of culture can be achieved by examining the *cultural web* of factors within an organisation which preserve and sustain commonly held core beliefs – the *recipe*. This section suggests how the elements of this cultural web might be analysed. This is important for two reasons in relation to later parts of the book. First, it provides the background against which an assessment of future strategic choices can be made (Chapter 7) both in relation to options which might be possible within the current 'recipe' and for those which would require more significant change. Second, where the recipe would need to be changed it also provides a background against which to assess how change might be achieved (Chapter 11).

To simplify the discussion in this section, different facets of the cultural web will be discussed in order to build up an analysis of the influence of culture on strategy. However, it must be remembered that it is the subtle interrelationships between these various facets which are of greatest importance and readers should not regard the following discussions as a series of unrelated issues. The impact of the cultural web on an organisation can be analysed by looking at the following issues (Figure 5.3).

Aspects of cultural web	Some useful questions
A. Stories and myths	1. What **core beliefs** do the stories reflect? 2. How **strongly held** are these beliefs with power holders? 3. How **pervasive** are the beliefs (through the levels)? 4. How do beliefs relate to **strengths** and **weaknesses**? 5. Who are the **heroes**? 6. Do the heroes **conform** to or **challenge** the beliefs?
B. Rituals and symbols	1. What **behaviour** is expected and rewarded (e,g, risk taking)? 2. What **language** is used to describe the organisation and its activities? 3. What is the dominant **attitude** towards each stakeholder group?
C. Leadership and management style	1. What are the **core beliefs** of the leadership? 2. Which aspects are stressed in public (e.g. annual reports)? 3. How do they regard structures (e.g. centralists or devolutionist) 4. What **type** of strategy is favoured (e.g. defensive or speculative?) 5. What attributes are sought in **new recruits**?
D. Structure and systems	1. Do structures/systems encourage **collaboration** or **competition**? 2. Which aspects of strategy are most closely **monitored** and **controlled**? 3. What **kind of training** is given?

Figure 5.3 Analysing the impact of the cultural web on strategy: a checklist.

HISTORY AND AGE (TRADITION)

The *stories, rituals and symbolic behaviour* in organisations provide valuable insights into the core beliefs of the organisation – the recipe – and can contribute towards strategic analysis.[4] These factors are a product of the history and age of the organisation since they arise and develop over time through the experiences of individuals and groups undertaking the day-to-day tasks of the organisation. The stories and myths distil the essence of the company's past strategies, legitimize types of behaviour of those individuals and groups currently within the organisation, and attitudes of outsiders towards that organisation, as seen in Illustration 5.2. For example, it has been argued that the dominant culture of the National Health Service within the UK is one of curing sickness rather than promoting health. Most of the stories within the Health Service concern spectacular developments in curing – particularly in terminal illnesses. In contrast, community medicine and preventative care are still the 'Cinderellas' of the Health Service and receive little attention and kudos. The heroes of the organisation are in curing not caring. And in oil companies the heroes are still the exploration teams.

Stinchcombe[5] found that the way that companies were organised and managed bore a strong relationship to the era in which that particular industry had its foundations. For example, the pre-Industrial Revolution industries, such as farming or construction, still retain many of the features associated with craft industries despite modern methods of operation. History and tradition can be a considerable problem where culture has developed in a way which threatens the survival of the organisation in the light of a changing environment – such as new technologies or competitors. The experiences in UK motor manufacturing industry (late 1970s) and the UK newspaper publishing industry (1980s) are both good examples of the immense difficulties which can be faced in such circumstances.

In analysing the impact of this history on an organisation's strategy – both past and future – there are several questions which can be posed. Some of these are set out in Figure 5.3. The answers should give a clearer understanding of the core beliefs. These range from whether the stories and myths are predominantly concerned with success or failure, change or stability, to the type of language used within the organisation. For example, when the hovercraft service started channel crossings in the late 1960s the companies deliberately mimicked airlines rather than ships and this was sustained throughout by the rituals and symbols – they had a 'pilot', dressed their 'cabin staff' as did airlines, had 'flights' not sailings, etc.

ILLUSTRATION 5.2

Woolies's changed image

A strong company culture and image is a two-edged sword. The traditional
strength of a company can soon become a major burden.

The refurbishing of Woolworth's 1950s headquarters in Marylebone Road, London in the mid 1980s was a richly symbolic event. Much of the decor and fittings had remained unchanged since the confident era when Woolies was the top merchandising power in the land. Until 1982s takeover under John Beckett, much of the management was also 1950s-style. The modernised building stood for the modernised firm – reorganised, repositioned and ready to assert itself in the high street. It took three years of hard labour for a new management team to gain the confidence to reshape the firm's physical appearance in its own image. It wasn't that people within Woolworth didn't know what needed to be done – they found it difficult to act on their plans. The reasons are an object lesson in the power of a corporate history.

Woolworth (founded in 1908) had an exemplary policy of internal promotion. Its boast was that a sweeper or doorman could become chairman. But for all the culture's coherence, this meant that when people ended up in the boardroom they were completely introverted – they had known nothing other than the Woolworth's system.

The Woolworth philosophy was very successful up to the 1960s. Then, however, it was unable to cope with the increased consumer sophistication. The new team in 1982 largely came from outside retailing and felt that to be an advantage in the circumstances. They had to eradicate the deep-worn grooves of habit. This was achieved largely by repositioning and creating a group of distinctive retailing ventures such as B & Q (DIY) and later Comet (electrical goods). Woolworth's core business was divided into property and retailing. The success of B & Q was used as a model of how competitive advantage could be gained by careful product/market positioning. But more importantly it demonstrated both internally and externally that a new Woolworth really had arrived at last.

Source: *Management Today*, March 1986.

LEADERSHIP AND MANAGEMENT STYLE

In later chapters it will be seen how important the leadership[6] of an organisation is in terms of shaping and changing culture to ensure survival and success. Accordingly it is important during strategic analysis to establish how previous and current leadership has contributed to the organisation's culture and development.

Miles and Snow,[7] whose findings were discussed in Chapter 2, categorise organisations into three basic types in terms of how they behave strategically (Table 5.1). When undertaking a strategic analysis this provides a means of assessing the dominant culture of the organisation. By reviewing the types of system and the historical choices of strategy, the analyst can distinguish between a defender and a prospector organisation, and hence judge the extent to which new strategies might fit the current 'recipe'. In the context of the current discussion on leadership, the central dilemma for organisations should now be clear. A cohesive culture almost demands, and often produces, 'cloning' within the organisation – where more and more like-minded individuals are selected into key leadership roles or become 'socialised' into the organisation's dominant beliefs and approaches. However, there are dangers of blindly following this 'recipe'. This issue is discussed more fully in Chapter 11 which looks at how culture can be managed and changed.

STRUCTURE AND SYSTEMS

The *structure* and *systems* of an organisation are also an important part of the cultural web and, as such, are influential on how individuals and groups perceive the organisation's strategies. Chapters 10 and 11 will discuss how the design and management of structure and systems is crucial to the successful implementation of strategy. However, at this stage it is worthwhile briefly highlighting ways in which

Table 5.1 Different types of organisation culture and their influences on policy making.

Organisation type	Characteristics of policy-making		
	Dominant objectives	*Preferred strategies*	*Planning and control systems*
1. Defenders	Desire for a secure and stable niche in market	Specialisation: cost-efficient production: marketing emphasises price and service to defend current business: tendency to vertical integration.	Centralised, detailed control Emphasis on cost efficiency Extensive use of formal planning.
2. Prospectors	Location and exploitation of new product and market opportunities	Growth through product and market development (often in spurts). Constant monitoring of environmental change. Multiple technologies.	Emphasis on flexibility, decentralised control, use of *ad hoc* measurements
3. Analysers	Desire to match new ventures to present shape of business	Steady growth through market penetration. Exploitation of applied research. Followers in the market.	Very complicated. Co-ordinating roles between functions (e.g. product managers). Intensive planning.

After R.E. Miles and C.C. Snow, *Organizational Strategy, Structure and Process*, McGraw-Hill, 1978.

structure and systems contribute to culture (Figure 5.3). For example, an organisation which is structured and managed as a series of separate and competitive units is likely to have a cohesive culture at the level of these subunits which makes collaborative ventures (between units) difficult. Indeed, in many such organisations the systems of control and reward are likely to have developed in a way which encourages and supports competitive (rather than collaborative) behaviour. It is not surprising, therefore, that individuals and groups are likely to favour strategies which can be pursued in a devolved rather than an integrated way.[8]

A close look at the control systems of the organisation can be very instructive in seeing which aspects are most closely monitored. Many public service organisations in the UK have been obsessed with 'stewardship of funds' rather than quality of service. This can be clearly seen in the bureaucratic procedures which are almost entirely concerned with accounting for spending and have little regard for 'outputs'. The training programmes of organisations can also give useful pointers to core beliefs. For example, some organisations only have training in the 'technical' skills of the job whereas others place more emphasis on the development of general skills and attitudes. In the 1980s many large accountancy firms in the UK extended into management consultancy from their traditional base of auditing. Nevertheless, by far the majority of their training remained in auditing skills.

5.3 COALITIONS AND STAKEHOLDERS

Although individuals may have a wide variety of personal aspirations, groups of individuals exist in most organisations within which the individuals have identifiably shared expectations. These groups can be formally identified as *stakeholders* (e.g. managers, banks, unions, shareholders, etc.). For example, in 1981 the shareholders of the Savoy Hotel in London resisted increasingly generous offers to sell out to Trust House Forte. They considered THF to be a 'down market' company which did not match their expectations. (See Illustration 5.3.) However, a better understanding will emerge if *coalitions*[9] (of common expectations) are identified. It will be seen in the sections which follow that coalitions tend to arise as a result of events rather than being enshrined within the formal systems of the organisation. Coalitions may occur within departments, geographical locations, different levels in the hierarchy, different age groups. Most individuals will 'belong' to more than one such coalition. In order to obtain any influence in decision making, individuals will need to identify themselves with the aims and ideals of these coalitions. Political parties, of course, represent this process in operation quite clearly, but readers need to recognise that a similar process occurs in virtually every organisation. Similarly external stakeholder groups will attempt to influence strategy, to a greater or lesser extent, through their links with internal groups or individuals.

5.3.1 Conflicts of expectations

Since the expectations of groups are likely to differ it is quite normal for conflict to exist within organisations regarding the importance and/or desirability of many aspects of

ILLUSTRATION 5.3

The Savoy Hotel – last bastion of gracious living?

When Sir Charles Forte offered to rescue the Savoy Hotel from its financial difficulties, his takeover bid was met with strong resistance.

The Savoy Hotel in London was once described by one of its shareholders as exuding 'A sense of history, a feeling that in a tinfoil and plastic world, there was still one last bastion of truly gracious living, a hotel where one could kick one's shoes off, look around, and say, "Hey, this place is pretty nice".'

For several years leading up to 1980, however, the Savoy had suffered a series of losses which had left it vulnerable to takeover bids. As 'an obvious commercial move' in 1981 Sir Charles Forte made a bid of £58 million to add the Savoy Group to the Trust House Forte chain of restaurants, cafés and hotels. The move was met with indignation from all who were associated with that noble clutch of hotels which had become synonymous with distinction and good tastes. The reason for their resistance to Sir Charles' offer of salvation was not so much on the grounds of commercial wisdom, however, but at the thought of the style and tradition of such a sacred institution being subjected to the rule of the King of the Motorway café.

As the squeals of protest echoed around him, Sir Charles retained an air of nonchalance: 'Why are people so excited because I am interested in the Savoy? Do they think I am going to fill the foyer with Coca Cola machines or something?'

Nevertheless, the underlying distress behind the protests were succinctly expressed by the Savoy management's public statement:

> On professional grounds we do not think a vast combine like Trusthouse Forte, which among other things, runs service stations on the main arterial roads, and airport catering, is qualified to run hotels of the quality of the Savoy.

By mid 1981 the THF offer for the Savoy Group had lapsed, but despite the Savoy's recommendation not to accept the offer, THF had still managed to acquire 61.9% of the Savoy's Equity and a 38.6% voting share.

Source: *Sunday Times*, 22 March 1981.

strategy. This section considers some of the typical expectations that exist and how they might conflict. The main points are summarised in Figure 5.4. In many different circumstances a compromise will need to be reached between expectations which cannot all be achieved simultaneously. This varies from the conflict between growth and profitability; growth and control/independence; cost efficiency and jobs; volume/mass provision versus quality/specialisation, through to the problems of suboptimisation where the development of one part of an organisation may be at the expense of another.

What emerges is the need to understand the expectations of different groups and weigh these in terms of the power that they exercise. For example, banks may not have a shareholding in a company but may well have a direct interest through the funds that they loan: their main expectation is to achieve a secure return on their investment in terms of interest, and a company with high borrowings may well discover that meeting the bank's expectation becomes a dominant requirement.

1. In order to grow, short term profitability, cash flow and pay levels may need to be sacrificed.

2. When family businesses grow, the owners may lose control if they need to appoint professional managers.

3. New developments may require additional funding through share issue or loans. In either case financial independence may be sacrificed.

4. Public ownership of shares will require more openness and accountability from the management.

5. Cost efficiency through capital investment can mean job losses.

6. Extending into mass markets may require decline in quality standards.

7. In public services a common conflict is between mass provision and specialist services (e.g. preventative dentistry or heart transplant).

8. In public services savings in one area (e.g. social security benefits) may result in increases elsewhere (e.g. school meals, medical care).

Figure 5.4 Some common conflicts of expectations.

Local government is an excellent example of how a variety of stakeholder groups with differing expectations attempt to influence the formulation of strategy. The electorate are able to influence the situation by allocating power to political parties. They in turn are subject to their own internal pressures from groupings with differing expectations and must reconcile their policies with the views of opposition parties and the administrators in the local government departments. Illustration 5.4 shows one example.

It is useful when analysing the strategic importance of expectations within a company to look for one of three commonly occurring situations:

1. *Where the parts are more important than the whole*. This is well illustrated by many local authorities where people tend to owe more allegiance to the individual committees (service areas) such as recreation, housing or education, than they do to the corporate entity. This can make interdepartmental ventures quite difficult, as with the use of sports centres by schools. In ICI,[10] for example, prior to the chairmanship of Sir John Harvey-Jones, many employees knew little of the corporate centre; indeed, it has been said that many did not know who the chairman was. They identified with their own division of Fibres, Chemicals, etc.

2. *Where the whole is more important than the parts*. This is often seen in family companies where the maintenance of a strong family identity is often achieved at the expense of the efficient running of the various parts of the company. Some large organisations such as Shell and IBM put a great deal of effort into sustaining identity with the company as a whole.

3. *Where external influences are very important*. This is best typified by many voluntary organisations whose members have strong demands on their time from other sources (home and work), or in organisations in which professionals such as doctors, lawyers or scientists, play an important part and see the maintenance of external codes of practice or standards as of overriding importance.[11] The way in which the organisation operates is dominated by these outside influences.

Such an analysis is important since it contributes significantly to the understanding of an organisation's core beliefs and its strategic position which is necessary when

ILLUSTRATION 5.4

Rochdale buy-local policy

Local authorities find themselves in the position of wearing several 'stakeholder' hats at the same time. This often leads to potential areas of conflict – for example between cost conscious purchasing policies and the desire to support local firms.

Encouraged by the apparent stupidity of a Rochdale manufacturer supplying Birmingham City Council with windows while Rochdale Metropolitan Borough Council (MBC) was using windows produced in Birmingham, Rochdale adopted a buy-local policy.

In 1986 Rochdale MBC Leader Richard Farnell said priority would be given to local companies in tendering for council contracts. The scheme was similar to a system that Glasgow City Council had been operating since August 1982, where local companies whose tenders were within 5% of the lowest acceptable price were given the opportunity of re-examining their costs with a view to reducing their price. If no tenders fell into this category, then companies in adjoining authorities and towns were offered the same opportunity.

Rochdale planned to run the scheme for a trial period of twelve months during which time it would be vigorously promoted and monitored by the council's Industrial Development and Advisory Centre. The scheme formed part of a total policy package, said Rochdale Industrial Development Officer Peter Woodhouse, similar to the programme which had proved very successful in Glasgow. The council planned to reduce the size of individual contracts so they could be handled by smaller companies and to hold a series of workshops where potential suppliers could talk directly to council purchasing officers. Stewart Ogg, a member of Glasgow's economic development unit, said that the policy had diverted in aggregate some £2 million of contracts in each year of operation. He warned, however, that Rochdale could expect some criticism from neighbouring authorities angered at the implementation of such a scheme.

Glasgow had also been careful to ascertain which companies were truly local. Mr Ogg said that although some companies were nominally local they could have production based abroad.

Source: *Local Government Chronicle*, 3 October 1986.

assessing future strategies. For those who wish to affect strategic changes it provides a valuable insight into the circumstances in which change would be affected, particularly when linked to an assessment of the power structure of the organisation (see below).

5.3.2 Identifying coalitions

It is one thing to talk about the way in which coalitions influence a company's strategies, but it can often, in practice, be quite difficult to identify coalitions. There is always the danger of concentrating too heavily on the formal structure of an organisation as a basis for identifying coalitions since this can be the easiest place to look for the divisions in expectations mentioned previously. It is, however, essential to unearth the 'informal' coalitions and assess their importance.

Other problems in analysis are that individuals tend to belong to more than one coalition, and coalitions will also line up in different groupings depending on the issue in hand. For example, marketing and production departments could well be united in the face of proposals to drop certain product lines whilst being in fierce opposition regarding plans to buy-in new items to the product range. It is often specific events which trigger-off the formation of coalitions. For this reason it is helpful to speculate on the degree of unity or diversity between the various coalitions if faced with a number of possible future events. In this respect this is also a tool of strategic evaluation. Nevertheless this process can be very helpful during strategic analysis in uncovering potential alliances or rifts which may be significant in thinking about future strategic choices.

Pfeffer[12] provides an interesting example of how such an analysis can be undertaken. Table 5.2 shows a typical analysis in the case of a company which operated on two sites (Nottingham and Lincoln). The various coalitions and external stakeholders are identified and the table is used to map out their expected reactions to a variety of possible changes. There are several useful points which emerge from this analysis:

- There will always be some events over which the majority of coalitions can unite. Such solidarity tends to occur during the early stages of development of new companies or when survival is threatened by such events as a possible takeover by a major competitor.
- New coalitions may become important in certain of the situations envisaged. For example, the proposal to close the Lincoln plant would meet resistance not only from the employees there but also from the local support which they were able to muster. Equally, computerisation would be resisted by clerical staff who had hitherto never been viewed as a cohesive group.
- In some cases there would be divided views within one of the coalitions. For example, the export section of the marketing department might be delighted by

Table 5.2 The attitudes of various 'coalitions' towards possible future changes.

Possible changes	A	B (internal coalitions)						C (external stakeholders)			
	Whole company	1 Market dept	2 Prod dept	3 Notts plant	4 Lincoln plant	5 Gradu-ates	6 Clerical staff	1 Suppl. A	2 Cust. X	3 Shr.hdr. M	4 Local comm.
1. Sell out to competitor	−	−	−	−	−	−	−	0	−	0	−
2. Introduce computerised systems	+	+	?	+	0	+	−	0	+	+	0
3. Close Lincoln plant	?	+	−	+	−	0	0	0	+	0	−
4. Develop new EEC markets	?	?	−	+	−	0	0	+	−	+	0
5. Subcontract production	?	+	−	−	−	0	0	−	0	−	−

+ = support   0 = neutral   − = oppose   ? = divided opinion

plans to expand sales in the EEC but not so their UK counterparts. Thus these would need to be viewed as separate coalitions in such circumstances.

● At this stage it is important to identify potential alliances between coalitions regarding any of these future options. In this example a particularly significant observation is that the possibility of closing the Lincoln plant could well see an alliance between the Nottingham plant and the marketing department with strong support from the major customer X. In any such move the Lincoln plant could only rely on production staff and local community action; others seem to be broadly indifferent.

5.4 POWER

The previous section was concerned with analysing how expectations are 'structured' within and around any organisation. Such an analysis is only useful alongside a parallel analysis of the power that individuals or groups possess. Power is the mechanism by which expectations are able to influence policy and is an important part of the cultural web. In most organisations power will be unequally shared between the various coalitions or stakeholders. In other words, policy making tends to be dominated by one group, usually by the management of the company.[13] Before proceeding, it is necessary to understand what is meant here by power.[14] In particular, a distinction needs to be drawn between the power that people or groups apparently have as a result of their position within the organisation as against the power that they actually possess due to other reasons. For the purposes of strategic analysis, power is best understood as *the extent to which individuals or groups are able to persuade, induce or coerce others into following certain courses of action.* This is the mechanism by which one set of expectations will dominate policy making or seek compromise with others. An analysis of power must, therefore, begin by an assessment of the sources of power.

5.4.1 Sources of power within organisations

Power within companies can be derived in a variety of ways, any of which may provide an avenue whereby the expectations of an individual or group may influence company policy. The following are the normally recognised sources of power (Figure 5.5).

1. *Hierarchy* provides people with formal power over others and is one method by which senior managers influence policy. In particular, if strategic decision making is confined to top management this can give them considerable power. However, it is important to remember that this type of power has a very limited effect if used in isolation. Many industrial disputes illustrate the impotence of management if they rely only on formal power.

2. *Influence* can be an important source of power and may arise from personal qualities (the charismatic leader) or because a high level of consensus exists within the group or company (i.e. people are willing to support the prevailing viewpoint). Indeed there is strong support for the view that the most important task of managers is to shape the culture of the organisation to suit its strategy.[15] It is important to recognise, however,

A. **Within organisations**	B. **For external stakeholders**
1. Hierarchy (formal power), e.g. autocratic decision making	1. Control of strategic resources, e.g. materials, labour, money
2. Influence (informal power), e.g. charismatic leadership	2. Involvement in strategic implementation, e.g. distribution outlets, agents
3. Control of strategic resources, e.g. strategic products (coal)	3. Possession of knowledge (skills), e.g. subcontractors
4. Possession of knowledge/skills, e.g. computer specialists	4. Through internal links, e.g. informal influence
5. Control of the environment, e.g. negotiating skills	
6. Involvement in strategic implementation, e.g. by exercising discretion	

Figure 5.5 Sources of power.

that the extent to which an individual or group can use their influence is determined by a number of other factors. For example, access to channels of communication (the media) is an essential requirement. In many situations prior commitments to principles or specific courses of action can give individuals influence. Some of these principles may be quite central to the organisation's mission. For example, the 'no redundancy' policy of many Labour-controlled local authorities can be used by individuals or groups within that authority to challenge courses of action proposed by senior management (such as productivity deals).

3. *Control of strategic resources* is a major source of power within companies. It should be remembered that the relative importance of different resources will change over time and hence power derived in this way can show dramatic changes. The power of organised labour is most potent when demand for output is high and labour supply short. The decline in the position of car workers in the wages league between 1970 and 1980 is evidence of the erosion of this source of power. Within any one company the extent to which the various departments are seen as powerful will vary with the company's circumstances. Design or R&D departments may be powerful in companies developing new products or processes, whereas marketing people may dominate companies which are primarily concerned with developing new markets.

4. *Knowledge/skills.* The logical extension of the previous point is that individuals can derive power from their specialist knowledge or skills. Certain individuals may be viewed as irreplaceable to the company, and some will jealously guard this privileged position by creating a mystique around their job. This can be a risky personal strategy since others in the organisation may be spurred to acquire these skills or to devise methods of bypassing them. The power of many organisations' computer specialists was threatened by the advent of microcomputers which provided others within the organisation with a means of bypassing those specialists.

5. *Control of the environment.* Most people know that events in the company's environment are likely to influence company performance. However, some groups will have significantly more knowledge of, contact with, and influence over the environment than others. This can become a source of power within the company, since these

groups are able to reduce the uncertainty experienced by others.[16] It is probably for this reason that financial and marketing managers have traditionally been seen as dominant in policy determination whilst production managers have taken a back seat.[17] This source of power becomes most important when the environment is hostile or unpredictable. Then most of the factions will unite behind those who are seen to be best able to protect the company, despite the fact that the 'medicine' which might be doled out might represent a denial of many of their expectations. Many would argue that Sir Michael Edwardes[18] derived much of his power within British Leyland in this way between 1977 and 1982.

6. *Exercising discretion.* This is a most significant source of power within all organis-ations which is very often overlooked. Individuals derive power because they are involved in the company's decision processes by the very nature of their jobs. The execution of strategy, by its very complexity, cannot be controlled in all its minutest detail by one person or group and hence many other people within the company will need to interpret and execute particular parts of that policy and, in doing so, will use their own personal discretion. This is a major source of power for middle-management in organisations. The extent to which discretion is allowed to influence policy is obviously related to the types of control system within the organisation. These will be discussed in Chapter 11.

5.4.2 Sources of power for external stakeholders.

As with internal groups, those outside the organisation may have a number of sources of power which help them influence the organisation's strategies. These are also summarised in Figure 5.5.

1. *Resource dependence* is the most common source of power. For example, major suppliers, banks and shareholders all derive power from this source. The short term survival of the company may be critically dependent on one or more of these stakeholders. As discussed in Section 3.4.2 of Chapter 3, the power that buyers or suppliers exercise over an organisation is also likely to depend on the extent to which they are able to exercise control over resource provision or acquisition.
2. *Involvement in implementation* through linkages between value chains can be an important source of power for suppliers, channels and buyers as mentioned in Chapters 3 and 4. One of the major changes since the 1960s in many industries has been the extent to which power has shifted from the manufacturing sector to the distribution sector. The greater knowledge that distribution companies have of trends in consumer tastes has allowed them to dictate terms to manufacturers rather than simply being outlets for goods designed and planned by manufacturing companies.
3. *Knowledge and skills* critical to the success of the company may be a source of power. A subcontractor, for example, may derive power in this way, if it performs a vital activity in the company's value chain.
4. *Internal links* can provide a route for external stakeholders to influence company strategy. This is determined by the policy making processes within the organisation. At one extreme a highly authoritarian organisation is likely to be hostile to any attempts by outside stakeholders to be formally involved in formulation of strategy,

and therefore any influence on policy must be derived in other ways. In contrast, some organisations actively seek to involve a wide variety of stakeholders in strategic decision making. *Industrial democracy*[19] is concerned with the extent to which stakeholders can be formally involved in policy making.

5.4.3 Methods of assessing power

Since there are many different sources of power and influence, and each is dependent upon circumstances, some managers find this type of political analysis quite bewildering. However, it is important to incorporate a political analysis into any strategic analysis and this section provides readers with some simple guidelines on how this can be done.

The analysis will, once again, rely heavily on Pfeffer[20] who argues that the best way to cope with this complex situation is by stepping back from the detail and looking for *indicators of power*. For simplicity, it is suggested that there are four major indicators of power:

1. The *status* of the individual or group. One measure of status might be position within the hierarchy, but others are equally important, for example, an individual's salary, or job grades of groups. Equally, the reputation that a group or individual holds with others will be very relevant.
2. The *claim on resources* as measured by the size of a department's budget, or the number of employees within that group. In particular, trends in the proportion of resources claimed by that group may be a useful indicator as to the extent to which their power is waxing or waning. The least powerful groups invariably see their resources eroded by the more powerful. A useful comparison can be made with similar groups in comparable organisations.
3. *Representation in powerful positions.* The best example of this is the composition of the board of directors and their particular specialisms. The weakness of the production function may result from lack of representation at board level. Within less hierarchical organisations representation on important committees could be a measure of power, although a simple 'head count' in this type of analysis would overlook the extent to which the individuals are influential. Here individual status should be taken into consideration.
4. *Symbols of power.* Internal division of power may be indicated in a variety of ways. Such physical symbols as the size and location of people's offices, whether they have a secretary, carpets, a private telephone, or newspapers delivered each morning are all important clues. Whether individuals are addressed by their first or second names, even the way they dress, may be symbols of power. In more bureaucratic organisations, the existence of 'distribution lists' for internal memoranda and other information can give useful clues to the power structure. Surprisingly, these lists do not always neatly reflect the formal hierarchical structure and may provide pointers as to who really is viewed as powerful within the organisation.

It should be remembered that none of these four indicators is by itself likely to uncover fully the structure of power within a company. However, by looking at all four it may be possible to identify which people or groups appear to have power by a number of these measures. Table 5.3 illustrates how such an analysis might be performed to assess the relative power of the marketing and production departments, and the Nottingham and Lincoln plants of the previous example (Table 5.2). It is clear that the marketing department is seen as powerful by all measures and the production department universally weak. Equally, the Nottingham plant looks particularly powerful in relation to Lincoln.

Alongside this internal assessment of power a similar analysis of the power held by *external stakeholders* needs to be carried out. The indicators of power are slightly different.

Table 5.3 Assessing the relative power of coalitions.

1. Internal coalitions

Indicators of power	*1* *Marketing* *dept*★	*2* *Production*★	*3* *Nottingham* *plant*★	*4* *Lincoln* *plant*★
A. *Status*				
1. Position in hierarchy (closeness to board)	H	L	H	M
2. Salary of top manager	H	L	H	L
3. Average grade of staff	H	M	H	L
B. *Claim on resources*				
1. Number of staff	M	H	M	M
2. Size of similar company	H	L	H	L
3. Budget as % of total	H	M	H	L
C. *Representation*				
1. Number of directors	H	None	M	None
2. Most influential directors	H	None	M	None
D. *Symbols*				
1. Quality of accommodation	H	L	M	M
2. Support services	H	L	H	L

2. External stakeholders

Indicators of power	*Supplier A*★	*Customer X*★	*Shareholder M*★
1. Status	H	H	L
2. Resource dependence	L	H	H
3. Negotiating arrangements	M	H	L
4. Symbols	H	H	L

★ These are examples – the list will clearly vary from one situation to another.
  H = high   M = medium   L = low

1. The *status* of an external party such as a supplier is usually indicated in the way that they are discussed amongst company employees and whether they respond quickly to the supplier's demands.
2. *Resource dependence* can often be measured directly. For example, the proportion of a company's business tied up with any one customer, or a similar dependence on suppliers can normally be easily measured. Perhaps the key indicator is the ease with which that supplier, financier or customer could be replaced at short notice.
3. *Negotiating arrangements.* Whether external parties are treated at arms length or are actively involved in negotiations with the company. For example, a customer who is invited to negotiate over the price of a contract is in a more powerful position than a similar company who is given a fixed price on a take-it-or-leave-it basis.
4. *Symbols* are equally valuable clues. Whether the management team wines and dines some customer or supplier, or the level of person in the company who deals with a particular supplier. The care and attention paid to correspondence with outsiders will tend to differ from one party to another.

Again, no single measure will give a full understanding of the extent of the power held by external groups, but the combined analysis will be very useful. Part 2 of Table 5.3 illustrates how an analysis of the power of external stakeholders can be performed (using the data from Table 5.2).

This extended example has been used to illustrate how an analysis of both the expectations and power structures in an organisation can be undertaken as part of a strategic analysis. To gain maximum benefit from this type of analysis readers need to look for a combination of strongly held expectations and the power to exercise them. For example, customer X may well pose a significant problem to a strategy of entering new EEC markets – the company may lose X's business on which they are highly dependent. Furthermore, the survival of the Lincoln plant looks even more precarious when this analysis of power is added to the previous assessment of the attitudes of coalitions. Not only does Lincoln appear to be isolated (from the previous analysis) but the most powerful groups (marketing and customer X) would welcome closure. In contrast, both Lincoln and its major potential ally (production), have little power themselves.

5.5 ORGANISATIONAL OBJECTIVES

Many, if not all, organisations will have formally stated objectives. However, it is important to recognise that objectives are set by somebody or some group of individuals. Referring back to Figure 5.1, it can be seen that organisational objectives result from the expectations of individuals and groups within and around the organisation together with the power that these groups have in influencing the overall objectives of the organisation. So objectives tend to be shaped by those who have most power – normally the organisation's management.

However, this dominant coalition is likely to be influenced by the expectations of other stakeholders, and in particular the power which they perceive these groups to have when objectives are being formulated. Some stakeholder groups do not seek to impose objectives as such on an organisation but they do insist on imposing constraints.

A local authority may not have the power or desire to impose objectives on a company in its area; it can, however, impose constraints on such matters as pollution control and planning permission. The influence of the stock market may be regarded as a constraint: if a company does not perform to expectations then it is likely to suffer a reduction in

---

ILLUSTRATION 5.5

Types of objective

Organisations' objectives are of different kinds and vary in the extent to which they are specific.

1. Mission

What is our mission statement? It's easy – we will be the most honest cosmetic company around. How will we do it? That's easy too – we will go diametrically in the opposite direction to the cosmetic industry.

Anita Roddick from The Body Shop
Marketing, 1986

2. Corporate: Open.

The primary aims of the Westland Group are to provide a sound investment for our shareholders and also worthwhile job prospects for our employees. Our objectives are customer satisfaction, real growth in earnings per share and a competitive return on capital employed.

Westland Group Annual Report 1986

3. Corporate: Closed.

The most important objective remains the achievement of a minimum return of 20% on average capital employed with a target return of 25%.

United Biscuits Annual Report 1985

4. Unit: Open.

One of the main aims for one of the business areas in which the company is involved is to play a leading role in meeting the requirements of the widening and expanding home entertainments industry.

Sir Richard Cave, Chairman, Thorn EMI
1980

5. Unit: Closed.

In the UK, Costain Homes is budgeting to sell 2,500 homes in 1987 – a figure that will put it among the top ten housebuilders.

Report on Costain Homes
Costain Group plc Annual Report 1986

share price. National government may argue that it is not its intention to influence the policies of private companies but may impose sanctions if that company defies a trading embargo for example. Given that objectives arise out of these differences of expectations, it is unwise to regard objectives as permanent or preordained.[21] They are a product of the cultural and political processes discussed above and should be regarded as such in the analysis and formulation of strategy.

Illustration 5.5 shows the sort of formal objectives stated by companies. Just a brief glance shows that there are differences in their content and in the extent to which they are specific. They all have two things in common: they express desired ends to be achieved, and they are expressed as formal organisational aims. However, they are different types of statement about desired ends. These differences can be thought of as a hierarchy of objectives.[22] Objective 1 is an expression of what might be called *mission*; 2 and 3 are expressions of *corporate objectives*; and 4 and 5 are expressions of *unit objectives*. The discussion which follows is summarised in Table 5.4.

5.5.1 Mission

The mission of an organisation is the most generalised type of objective and can be thought of as an expression of its *raison d'être*. Richards[23] calls it the 'master strategy' and says it is 'a visionary projection of the central and overriding concepts on which the organisation is based'. He goes on to say that it 'should not focus on what the firm is doing in terms of products and markets currently served, but rather upon the services and utility within the firm'. If there is substantial disagreement within the organisation as to its mission, it may well give rise to real problems in resolving the strategic direction of the organisation.

5.5.2 Corporate objectives

Corporate objectives and unit objectives are distinguished in this chapter because there are different 'levels' of objectives with different characteristics in organisations. *Corporate objectives* are often expressed in financial terms. They could be the expression of desired sales or profit levels or rates of growth, dividend levels or share valuations. Increasingly, however, organisations have corporate objectives of a non-financial

Table 5.4 The nature of objectives.

Types of objective	Common characteristics	
1. Mission	General Visionary Central and overriding Often unwritten	Open
2. Corporate	Often expressed financially Express stakeholder expectations Formulated by senior management	Open or closed
3. Unit	Specific to units of organisation Operational Often multiple	Open or closed

nature, such as employee welfare or technological advance, but it is rare for these to be unaccompanied by financial objectives. They are frequently formal statements of *stakeholder expectations*. Traditionally, this may have meant the shareholders, so the corporate objective may have been a statement about the required return to share-holders. However, as it is becoming increasingly recognised that stakeholders might also be employees, customers, suppliers, the local community and so on, there could be formal statements of objectives to be met on their behalf.

Corporate objectives are usually formulated by senior members of the board or even the chairman or chief executive. They are more likely to be handed down to, rather than be formulated by, lower levels of management. In a divisionalised company, for example, corporate objectives may be set by the board at head office and then translated into divisional objectives which become financial targets for the division.

5.5.3 Unit objectives

Unit objectives are here distinguished from corporate objectives in so far as they are likely to have the following characteristics:

- They relate to the individual units of the organisation. For example, they may be the objectives of a division or of one company within a holding company. In the case of public sector organisations, the unit could be a department of a local authority or a hospital in a particular health authority.
- They may be financial objectives stated in much the same way as corporate objectives, but at a unit level. A corporate objective of a given growth in profit after tax might be translated into an objective for each business unit. They are likely to be more operational in nature than corporate objectives. In this sense they are to do with the planning of operational activity, which is discussed in the next section.
- Multiple objectives might well be more common at the unit level than at the corporate level. This is likely to be the case if objectives are conceived of in operational terms since the operations of a business are multi-faceted.

5.5.4 The precision of objectives

Illustration 5.5 may be looked at in another way. Some objectives (numbers 2 and 4) can be measured: it is possible to say they can be achieved at some future time. These are 'closed' objectives. Others (1, 3 and 5) are objectives which can never be achieved since they will always persist. These are 'open' objectives.

Many writers[24] have argued that objectives are not helpful unless they are capable of being measured and achieved – unless they are closed. This view is not taken here. Open statements may in fact be just as helpful as closed statements. For example, mission should be a very important influence on strategy: it may concentrate people's perception of their operation on the needs of customers and the utility of the service, for example, and at the same time set the boundaries within which they see the business developing. But statements of mission are very difficult to make in closed terms. The role of this sort of objective is very much to do with focusing strategy rather than deciding when it has been 'achieved'. In addition, there may be some objectives which are important but are difficult to quantify or express in measurable terms. An objective such as 'to be a leader in technology' may be highly relevant in today's technological environment, but may become absurd if it has to be expressed in some measurable way. Illustration 5.6 shows how one organisation used its statements of mission and objectives positively.

However, there are times when specific objectives are required. These are likely to be when urgent action is needed, such as in a crisis or at times of major (usually strategic) transition, and it becomes essential for management to focus its attention a limited number of priority requirements. An extreme example would be in a *turnaround* situation. If the choice is between going out of business and surviving, then there is no room for latitude through vaguely stated requirements.

It is also helpful to have closed objectives for planning purposes. Here the objective

---

ILLUSTRATION 5.6

Organisational culture and values are a critical part of strategy. This is particularly so in organisations where members of the company are physically separated.

F International was a group of companies staffed mainly by home-workers. It was founded by Steve Shirley when she first had young children which prevented her from seeking normal office work. By 1985 it was operating in many countries, largely in the area of computer software design and programming. The following is an extract from the company charter published in 1984.

Mission
F International's mission is to stay a leader in the rapidly growing and highly profitable, knowledge intensive software industry. It aims to achieve this by developing, through modern telecommunications, the unutilised intellectual energy of individuals and groups unable to work in a conventional environment.

Strategy
F International's strategy is to maximise the value of its unusual asset base by establishing a competitive advantage over conventionally organised firms, and imitators of its approach, through cost and quality competitiveness. This occurs by the development of a methodology which ensures quality and by establishing a company ethos which binds people who work largely independently and often alone.

Values
People are vital to any knowledge intensive industry. The skills and loyalty of our workforce are our main asset. Equally important is the knowledge which comes from the exchange of ideas with our clients and their personnel. It follows that human and ethical values play a pivotal role in the way in which an organization like F International conducts itself. This is even more true in a structure as open and free as F International. To maintain a high level of creativity, productivity and coherence in such an environment requires a set of high ethical values and professional standards that any member of the organisation can identify with and see realised, and reinforced, in the organisation's behaviour. F International has defined for itself such a charter of values.

becomes a target to be achieved. Suppose a company is seeking to develop and launch new products: it is helpful for managers to have some yardstick, of profitability perhaps, against which to judge the success of the new venture.

5.6 SOCIAL RESPONSIBILITY[25]

Whereas the dominant objectives of commercial organisations are invariably expressed in terms of financial performance, it should be clear from discussions in this chapter that organisations never pursue a single objective to the exclusion of all other considerations.

F International

1. Professional excellence
Our long term aim is to improve our professional abilities so as to maintain a quality product for our clients. It is also our aim to develop fully our professional potential as people and to develop our organization in a way which reflects our own individuality and special approach.

2. Growth
We aim to grow our organization to its full potential, nationally and internationally. We aim to grow at least as rapidly as the software industry as a whole in order to maintain our own position as an attractive employer and a competitive supplier.

3. Economic and psychological reward
We also aim to realise and enjoy fully the economic and psychological rewards of our efforts resulting from the development of the unique competitive advantage of our structure and capabilities. We aim to achieve profits, reward our workforce, maintain the Employee Trust and provide an attractive return to our shareholders.

4. Integrated diversity
We have a commitment to consistent procedures worldwide as a means of lowering cost, but aim to conduct ourselves as a national of each country in which we operate.

5. Universal ethics
We respect local customs and laws, but see ourselves as members of a world society with respect for human dignity and ethical conduct beyond the profit motive and local circumstances.

6. Goodwill
An extension of our ethical view is a belief in the goodwill of others: colleagues, clients and vendors. We also believe that goodwill results in positive, long term relationships.

7. Enthusiasm
Finally we believe that enthusiasm for our people and our product, and that ability to engender that enthusiasm in others, is the most essential quality of leadership within the organization. Enthusiasm promotes creativity, co-operation and profit.

Source: Company Charter.

In the past twenty years or so there has been an increasing acceptance by management of the diversity of stakeholder interests and expectations to be accommodated. This has given rise to the notion of *social responsibility*, by which is meant the acceptance by management of organisational responsibilities of a social nature wider than the legal minimum which it is bound to fulfil. There is a wide variety of issues[26] which can be considered to fall under this broad heading. These are summarised in Figure 5.6.

How organisations respond to these issues varies considerably and may be summarised as shown in Table 5.5. Within the ten categories shown there are four broad groupings of response, each of which may give rise to conflicts of objectives and policy.[27]

1. At one extreme there are organisations which largely conform to Milton Friedman's maxim that 'the business of business is business', and that the 'only social responsibility of business is to increase its profit'.[28] These are in categories 1 to 3 of Table 5.5. The holders of these beliefs argue that not only is it not the duty of business to be concerned about social issues but that in doing so they would detract from the primary way in which they should be contributing to society, that is by operating businesses which are economically efficient. Social responsibility, they argue, is the domain of government which should prescribe, through legislation, the constraints which society chooses to impose on business in their pursuit of economic efficiency. Expecting companies to exercise these duties can, in extreme cases, undermine the authority of government and give business organisations even more power. Somewhat paradoxically, however, it is often devotees of this school of thought that most resent government 'interference' in business affairs.

Should organisations be responsible for ...

Employee welfare
... providing medical care, assistance with mortgages, extended sickness leave, assistance for dependents, etc?

Working conditions
... enhanced working surroundings, social and sporting clubs, above minimum safety standards, etc?

Job design
... designing jobs to the increased satisfaction of workers rather than economic efficiency?

Internal aspects

Pollution
... reducing pollution below legal standards if competitors are not doing so?

Product safety
... danger arising from the careless use of product by consumers?

Marketing practices
... curtailing advertising which promotes products which harm health (e.g. tobacco and sweets)?

Employment
... positive discrimination in favour of minorities

Community activity
... sponsoring local events and supporting local good works?

External aspects

Figure 5.6 Some questions of social responsibility.

2. The next group are in categories 4 to 7 of Table 5.5. Here social responsibility is exercised in a careful, selective way and usually justified in terms of economic commonsense. Sponsorship or welfare provision would be rationalised as sensible expenditures akin to any other form of investment or promotion expenditure. Many companies recognise that this careful attention to aspects of social responsibility could be in the long term interests of the company. For example, the avoidance of 'shady' marketing practices will prevent the need for yet more legislation in that area. They argue that if managers wish to maintain discretion in the long run over issues such as marketing practices, then they are wise to operate responsibly in the short term. Within this category lie companies who would agree with an industrial journalist[29] who, when asked why some companies behave more responsibly than others, replied 'because

Table 5.5 Social responsibility: ten roles of the firm.

Role	Behaviour and attitude		
	Economic	*Social*	*Political*
1. Profit maximiser	Profit dominates	Regarded as an impediment to profit	Actively avoids involvement with political system
2. Profit satisficer	Growth dominates	Reacts against societal and social pressures as incursions	Avoids interaction with political system
3. Defender of free enterprise	The business of busness is business	Reacts against social component as being not within firm's proper scope	Stands up for 'free enterprise'
4. The lone wolf	Prime emphasis on profit	Voluntarily but uni-laterally assumes responsibility	Avoids involvement unless cornered
5. Societally engaged	Prime emphasis on profit	Interactively engaged	Engaged only in negotiation of the rules of the game
6. Societally progressive	Prime emphasis on profit	Interactively engaged	Positively involved in formulation of national industrial policies
7. Global actor	Prime emphasis on profit	Interactively engaged	Assumes a responsibility to foster a balance between national and international economic policies
8. Developer of society	Financial self-sufficiency	Produces changes in the lives of mankind through innovation	Positively involved with emphasis on planned develop-ment of social infrastructures
9. Social servant	Secondary to societal obligations	Provides essential but non-economic goods and services	Positively involved in formation of national industrial policies with emphasis on social matters
10. Employment provider	Subsidised operation	Provides jobs	Subsidised and supported by government

Source: from *Facing Realities: The European Societal Strategy Project*, p.14, summary report produced by the European Foundation for Management Development and the European Institute for Advanced Studies in Management, 1981.

some companies are smarter than others'. They would argue that management ignores social influences at its peril and the 'smarter' companies are those that recognise and cope with these issues in policy making. The conflicts of responsibility which arise here are, for example, between pollution control and job provision. Extra costs in pollution control could mean uncompetitive costs and thus threaten plant closure and job losses.

3. The third category is the 'progressive' organisation which regards a wide variety of social responsibility issues as an important influence on policy making. These are in category 8 of Table 5.5. The Quaker companies of the last century are a good example and, to a considerable extent, the attitudes of these companies have remained more progressive than others into this century. Companies in this category might argue that they would retain uneconomic units to preserve jobs, would avoid manufacturing 'anti-social' products, and would be prepared to bear reductions in profitability for the social good. But to what extent would they be prepared to do so? At some point there could be a conflict between social responsibility and survival, or between social responsibility and the expectations of shareholders.

There are also organisations which are quite specifically founded and run as a response to community needs. Societal needs are paramount and profits secondary or a constraint. These are categories 9 and 10 in Table 5.5 and include many public services, charities, the church and so on. The problem these organisations face may be to do with how 'commercial' they are prepared to be in order to carry out their social role. For example, charities are often accused of spending too high a percentage of their funds on internal administration. Illustration 5.7 shows an organisation whose business was social responsibility.

5.7 SUMMARY

This chapter has analysed how the expectations of individuals and groups might influence an organisation's strategies. It has been necessary to look at the expectations of people both inside and outside the organisation (e.g. customers, suppliers, financiers). So, what people want an organisation to do or to be like can influence strategy provided those individuals or groups have sufficient *power*. This has long been thought of in strategic terms under the label of 'objectives'. However, it is misleading to regard objectives in a traditional way of being 'handed down from on high'. Preordained objectives are rarely used in formulating strategy except in a very general sense (e.g. the organisation's mission).

Objectives and, indeed, strategies are better thought of as the product of a complex interplay between the issues discussed in this chapter; the expectations of individuals and groups, the values of society, organised groups and the dominant culture of the organisation. These cultural and political issues pervade the organisation's structure and systems, influencing the way in which people behave and the type of person selected into the organisation. They need to be understood and analysed as an essential background against which strategic change can be planned and effected successfully. This theme will be discussed further in later chapters.

ILLUSTRATION 5.7

Business in the Community

Although social responsibility is usually thought of in terms of individual businesses, *Business in the Community* has social responsibility as its business.

Business in the Community (BIC) was set up in 1981 under the directorship of Stephen O'Brien, to combine corporate money and business expertise with local communities to regenerate depressed areas. It was most well known for its work in setting up enterprise agencies which became a feature of most of Britain's unemployment blackspots by the mid 1980s. Much of its work was concentrated on providing advice, moral support, and sometimes financial backing to local entrepreneurs. In 1985 contributors gave £11m which helped to create 20,000 new businesses and 75,000 new jobs, claimed BIC.

O'Brien had a simple approach to BIC, based on his previously successful career selling money. 'I spend my time spreading the message that it is in the company's commercial interests to get involved in their communities', he said. 'Companies will only be able to sell their goods and services if their communities are prosperous.' In the first five years he managed to sign up 160 companies as BIC members including Shell, IBM, Marks and Spencer, and Scottish and Newcastle breweries. The list of members also included a number of accountancy firms, management consultancies and building societies.

Motives for joining varied. Often companies joined to soften the effects of their own redundancies. The idea of the enterprise agency was pioneered by Pilkington in its attempt to cushion the effect of large redundancies in its manufacturing plants in St Helens. For some companies, such as Barclays Bank, corporate image was a key motivating factor, while for others it was the simple realisation that impoverished local communities mean poor sales.

Some of the plans for BIC included campaigns to persuade large companies to buy locally and to 'loan' their executives or management trainees for temporary assignment in BIC sponsored enterprise agencies.

Source: *Management Today*, September 1986.

REFERENCES

1. G. Hofstede, *Cultures Consequences*, Sage, 1980. An abridged version of the findings relevant to this chapter can be found in his article 'Motivation, leadership and organisation: do American theories apply abroad?', *Organisational Dynamics*, Summer, 1980.

2. P. T. Terry, 'The English in management', *Management Today*, Nov. 1979.

3. For example: Huw Beynon, *Working for Ford*, Pelican, 1984. Also Michael Edwardes, *Back from the Brink*, Pan, 1983.

4. The importance of symbolic behaviour is underlined by many authors. For example: T. Peters and N. Austin, *A Passion for Excellence*, chapter 16, Collins, 1985; T. C. Dandridge, I. Mitroff and W. Joyce, 'Organisational symbolism: a topic to expand organisational analysis, *Academy of Management Review*, **5**: 77–82, 1980.

5. A. L. Stinchcombe, 'Social Structure and Organisation', in J. D. March (ed.), *Handbook of Organisation*, Rand McNally, 1965.

6. The importance of leadership in shaping culture is underlined by Peters and Austin (reference 4), and E. H. Schein, *Organisational Culture and Leadership*, Jossey Bass, 1985, amongst others.

7. R. E. Miles and C. C. Snow, *Organisational Strategy: Structure and process*, McGraw-Hill, 1978.

8. M. Kanter, '*The Change Masters: Innovation for productivity in the American corporation*', Simon & Schuster, 1983, has called these 'segmentalist' structures.

9. A number of writers have influenced how we view coalitions in organisations. The following references should be useful for readers interested in pursuing this area:
   - R. M. Cyert and J. G. March, *A Behavioural Theory of the Firm*, Prentice Hall, 1964.
   - D. Katz and R. L. Kahn, *The Social Psychology of Organisations*, John Wiley, 1966.
   - J. D. March and H. A. Simon, *Organisations*, John Wiley, 1967.
   - J. D. Thompson, *Organisations in Action*, McGraw-Hill, 1967.
   - A. M. Pettigrew, 'Strategy formulation as a political process', *International Studies of Management and Organisation*, **VIII**(2), 1977.

10. A. M. Pettigrew, *The Awakening Giant*, Basil Blackwell, 1985.

11. For a discussion of the influence of the professional on the values and practices of management see the following texts by R. H. Hall: 'Professionisation and bureaucratisation', *American Sociological Review*, **33**: 92–104, 1968, and *Organizations: Structure and process*, Prentice Hall, 1972. Also, J. Pfeffer, *Power in Organisations*, p. 157, Pitman, 1981.

12. J. Pfeffer, *Power in Organisations*, pp. 37–43, Pitman, 1981, includes an example concerned with educational planning at New York University which is useful in understanding the approach.

13. R. M. Cyert and J. G. March (reference 9) argue that management is usually the dominant stakeholder and its expectations (often growth) tend to influence strategy most strongly.

14. I. C. Macmillan and P. E. Jones, *Strategy Formulation: Power and politics* (2nd edn), p. 14, West, 1986, provides some useful definitions of the words 'power', 'influence' and 'authority'. Readers should note that in this book the word 'power' is used in a much wider sense than their definition, in fact much nearer to their definition of 'authority'. The choice was made since it more closely resembles the normal usage of the word 'power' within the UK. The central point to remember is that formal lines of authority do not always describe the *actual* power structure – a point made by M. Dalton, in *Men who Manage*, Wiley, 1959.

15. See for example T. Peters and N. Austin (reference 4).

16. See for example: D. J. Hickson *et al.*, 'A strategic contingency theory of intraorganisational power, *Administrative Science Quarterly*, **16**(2), 1971; and D. C. Hambrick, 'Environment, strategy and power within top management teams, *Administrative Science Quarterly*, **26**, 1981.

17. Certainly this was found to be the case by J. M. Godiwalla, W. A. Meinhart and W. D. Warde in their research documented in *Corporate Strategy and Functional Management* (Praeger, 1979), although Miles and Snow (reference 7) do point out that in defender-type companies, production managers may also exercise considerable influence. T. Hill, *Manufacturing Strategy*, Open University, 1985, cites this as a major shortcoming of UK companies compared to many other economies.

18. Michael Edwardes (reference 3).

19. *Report of the Committee of Inquiry on Industrial Democracy* (Bullock Report), Chairman: Lord Bullock, HMSO, 1977.

20. J. Pfeffer's (reference 12) chapter 2 is a most interesting discussion of the problems and approaches to assessing power in organisations.

21. An interesting account of the variety and differences of the objectives of managers may be found in D. Norburn and P. Grinyer, 'Directors without direction', *Journal of General Management*, **1**(2), 1973/74.

22. The idea of a hierarchy of objectives has been used by many writers. For an early example see C. H. Granger, 'Hierarchy of objectives', *Harvard Business Review*, **42**(3), 1964.

23. See M. Richards, *Organisational Goal Structures*, West, 1978.

24. See, for example, I. Ansoff, *Corporate Strategy*, p. 44, Penguin, 1968, says: 'We define an objective as a measure of efficiency of the resource conversion process. An objective contains three elements: the particular attribute that is chosen as a measure of efficiency, the yardstick or scale by which the attribute is measured and the goal – the particular value on the scale which the firm seeks to attain.'

25. For a fuller discussion of the issues of social responsibility see K. Davis, 'The arguments for and against corporate social responsibility', *Academy of Management Journal*, **16**(2), 1973. Also, E. K. Morgan, 'Social responsibility and private enterprise in Great Britain', *National Westminster Bank Quarterly Review*, May, 1977.

26. See, for example, D. Clutterbuck, *How to be a Good Corporate Citizen: Managers' guide to making social responsibility work – and pay*, McGraw-Hill, 1981. A brief summary is also given in *International Management*, pp. 38–40, May, 1981.

27. Many of the problems arising from differing conceptions of the social roles of organisations in a changing environment are discussed in the report *Facing Realities* published by the European Societal Strategy Project, 1981.

28. This argument is well illustrated by Milton Friedman in 'The social responsibility of business is to increase its profits', reported by D. J. McCarthy, R. J. Minichiello and J. R. Curran in *Business Policy and Strategy* (3rd edn), Irwin, 1979.

29. These comments were made by F. Wright, Business Editor of the *Morning Telegraph*, Sheffield, on a video documentary entitled *Social Responsibility of Companies*, made by K. Scholes and A. Wood and produced by Sheffield City Polytechnic Education Services Department, 1979.

Recommended key readings

- Readers should be familiar with the political context of organisational decision making. We recommend either I. C. Macmillan and P. E. Jones, *Strategy Formulation: Power and politics* (2nd edn), West, 1986, or J. Pfeffer, *Power in Organisations*, Pitman, 1981.

- Books which deal usefully with strategy as a product of organisational culture are R. E. Miles and C. C. Snow, *Organisational Strategy: Structure and Process*, McGraw-Hill, 1978, and E. H. Schein, *Organizational Culture and Leadership*, Jossey Bass, 1985.

- T. Peters and R. Waterman, *In Search of Excellence*, Harper & Row, 1982, and T. Peters and N. Austin, *A Passion for Excellence*, Collins, 1984, both stress the critical importance of understanding and managing organisational culture in successful organisations.

- A more traditional approach to the idea and use of corporate objectives might be useful. The following will help: I. Ansoff, *Corporate Strategy*, chapters 3 and 4, Penguin, 1968, or chapters on objective setting in books by J. Argenti such as *Practical Corporate Planning*, George Allen & Unwin, 1980 or *Corporate Planning*, George Allen & Unwin, 1968.

Part III

STRATEGIC
CHOICE

In many ways strategic choice is the core of corporate strategy. It is concerned with decisions about an organisation's future and the way in which it needs to respond to the many pressures and influences identified in the strategic analysis. In turn the consideration of future strategy must be mindful of the realities of strategy implementation which can be a significant constraint on strategic choice.

Chapter 2 showed that organisations are continually attempting to readjust to their environment, and one of the major criticisms which can be made of managers concerns their inability or unwillingness to consider the variety of strategic options open to the company. Rather they tend to remain bound by their recipes and resistant to change. It is for this reason that this part of the book presents a systematic way of looking at strategic choice. The steps outlined here help to promote a wider consideration of strategy and the appropriateness and consequences of options available to the organisation.

The discussion of strategic choice has been divided into three chapters:

- Chapter 6 looks at the strategic options which are available to organisations and the reasons why some strategies might be viewed more favourably than others.
- Chapter 7 establishes some general criteria (suitability, feasibility and acceptability) against which strategic options might be judged. It also outlines some approaches to assessing the merits of different types of strategy in terms of both their strategic logic and their cultural fit to the organisation.
- Chapter 8 looks at techniques which might be helpful in evaluating specific options within the broad framework developed in Chapters 6 and 7. The chapter also discusses the ways in which strategies might be selected for implementation.

Part III

STRATEGIC CHOICE

Chapter 6
STRATEGIC OPTIONS

6.1 INTRODUCTION

The purpose of this chapter is to identify the various strategic options that organisations might pursue. The choice between development options is strongly dependent on the particular circumstances of any one organisation and this will be discussed in Chapters 7 and 8.

Much of the discussion of strategic choice has been built around the assumption that organisations are concerned with growth as a major objective. Clearly, if organisations wish to grow they need to seek out new opportunities. Whereas this justification of strategic choice is undoubtedly relevant to a large number of companies, there are also many organisations which, either by choice or circumstances, would not feature growth as a major objective. In fact, during periods of recession many managers will be mainly concerned with the process of managing the organisation through a period of retrenchment.

The approach in this chapter, therefore, is to argue that the process of strategic choice must address itself to a wide variety of situations. Growth is not the reason for strategic choice being necessary; rather the need lies in the fact that an organisation's internal and external circumstances are constantly changing. Change is a prerequisite of long term survival. The emphasis in this chapter is, therefore, on *development strategies* rather than narrower growth strategies.

In reviewing strategic options it is important to distinguish between three separate aspects of any strategy, all of which need consideration:

1. The *generic strategy* to be pursued, i.e. the basis on which the organisation will compete or sustain excellence.
2. The alternative *directions* in which the organisation may choose to develop.
3. The alternative *methods* by which any direction of development might be achieved.

Figure 6.1 illustrates this point and also provides a structure for this chapter. Whereas decisions on *generic strategy, direction, and method* are not independent of each other, they do benefit from separate discussion. For example, an organisation pursuing cost leadership may choose to achieve this whilst pursuing a strategy of market development. However, this still leaves a further choice as to whether entry to new markets is best achieved by acquisition of companies already operating in those markets, through the company's own efforts or jointly with other organisations.

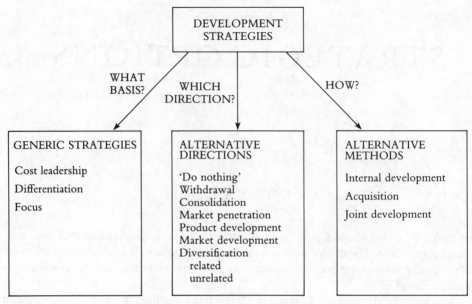

Figure 6.1 Development strategies.

To help readers cope with these various complexities the chapter follows a step-by-step discussion of strategic options in the following way:

- The *generic strategies* whereby organisations will compete and survive will first be reviewed. There are important links to the concept of the value chain introduced in Chapter 4.
- Strategic options will then be identified in general categories (such as 'product' or 'market' development) without discussion of the various methods through which those options might be undertaken.
- These general categories will be discussed in simple product/market terms – in effect taking the stance of a highly specialised organisation attempting to review its options. This is not because the majority of companies are in this situation (research, in fact, shows quite the opposite) but because it helps illustrate the *principles* of identifying options which are universally applicable.
- The different *methods* of development will then be discussed – again in general terms without specific reference to any particular development direction.
- Chapter 6 will conclude by summarising the variety of options available to organisations when these aspects are combined. For example, market development by joint development may be achieved by a number of strategies which will be listed.

6.2 GENERIC STRATEGIES

Before considering the development directions it is important to give some thought to the basis on which the organisation will compete and/or sustain a superior level of performance – to the *generic strategy* which the organisation will follow. This section will review these generic strategies drawing on previous discussions concerning the value chain (Chapter 4) and look forward to the next chapter on the evaluation of strategies.

For commercial organisations the discussions in this section are concerned with establishing the basis on which a company will build and *sustain* competitive advantage. For public service organisations it is concerned with the equivalent issue, namely the basis on which the organisation will choose to sustain the quality of its services within agreed budgets. Porter's[1] work is of central importance to this section. The purpose of defining the generic strategy of an organisation is to ensure that deliberate choices are made about the type of competitive advantage it seeks to attain and the scope within which this will be done (see Figure 6.2). Attempting to be all things to all people is normally a recipe for mediocrity. (Porter calls this being 'stuck in the middle'.)

It can be seen from the figure that there are essentially three generic strategies which an organisation can follow: cost leadership, differentiation and focus. These will now be discussed.

6.2.1 Cost leadership

There are many organisations who sustain their competitive advantage through continued attention to their cost structure *vis-à-vis* competition. For example, cost structure often provides an insuperable barrier to entry through economies of scale in production, R&D or marketing expenditure. Equally, the concept of the *experience curve*[2] (see Chapter 4) suggested that cost structure improves markedly as organisations become experienced with new technologies and/or markets. If organisations are to sustain cost leadership successfully across their range of activities they must be clear on how this is to be achieved through the various elements of the value chain. For

COMPETITIVE ADVANTAGE

		Lower cost	Differentiation
COMPETITIVE SCOPE	Broad Target	1. Cost leadership	2. Differentiation
	Narrow Target	3A. Cost focus	3B. Differentiation focus

Figure 6.2 Three generic strategies. (From M.E. Porter, *Competitive Advantage: Creating and sustaining superior performance*, Free Press, 1985. Used with permission of The Free Press, a Division of Macmillan, Inc. Copyright 1985 Michael E. Porter.)

example, a company may gain cost advantage through its access to low cost sources of raw materials (perhaps achieved through backward integration). Sometimes this applies to other important inputs such as people's time. In many 'start-up' situations within large organisations this time may be 'loaned' from mainstream activities – or simply not accounted for.

In other organisations cost advantage is gained within the organisation's own operations – perhaps because of its special skills, technologies or systems, or high levels of capacity utilisation.

In other circumstances it is the marketing activities which provide the opportunity for cost advantage. For example, an organisation which already has an extensive field salesforce is better placed to introduce new products through this sales network than is an organisation starting up anew. Many public services have found it possible to spread their range of activities at little cost simply because the infrastructure is already in place (e.g. new sports activities in leisure centres). There are also circumstances where cost advantage can be gained through the special linkages which exist between an organisation's value chain and that of channels or customers. Porter argues that these linkages are crucial to defending the organisation's position against competition.

For example, some of the most notable business successes in the UK have been organisations which have found cost advantage in new forms of distribution which do not respect the 'traditional' demarcation lines. So, for example, the multiple chains in groceries, electrical goods and DIY transformed those industries during the 1970s and 1980s.

It should be clear from these few examples that cost leadership, as a generic strategy could be applied to any of the specific development directions outlined below. Therefore, when thinking through the merits of various strategies this overview is important. It is necessary to be clear that a strategy of product development or backward integration, etc. would actually contribute to the organisation's *overall* generic strategy.

6.2.2 Differentiation

Cost leadership is not the only way in which organisations can sustain their competitive advantage or superior performance. A quite different type of generic strategy is that of *differentiation* of the organisation's strategies from that of major competitors or (in public services) other providers. Illustration 6.1 gives an example of differentiation in retailing. The concept of the value chain should remind readers that differentiation is only of strategic importance if it is recognised and valued by consumers/users. Differentiation can be achieved in many different ways within the value chain or in terms of the linkages with the value chains of suppliers channels or customers. For example, a restaurant may differentiate itself in terms of quality of food, or service or ethnic cuisines. A building society may choose to have longer opening hours than banks, a manufacturer may provide an ex-stock delivery service; a dentist may provide special orthodontic treatment. Often it is linkages between different activities within an organisation's value chain which are of most importance in sustaining advantage – new strategic directions may well provide an opportunity to strengthen these linkages or even become a new basis of differentiation from other providers.

6.2.3 Focus

The discussion so far has assumed that generic strategies will be applied widely in the 'market'. In many cases this is not so and a key ingredient of the organisation's strategic success is the way in which the strategy is *focused*[3] at particular parts of the market. Clearly, when this is combined with either cost leadership or differentiation there are different subcategories of a 'focus' strategy. There are, once again, many forms of this generic strategy. For example, aiming a product or service at a particular buyer group, segment of the product line, or smaller geographical area are all common (and successful) ways of focusing. However, an organisation then needs to determine whether within this smaller part of the total market they will compete through cost leadership or differentiation. The arguments above are then relevant to this decision. So, a local brewery may be able to compete against the nationals in its own area by sustaining a better cost structure (due to reduced distribution and marketing costs). Or

---

ILLUSTRATION 6.1

Convenience stores

> Even in the days of the national multiple grocery retailer (Sainsbury, Tesco, etc.),
> there is a growing place for others who have a carefully differentiated strategy.

Convenience stores are loosely defined as occupying between 50 and 300 square metres floorspace and the concept of convenience is expressed in a number of ways. Stores are generally open long hours (up to fifteen hours per day) seven days per week, allow for quick self-service shopping and carry a wide range of convenience items (e.g. groceries, fresh fruit and vegetables, confectionery, wines, beers and spirits, toiletries, tobacco, newspapers, paperbacks, small DIY items and fast food as well as photographic printing, video hire and dry cleaning services – in some stores.

The stores have their origin in the American experience where the number of such stores grew from 3,000 in 1960 to 70,000 in the mid 1980s. Of course, convenience trading *per se* is not new in the UK – many traditional corner shops and off-licences were forced to develop in this way to survive the onslaught of the supermarkets with their emphasis in low prices. However, whereas these traditional shops tend to be single outlet owner-managed businesses, the new wave of convenience stores are developing as specialist multiple groups. In addition, 'voluntary' groups – like the Spar shops (some 3,000) – are starting to convert many outlets to convenience stores by a careful review of product range and customer service in favourably located stores.

Another major development, again following American trends, is that of the petrol forecourt stores – in the USA 50% of convenience stores are in petrol forecourts. British Petroleum plans a network of 100 'food plus' stores in the UK by 1990 and argue that petrol and convenience stores are a perfect mix. Petrol stations are already open some sixteen hours per day and existing staff would be able to cope with both food and petrol sales for at least half of that time. However, the petrol companies are aware that they would need to attract pedestrians from surrounding areas if the convenience stores are to prove successful.

Source: *Housing and Planning Review*, 5 October 1985.

it may be the local image of the brewery's products which could be the basis of competitive advantage – in which case cutting back on local marketing expenditure would be a mistake.

Within public service organisations there are often some very difficult decisions concerning the 'focus' of strategies. For example, a public library service could undoubtedly be run more cost efficiently if it were to pull out of low demand areas and put more resources into its popular branch libraries. It might also find that an extension of its services into audio and video tapes or new forms of public information services would prove popular. However, the extent to which these strategies would be regarded as within the library's remit might be hotly debated. In other words, the objectives of an organisation usually prescribe some boundaries to the types of generic strategy to be followed – particularly so in the public services as seen in Illustration 6.2

ILLUSTRATION 6.2

Swimming pools or leisure lagoons – the planners' dilemma

Strategic choice in public service provision can prove to be a difficult process as a limited resource is available to serve a variety of needs.

The first public bathing establishments in relatively recent history followed the passing of the 1846 *Baths and Wash House Act*. The need at that time was to enable people to keep clean and thus inhibit the spread of disease and infection. Indoor swimming, as such, was a secondary activity until the late nineteenth century when the first great building boom occurred. There was a further boom in the 1960s which saw the building of functional box-like swimming pools in most towns and cities.

In the 1970s came a new concept – the leisure pool – where often no special provision was made for the competition swimmer – the emphasis being on enjoyment – more like a beach. Some centres installed wave-machines, palm trees and deck chairs. By the 1980s the funds available for expansion became much tighter and some hard thinking was needed on how best to develop the service.

The dilemma lay in the wide variety of 'consumer' requirements. For example, the competitive swimmer needed a laned pool of standard length, not too shallow at either end and spectator facilities. In contrast, the learner or the disabled needed shallow water with easy access. The recreational 'swimmer' was more concerned with ambience, from equipment (slides, rafts, rings, etc.) and refreshment areas.

In order to satisfy these varying needs, local authorities had several options open to them. The larger authorities could follow a policy of specialised pools strategically located throughout the area (particularly in relation to public transport). This gave people genuine choice. Other authorities decided that multipurpose pools were desirable and more cost efficient. They provided for the serious competitor and the fun-swimmer in the same building.

One factor which often determined the choice between these alternatives was the practicalities of converting existing pools as against constructing new purpose-built facilities. Normally, those authorities who chose (or were required) to convert found difficulty in providing genuine multipurpose pools.

Source: *Leisure Management*, September 1986.

For multinational corporations[4] it is important to establish whether the differences between countries/markets are best served by separate 'national' strategies (i.e. focus) or whether the potential cost advantage of operating as a truly integrated multinational corporation will provide a more successful strategy for the organisation. Some multinational organisations pursue what has been called a *multi-focus* strategy which seeks to combine the benefits of global integration and separate national strategies. For example, in the motor car industry although the production of major components (e.g. an engine) may be concentrated on a few locations, the supply of materials, components and services for production are organised locally. This usually proves to be the most cost effective way and also provides the necessary control to maintain reliable schedules and short delivery times. This would be extremely difficult to achieve if the supply of every small component was organised globally.

Small companies often follow very focused strategies with great success. This is usually referred to as a *niche*[5] strategy where an organisation is so specialised to the needs of a very small part of the market that it is secure against competition from large organisations.

In considering the basis on which an organisation should operate and compete, that organisation is invariably forced to review the underlying justifications for its choice of strategies. This is an important aspect of strategic evaluation and, as such, is an issue which will be given considerable discussion in Chapter 7. The brief introduction to 'generic strategies' will provide a background to those further considerations.

6.3 ALTERNATIVE DIRECTIONS FOR STRATEGY DEVELOPMENT

This section will set out the strategic directions that an organisation could take. The *methods* by which any alternative might be developed will be discussed in later sections. Figure 6.3 summarises the various alternatives.

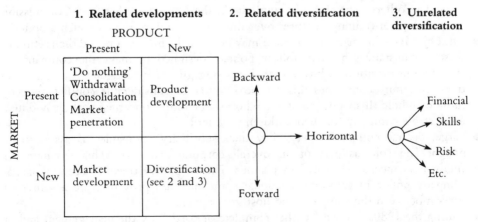

Figure 6.3 Alternative directions for development. (Adapted from H. Igor Ansoff, *Corporate Strategy*, p.99, Penguin, 1968.)

6.3.1 'Do nothing'

It will be seen in Chapter 8 that the evaluation of strategic options will require some useful basis against which to assess the merits of those options. A valuable base is the 'do nothing' situation since this helps with the assessment of whether an organisation would have sufficient incentive to change from its current activities. 'Do nothing' represents the situation whereby a company continues to follow, in broad terms, its current strategies whilst events around it change. It would, however, allow for the normal operational changes which occur in any business like replacing operatives who leave or continuing to advertise at the same level and in the same manner as before.

Since most businesses and public service organisations are facing considerable changes – both internally and externally – it is rare for 'do nothing' to be a viable strategy beyond the very short term. 'Do nothing' is not really a strategy in the same sense as product development or diversification, but a basis against which these other strategies can be assessed. Nevertheless, for planning purposes[6] it is helpful to include 'do nothing' in the range of options so that it is evaluated alongside the strategic options under consideration. This provides a discipline in the planning which ensures that the 'do nothing' situation is not disregarded.

6.3.2 Withdrawal

This is an option which is often overlooked, although there are many circumstances where complete or partial withdrawal from a market would be the most sensible course of action. Some examples make the point.

- In certain markets the value of a company's products or assets are subject to considerable changes over time and a central issue in policy making may be the astute acquisition and disposal of these products, assets, or businesses. This is particularly important for companies operating in markets which are subject to speculation such as energy, metals, commodities, land or property.
- In many public service organisations it is important to keep under review the range of activities being provided; since withdrawal from one area would release funds to expand in others. The shifts in emphasis in the Manpower Services Commission sponsorships of training ventures over time are a good example of such a policy.
- The objective of a small entrepreneur may be to 'make his million' and then retire. In these circumstances he may follow policies designed to make the company an attractive proposition to buy rather than being guided by longer term considerations. In family companies this can be a source of considerable conflict between those who hold this view and others who may be more concerned with providing a more stable company for their children to inherit.
- Large, diverse companies may view their subsidiary companies as assets to be bought and sold as part of an overall corporate strategy. This *divestment* or *disinvestment*[7] needs to be carefully planned. The use of divestment as a central part of company policy in some multinational companies has proved to be a source of friction between the company and host government.
- During the 1980s *buy-outs*[8] (either complete or partial) by the management and/or employees became quite common in the UK. Often they were triggered by the privatisation of companies in the pubic sector. Illustration 6.3 expands this point.

ILLUSTRATION 6.3

Management buy-outs

Companies wishing to divest parts of their operation could do so by liquidation or outright sale to a third party. However, a third option of selling to the management and/or employees of the unit – often called a 'leveraged buy-out'.

Although management buy-outs have hitherto been more prevalent in the USA than the UK, there are already some examples around which illustrate the general reasons why buy-outs might prove popular.

In some cases the buy-out might prove to be the most politically acceptable solution. Many would argue that the partial management/employee buy-out of Jaguar cars from the BL group in 1985 was much more acceptable than a third party sale (particularly to an American company – General Motors, which seemed possible).

When Trafalgar House made a takeover bid for electrical engineers (Haden) in 1985, senior managers leapt to the company's defence and arranged a buy-out to avoid what they regarded as an 'opportunistic and unwelcome takeover' – presumably a euphemism for fears of asset stripping (although that was not normally the Trafalgar House style).

In 1984 Unilever took over the Brooke Bond company – most of whose products fitted the food-related theme of Unilever's business. Frank Andrew led a £90 million buy-out of a Brooke Bond subsidiary Mallinson-Denny (timber specialists) fearing the neglect which might occur as an unrelated part of a food empire. Another well publicised buy-out was that of the Mecca Leisure empire from Grand Metropolitan in 1985.

Perhaps the strangest and most controversial buy-out (or sell-out depending on opinion) was the sale of the Trustee Savings Bank (TSB) in 1986. This followed a long, and interesting, debate about who actually owned the bank – the government, the depositors, the trustees or the employees. Eventually it was agreed that it was owned by no-one!

Source: *Management Today*, January 1986.

- Sometimes organisations will partially withdraw from a market by licensing the rights to other organisations. This became common in the public sector where particular services have been privatised (e.g. laundry services in hospitals).
- The most extreme form of withdrawal is when an organisation's position becomes so untenable that voluntary or forced *liquidation* may be the only possible course of action.

6.3.3 Consolidation

Consolidation should not be confused with the 'do nothing' situation discussed above. Consolidation implies changes in the specific way the company operates, although the range of products and markets may remain unchanged (see Illustration 6.4). Consolidation is equally relevant to growing, static, or declining markets and may take several forms.

1. *Maintaining share in a growing market.* A company which is operating in markets showing high levels of growth may wish to maintain market share by growing with

the market. In fact the Boston Consulting Group's work[9] (see Chapter 4) suggests that the pursuit of growth to achieve dominant market share makes strategic sense: the failure to grow in line with competition is likely to mean that the firm ends up with an uncompetitive cost structure and, when the market reaches maturity, a very difficult task in recovering market share, or achieving a competitive cost base.

Public services trying to follow any 'natural' growth in demand for particular services can face difficult choices. Unless funds can be diverted from other areas then quality of service may decline (e.g. longer waiting lists), 'rationing' arrangements may need to be applied or the service may be withdrawn from particular areas or groups. Other alternatives have also proved necessary such as fund raising and the introduction of charges (e.g. prescription charges). Contrary to immediate post-war beliefs, many public services have an almost limitless demand which simply grows as the quality of provision increases.

ILLUSTRATION 6.4

Consolidation does not mean standing still

When protective patents expired Rank Xerox had to take positive steps to retain its position as market leader in the photocopying business.

For over two decades, up to the early 1970s, the basis of the Xerox Corporation's fortunes had been with photocopying technology, which they had developed and fully patented. When the patents ran out, Xerox, and with it Rank Xerox, its UK subsidiary, faced stiff competition from large multinationals such as Kodak, IBM, and various Japanese companies who had been patiently waiting with their own machines to capitalise on Xerox's success. It was clear that if they were to remain market leaders, Xerox would have to re-examine its strategies in the light of this new threat and take action accordingly to consolidate its position.

Xerox had always rented out its machines to companies until the patents expired, but a change in marketing tactics in 1976 to sell machines as well as rent them proved to be an effective method of strengthening their market position. Coinciding with this selling strategy, reorganisation of the salesforce around nine business areas in the UK was aimed at improving the responsiveness of the service and salesforce to the customers' needs. Additional selling programmes included experimenting with telephone sales which could be followed up by salespeople and the introduction of high street showrooms where a whole range of office equipment could be sold off the shelf. Copy bureaux undertook a wide range of light printing jobs which could be performed on Xerox machines.

The Japanese always sold copiers through dealers who were able to offer various trade discounts to customers. Because Xerox sold from price lists, their various discounts were generally only for large customers, and although they aimed to remain price competitive, they hoped to gain their edge over the Japanese by providing an unrivalled back-up service to customers. This was done by operating a decentralised field service force which aimed to carry out repairs to rented machines within an average of four hours of any breakdown.

By improving their sales techniques and service back-up, Xerox and Rank Xerox were able to consolidate their position as market leaders and remain ahead of competitors.

Source: *Management Today*, June 1980.

2. *Consolidation in mature markets* provides different strategic challenges and needs to be addressed in different ways. It is common for organisations to *defend* their position by an increased emphasis on *quality* (of product or service), by increased marketing activity or by improving cost structure through productivity gains and/or increasing capital intensity. Any of these can provide barriers to entry of new competitors. The extent to which these approaches will be appropriate will be dependent on the basis on which the organisation will choose to compete or secure its position (e.g. cost competition or differentiation from competitors). It is interesting to note that the tightening of the public funds available to many public services during the 1980s required a major reassessment of these issues of quality, marketing and productivity.

3. In *declining markets*[10] consolidation may require significant changes. For example, it might be sensible to buy-up the order book of companies which leave the market; distributors may need to seek new sources of supply; new internal agreements may need to be developed to ensure continuing cost competitiveness in the smaller market. In both public and private sectors one of the most difficult decisions is whether to reduce capacity, either temporarily (moth-balling) or permanently.

Often during the transition from a mature to a declining market an organisation will follow a strategy of *harvesting*, i.e. gaining maximum pay-off from its strong position. This can be done through licensing of technology or distribution rights, leasing of facilities, etc. One of the most difficult strategic decisions is on how long to remain in products/markets which are in short term decline but where there is some hope of a market recovery. If *turnaround*[11] cannot be achieved fairly quickly it is likely that exit from the product/market will be necessary.

6.3.4 Market penetration

The previous section has been concerned with options which would maintain a company's market share in its present markets. Opportunities often exist for gaining market share as a deliberate strategy and this is normally referred to as market penetration. Much of the previous discussion is relevant to this option since, for example, improving quality or productivity, or increasing marketing activity could all be means of achieving market penetration. Equally the arguments concerning the long term desirability of obtaining a dominant market share are relevant. However, the ease with which a company can pursue a policy of market penetration will be dependent on the nature of the market and the competitive position which prevails.

When the overall market is growing or can be induced to grow, it may be relatively easy for companies with a small market share, or even new entrants, to gain market share fairly rapidly. This is because the absolute level of sales of the established companies may still be growing and indeed, in some instances, those companies may be unable or unwilling to meet the new demand. Import penetration into some industries can be traced back to the early 1970s when companies were unable to supply the peak demand occurring during booms and their customers had to seek alternative sources overseas. Once established with overseas suppliers, many UK users were reluctant to revert to UK sourcing. When the boom was over the importers held on to their market share. Organisations which had failed to follow the natural growth of a market may need to *catch-up* at a later date which can often prove more difficult.

In contrast, market penetration in static markets can be much more difficult to achieve. The lessons of the experience curve would, of course, emphasise the difficulty of market penetration in mature markets since the advantageous cost structure of market leaders should prevent the incursion of lower market share competitors. In declining markets it is difficult to generalise on the difficulties of pursuing a policy of market penetration. A company which is determined to confine its interests to one product/market area and unwilling to permit a decline in sales will need to gain market share. If other companies are leaving the market, penetration could prove easy although the wisdom of the strategy may be in some doubt. Often market penetration, particularly in mature markets, can only be achieved through collaboration with others. For example, one response to tightening budgets in the public sector has been to reserve part of the available funding to back collaborative ventures – particularly where it is felt that value for money would be increased, e.g. recreational use of school facilities.

6.3.5 Product development

Often companies will feel that consolidation in their present products/markets does not present adequate opportunities and will search for alternatives which build upon the company's present knowledge and skills. In the case of product development the company maintains the security of its present markets whilst changing and developing new products. Some, examples will illustrate the many reasons why companies might show a preference for product development. Companies in retailing will follow the changing needs of their customers by a continuing policy of introducing new product lines. In the same way local authorities need to shift their pattern of services as local needs change. Sometimes product development is preferred because the company is particularly good at R&D or because it has structured itself around product divisions. When product lifecycles are short – as with consumer electronics – product development needs to be a central part of company strategy.

Nevertheless, product development raises uncomfortable dilemmas for firms. Whilst new products may be vital to the future of the firm, the process of creating a broad product line is expensive, risky and potentially unprofitable. For these reasons there has been an increased trend towards technology transfer and collaborative ventures. Also, many organisations choose to renew the competitiveness of current products through modifications or new marketing approaches.

6.3.6 Market development

In the case of market development the organisation maintains the security of its present products whilst venturing into new market areas. Market development can include entering new *market segments*, exploiting *new uses* for the product or spreading into new *geographical areas*.

Just as companies have good reasons to prefer product development, other companies might have a strong preference for market development. In capital intensive industries many of the company's assets (money, plant, skilled people) will be specifically devoted to the technology of a particular product. These assets cannot easily be switched to produce other products. In this situation the company's *distinctive competence* lies with the product and not the market and hence the continued exploitation of the product by market development would normally be preferred. Most capital goods companies have developed this way by opening up more overseas markets as old markets become saturated. A similar argument applies to organisations whose distinctive competence is in R&D. The rapid worldwide exploitation of microelectronic technology is a good example. Many service industries such as insurance, banking and, recently, advertising companies have been pulled towards globalisation – often because some of their major customers are large multinational corporations.

Exporting is an important method of market development. There are various reasons why organisations might want to develop beyond exporting and internation-alise[12] by locating some of their manufacturing, distribution or marketing operations overseas. For example, an organisation may need to do so for *defensive* reasons – tariff barriers may have been raised or import controls introduced in important overseas markets. There may be operational or logistical reasons which make the international option more favourable, such as changes in the relative costs of labour, or transport or supplies. In contrast, other organisations may be positively seeking international markets to stave off decline in home-based demand – for example in the capital goods industry. The basis on which international expansion could be pursued will be considered more fully below.

Public service organisations, too, have often chosen to develop into new markets as the demand for traditional services has moved (particularly due to demographic changes). Developments have been particularly sought where they would attract significant additional revenue. For example, higher education institutions in the UK developed into new market sectors (e.g. mature students, in-company work, etc.) and also overseas as the numbers in the traditional age group (18–22) began to fall rapidly beyond the mid 1980s and public funding remained relatively static.

6.3.7 Diversification

Diversification as a description of strategy is used in different ways by different people. In this chapter the word will be used in a fairly general way to identify all directions of development which take the organisation away from its present products and its present market at the same time.[13] However, it is convenient to divide the considera-tion of diversification into two broad types:

- *Related diversification* which represents development beyond the present product and market but still within the broad confines of the 'industry' within which the company operates. For example, Thornton the specialist confectionery company, distributed its chocolates through its own shops.
- *Unrelated diversification* is development beyond the present industry into pro-ducts/markets which, at face value, bear no clear relationship to the present product/market. For example, companies like Hanson Trust developed rapidly in this way in the 1980s.

Sections 6.3.8 and 6.3.9 discuss diversification, its different forms, and the advantages and disadvantages of developing by diversification. It should be remem-bered, however, that many organisations are already very diverse and may sensibly be needing to ask the reverse question, namely how far should they specialise their activities. It is not intended to give separate discussion to *specialisation* as an alternative since the arguments are essentially the reverse of those used in diversification. Readers should bear this in mind when reading the sections which follow, and view them as a discussion of the relative merits of specialisation and diversification.

6.3.8 Related diversification

Referring back to Figure 6.3, it can be seen that even though related diversification takes a company beyond its present products and markets, it still keeps the company in areas where it has some knowledge. The new alternatives are within the industry in which the company presently operates. It is important to be clear what is meant by 'industry' and to understand some of the terminology which is commonly used.

- *Industry* refers to all the steps of manufacturing, distribution and servicing which go into the production and marketing of a company's products and other products of which they form a part. This is a very broad definition in some cases since, for example, a manufacturer of nylon cloth might be viewed, for this purpose, as being in the same industry as chemical companies, synthetic fibre producers, clothing manufacturers, designers, retail outlets, to name but a few. In public services the term 'industry' is equally relevant and refers to all the necessary activities to design, create, operate and deliver the services. Readers should note the important link to the concept of the *value system* introduced in Chapter 4. Essentially, related diversification refers to developments which increase the range of activities within the value system which the organisation undertakes itself. Importantly it builds linkages which may be unique and be a crucial means of sustaining competitive advantage.
- *Backward integration* refers to development into activities which are concerned with the inputs into the company's present business (i.e. are further back in the value system). For example, raw materials, machinery and labour are all important inputs into a manufacturing company.
- *Forward integration* refers to development into activities which are concerned with a company's outputs (i.e. are further forward in the value system). Transport, distribution, repairs and servicing are examples.
- *Vertical integration* is a broader term used to describe either backward or forward integration (or both together).
- *Horizontal integration* refers to development into activities which are either competitive with, or directly complementary to, a company's present activities. A lending library's extension into a tourist information service or video cassette material would be examples.

To simplify reasons why organisations might view related diversification favourably, the case of a manufacturing company can be considered. There are many value activities which occur both before and after the company's own operations and which are candidates for related diversification. These are shown in Figure 6.4. Figure 6.5 summarises the major advantages and disadvantages of such diversifications. Equally, highly diversified companies might see any of these as reasons to increase their degree of specialisation. For example, it may be decided that supplies of raw materials have become available from a reliable low-cost source and this provides a good reason to cease the manufacture of those materials within the company.

6.3.9 Unrelated diversification

Unrelated diversification refers to options which lie beyond the boundaries of the industry within which the company presently operates. At face value these options may bear no logical relationship to the organisation's activities.

Synergy[14] is a commonly quoted reason for unrelated diversification. Synergy can occur in situations where two or more activities or processes complement each other to the extent that their combined effect is greater than the 'sum of the parts'. Although the success of product and market development strategies can also depend upon synergy, it is a particularly important idea in the case of unrelated diversification. Synergy may result for financial reasons where, for example, one activity generates a short term positive cash flow and another needs such a source of cash. Equally, the good image of a company may be used as a platform to develop into a new line of business which might

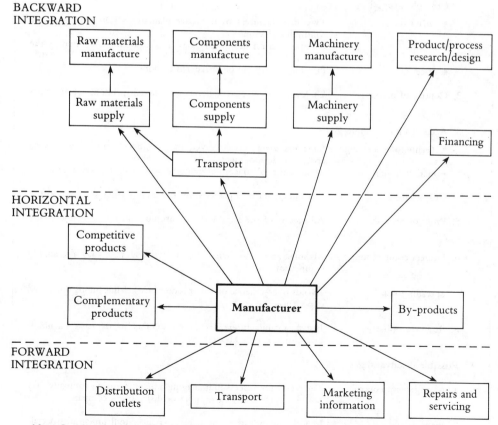

Note: Some companies will manufacture components or semi-finished items. In those cases there will be additional integration opportunities into assembly or finished product manufacture.

Figure 6.4 Alternatives open to a manufacturer to develop by related diversification.

have proved very difficult without such a support. The estimation of the likely benefits which synergy can bring can be a method of evaluation of strategy and is discussed in Chapter 7.

Other reasons for unrelated diversification may be related to the aspirations of decision makers, the opportunity to employ existing under-utilised resources in a new field, or the desire to move into a different area of activity perhaps because the present one is in decline. These and other reasons are summarised with brief examples in Figure 6.6.

Strategies of diversification raise a number of potential problems as suggested in Figure 6.5. They therefore require organisations to be clear on how the diversified operations will be managed. In particular, there are important decisions concerning the extent to which new activities are integrated with or separated from current operations. These are issues which are discussed in Chapter 10.

A. Possible advantages	**Examples/comments**
1. Control of supplies	
• Quantity	Tyre manufacturers own rubber plantations (Dunlop) to secure continuity of supply.
• Quality	Components for motor cars may need to be manufactured by the company.
• Price	Printing facility can be cheaper if in-house.
2. Control of markets	Unilever bought Mac-fisheries to help sell products of Hebrides fishing fleet.
3. Access to information	
• Technological change	Shoe manufacturers involved in machinery companies to keep abreast of developments.
• market trends	Manufacturers' concern at being isolated from market trends.
4. Cost savings	Full integrated steel plants save cost on reheating and transport.
5. Profit or growth	All sectors of the same industry are not equally profitable at any time.
6. Indirect competition	Manufacturer who owns a raw material supplier may also supply competitors.
7. Spreading risk	Avoids over-reliance on one product/market but builds on related experience.
8. Resource utilisation	British manufacturers act as consultants to overseas clients – capitalising on the know-how.
B. Possible disadvantages	
1. Management control	The recipe for success in managing a manufacturing company may not be transferable to a supplier or distribution company.
2. Inefficiencies	In declining industries companies may need to disintegrate (specialise) as the scale of production declines.

Figure 6.5 Some reasons for related diversification.

Possible advantages	Examples/comments
1. Need to use excess cash or safeguard profit	Buying a tax loss situation (Trafalgar House purchase of Cunard)
2. Personal values or objectives of powerful figures	Personal image locally or nationally may be a strong motive Many successful business people sink their fortunes into football clubs Some business ventures are described as 'buying a knighthood'
3. Exploiting under-utilised resources	Farmers use fields for camp sites Local authorities use plastic-waste for new materials Coal industry makes building materials from coal waste
4. Escape from present business	A company's products may be in decline and unrelated diversification presents the only possible 'escape'
5. Spreading risk	Some companies believe that it is good sense not to have all their 'eggs in one basket' and so diversify into unrelated areas
6. To benefit from synergistic effects	See text

Figure 6.6 Some reasons for unrelated diversification.

6.4 ALTERNATIVE METHODS OF STRATEGY DEVELOPMENT

The previous sections have been concerned with alternative directions in which organisations might develop and the basis on which they could sustain superior performance. However, for each of these alternatives a further choice is also needed, namely, the *method* by which that direction is to be developed. These methods can be divided into three 'pure' types: *internal development*, *acquisition*, and *joint development*.

Like most strategic decisions the choice between these methods is a trade-off between a number of factors such as cost, speed and risk. How this trade-off is viewed in any one situation will depend not only on the circumstances of the company but also on the attitudes of those making the decision. This should be apparent since companies within the same industry often have quite different, and long standing, approaches to development – some always preferring to develop internally, others by acquisition. Before reviewing these alternatives in more detail it is worthwhile looking at the information available concerning the popularity of these alternatives as methods of development.

Both Channon[15] and Sutton[16] have provided a detailed picture of the role of acquisition/mergers as a means of strategic development in British industry. Their major conclusions are that development by acquisition tends to go in waves (for example, 1898–1900, 1926–1929, 1967–1973 and 1985–1987) interspersed with long periods where most development (as measured by new investment) occurs internally. Moreover, these merger booms tend to be selective in terms of industry sector. For example, in the UK the 1960s boom was particularly important in brewing, electrical engineering (GEC) and textiles (Courtaulds). Between 1985 and 1987 high street retailing takeovers were significant (Dixon, Burton, Harris/Queensway etc.). Similar patterns of activity have been observed in the USA and other developed countries particularly in service industries such as catering or household services, although there has been little written about its extent. The discussion which follows will attempt to cast some light on the advantages and disadvantages of development internally by acquisition or jointly.

6.4.1 Internal development

For many organisations internal development has always been the primary method by which strategy has developed and there are some compelling reasons why this should be so. Very often, particularly with products which are highly technical in design or method of manufacture, companies will choose to develop new products themselves since the process of development is seen as the best way of acquiring the necessary skills and knowledge to exploit the product and compete successfully in the market place. A parallel argument would apply to the development of new markets by direct involvement. For example, many manufacturers still choose to forego the use of agents within the UK and export markets since they feel that the direct involvement (which they gain from having their own salesforce) is of considerable advantage in terms of gaining a full understanding of the market.

Although the final cost of developing new activities internally may be greater than by acquiring other companies the spread of cost may be more favourable and realistic. This is obviously a strong argument in favour of internal development for small companies who simply do not have the resources available, in the short term, to develop in any other way. A related issue is that of minimising disruption to other activities. The slower rate of change which internal development brings usually makes it favourable in this respect.

It is often forgotten that a company may have no choice on how new ventures are developed. Companies that are breaking new ground are not in a position to develop by acquisition or joint development since they are the only ones in the field. But this problem is not confined to such extreme situations. On may occasions, organisations that would prefer to develop by acquisition cannot do so since they cannot find a suitable company willing to be bought out. This has been cited as a particular difficulty for foreign companies attempting to enter Japan.[17] Internal development avoids the often traumatic behavioural problems arising from acquisition.[18] The cultures of the acquiring and acquired companies may be incompatible.

There are also many reasons why companies find it difficult or inappropriate to develop new strategies internally. These reasons will be discussed in the next section since the shortcomings of internal development are very often the reasons for preferring acquisition as a method of development.

6.4.2 Acquisition

Perhaps the most compelling reason to develop by acquisition is the speed with which it allows the company to enter new product/market areas. In some cases the product and/or market are changing so rapidly that this becomes the only way of successfully entering the market since the process of internal development is too slow by comparison. Another common reason for acquisition is the lack of knowledge or resources to develop certain strategies internally. For example, a company may be acquired for its R&D expertise, or its knowledge of property speculation, or a particular type of production system.

The overall cost of developing by acquisition may, in certain circumstances be particularly advantageous. Companies going into liquidation may be a good buy. An extreme example is asset stripping where the sole motive for the acquisition is short term gain by buying up undervalued assets and disposing of them piecemeal.

The competitive situation may influence a company to choose acquisition. In markets which are static and market shares of companies reasonably steady, it is often a difficult proposition for a totally new company to enter the market since its presence would upset the equilibrium. If, however, the new company chooses to enter by acquisition, the risk of competitive reaction is reduced. The same arguments also apply when an established supplier in an industry acquires a competitor either for the latter's order book (market share) or in some cases to shut down its capacity to help restore a situation where supply/demand is more balanced and trading conditions more favourable.

Sometimes there are reasons of cost efficiency which would make acquisition more favourable. This cost efficiency could arise from the fact that a company which is established and running may already be a long way down the learning curve and have achieved efficiencies which would be difficult to match quickly by internal development. In public services cost efficiency is usually the stated reason for merging units and/or rationalising provision.

Many of the problems associated with acquisition have been hinted at in the discussion of internal development. In essence, the overriding problem with acquisition lies in the ability to integrate the new company into the activities of the old[19] – an issue which will be given fuller consideration in later chapters.

6.4.3 Joint development

Joint development of new products/markets has become increasingly popular in the UK since the early 1970s largely as a result of North American influence. The advantages of joint development can best be illustrated by describing some of the different types of joint development which occur.

1. *Consortia* are formal agreements between two or more organisations to undertake a new venture together. There are many different circumstances where consortia are commonly used. Large civil engineering projects (such as the Thames flood barrier) normally require a pooling of several specialist skills as do major aerospace undertakings (e.g. Concorde). Consortia are very common in the opening up of new overseas markets, and are also quite common in the public sector – for example following the dissolution of the Metropolitan County Councils (1986) many of their functions were taken over by a co-ordinating consortium (e.g. public transport), and also between the private and public sectors as shown in Illustration 6.5.

2. *Franchising*[21] is perhaps the best known and most common type of joint development. The details of a franchise agreement can vary considerably but the underlying

rationale is the same. The advantages of franchising arise from the fact that each party has only a particular strength or interest in part of the development process and that these two interests are complementary. Perhaps the best known franchising system internationally is Coca Cola. Here the Coca Cola company's part of the development is through the product, its unrivalled brand name, and the mass consumer advertising. Against this, franchise holders will be responsible for manufacturing, bottling, distribution and selling of Coca Cola (or just some of these activities). By this means, both parties benefit since it allows them to use their own limited resources to greater overall effect.

ILLUSTRATION 6.5

Heritage and leisure – working together

Although joint ventures can start in small ways – perhaps through some joint planning and co-ordination – this is often the basis for a much broader sharing of resources to mutual benefit.

The West Glamorgan Heritage Attractions Group was launched in West Wales in 1983. It represented a unique collaboration between private, public and voluntary sector organisations to organise and promote a range of heritage and leisure facilities for tourism. The idea started with the desire to better exploit the tourist potential of the areas 'museums' (both public and private). Originally the venture was limited to eight such museums in Swansea and West Glamorgan. Subsequently the membership was extended – both geographically and, more importantly, into new types of leisure and heritage organisation. A further thirteen organisations joined by 1986, including such diverse activities as the Dan Yr Ogof Caves (private), Margam Abbey (Church of Wales and Aberdulais Falls (National Trust).

The early work of the group focused upon the basic exchange of information about each others' facilities and the development of cross-referral opportunities – passing visitors from one site to another. A marketing slogan, 'Enjoy our Heritage', was used in the joint promotion leaflet in 1984. The economies of scale achieved in this promotion, together with a favourable market response to the notion, stimulated a more ambitious approach in 1985. A symbol was designed to provide corporate identity and was used on car stickers, entry points, leaflets and letterheads. A marketing subcommittee was formed and took advantage of Wales Tourist Board's Marketing Support funds. Thus for £600 each member gained the benefit of a £20,000 campaign including leaflets, promotional video, mobile exhibition and site display panels.

Other advantages extended to discounts through joint purchasing power, hospitality costs for journalists were spread and thematic tours could be arranged for customers covering several facilities. The group was also exploring a more co-ordinated approach to souvenirs.

Importantly the group also committed itself to the setting and monitoring of customer service standards, and commissioned market research to test customer reactions. A counselling service was provided to discuss any areas of poor performance. Finally, the group had also concerned itself with the training of managers and staff. Indeed they sought and obtained funds from the Manpower Services Commission to fund this training.

Source: *Leisure Management*, August 1986.

3. *Licensing*[22] arrangements are a form of franchising which is common in science-based industries such as chemicals. The R&D department of a chemical company may develop and patent more products than the company is able to manufacture itself. Licences are, therefore, granted to other manufacturers who pay a fee (percentage of turnover) to the patent holder. Licensing is also used as a means of developing overseas markets without being involved in local manufacture or exporting from the UK.

4. *Agents* have been used in joint developments for many years. Many UK companies develop overseas markets by use of local agents not only on the grounds of their better local knowledge but also because this is the most cost efficient way to operate. This is particularly true in markets where levels of sales are relatively low and hence do not justify the full-time attention of even one sales representative.

The attractiveness of joint ventures could, arguably, increase as environmental change

Table 6.1 Summary of strategic options.

Development directions	Development methods		
	Internal	*Acquisition*	*Joint*
1. 'Do nothing'	–	–	–
2. Withdraw	Liquidate	Complete sell-out Partial divestment Management buyout	Licensing Subcontracting
3. Consolidation	Grow with market Increase: quality productivity marketing Capacity reduction/ rationing	Buy and shut down	Technology transfer Subcontracting
4. Market penetration	Increase quality productivity marketing	Buy market share Industry rationalisation	Collaboration
5. Product/service development	R&D Modifications Extensions	Buy-in products	Licensing Franchising Consortia Lease facilities
6. Market development	Extend sales area Export New segments New uses	Buy competitors	New agents Licensing Consortia
7. Backward integration	Switch 'focus'	Minority holdings	Technology sharing Exclusive agreements
8. Horizontal integration	New units	Buy subsidiaries	Tied arrangements
9. Forward integration	Create subsidiaries		Franchising Consortia
10. Unrelated diversification			

accelerates. For example, given the rate of obsolescence of plant due to technological innovation, it could well be advantageous for a company to consider becoming a marketing and distribution operation working on a joint venture basis with a manufacturer who is more specialised in the necessary field of technology.

6.5 SUMMARY

This chapter has been confined to an identification of the strategic options available to organisations as they develop and change. Before reviewing specific options it is valuable to establish the *generic strategy* on which the organisation will sustain its competitive advantage or excellence. Options have also been reviewed in terms of both development *directions* and *methods* of development. Table 6.1 pulls together both of these facets and provides a summary of the options considered in the chapter.

It needs to be recognised that such a listing of options is only the beginning of the process of strategic choice since the appropriateness of these various options will need to be assessed in the light of an organisation's circumstances. The next two chapters will deal with this process of *evaluation* in two stages. Chapter 7 establishes the broad criteria and rationale for matching options with circumstances whilst Chapter 8 reviews a range of useful evaluation methods for specific options and assesses the methods by which organisations actually select strategies.

REFERENCES

1. Michael Porter discusses generic strategies in chapter 2 of *Competitive Strategy*, Free Press, 1980 and in *Competitive Advantage*, Free Press, 1985.

2. P. Conley, *Experience Curves as a Planning tool*, 1978. (Pamphlet available from the Boston Consulting Group.)

3. Marketing strategy has long acknowledged the importance of market segmentation, a common form of focus strategy. For example, P. Kotler, *Marketing Management* (4th edn), chapter 8, Prentice Hall, 1980.

4. See Y. Doz, *Strategic Management in Multinational Companies*, Pergamon, 1986.

5. P. Modiano and O. Ni-Chionna, 'Breaking into the big time', *Management Today*, Nov., 1986 looked at the growth of sixteen companies in the UK electronics industry and cite 'niche' strategies as a critically important ingredient of their competitive strategy.

6. For example the 'do nothing' situation can be used as a base line when undertaking financial assessments of strategic options, e.g. through discounted cash flow.

7. S. Slatter, *Corporate Recovery*, chapter 7, Penguin, 1984. J. Coyne and M. Wright (eds), *Divestment and Strategic Change*, Philip Allan, 1986.

8. See H. Parker, 'How to buy out', *Management Today*, Jan., 1986, for a discussion of buy-outs.

9. See references in Chapter 4.

10. M. E. Porter, 1980 (reference 1), Chapter 12. Also K. R. Harrigan, 'Strategies for declining industries', DBA dissertation, Havard, 1979, on which parts of the chapter are based.

11. See Slatter (reference 7).

12. See Doz (reference 4).

13. Our use of the term 'diversification' is similar to that used by I. Ansoff in *Corporate Strategy*, Penguin, 1968. In Chapter 7 Ansoff identifies general reasons why firms might choose diversification as a method of development.

14. The idea of synergy is well explained by I. Ansoff in *Corporate Strategy*, Penguin, 1968. Also I. Ansoff, *Implanting Strategic Management*, pp. 80–4, Prentice Hall, 1984.

15. D. Channon, *Strategy and Structure of Business Enterprise*, Macmillan, 1973, based his research on an analysis of the 'Times Top 500' companies in an attempt to replicate earlier studies in the USA, notably by Chandler (1962). His findings on the relationship between strategy and structure will be discussed in Chapter 10. At this stage his observations of how acquisition and merger has been part of the development of UK companies is interesting.

16. See C. J. Sutton, *Economics and Corporate Strategy*, chapter 7, Cambridge University Press, 1980.

17. J. Capito, 'Joining with Japan', *Management Today*, April, 1983, reviews many of the difficulties which foreign companies can face in attempting to acquire Japanese companies. However, he also cites successful examples of such acquisitions.

18. For interesting examples of the turmoil that can result from acquisition see:

   • M. Fenton, *Management Today*, Sep., 1979.
   • A. van de Vliet and D. Isaac, 'The mayhem in mergers', *Management Today*, Feb., 1986.
   • R. Heller, 'The agonies of agglomeration', *Management Today*, Feb., 1986.

19. See reference 18.

20. For a comprehensive review of the management of joint ventures, see K. R. Harrigan, *Managing for Joint Venture Success*, Lexington Books, 1986.

21. See N. Mendelsohn, *Guide to Franchising* (3rd edn), Pergamon, 1982, or W. L. Seigel, *Franchising*, John Wiley, 1983.

22. C. Edge, 'Britain's innovation trap', *Management Today*, Nov., 1985, cites collaborative ventures and technology transfer as important ingredients in the R&D strategies of many companies.

Recommended key readings

• For an interesting discussion of strategies appropriate to companies in differing market environments see M. E. Porter, *Competitive Strategy*, Free Press, 1980.

• Porter (1980, chapter 2) also reviews the generic strategies available to organisations. This discussion is repeated in M. E. Porter, *Competitive Advantage*, Free Press, 1985.

• The discussion to be found in chapter 7 of Igor Ansoff's *Corporate Strategy* (Penguin, 1968) still provides an excellent exposition of the logic of diversification.

Chapter 7

STRATEGY EVALUATION
CRITERIA AND APPROACHES

7.1 INTRODUCTION

The previous chapter has identified a variety of ways in which organisations may choose to develop. The purpose of this chapter is to discuss some general approaches to evaluating these options. However, it is first necessary to establish the criteria against which organisations would 'judge' the merits of particular options. It will be seen that these criteria often conflict with each other and evaluation usually requires sensible judgements on how these differing requirements should be weighed.

In order to clarify how organisations might approach these difficult issues of strategy evaluation the discussion has been divided into two parts. Chapter 7 will look at some general approaches to strategy evaluation. In particular there will be an emphasis on how an organisation's circumstances might dictate the types of strategy that they follow. Chapter 8 will look at methods and techniques for evaluating specific options.

7.2 EVALUATION CRITERIA

A useful way of looking at evaluation criteria is to view them as falling into three categories:

1. Criteria of *suitability* which attempt to measure how far proposed strategies fit the situation identified in the strategic analysis. Does the strategy, for example, capitalise on the company's strengths, overcome or avoid weaknesses and counter environmental threats?
2. Criteria of *feasibility* which assess how any strategy might work in practice. For example, whether the strategy is achievable in resource terms.
3. Criteria of *acceptability* which assess whether the consequences of proceeding with a strategy are acceptable. For example, will it be sufficiently profitable or generate the growth expected by senior management, shareholders or other stakeholders? Another important measure of acceptability is the level of risk involved in any strategy.

The review of evaluation techniques in Chapter 8 will show that different methods tend to focus on one or perhaps two of these criteria. Firstly, however, a little more needs to be said about the criteria.

7.2.1 Suitability

One of the prime purposes of strategic analysis is to provide a clear picture of the organisation and the environment in which it is operating. A useful summary of this situation might include a listing of the major opportunities and threats which face the organisation, its particular strengths and weaknesses and any objectives which are a particularly important influence on policy.[1]

One important measure of evaluation is the extent to which any strategy addresses itself to the situation described in the strategic analysis. Some authors[2] have referred to this as 'consistency'. Certain questions need to be asked about any strategic option, such as:

- How far does it overcome the difficulties identified in the strategic analysis (resource *weaknesses* and environmental *threats*)? For example, is the strategy likely to improve the organisation's competitive standing or resolve the company's liquidity problems, or decrease dependence on a particular supplier?
- Does it exploit the company *strengths* and environmental *opportunities*? For example, will the proposed strategy provide appropriate work for skilled craftsmen, or help establish the company in new growth sectors of the market, or utilise the present, highly efficient, distribution system?
- Does it fit in with the organisation's *objectives*. For example, would the strategy be likely to achieve profit targets, achieve growth expectations or retain control for an owner manager?

7.2.2 Feasibility

An assessment of the feasibility[3] of any strategy is concerned with whether it can be implemented. For example, the scale of the proposed changes needs to be achievable in resource terms. As suggested earlier, this process will already have started during the identification of options and will continue through into the process of assessing the details of implementation. However, at the evaluation stage there are a number of fundamental questions which need to be asked when assessing feasibility:

- Can the strategy be *funded*?
- Is the organisation capable of performing to the *required level* (e.g. quality level, service level)?
- Can the necessary *market position* be achieved and will the necessary marketing skills be available?
- Can *competitive reactions* be coped with?
- How will the organisation ensure that the required *skills* at both managerial and operative level are available?
- Will the *technology* (both product and process) to compete effectively be available?
- Can the necessary *materials* and services be obtained?

This is not a definitive list but does illustrate the broad range of questions which need answering. It is also important to consider all of these questions with respect to *timing* of the required changes.

7.2.3 Acceptability

Alongside the analysis of suitability and feasibility is the third measure, acceptability. This can be a difficult area since acceptability is strongly related to people's expectations, and therefore the issue of 'acceptable to whom' requires the analysis to be thought through carefully. Some of the questions that will help identify the likely consequences of any strategy are:

● What will be the financial performance of the company in *profitability* terms? The parallel in the public sector would be *cost/benefit* assessment.
● How will the *financial risk* (e.g. liquidity) change?

ILLUSTRATION 7.1

Supergrip Tools was formed in 1979 when four junior managers in an old-established (Sheffield) tool company decided to buy the firm with the aid of a £350,000 bank loan, following liquidation. The new management team were energetic and enthusiastic, and succeeded in keeping the firm going, but over the first five years they were faced with major difficulties:

1. The old company had been family owned and controlled. Working practices were orientated towards providing a living and an easy existence for the family. Several managers were coasting in anticipation of their pension. On the positive side, many of the seventy-five staff were loyal and highly skilled toolmakers, on whom the firm's reputation for quality workmanship depended.
2. The history of the company had led to a large and fragmented product range. The company manufactured a total of 1,750 different products, ranging from heavy hand tools such as vices, to lighter items such as chisels.
3. The company had 1,500 customers but only 250 of these had sizable accounts. They

A. Rationalise existing product range and customers

Suitability	Supergrip could economise on:
	1. Sales and administration by concentrating on those customers with larger orders
	2. Eliminating short productions runs
	3. Only selling under own brand name
	Does **not** address problem of static UK market.
Acceptability	Would salespeople be prepared to acquire right skills to specialise? Workforce would need to adapt to narrow product range. Some skills would be redundant.
Feasibility	Does company have skills to assess market – which tools and customers to concentrate on and which to eliminate? New investment needed as existing machinery cannot cope with long production runs, but this is the 'cheaper' alternative.
Conclusion	Not particularly suitable, but more acceptable and feasible given the existing resources than (B).

Source: Case study by P. Jennings, Sheffield City Polytechnic.

- What will be the effect on *capital structure* (e.g. gearing or share ownership)?
- Will any proposed changes be acceptable to the general *expectations* within the organisation (e.g. attitudes to greater levels of risk)?
- Will the *function* of any department, group or individual change significantly?
- Will the organisation's relationship with outside *stakeholders* (e.g. suppliers, government, unions, customers) need to change?
- Will the strategy be acceptable in the organisation's *environment* (e.g. will the local community accept higher levels of noise)?
- Will the proposed strategy *fit existing systems* or will it require major changes?

Supergrip tools – assessment of options

ranged from those who bought Supergrip tools but sold under their own brand name, to wholesalers, retailers, and even the Ministry of Defence. The salespeople were expected to sell all products to all potential buyers in their particular area of the UK (no exports).

4. When the old company went into liquidation many of the creditors remained unpaid. This made it difficult to get supplies. Similarly, many customers were reluctant to begin trading again, fearing that the new company would not survive for long.

5. Although the factory buildings were acceptable, much of the machinery used to manufacture the tools was old and inefficient.

The 'rescue' operation for Supergrip had been successful, and a satisfactory level of sales maintained. However, the management was aware of the desperate need for new investments and developments for long term survival, especially in the light of the static UK market demand for tools, and increasing import penetration. Two major options are considered below in terms of their suitability, acceptability and feasibility.

B. Expand into export market

Would give access to developing markets for quality tools, particularly the Middle East and thus solve problems of static demand.

Would require major changes in skills and approach for a traditional company. Management team needs to be prepared to take risks, travel and develop contacts. Workers would have to adapt to make types of tool needed for export market.

Major difficulty in acquiring necessary exporting skills.
Possible retraining or buying an already-established export manager.
Would need considerable financial backing, high set-up costs for export drive; also payment delays.
Could they gain foothold in this very competitive market?

The most suitable solution, but greater element of risk.
Acceptability and feasibility in doubt.

Clearly a new strategy is unlikely to be the ideal choice of all stakeholders. The management of stakeholder expectations is therefore crucial and will be discussed in Chapter 11.

Illustration 7.1 shows how the criteria of suitability, feasibility and acceptability can be used to help evaluate a strategic option.

7.3 ASSESSING THE SUITABILITY OF OPTIONS

Chapter 8 will review a variety of methods whereby strategic options can be evaluated – either separately or against each other. However, the sheer number of considerations involved in evaluating a range of options can be quite bewildering. For this reason organisations need to be clear on which types of option make sense in their particular circumstances and to establish the *rationale*[4] for pursuing one or more of these. It is at that stage – effectively a shortlist – that more detailed evaluation is both necessary and practical. Options are only given further consideration (at least in the first instance) if they would appear to suitably address the situation identified in the strategic analysis. Figure 7.1 outlines the approach taken to evaluation in these two chapters.

In Part II of this book there has been a continuing emphasis on strategy-making as a process of balancing the (often conflicting) demands of the environment, an organisation's resource capability and the expectations that people have of the

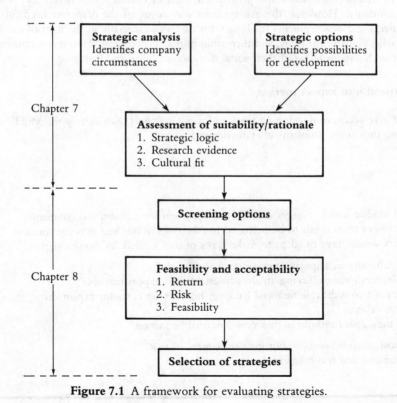

Figure 7.1 A framework for evaluating strategies.

organisation and its development. This same theme is of equal importance during strategic choice.

Good choices of strategy are ones which pay appropriate attention to each of these 'pressures' from the environment, resources and expectations. It should be made clear that 'proper attention' does not normally mean equal attention. It is usual that one of these factors is taken as the perspective from which strategies are reviewed, with the other two factors being regarded as constraints. There is a danger in assuming that a product/market (environment-led) perspective is the only way of assessing strategic options. The dominance of such a viewpoint in the literature is undoubtedly due to the excessive attention which has been paid to strategic development during growth – at the expense of a fuller consideration of a range of different circumstances.

Organisations operating in very stable environments may be mainly concerned with resource *utilisation* and this will be a more relevant perspective from which to review options (see Table 7.1). The idea of *distinctive competence* discussed in Chapter 4 may be the main issue steering company strategy (see Illustration 7.2). Product/market opportunities and expectations become constraints upon the company in attempting to capitalise on this distinctive competence.

For many public service organisations strategic development centres around the issue of how limited resources should best be used since there may be many more demands than can be satisfied. In these circumstances strategic choice is either dominated by resource capability (i.e. what the organisation is best and/or most efficient at providing) or by the expectations of those with most power who will dictate priorities.

Similarly, there are many other circumstances when the dominant expectations of an organisation are the appropriate perspective from which to assess options. New business ventures tend to be dominated by the expectations of the founder, which are not always expressed in product/market terms. The desire to be independent or successful can be very important. A similar situation can recur in an organisation at a later date, triggered off by unexpected or difficult events such as the loss of a major customer or supplier: short term survival, at almost any cost, dominates company strategy. In such a *turnaround* situation strategic options are assessed primarily by this measure.

In order to provide a properly balanced view of the different approaches to

Table 7.1 Different perspectives for assessing strategic options.

Perspectives	Options concerned with	Constraints	Most applicable to situation of
1. Environment (product/market)	Satisfying market opportunities	Resource utilisation Expectations	Growth Retrenchment
2. Resource utilisation	Capitalising on the company's distinctive competence	Environmental opportunities Expectations	Stability Limited resource
3. Culture/expectations	Meeting the needs of powerful individuals or groups	Environmental opportunities Resource utilisation	New companies Turnaround Sudden change Limited resource

strategic evaluation the remainder of this chapter will present a variety of approaches which reflect different perspectives. For convenience these approaches have been divided into three groups:

1. Approaches which attempt to establish a *strategic logic* which links the nature of the product/markets and the resource capability of the organisation to the suitability of particular types of strategy.
2. Approaches based upon the *research evidence* of how organisational performance is related to choice of strategy.
3. *Cultural fit* approaches where the emphasis is on understanding how well strategies fit the culture and expectations of the organisation and the extent of cultural change which would be required to make that strategy work.

Although in general each approach might be more or less useful in different

---

ILLUSTRATION 7.2

Weir's engineering solution

> Many organisation's long term development is driven by their technological
> know-how. Sometimes this can lead the company in unexpected directions.

Like many UK engineering companies, the Weir group suffered a traumatic shock during the early 1980s recession but survived, albeit in a somewhat slimmed-down and reorientated form. In fact, the history of Weir is one of significant shifts in emphasis as markets rose and waned.

In the mid 1980s the company was the largest UK producer of pumps of the kind employed for feeding power station boilers and for other applications in oil, chemicals and aboard ships. This was where the company began: manufacturing feed pumps and related machinery for the steam engines in the Clyde-built ships of the nineteenth century. From this developed a steel castings business, originally set up to produce their own pump-making needs and then expanded by acquisition. The third major (and more recent) part of the business was the design and supply of desalination plants (mainly to the Middle East). This too evolved from company technology – an evaporator which allowed the use of sea water in ships' boilers.

Over the years the company had managed to exploit these skills in many ways. They had been in and out of motor vehicles, aircraft and armaments, industrialised housing, packaging machinery, valves and other engineering products. But pumps and maritime equipment remained the core products of the group and when British shipbuilding finally slipped beneath the waves the group found alternative outlets for its skills in the power generation industry. But even this did not insulate them from the traumas of the early 1980s recession – the group was rescued by extensive restructuring and refinancing.

The strategic options at that stage were limited, being a medium sized company with limited resources. They decided to sell specialist skills and services as well as products – again this exploited the expertise of the desalination group which (as a contract company) had been in that business for some time. The services business expanded through computer aided design/project management into technical assistance, instrumentation, technical consultancy and equipment maintenance and servicing (e.g. in power station).

Source: *Management Today*, March 1986.

circumstances it must be stressed that essentially they are not alternative approaches. Indeed it is hoped that readers will feel that strategic evaluation will be improved if a number of approaches are taken since they provide valuable, and complementary, insights into the appropriateness of various strategies.

7.3.1 Strategic logic

The literature on strategic evaluation has been dominated since the 1950s by rational/ economic assessments of strategic logic. In this section the discussions will be limited to reviewing a small number of these frameworks which are indicative of the general approach to strategy evaluation taken by such assessments. Essentially they are all concerned with matching particular strategic options with an organisation's market situation and its relative strategic capabilities. The following four approaches will be briefly reviewed:

1. *Product portfolio analyses* which place emphasis on the nature of the markets (particularly growth rate) and an organisation's competitive standing.
2. *Lifecycle analyses* which are a refinement and extension of product portfolio analyses and pay more detailed attention to the stage in an industry lifecycle.
3. *Competitive advantage* analysis which further refines the consideration of an organisation's ability to sustain its competitive advantage.
4. *Synergy* which is concerned with assessing the value which can be created from a given resource-base – particularly in circumstances where different ventures may be 'pulled together' (e.g. mergers, rationalisations, etc.).

Although most of the literature is concerned with private sector profit-seeking organisations, the lessons are equally valid in the public sector. The following sections will attempt to interpret the discussion in this context.

PRODUCT PORTFOLIO ANALYSES
Most of the discussion in Chapter 6 was concerned with the analysis of competitive strategies or activities of single organisational units. However, much of the strategy evaluation at the centre of large, diverse organisations takes a somewhat different perspective from that at the level of the individual business unit. American literature[5] in the field of corporate strategy draws strong distinctions between the former which they call 'corporate strategy' as against the latter which they refer to as 'business strategy'. In a large and diverse organisation a prime concern of evaluation at the corporate level is that of achieving a balanced range (or portfolio) of businesses or activities. The product portfolio concept has already been mentioned in Chapter 6 as a possible justification for unrelated diversification. The idea evolved from the work on experience curves by the Boston Consulting Group (BCG) as described in Chapter 4. Figure 7.2 (A) illustrates the simple BCG matrix which is used to indicate where each business activity lies in relation to two factors: market growth rate and market share. It should be remembered that this type of analysis can be used to look at whole businesses (e.g. within a group) or to look at business activities (e.g. products) within any one company. Future options can be plotted onto the matrix in the same way. This matrix can then be used as a guide on a number of important strategic questions relating to the evaluation of future strategies.

- How far will the proposed new strategy improve the company's portfolio of interests? For example, will it help develop business growth areas whilst removing the dogs that drain cash flow for no long term reward?
- Since stars generally require an investment of funds will there be sufficient cash cows to provide this necessary investment? This is an important question about the balance of the portfolio. For example, a major reason for company bankruptcies is that a firm may be investing heavily in the promotion and stocking policy for products in rapid growth without profitable and well established products from which it can fund these new ventures.

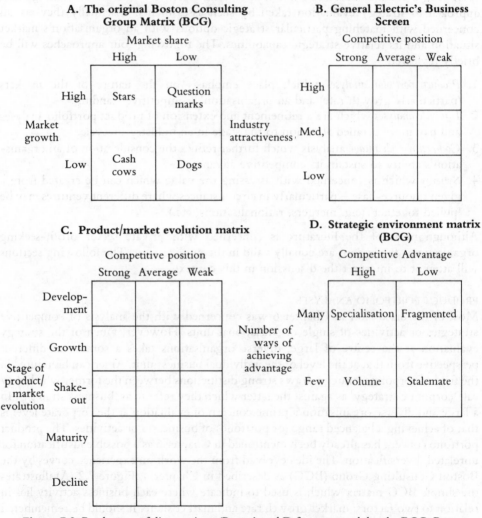

Figure 7.2 Product portfolio matrices. (Parts A and D from research by the BCG. Part B adapted from C. Hofer and D. Schendel, *Strategy Formulation: Analytical concepts*, copyright 1978 by West Publishing Co. Part C from C. Hofer, *Conceptual Constructs for Formulating Corporate and Business Strategies*, p.3, Intercollegiate Case Clearing House, Boston, no. 9-378-754, 1977, and adapted by C. Hofer and D. Schendel, *Strategy Formulation: Analytical concepts*, p.34, West Publishing Co., 1978.)

- In the public services[6] it is important to have a balance of activities which matches the range of skills within the organisation, otherwise certain groups are badly overstretched whilst others remain underemployed.
- Another issue of importance in the public services is the political acceptability of the portfolio of activities. Often the more exciting developments will only be sanctioned if sufficient resource and attention is being paid to the mundane everyday activities/services.
- There are some situations where dogs may need to be kept since they provide a necessary platform for the successful development of the stars or to keep competitors' cash cows under threat. A car manufacturer might argue that it needs to be involved in the low profitability bulk market if it wishes to operate in the more specialist, profitable sectors of the market. It is in the former activity that the skill of making cars is learned and improved.
- The long term rationale of product or business development can be highlighted by the matrix. Which strategies are most likely to ensure a move from question marks through to stars and eventually cash cows? In short, is the company likely to dominate its particular markets?
- The matrix can also help in thinking about acquisition strategy. Companies that embark on acquisition programmes often forget that the most likely targets for acquisition are not the stars and cash cows of the business world but the question marks or dogs. There may be nothing wrong with acquiring a question mark provided the resources are there to move it towards star-dom, bearing in mind the real costs and difficulties of acquisition as pointed out in Chapter 6.

There have been a number of refinements and modifications to the original BCG matrix, three of which are also illustrated in Figure 7.2 and can be followed up in the references.[7] These matrices can be used in much the same way as described above.

Product portfolio analysis is not a comprehensive evaluation technique. As an evaluation technique its scope is limited. It is a preliminary step in any evaluation and helps to raise questions about the rationale of any strategy. More detailed techniques of evaluation need to be used to assess the overall desirability of strategy which seems to fit the product portfolio. Readers should also note that some writers have cast doubt on the practical value of the approach.[8]

LIFECYCLE ANALYSIS

It was mentioned in the previous section that one particular development of the product portfolio concept has been used extensively. This is often referred to as *lifecycle analysis* (or product/market evolution analysis as in Figure 7.2). This section will review one such approach as presented and used by the business consultants, Arthur D. Little.[9] Figure 7.3 is a summary of their lifecycle portfolio matrix and consists of two dimensions. The market situation is described in four stages – from embryonic to aging; the competitive position in five categories ranging from weak to dominant. The purpose of this matrix is to establish the appropriateness of particular strategies in relation to these two dimensions.

Clearly, if this approach is to provide a strategic logic for the development direction of a specific organisation the crucial issue is establishing where that organisation is currently positioned on the matrix.

Stages of Industry Maturity

Competitive position	Embryonic	Growth	Mature	Ageing
Dominant	Fast grow Start-up	Fast grow Attain cost leadership Renew Defend position	Defend position Attain cost leadership Renew Fast grew	Defend position Focus Renew Grow with industry
Strong	Start-up Differentiate Fast grow	Fast grow Catch-up Attain cost leadership Differentiate	Attain cost leadership Renew, focus Differentiate Grow with industry	Find niche Hold niche Hang-in Grow with industry Harvest
Favourable	Start-up Differentiate Focus Fast grow	Differentiate, focus Catch-up Grow with industry	Harvest, hang-in Find niche, hold niche Renew, turnaround Differentiate, focus Grow with industry	Retrench Turnaround
Tenable	Start-up Grow with industry Focus	Harvest, catch-up Hold niche, hang-in Find niche Turnaround Focus Grow with industry	Harvest Turnaround Find niche Retrench	Divest Retrench
Weak	Find niche Catch-up Grow with industry	Turnaround Retrench	Withdraw Divest	Withdraw

Figure 7.3 The lifecycle portfolio matrix. (From Arthur D. Little.)

1. The *position within the lifecycle* is determined in relation to eight external factors or 'descriptors' of the evolutionary stage of the industry. These are: market growth rate, growth potential, breadth of product lines, number of competitors, spread of market share between these competitors, customer loyalty, entry barriers, and technology. It is the balance of these factors which determines the lifecycle stage. For example, an *embryonic* industry is characterised by rapid growth, changes in technology, fragmented market shares and pursuit of new customers. In contrast, *ageing* industries are best described by falling demand, declining number of competitors and, often, a narrow product line.

2. The *competitive position* of the organisation within its industry can also be established by looking at the characteristics of each category in Figure 7.3. A *dominant* position is rare in the private sector and usually results from a quasi-monopoly. In the public sector this may be a legalised monopoly status (e.g. public utilities). *Strong* organis-ations are those that can follow strategies of their own choice without too much concern for competition. A *favourable* position is where no single competitor stands out but the leaders are better placed (e.g. UK grocery retailing). A *tenable* position is that which can be maintained by specialisation or focus. *Weak* competitors are ones who are too small to survive independently in the long run.

Despite the fact that even such a detailed matrix can suggest that strategic choice is a simplistic and easy affair (which it is not), the A. D. Little matrix can be helpful in guiding strategic choice. Given the wide variety of strategic options discussed in Chapter 6, the main value of this matrix is in narrowing down this range of options to those which are worthy of further consideration given the organisation's circum-stances. For example (referring to Figure 7.3), the following general relationships would normally hold good.

1. Where growth is occurring and/or a favourable (or better) competitive position exists organisations are well placed to follow the '*natural*' development of the market, although this may be achieved in different ways. The extreme case is clearly a dominant organisation in an embryonic industry which is likely to be creating the natural growth through its own efforts which it will seek to defend during growth by moving faster than competition or by cost leadership (through size or experience). Indeed, a dominant company may well be able to defend its position through the whole lifecycle of the industry by carefully planned shifts in strategy (for example, through renewing the market strength of a product to avoid competition from innovation).

2. In contrast weak organisations are unlikely to survive through the lifecycle unless they identify and exploit a market *niche* and, effectively, become a strong supplier within that niche. As growth declines, organisations will need to be more selective in their choice of strategy. This is particularly important if the organisation is not in a strong competitive position. Indeed, many of the strategies discussed in Chapter 6 allow organisations to be selective and prosper. The concepts of *focus* as an important generic strategy (and a niche strategy is an extreme example of focus) are clearly of primary importance. However, in more difficult situations (towards the bottom right-hand corner of the matrix) important judgements will need to be made as to which product/markets should be pursued and which discontinued. So a strategy of *retrenchment* would normally be the first step down this road but may need to be

followed by attempts to *turnaround* the organisation's performance or to *divest* parts of the organisation or even *withdraw* entirely from particular products/markets.

3. It is important to recognise that some of the strategic options discussed in Chapter 6 will take on different forms depending on the position on the matrix. For example, a strategy of *market development* for a dominant company is likely to be achieved by the organisation's own stimulation of new demand. In contrast, in more mature markets and weaker competitive position market development would need to be achieved much more selectively by targeting new segments or moving into new markets where the conditions were more favourable (e.g. overseas development).

4. In the public services the strategy of a state-owned monopoly (such as the Post Office) in an aging market is largely defensive – although its position is protected by its monopoly status. It has been argued that this is necessary since the natural response in an openly competitive situation would be to follow more selective strategies – in particular to reduce levels of service in the unprofitable (rural) areas and concentrate on cost efficient operations in large cities.

5. It is also interesting to note how many public services in the UK started to refine, prioritise and differentiate their activities after the long period of growth of the 1960s and 1970s. This was largely achieved by increasing cost efficiency, quality improvements and discontinuing certain services which were better provided by other bodies.

COMPETITIVE ADVANTAGE ANALYSIS
Porter[10] has extended the considerations of the lifecycle portfolio by looking at the relationship between the development stage of the industry, whether it be in growth,

	Stage of 'industry' development		
	Growth	Maturity	Decline
Leader	Keeping ahead of the field	Cost leadership Raise barriers Deter competitors	Redefine scope Divest peripherals Encourage departures
Follower	Imitation at lower cost Joint ventures	Differentiation Focus	Differentiation New opportunities

Strategic position of organisation (row label at left spanning both rows)

Figure 7.4 Competitive strategies for leaders and followers. (From M.E. Porter, *Competitive Advantage: Creating and sustaining superior performance*, Free Press, 1985. Used with permission of The Free Press, a Division of Macmillan, Inc. Copyright 1985 Michael E. Porter.)

maturity or decline, and the strategic position of the individual organisation, leader or follower within the industry.

It should be noted that the terms 'leader' and 'follower' are not synonymous with positions of dominance and weakness and hence Porter's analysis provides an additional perspective on the issue of competitive choice. The following provides a résumé of the analysis. (See Figure 7.4).

(a) Growth

Much of the traditional literature about strategic development has taken the stance of an industry leader operating in growth markets (or in the case of public services in a position of expanding budgets). Developments tend to occur by chasing growth as close to current product/market strategies as possible – but inevitably being forced towards increased diversification as growth opportunities dry up. Illustration 7.3

ILLUSTRATION 7.3

Asda/MFI

Even for companies which have followed a successful product/market strategy for many years, there may come a time when more unrelated diversification looks attractive.

After a long period of impressive growth within the same industry, Asda, one of the 'big three' UK food retailers, acquired MFI Furniture, a consistent growth star in its own right.

From the late 1950s through to the early 1980s Asda was transformed from a small dairy and pork farm business to a major retail grocery chain, with particular strong market presence in the north of England. The company had seen the impact that car ownership would have on shopping habits and created the concept of the out-of-town supermarket catering for all categories of shopper, particularly the car owner. As this formula was copied by others they kept ahead of the field by rapid geographical expansion in the north of England and improving the quality of their operation.

By the late 1970s they faced the head-on competition of their major rivals, Tesco and Sainsbury, as Asda ventured south. But this process of market development became increasingly tough as the competitive rivalry between the big three increased.

For these reasons in 1985 Asda made a controversial move in acquiring MFI Furniture, itself a consistent growth star in its own right. This allowed the company growth and development to continue in new areas of retailing furniture and carpets.

After so many years of growth and development by 'sticking to the knitting' there were many who questioned the wisdom of this unrelated diversification. However, others believed that one of the motivations for the move was to ensure satisfactory succession for the Asda chairman, Noel Stockdale, who had been with Asda for over forty-five years. MFI's chairman, Derek Hunt, became Chief Executive, with a young board (average age under 50). MFI also opened up new options, particularly in overseas expansion.

However, operating synergy seemed hard to find, and Asda/MFI shares under-performed in 1985, 1986 and 1987. In 1987 Derek Hunt resigned as an Asda director and led a £505 million management buy-out of MFI. Asda, for its part, returned to its superstore strategy, concentrating on store refurbishment, geographical expansion and a move into own-brand products.

Sources: *Management Today*, April 1986, and financial press.

shows this process very well and the development of many public services during the 1960s and 1970s was very similar. During growth, industry leaders are often compelled to develop the business internally (at least during the early stages) since there are few suitable candidates for acquisition or to work as partners.

The competitive advantage of leaders during growth stems from staying ahead of the field (for example) in offering unique products or services or in the cost advantages they have gained through their relative size or experience.

The position for followers in the industry is somewhat different. They may, of course, have entered the industry as a result of the leader(s) being unable (or unwilling) to cope with the potential demand. The proliferation of home computer systems in the early 1980s was a good example. Where rapid growth is occurring the followers, at this stage, may well be able to develop by imitation of the leader's strategy – indeed the market may be so unsophisticated as to demand imitation. Imitation can be most effective if done at lower cost (e.g. own-brand supplies). Sometimes followers are able to enter the industry through joint ventures with leaders who may be hard-pressed to serve the market alone. Subcontracting is an example of such a situation – and can prove to be a low-risk way of gaining experience of the industry. Larger organisations which feel that they have missed a major development may well acquire one or more of the smaller follower organisations as a means of catching-up. The major danger for followers during growth is that they fail to understand that a strategy of imitation, although perhaps adequate during growth, is likely to be disastrous as the industry approaches maturity and buyers become more discerning.

(b) Maturity

The onset of maturity in any industry (or public service) is a difficult period for many organisations, where expectations need to be adjusted and the strategic role of the organisation in the industry given careful thought.[11] In essence each organisation needs to assess how it can choose a strategic approach which best matches its distinctive competence *vis-à-vis* competitors. In grocery retailing, although a mature industry, there has therefore been much change as the major retailers have adjusted their strategies to build on competitive advantages of buying power, and store size and location. In public services too a realisation that the service cannot hope to be a monopoly supplier with complete 'market' coverage has forced managers to define the boundaries of their activities and to allow others to serve the remaining demand/need. The speight of privatisations within public services (e.g. ancillary services in hospitals) is an example.

Leaders in an industry may choose to consolidate their position in a number of ways which help them gain competitive advantage by virtue of their leadership:

- By exploiting their superior *cost structure* usually through highly competitive pricing.
- By raising the *structural barriers* – for example through high levels of marketing expenditure, geographical spread (e.g. globalisation)[12] or blocking access to distribution channels or suppliers; or even encouraging government policies (e.g. new regulations) which would make entry more difficult.
- By making it less attractive or more risky for others to challenge the leader's position. This could be through threatening retaliation, or perhaps by promising to

match any offering of the followers. (The 'never knowingly undersold' policy of the John Lewis partnership stores is a good example.)

The position for followers during maturity is almost the reverse. The most successful strategies of followers are where they are able to *differentiate* themselves from the leaders. This is usually combined with a quite deliberate strategy of *focusing* on particular parts of the market (*segmentation* or *niche*). Readers are reminded of the discussions in Chapter 6 which explained how this process of differentiation and focus can only be a means to genuine competitive advantage if conceived of throughout the *value chain*. Porter[13] provides a useful framework for identifying the various ways in which this differentiation can be achieved effectively by followers and used to their advantage. This is shown in Figure 7.5. The underlying purpose of a follower strategy must be to nullify the competitive advantage of the leader (discussed above) whilst minimising the threat of retaliation. The essential messages are:

- Imitation of the leader can only be sustained by 'pure spending' (e.g. price wars) and is unlikely to succeed unless the follower organisation has substantial financial resources (e.g. from a parent company).
- Followers can compete in the same product/market as a leader by reconfiguring part of all of the value chain. For example, they may reduce supply costs by re-sourcing or use different outlets, or lower cost marketing methods (e.g. own-label suppliers). However, these differences must be genuinely valuable to customers in some way or other.
- Another alternative is to redefine the competitive scope of the organisation *vis-à-vis*

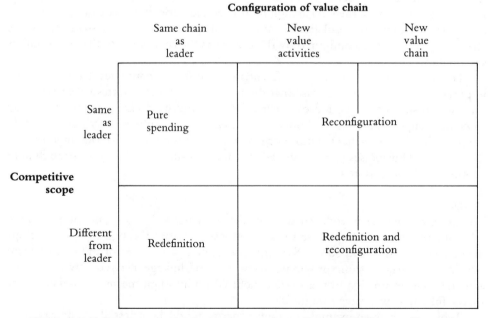

Figure 7.5 Follower strategies for mature markets. (From M.E. Porter, *Competitive Advantage: Creating and sustaining superior performance*, Free Press, 1985. Used with permission of The Free Press, a Division of Macmillan, Inc. Copyright 1985 Michael E. Porter.)

the leader. The best known form of redefinition is by narrowing the focus of the organisation, i.e. *market segmentation* (or *niche* strategies). So the follower becomes a leader within that segment or niche. Advantage can also be gained by *horizontal integration* (or vice versa) again making the company different from the leader. So a 'property shop' providing all the services needed to change house may compete successfully with the leaders of the separate services (estate agents, solicitors, insurance). *Vertical integration* may also provide advantage (e.g. the small specialist retailer may provide better after-sales service than the high street multiples).

Geographical spread on an area by area basis is the route whereby Japanese companies[14] have gradually challenged and displaced the incumbent leaders in other countries (e.g. motorbikes, cars and consumer electronics). Interestingly enough this globalisation process was helped along by a very clear market segmentation (focus) approach. Typically, Japanese would enter the bottom end of the market (which was badly defended) and gradually displace the leaders by trading-up from this bridge-head.

(c) Decline

Many of the principles concerning competitive strategy in maturity are similar during decline and will not be repeated. However, there are some additional factors which are special to decline.[15] The most obvious one is that when demand is reducing, options such as *divestment* or *withdrawal* tend to be of pressing concern. Leaders have some difficult decisions to make; in particular the viability of their venture is likely to be threatened unless some other organisations leave the industry. It is quite common for leaders to induce this process by buying competitors and closing-down their capacity. In other circumstances (the steel and oil industries and agriculture are examples) leaders push hard for industry regulation – either voluntary or imposed. Usually the value chain will have to be reconfigured by the leaders as the economics of the chain shift as scale reduces.

For followers the need to differentiate themselves continues to be of vital importance and it is often the case that the followers (who are more specialist) are the ones which survive the period of decline the best. Indeed decline usually throws up some new opportunities as the leaders shed their more peripheral activities. Certainly many of the service elements within organisations are now provided out-of-house by thriving small businesses (e.g. design, advertising, consultancy, R&D) or through joint ventures such as consortia.

SYNERGY

The previous chapter introduced the concept of synergy[16] as a means of explaining why organisations might choose to take on new activities through market development, diversification and so on. Synergy was seen as a measure of the extra benefit which could accrue from providing some sort of linkage between two or more activities. The estimation of this extra benefit is an important means of assessing how successful any new strategy might be.

Table 7.2 gives an example of how synergy might be assessed in the case of a single-outlet grocery retailer wishing to increase the overall size of his business. The company wants to assess the degree of synergy between the present business and three alternative methods of development: buying more grocery shops, expanding the

Table 7.2 The assessment of synergy for a grocery retailer.

Degree of synergy with present activities	Strategy 1 Buy more shops	Strategy 2 Expand into alcoholic drink	Strategy 3 Open cash and carry wholesaler
1. Use of cash	Produces profit from idle cash	Produces profit from idle cash	Produces profit from idle cash
2. Use of premises	None	More turnover/ floor space	None
3. Use of stock	Perhaps small gains from moving stock between shops	None	Reduction of stock in shops as quick delivery guaranteed
4. Purchasing	Possible discounts for bulk	None	Reduced prices to shops
5. Market image	Good name helps launch (i.e. cost of launch reduced)	None	Little

product range into alcoholic drinks, and opening a cash and carry wholesaler. The factors identified in the table are intended to illustrate the possible areas where synergy might occur (use of cash, stock, premises or in purchasing, etc.). This analysis attempts to assess the contribution of each of these factors towards the relative merits of each option. For example, the fact that the retailer has a good name in the locality should reduce the launch cost of new shops compared with a totally unknown retailer setting up in the area. The detailed assessment of how much these savings might be would then evolve from a consideration of the advertising and promotional campaign details (at a later stage).

The idea of synergy is particularly helpful if it is related to previous discussions about the value chain. In that sense synergy is a measure of the benefits which can accrue through pursuing linkages between the value chains of two separate activities or businesses. It is often used as an explanation as to why a takeover might 'make sense' (see Illustration 7.4). So the grocery retailer hopes to gain cost advantage through the increased buying power which would result in the multiple chain strategy. In contrast, strategy 2 (moving into alcoholic drinks) would seek competitive advantage through differentiation from competitors. Often synergy results from more intangible sources when two or more value chains are linked. For example, in many acquisitions the predator company would attempt to impose a tried and tested management recipe in order to transform the financial performance of the companies acquired.

In some industries companies are forced to seek synergy because their competitors are doing so. The changing face of the UK financial services industry in the late 1980s was an example. In particular, building societies extended into many related services such as insurance, estate agencies, equity plans, etc. following a change in legislation in late 1986.

Readers should note that the theoretical benefits of synergy are often difficult to accrue in practice – particularly following mergers or acquisitions as discussed in Chapter 6,[17] and shown in Illustration 7.5.

ILLUSTRATION 7.4

Synergy

During takeover bids synergy is often presented as the major reason why the takeover could 'make sense'.

In 1986 the Imperial Group fought to take over United Biscuits (prior to their own takeover by Hanson Trust). The advertisement below shows how the synergy argument was used.

Consider these 500 words carefully.
Each one could be worth £12 million.

There are 500 words in this advertisement.

Each one is worth reading very, very carefully. Because they develop an argument which, when followed through to its logical conclusion, could lead the way to the formation of a new company with an annual turnover well over £6,000,000,000. (Half of which comes from related businesses.)

The two companies are United Biscuits and Imperial.

United Biscuits are front-runners in the food market and expanding fast in leisure.

Imperial are leaders in the food, leisure and tobacco markets. (See? Common ground already.)

By joining forces, our combined turnover, based on 1985 sales, will be well above £6 billion.

One and one is more than two.

From this point on, the words grow progressively more valuable.

If our combination stood only for a pooling of sales, our argument would be strong.

What makes it incontrovertible and so potentially fruitful is how those common resources could be exploited.

Imperial presently control over 6,000 pubs, restaurants and shops.

Ready markets for United Biscuits' crisps, snacks, confectionery, pizzas and burgers.

Simply by coming together, we could substantially increase our penetration into these outlets.

Two vans can't live as cheaply as one.

All those pubs and restaurants, as well as a nationwide network of tobacconists, need regular replenishment.

By bringing together our distribution and wholesale operations, we anticipate an impressive reduction in overheads.

Imperial's strong cash flow will provide a rich source of funds to invest back into our brands both at home and in the United States of America.

One of those brands is Pizzaland whose restaurant opening programme will be accelerated.

On the subject of overseas markets, United's growing presence in North America, Hong Kong, Japan and the Third World will open new doors for Imperial. Much as their world markets will be introduced to us.

Two frozen peas in a pod.

One of the fastest growing world markets is Frozen Foods.

The home market as much as the catering market.

Imperial, with Ross and Youngs, are strong in supermarkets, We're both growing fast in the catering trade.

Together, we can consolidate our successes and create a giant bigger than the jolly green one.

Even more resourceful.

As you read this, there's a team of people at United Biscuits working hard on new product development. Our record testifies to their successes in the past.

Round the corner, at Imperial, another team is busy on their new product development.

It's easy to imagine how the pooling of those resources could benefit both companies.

Ask the other half.

It's not just United who want Imperial.

It's Imperial who want United.

Both of us know just how well suited we are to each other.

Just how powerful a force we can be together.

However many words others may give you, in the long term they just can't add up to the same value.

And in the long run, it's not words that count.

But the value behind them.

United Imperial

THE LONGER YOU LOOK AT IT, THE MORE IT MAKES SENSE.

7.3.2 Strategy and performance: research evidence

The analyses in the previous section have attempted to establish a strategic logic or rationale which will explain why some strategies might be more suitable than others. An additional approach to assessing the suitability of options is to review the research evidence which is available on the relationship between the choice of strategy and the performance of organisations. In this context the continuing work of the Strategic Planning Institute (SPI) through its PIMS databank is important. This databank contains the experiences of some three thousand businesses (both products and services). These are documented in terms of the actions taken by the business (i.e. choice of strategic options), the nature of the market and competitive environment and the financial results.[18] Some of the more important PIMS findings, together with other research, will be summarised in this section, for further information readers should follow up the references. There have also been other studies which have sought to clarify the relationship between choice of strategy and organisational performance and they will be reviewed too.

THE IMPORTANCE OF MARKET SHARE

In the discussion of the strategic environment in Chapter 3 the strategic importance of 'market power' was introduced. In understanding the likely impact of the environment on any one organisation this market power is a crucial factor to understand. Likewise when looking at the choices open to organisations in the future the extent to which they are likely to increase or decrease this market power needs careful assessment.

Much of the research in this area has used market share as a measure of market power and there is much evidence that market share and profitability are linked. The Boston Consulting Group argue this on the basis of the experience curve and the superior cost structure of market leaders (see Chapter 4) and this assertion is also supported by the findings of the PIMS study, as shown in Figure 7.6. Return on investment rises steadily in line with market share.[19]

The PIMS researchers suggest a number of main reasons why market share and ROI should be linked.[20] They are largely concerned with the cost benefits which market share brings. The purchase to sales ratio differences between high and low market share firms are startling – high market share companies seem to be able to buy more competitively or produce components economically 'in-house'. Also some economies of scale benefit firms with high market shares. For example, marketing costs tend to decline as a percentage of sales with increased share. The indications are also that high market share firms develop strategies of higher price/higher quality than low share competitors. This phenomenon may, in fact, be somewhat circular. High share firms tend to be more profitable, thus providing the cash resources for R&D to improve and differentiate products, thus enhancing their market position and also justifying higher prices which in turn increase profits. It must be remembered that high market share and size are not always the same. There are large firms which do not dominate the markets in which they operate; and there are small firms which dominate segments of markets.

ILLUSTRATION 7.5

Why predators may get indigestion

Acquisition needs to be properly planned to avoid post-takeover problems.

On past form, 1990 could turn out to be disaster year for many of the European companies which had joined the great American takeover stampede of 1986. Though some transatlantic takeovers had been undoubted successes – notably in the food and chemical industries – the nightmare that had come to haunt most predators was that they would join the long list of European companies with troublesome US subsidiaries.

Richard Hickinbotham, an analyst at London stockbrokers Hoare Govett, made no bones about it: 'The tradition is that British companies buying in the States don't know how to manage things, and generally uncover a can of worms'. Crocker Bank was an arch example: it was poorly vetted before takeover, and produced one nasty surprise after another until Midland Bank managed to knock it into shape, before selling it in 1985.

The prime half-dozen reasons for failure are:

1. Inadequate assessment of the strengths and weaknesses of a prey before the bid is made (one of Midland's many errors).
2. A similar lack of attention to the attractiveness or otherwise of the industry in which it operates.
3. Lack of consideration about whether the takeover price can really be recouped in additional future earnings.
4. Lack of clarity about whether one's intention is to move into technologies or products and markets which are related to one's existing core businesses.
5. Inadequate attention to how this affects the vital question of how far, and how, to integrate the new subsidiary into one's own organisation and culture.
6. This last point is linked with a host of other difficult decisions about the maintenance or replacement of existing managers, systems and ways of doing things.

None of these problems is peculiar to transatlantic takeovers; they also govern the success or failure of purely national acquisitions, whether the country in question is the US, Britain, Germany or anywhere else. These and other problems are so common that takeovers of all kinds have an average failure rate of about fifty per cent, according to most research studies, with unrelated acquisitions coming off especially badly.

If these pitfalls are difficult to avoid in one's own backyard, they are downright deadly at a distance of several thousand miles, in a culture and market that are far harder to understand than most foreign companies realise until they learn by bitter experience.

What is worse for transatlantic acquirers is the failure of many Europeans to realise that the US market is more regional than it looks; that distribution, service and advertising patterns tend to differ from Europe's; that American organisations are less collegiate than (most of) Europe's, with the chief executive often wielding overriding power; that most US subsidiaries will be difficult to control (witness Unilever's long-standing problems with Lever Brothers); and that ownership of less than 100% may therefore be ineffective.

The latter was part of Midland's problem with Crocker, as well as Shell's with Shell Oil. Both eventually bought full control. BP, which still owns only 55% of its troublesome Sohio subsidiary, had to mount a boardroom coup in 1986 in order to achieve managerial control.

Source: Abridged from *Financial Times*, 19 December 1986.

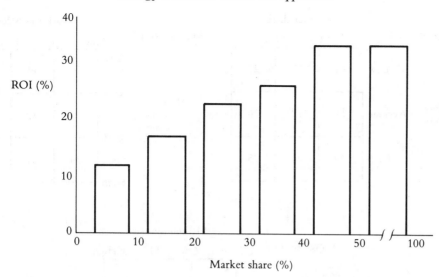

Figure 7.6 The relationship between market share and ROI. (From B.T. Gale and B. Branch, 'The dispute about high-share businesses', *Pimsletter*, No.19, The Strategic Planning Institute. Reprinted with permission of the SPI.)

CONSOLIDATION STRATEGIES

PIMS research findings provide a useful insight into the likely outcomes of pursuing a wide variety of strategies. Figure 7.7 summarises some of the findings relating to various types of consolidation strategy discussed in Chapter 6. For example, a common consolidation strategy is the upgrading of product or service quality. The evidence is that quality is of very real significance in the improvement of profit performance.[21] The best situation appears to be a combination of high share and high product quality, but even firms with low market shares demonstrate significantly higher profit performance if they have products of superior quality. (In this sense quality can be a partial substitute for market share in sustaining advantage.)

Figure 7.7(b) suggests that a reliance on increased marketing spending to consolidate an organisation's position in its markets does not appear in itself to be a satisfactory way of improving performance. Heavy marketing expenditure (as a percentage of sales) may actually damage ROI for firms with low market shares. This does, of course, pose a problem for a firm that is trying to improve or maintain its standing within its existing product/market: trying to do so by increasing marketing expenditure is likely to result in reduced profitability: in other words, attempting to 'buy market share' is unlikely to be successful.

The combined effect of marketing expenditure and product quality have also been studied. High marketing expenditure is not a substitute for quality:[22] indeed it appears that high marketing expenditure damages ROI particularly when quality is low (Figure 7.7(c)). It must be concluded that simply gearing up marketing expenditure as a means of consolidating a company's position is not sufficient.

Another common consolidation strategy is to seek improved productivity through capital investment – for example by the mechanisation of routine tasks. This has become so much a part of accepted 'management wisdom' that it might come as

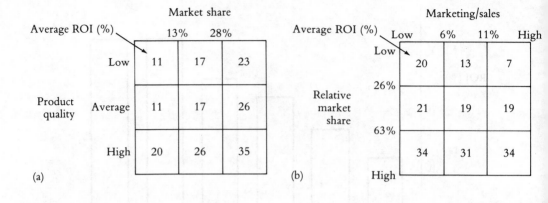

(a)

(b)

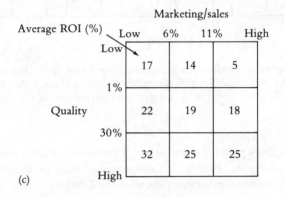

(c)

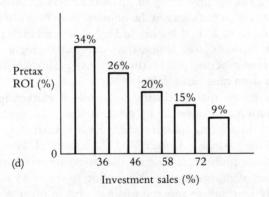

(d)

N.b. 'Investment' includes both working
capital and fixed capital at net book value.
The figures are four-year averages.

Figure 7.7 Consolidation strategies: PIMS findings. (a) Quality, market share and
return on investment (from R.D. Buzzell, 'Product quality', *Pimsletter*, No.4, SPI, 1984).
(b) Heavy marketing is not profitable for low share business (from SPI, A Program of
..., 1977). (c) High marketing expenditures hurt profits especially when quality is low
(from SPI, *A Program of* ..., 1977). (d) Investment intensity and ROI (from S. Schoeffler,
'The unprofitability of "modern" technology and what to do about it', *Pimsletter*, No.2,
SPI, 1980). All parts reprinted with permission of the Strategic Planning Institute.

something of a shock to learn that there is evidence to suggest that increased capital intensity can damage return on investment[23] as shown in Figure 7.7(d). The reasons for this are important to understand. Managers may expect reduced costs through mechanisation and reduced labour input, but assume that revenue will remain constant or rise. However, in capital intensive industries, companies are especially keen to ensure that capacity is fully loaded and may cut prices to keep volume, thus actually reducing overall margins; or undertake uneconomic production runs to keep customers happy; or even raise marketing expenditure to wrestle volume from competition. Since high capital investment is also a barrier to exit those suffering from low margins are reluctant to get out so they continue to battle on and make the situation worse. Indeed, raising capital intensity in an attempt to improve profit returns is most likely to be successful for companies who already have a strong position in the market, are unlikely to meet fierce price competition, and who are able to make real reductions in layout and production costs.[24] It is for some of these reasons that many organisations have preferred subcontracting as a means of improving productivity.

RELATED DEVELOPMENTS

Figure 7.8 summarises some PIMS findings relating to other types of related development. It has been argued in the previous section that high market share is very often of strategic advantage to organisations. However, the process of building market share (*market penetration*) is not without its costs[25] as seen in Figure 7.8(a). Short term profits are likely to be sacrificed, particularly when trying to build share from a low base. Similarly *product development* can bring uncomfortable dilemmas to many organisations.[26] New products/services may be absolutely vital to the organisation's future. The problem is that this may prove expensive and unprofitable (particularly in the short run). This is why a balanced portfolio of products is important. *Cash cows* can fund these developments, and avoid unnecessarily increasing the investment intensity of the company. Product development may require a commitment to high levels of spending on R&D. Figure 7.8(b) shows that whilst high market share companies may benefit in profit terms from relatively high levels of R&D expenditure, companies in a weak market position with high expenditure may suffer badly.

It is evidence of this type which has convinced many organisations to look seriously at *technology transfer* or acquisition of smaller companies as alternative to their own R&D efforts. Interestingly enough the success of many Japanese companies since the late 1950s has been built on such an approach.

Figure 7.8(c) also confirms that profitability can be depressed by over-rapid rates of new product introductions as organisations debug production, train sales people, educate customers and establish new channels.

DIVERSIFICATION AND PERFORMANCE

There has been a number of attempts to assess the extent to which diversification is related to performance. Table 7.3 shows two of these studies from the USA[27] and UK[28] as indicative of the findings. Readers are encouraged to follow up the references[29] for a full review of the range of research findings on this topic. However,

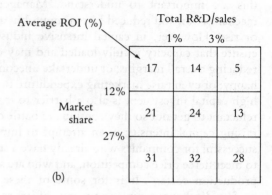

Cash flow % investment

Percentage change in market share

Beginning market share	−2 Steady	+2 Gain
Low	0	−4
12%	7	2
27%	10	7
High		

(a)

Average ROI (%)

Total R&D/sales

Market share	1%		3%
	17	14	5
12%	21	24	13
27%	31	32	28

(b)

The figures in the boxes show the cash flow generated as a percentage of the investment which has been made. This is greatest when a company already has a high market share which it is consolidating (10%) and lowest where the investment has been used to gain market share from a low starting position (−4%).

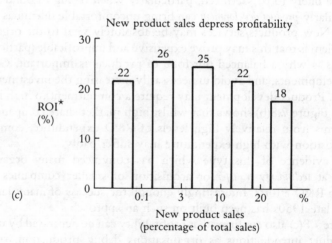

New product sales depress profitability

(c)

ROI* (%)

New product sales (percentage of total sales)	ROI* (%)
0.1	22
3	26
10	25
20	22
%	18

*Pretax and before financial charges.

Figure 7.8 Other related strategies: PIMS findings. (a) The cost of growth in market share (from V. Kijewski, 'Market-share strategy: beliefs v actions', *Pimsletter*, No. 9, SPI, 1983). (b) R&D expenditure, market share and ROI (from S. Schoeffler, 'Market position: build, hold or harvest?', *Pimsletter*, No.3, 1984). (c) New-product sales depress profitability (from R. Morrison and D. Tavel, 'New products and market position', *Pimsletter*, No.28, SPI, 1982). All parts reprinted with permission of the Strategic Planning Institute.

some of the most important conclusions of research findings to date are:

- That more diversified businesses grow faster and that growth tends to be greatest when diversification is of an unrelated nature.
- That related diversifications tend to prove more profitable than unrelated. This may not be due to the inherent superiority of related strategies but may be due to the difficulties of comprehending and coping with the more complex requirements of an unrelated strategy.
- Although a major justification for diversifications is to 'add value' through new linkages between value chains of the separate activities this usually proves to be a disappointment to companies. In other words, the practicalities of achieving these theoretical benefits often elude companies.

Table 7.3 Financial consequences of product strategies.
(a) USA 1960–1969†. (b) UK 1970–1980‡.

(a)

	Company product strategy*			
	Single product	Dominant product	Related products	Unrelated products
Sales growth (% p.a.)	7.2	8.0	9.1	14.2
Earnings growth (% p.a.)	4.8	8.0	9.4	13.9
Earnings growth per share (% p.a.)	3.9	6.0	7.6	7.9
P/E	14.6	15.7	19.2	15.8
Return on investment (%)	10.8	9.6	11.5	9.5
Return on equity (%)	13.2	11.6	13.6	11.9

(b)

	Company product strategy*			
	Single product	Dominant product	Related products	Unrelated products
Sales growth (% p.a.)	1.0	1.5	1.3	2.1
Profit growth before interest and tax (% p.a.)	0.09	0.75	0.67	1.31
Share growth (capital value % p.a.)	− 3.65	− 3.54	− 3.58	− 3.44
Return on capital employed (%)	18.1	19.1	16.9	16.7

*These product groups describe strategies which are progressively more diversified. So for example, the 'dominant product' situation refers to companies which have 70% or more of their sales in one product area and 'related' to companies with less than 70% in one product area. Highest profit returns were found for related strategies where diversification remained associated with core skills of the business (termed 'related constrained').

† From Richard P. Rumelt, *Strategy, Structure and Economic Performance*, Table 3-1, p.91, Boston, Mass.: Division of Research, Harvard Business School, 1974. Used with permission.

‡ R. Reed and G Luffman (see reference 28).

● It is often argued that unrelated diversification can be an important means of spreading the investment risk of shareholders. However, research evidence so far does not show this to be a significant benefit in practice.

Care needs to be taken in interpreting many of these research findings. For example the data bases are not necessarily directly comparable and often come from different countries and different times. For example in Table 7.3 it is possible that the results reflect the trading conditions of the time. Related diversification might be more suited to firms when there are opportunities for expansion in a growing economy. On the other hand, in times of little or no economic growth, a strategy of concentration on mainline products rather than the spreading of interests might make more sense. The balance of evidence does warn against unconstrained diversification.[29] As with product development, it is one thing to show that diversified companies can be profitable but it also has to be pointed out that the process of diversification can be very difficult and costly. A firm that follows a strategy of launching new businesses is likely to suffer a major drain on its cash resources: the average length of time it takes to move into profit is eight years and severe losses can be expected for four years.

7.3.3 Cultural fit

Although establishing the strategic logic of options is very valuable, it is also important to review those options within the political and cultural realities of the organisation. This section is concerned with how options might be assessed in terms of their *cultural fit*. In other words the extent to which particular types of strategy might be more or less assimilated by an organisation. This is not to suggest that the culture of an organisation should have pre-eminence in determining strategy. Indeed, one of the key roles of the leadership of organisations is to shape and change culture to better fit preferred strategies.

Perhaps these issues are best understood in terms of the previous discussions (Chapters 2 and 5) about the *cultural web* of an organisation and how it legitimises and sustains the *recipe* of the organisation. It is clear that, on the whole, organisations will seek out strategies which can be delivered without unduly challenging the recipe – managers find such strategies easiest to comprehend and pursue. However, the key judgement is whether or not such strategies are suitable in the face of the organisation's current situation – particularly if significant environmental change has occurred. The analyses outlined in the previous sections will give strong indications of whether or not the organisation's recipe does require some fundamental change if the organisation is to survive and prosper.

Whether recipe change is required or not, the assessment of strategic options in terms of cultural fit is valuable. If the organisation is developing within the current recipe then these analyses help to identify those strategies which would be most easily assimilated. In contrast, if the recipe will need to change then the analyses help in establishing which ways culture will need to adapt to embrace new types of strategy. This will be valuable analysis when planning implementation (see Chapter 11).

One of the key determinants on how culture might influence strategic choice is, again, the stage that an organisation is currently at in its lifecycle. Schein[30] provides a valuable discussion of this relationship between lifecycle, culture and strategy which

Table 7.4 Culture, the lifecycle and strategic choices.

Lifecycle stage	Key cultural features	Implications to strategic choice
1. Embryonic	1. Cohesive culture 2. Founders dominant 3. Outside help not valued	1. Try to repeat successes 2. Related developments favoured
2. Growth	1. Cultural cohesion less 2. Mismatched and tensions arise	1. Diversification often possible 2. Vulnerability to takeover 3. Structural change needed for new developments 4. New developments need protection
3. Maturity	1. Culture institutionalised 2. Culture breeds inertia 3. Strategic logic may be rejected	1. Related developments favoured 2. Incrementalism favoured
4. Decline	1. Culture becomes a defence	1. Readjustment necessary but difficult 2. Divestment may prove necessary

will be summarised here, and can be usefully linked to the lifecycle models discussed in Section 7.3.1 above. A combination of these two perspectives on different stages in the lifecycle can prove valuable in establishing options which fit both the strategic logic and the cultural situation. The key points of the ensuing discussion are summarised in Table 7.4.

EMBRYONIC STAGE

The culture of an organisation in its embryonic stage is shaped by the founders. Once the organisation survives, these personal beliefs become strongly embedded in the organisation and shape the types of development which subsequently occur. In other words, those core beliefs hold the organisation together and become a key part of its distinctive competence. Organisations will typically seek out developments which fit this culture. So, for example, an organisation which has been founded to exploit a particular technological expertise will tend to seek further developments which fit this self-image of a technology-driven organisation. They will favour product or process development when often the economic logic would suggest they would be better advised to seek additional markets to exploit their current assets. Not only do they not possess these 'marketing' skills, they do not see the organisation in that way – they are excited by the technology and this pervades the way in which the organisation is managed and the strategic choices it makes.

The strength and cohesion of culture in embryonic organisations has also frustrated the attempts of agencies established to help and advise small businesses on their development. The internal culture may reject the idea of outside help even when it might make economic sense.

GROWTH

The growth phase of organisations involves a very large variety of cultural changes in different circumstances. However, there are some commonly occurring situations which illustrate how cultural developments dictate strategic choice.

- The cohesiveness of culture seen in the embryonic stage tends to dissipate (to a greater or lesser degree) into subcultures, each of which may favour different kinds of development. It is at this stage, therefore, that the historical base of the company may be less of a guide to the choices that may be made. Indeed, it may well be that adequate resources are available to pursue more than one strategy – hence some degree of diversification may be sanctioned in order to keep the peace.
- The growth phase also marks the introduction of significant numbers of new people into the organisation and the emergence of a middle management. This, in turn, can reinforce the diversity of expectations within the organisation and the diffusion of a single dominant culture and preference for one type of strategy.
- Some organisations in growing markets face uncomfortable dilemmas. The strategic logic may dictate that they should follow the natural growth in the market or risk

---

ILLUSTRATION 7.6

Chevron Foods Ltd

The owner of a small company faces a conflict between personal preferences and competitive threats.

A small business, two years old in 1977, had been successfully and profitably established importing fruit juice and a dispensing system from the USA and marketing it to hotels, mainly in London. The business had been run as a marketing-only operation, relying on subcontract distribution of juice and servicing of the dispensers. Because the operation was limited to London, direct personal control was retained by the owner of all operations. However, by the end of 1977, he faced a dilemma.

> I have no particular desire to create a multi-million pound company, nor go for growth for its own sake. I suppose that the main reason I'm in business is because I enjoy what I'm doing and it makes me quite a nice living.
>
> But I am concerned about some things. My objective is to keep a slim operation: I don't like the idea of lots of levels of management and increasing overheads; and some of the developments could point that way. For instance, I just cannot get some business simply because we're not national.
>
> Trust House Forte and British Transport, two of the largest hotel groups, require a national service – and I can't give it. If I do, what will it do to my ideas of a slim operation? And if I don't – well, they have to get juice from someone and although no one else is distributing post-mix now, that is not to say someone won't in the future.

On the one hand was the objective of remaining slim, arising from personal values concerned with ownership and control. On the other was the owner's perception of the threat of competition if he did not expand geographically.

By 1979 the owner had decided that, despite his personal inclinations to limit growth, it was essential to develop the geographical coverage of the business. If he did not, the chances of competitors entering the market were too high, and could have resulted in a threat to the survival of the company he had established.

Source: 'Chevron Foods Ltd', case study by G. Johnson (1980). Available from the Case Study Clearing House of GB, Cranfield.

being uncompetitive once growth starts to ease. However, growth may challenge many of the other beliefs of the organisation like the desire to maintain a 'family' atmosphere and approach (as seen in Illustration 7.6).

- Many organisations, and particularly the public services, decide that development strategies requiring growth are difficult to foster and deliver within the confines of a predominantly low-risk bureaucratic culture. Therefore, they either reject such developments *or* decide to develop them in a protected way. This issue will receive fuller discussion in Chapter 11.

MATURITY

By the time that organisations reach maturity their culture tends to have been institutionalised to the extent that people tend not to be aware of it or even find it difficult to conceptualise culture as a meaningful concept. It is only when some crisis threatens the organisation that the strength of the culture becomes apparent (for example, the threatened takeover of Pilkington by BTR in 1986).

As a general rule, mature organisations are likely to favour developments which minimise change and are evolutionary from the current situation. This, of course, is why incremental (as against global) change is so commonly found within organisations. However, whereas incremental developments may be easier from the cultural point of view they may well prove wholly inadequate if environmental circumstances are deteriorating rapidly as mentioned above.

DECLINE

To a large extent the issues of cultural fit during decline are a natural extension of those faced during maturity. A cohesive culture may be seen as a key defence against a hostile environment. Organisations face very difficult decisions concerning retrenchment, divestment and withdrawal from products/markets which are ingrained in the culture of the organisation. Sometimes this adjustment in strategies can take many years particularly when the external image of the organisation reinforces this dominant internal situation. Woolworth is an extensively quoted example of this particular strategic problem as previously seen in Illustration 5.2. In some situations the difficulties of adjustment can be so great that the organisation's owners choose to sell out to another organisation who may then be able to instigate radical changes (the history of the UK newspaper publishing industry is littered with ownership changes of this kind).

7.4 SUMMARY

This chapter has been concerned with reviewing ways in which the *suitability* of various strategic options might be analysed. This is an important process since it requires managers to be explicit as to the underlying *rationale* behind particular strategies and to try to understand why those strategies might succeed or fail. Rather than provide a single framework for an analysis of suitability it has been suggested that a variety of different perspectives is more helpful. This relates to the central theme of this book, namely that strategic development within organisations is subject to a variety of different influences which, for convenience, have been grouped under three headings – the environment, resources, and expectations/culture.

The extent to which different types of strategy may suit an organisation's circumstances have been reviewed in relation to those various factors. It has been seen that one common thread is the stage of an organisation in its lifecycle which affects both the strategic logic of various options and the cultural climate in which strategic developments are taking place.

The next chapter considers strategic evaluation at a more detailed level where assessments concerning the feasibility and acceptability of *specific* strategies need to be sharpened up.

REFERENCES

1. See Chapter 4 for a discussion of SWOT analysis.

2. The idea of consistency of strategy was used by S. Tilles, 'How to evaluate corporate strategy', *Harvard Business Review*, July/Aug., 1963, to describe 'the efficiency of policies with respect to the environment'. He also referred to the extent to which strategy was appropriate in terms of resources available. These ideas of consistency and appropriateness are encapsulated in the term 'suitability' used in this book.

3. The term 'feasibility' has much the same meaning as Tilles' (reference 2) criterion of 'workability', i.e. is there a likelihood that the strategy can be made to work?

4. This idea that establishing the underlying rationale is an important preliminary analysis is similar to Rumelt's idea of the 'strategic frame' discussed in Chapter 2. Rumelt describes this step as follows: 'Before one can decide whether or not a given strategy will work, some indication that the right issues are being worked on is needed'. See 'Evaluation of strategy: theory and models', in D. E. Schendel and C. W. Hofer (eds), *Strategic Management*, Little Brown, 1979.

5. For example, C. W. Hofer and D. Schendel, *Strategy Formulation: Analytical concepts*, West, 1978, structure their chapters around this distinction between 'corporate level' and 'business level' strategies.

6. R. Gruber and M. Mohr, 'Strategic management for multi-program non-profit organisa-tions', *California Management Review*, Spring, 1982.

7. Hofer and Schendel (reference 5) provide a good review of portfolio matrices. Also 'The strategic environments matrix – BCG's new tool', *Financial Times*, 20 Nov., 1981.

8. Reservations about the use of the Boston Consulting Group's concepts and proposals are to be found in S. Slatter, 'Common Pitfalls in Using the BCG Product Portfolio Matrix', *London Business School Journal*, Winter, 1980.

9. The techniques built around the lifecycle concept described in this chapter have been developed and explained by the consultants Arthur D. Little in a series of booklets, the first of which was *A System of Managing Diversity* by R. V. L. Wright, published in 1974 by Arthur D. Little.

10. Michael Porter, *Competitive Advantage*, chapters 14 and 15, Free Press, 1985, reviews the

strategies appropriate to leaders and followers at different stages of an industry's development.

11. Michael Porter, *Competitive Strategy*, chapter 11, Free Press, 1980, discusses the special problems associated with the onset of industry maturity.

12. S. Segal-Horn, *Strategic Issues in the Globalisation of Service Industries*, EIASM Workshop, Brussels, May, 1987.

13. See reference 10 for a discussion of how followers in an industry might compete through differentiation.

14. Y. Doz, *Strategic Management in Multinational Companies*, p. 155, Pergamon, 1986.

15. Porter (reference 11, chapter 12) reviews strategies for declining industries.

16. See I. Ansoff, *Implanting Strategic Management*, pp. 80–4, Prentice Hall, 1984, for a discussion of synergy.

17. See A. van de Vliet and D. Isaac, 'The mayhem in mergers', *Management Today*, Feb., 1986, and R. Heller, 'The agonies of agglomeration', *Management Today*, Feb., 1986.

18. The PIMS data are collected from organisations which subscribe to the services offered by the Strategic Planning Institute. The data shown here are aggregate data, but subscribing organisations are able to access data more specific to their industry sector and use them to analyse their performance relative to that industry sector.

19. These data are further discussed in B. T. Gale, 'Planning for profit', *Planning Review*, Jan., 1978.

20. See R. D. Buzzell, B. Gale and R. Sutton, 'Market share: a key to profitability', *Harvard Business Review*, Jan./Feb., 1975.

21. This is discussed in one of the major articles describing the PIMS findings: S. Schoeffler, R. D. Buzzell and D. F. Heany, 'Impact of strategic planning on profit performance', *Harvard Business Review*, Mar./Apr., 1974.

22. See reference 21.

23. For a more thorough discussion of the impact on profit performance of capital intensity see S. Schoeffler, 'Capital-intensive technology-vs-ROI: a strategic assessment', *Management Review*, Sept., 1978, and S. Schoeffler, 'The unprofitability of modern technology', *Pimsletter*, No. 2., 1984.

24. This is dealt with in another article dealing with the issue of capital intensity, B. T. Gale, 'Can more capital buy higher productivity', *Harvard Business Review*, July/Aug., 1980. Also *Make Ready for Success*, NEDO, 1981 – a report on the UK printing industry between 1974 and 1981 – draws similar conclusions.

25. V. Kijewski, 'Market share strategy: beliefs vs actions', *Pimsletter*, No. 9, 1983.

26. S. Schoeffler, 'Market position: build, hold or harvest? *Pimsletter*, No. 3, 1984, and R. Morrison and D. Tavel, 'New products and market position', *Pimsletter*, No. 28, 1982.

27. These findings are from the work of R. Rumelt, *Strategy, Structure and Economic Performance*, Harvard Press, 1974, also summarised in an article by Bruce Scott entitled 'The industrial state: old myths and new realities', *Harvard Business Review*, Mar., 1973. Readers should be careful about drawing fine distinctions between Rumelt's categories since the sample size of one hundred is small and such distinctions would not be statistically significant.

28. R. Reed and G. Luffman, 'Diversification the growing confusion', *Strategic Management Journal*, 1986. Their results were derived from inflation adjusted data for British industry over the period 1970 to 1980. The top 1,000 UK companies were used to produce a sample of 349 who had not changed their product market base over the ten years. The sample included manufacturing and service companies. Significant deletions from the top 100 included non-British companies, those subject to takeover or liquidation during the period, financial institutions, non-public companies and those which government owned or controlled.

29. For readers who wish to examine the issue of diversification more fully, refer to:
    - H. K. Christensen and C. A. Montgomery, 'Corporate economic performance: diversification strategy versus market structure', *Strategic Management Journal*, **2**, 1981.
    - R. A. Bettis, 'Performance differences in related and unrelated diversified firms', *Strategic Management Journal*, **2**, 1981.
    - R. P. Rumelt, 'Diversification strategy and profitability', *Strategic Management Journal*, **3**, 1982.
    - C. A. Montgomery, 'Product – market diversification and market power', *Strategic Management Journal*, **6**, 1985.
    - C. K. Prahalad and R. Bettis, 'The dominant logic: a new linkage between diversity and performance', *Strategic Management Journal*, **7**, 1986.

30. E. Schein, *Organization Culture and Leadership*, Jossey Bass, 1985.

Recommended key readings

- In Part III of *Competitive Strategy* (Free Press/Collier Macmillan, 1980) Michael Porter reviews the rationale behind generic competitive strategies in different industry environments.

- C. W. Hofer and D. Schendel, *Strategy Formulation: Analytical concepts*, West, 1978, provides a useful review of portfolio analyses in chapter 4.

- The work of the PIMS project and many of the findings are summarised in R. D. Buzzell and B. T. Gale, *The PIMS Principles: Linking strategy to performance*, Macmillan, 1987.

- E. Schein, *Organization Culture and Leadership*, Jossey Bass, 1985, relates culture, lifecycle, and strategic choices.

Chapter 8

STRATEGY EVALUATION
TECHNIQUES

8.1 INTRODUCTION

The previous chapter introduced evaluation criteria (suitability, feasibility and accept-ability) and considered ways in which the suitability of particular types of strategy might be established in terms of their strategic logic, the cultural fit with the organisation and the research evidence available linking the choice of strategy to organisational performance.

This chapter is concerned with how specific options can be evaluated against the background of discussion in chapter 7, and considers the following:

- The *screening* of options prior to more detailed analyses of specific strategies.
- Methods of assessing the acceptability and feasibility of specific options against different measures:
  (i) The *return* which a strategy is expected to produce for the costs which it would incur.
  (ii) The degree of *risk* which a strategy would imply.
  (iii) The extent to which the strategy appears *feasible*.
- A critical review of how organisations *select* future strategies.

Readers are referred back to Figure 7.1 as a reminder of how these various aspects of evaluation relate to each other.

8.2 SCREENING OPTIONS

One of the benefits which should emerge from the assessments of suitability discussed in Chapter 7 is an understanding of the underlying *rationale* behind particular types of strategy. However, within these broad types there are likely to be different specific strategies which an organisation could follow, and the process of evaluation normally requires a narrowing down of these various options before a detailed assessment can be undertaken. This is not to suggest that options eliminated at this stage will not be given further consideration later. This section begins by reviewing the basis on which specific strategies can be assessed – whether options are to be judged on an absolute basis, against each other, or against the 'do nothing' situation (introduced in Chapter 6).

The section then outlines three contrasting approaches to the screening of options:

1. *Scoring* methods which rank options against a set of predetermined factors concerning the organisation's strategic situation. The extent to which specific options fit these criteria determines their position in this 'league table'.
2. *Decision trees* which also assess specific options against a list of key strategic factors. However, options are ranked by progressively eliminating others.
3. *Scenarios* which attempt to match specific options with a range of possible future outcomes and are particularly useful where a high degree of uncertainty exists (say in the environment as discussed in Chapter 3). Scenarios provide a means of keeping many more options under consideration.

8.2.1 Bases for comparison

Many of the methods of evaluation which follow are only of use if the analysis of any given strategy has some appropriate basis for comparison. Chapter 4 has already discussed the importance of establishing an appropriate basis for comparison (in assessing strategic capability).

There are problems in only using absolute measures or industry norms as bases for comparison. They assume that options are independent of each other: and more importantly, they do not address themselves to a central problem in strategic evaluation, namely the need to identify the incentive to change from the present strategy to a different strategy. Since strategy evaluation is concerned with assessing whether or not companies should change their present activities it is often helpful to use the 'do nothing' situation as a basis for comparison since this helps assess the company's incentive to change from present strategies. The 'do nothing' situation is the likely

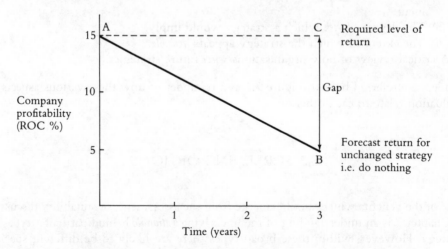

The company is currently operating at 15% return on capital and wishes to maintain that level. Increased competition, escalating labour costs and deteriorating machinery underlie the forecast of declining profitability unless current strategies are revised. BC represents the gap which is likely to exist in the three years' time between required performance and actual performance. The gap needs to be 'filled' by new strategies.

Figure 8.1 Gap analysis.

ILLUSTRATION 8.1

Ageing and public expenditure

Gap analysis is helpful in the development of public sector policies and spending plans.

One of the difficulties of public sector policy making is the long term nature of many commitments often supported by mandatory legal obligations to provide particular services. For this reason it is essential to predict the likely level of demand for the various public services many years ahead in order to establish the strategic implications to policy making and budgeting.

Planning is guided by an assessment of the *gap* which is likely to exist between current provision and expected future demands. These *gaps* vary by individual services and from one situation (e.g. country) to another.

One of the most important underlying trends which influences demand for public services is the age structure of a country's population. Analyses have predicted that by the year 2025 the ratio of government spending to Gross Domestic Product (GDP) will increase significantly in almost every advanced industrial country. This is attributed to the fact that people are living longer and producing fewer children, and the resultant growing costs of medical care and pensions are outstripping any possible declines in education costs.

Also, the pool of productive workers available to support the growing ranks of retired and elderly people will shrink, significantly raising the tax burden necessary to support social programmes.

Comparisons between different countries are quite startling in terms of the gap which needs to be bridged. For example, in Canada the social spending is likely to fall as a percentage of GDP until 2010 and then show a modest rise. In the United Kingdom a slow but steady rise is expected, accelerating beyond 2010 (post-war 'bulge' retirements). By 2025 the impact of demographic change on the Japanese economy is likely to be the most extreme. This reflects the lateness and rapidity with which Japan began the demographic transition to a lower fertility rate and a higher life expectancy. Social spending is predicted to increase some 80% (as a percentage of GDP) by 2025.

The policy implications in terms of bridging these gaps are significant. For example, the possible need to contain the real increase in per capita benefits; to limit the growth in medical costs; the possibility of higher tax rates; the desirability of raising savings and investment rates.

This policy debate at national level clearly has to be paralleled at local/regional level – where the picture is further complicated by population movements and major differences from the average countrywide demography. Equally the planning taking place in individual service departments will be strongly influenced by this changing population structure and policy priorities.

Source: 'Aging and social expenditure in the major industrial countries 1980–2025', IMF Occasional Paper, no. 47, 1986.

outcome if the organisation were to continue with current strategies disregarding any changes occurring in the environment or resource position of the company. The easiest way to incorporate this situation into an evaluation is by including it as a strategy option to be evaluated alongside others, as will be seen in the later discussions. However, it must be remembered that 'do nothing' is not an option *per se* – it merely provides a valuable base line against which to assess the incentive to change.

A useful technique which incorporates this approach is *gap analysis*[1] which can be used to identify the extent to which existing strategies will fail to meet the performance objectives in the future.

Figure 8.1 outlines the analysis for a single product/single market situation. Of course, this is a highly simplified example and readers must bear in mind that like any other forecasting process, gap analysis can be difficult and time consuming. In addition, it is usually necessary to apply measures other than profitability. Some of these may be easily quantifiable such as productivity or volume of sales, whereas others may be more subjective but nonetheless very important, such as levels of quality or service.

Gap analysis is also used extensively in public sector planning, although in a somewhat different way. Here the strategic problem is often concerned with whether the future demands on a public service are likely to change to such an extent that the current resource provision will prove wholly inadequate. This is particularly important when considering the statutory obligations of many public services such as hospitals, education or social services. Demographic information is often of central importance in attempting to assess the likely gaps in provision as can be seen from Illustration 8.1.

8.2.2 Scoring methods

Scoring methods are a systematic way of analysing *specific* options for their suitability or fit with the picture gained from the strategic analysis.

1. *Ranking* is the simplest type of scoring method where each option is assessed against a number of key factors which the strategic analysis identified in the organisation's environment, resources, and culture. Illustration 8.2 is an example of how such a ranking might be performed. One of the major benefits of ranking is that it helps the analyst to think through mismatches between a company's present position and the implications of the various strategic options. This is a useful preliminary step for a more detailed consideration. For example, one mismatch might be the lack of adequate production facilities to meet the output implied by a strategy. This would identify the need to assess the feasibility of a capital investment programme to bridge this gap using some of the techniques discussed below. More sophisticated approaches to ranking[2] assign weightings to each factor in recognition that some will be of more importance in that evaluation than others. The method can also be combined with sensitivity analysis (see below) to test out the likely impact on the company if the assumptions about each factor should change.

2. Chapter 4 discussed how the analysis of organisational resources in relation to the concept of the value chain could yield a picture of the organisation's *distinctive competence* and identify those value activities which are crucial to particular strategies. Such an analysis, if extended into the future, provides a means of scoring a strategy in resource terms as shown in Table 8.1. This is referred to as *resource deployment analysis*.

ILLUSTRATION 8.2

Ranking options – an example, Chevron Foods Ltd

Chevron Foods began trading in 1976 and grew rapidly in its first two years of operation to an annual turnover of about £0.5m by 1978. This small private company imported orange juice under licence from Florida and distributed the frozen juice to hotels in the UK together with a dispensing system which was installed and serviced free of charge. The key to the company's successful growth lay in this system which allowed hotels to serve high quality juice at the right temperature very quickly and efficiently during periods of high demand (breakfast). The company's sales had been largely confined to the larger hotels in the London area (with the exception of national chains which required a national service). The distribution of juice and installation/servicing of dispensers were subcontracted to independent operations.

In 1978 the company needed to decide to which of the many development alternatives they should give more detailed consideration, and a preliminary ranking of alternatives against a number of strategic factors were made (shown in the table).

Options	Desire for small company	Need to control quality of service	Dependency on supplier – licence – credit	Threat of competition	Need for 'big' outlets ('To 'pay' for cost of installation)	Need for high margins	Ranking
1. Do nothing (i.e. current strategy	✓	✓	Supplier wants growth(X)	X	✓	✓	C
2. Seek new suppliers	✓	✓	X	X	X	?	C
3. More customers of same type (in London)	X	✓	✓	Already large market share(X)	Best outlet already serviced(X)	✓	A
4. Expand nationally (in hotels)	X	Could lose X control	✓	✓	✓	✓	A
5. Expand product range (e.g. other juices)	✓	X	✓	X	X	✓	B
6. Seek new outlets (restaurants)	X	X	✓	May spread effort too widely(?)	Few large enough(X)	✓	A
7. Seek new outlets (hospitals)	X	X	✓	X	✓	X	B
8. Diversify (frozen foods)	?	X	X	X	X	?	B
9. Take over distribution and/or servicing	X	✓	?	X	X	?	C

✓ = Favourable influence   X = Unfavourable influence   ? = Uncertain or irrelevant
A = Appear most suitable   B = Moderately suitable   C = Appear least suitable

The ranking process is used to group the various options into three categories (A, B, C) in relation to their suitability. It should be noted that each strategic factor may not carry the same weight or importance: the need for growth to counter competition was in fact of overriding importance, so options 4 and 6 were identified as most suitable despite their lack of fit with other factors.

Source: 'Chevron Foods Ltd', case study by G. Johnson (1980). Available from the Case Study Clearing House of GB, Cranfield.

Table 8.1 Resource deployment analysis.

(a) Key resource areas	(b) Present company situation	Resource implications (c)		
		Strategy A (extend product range)	Strategy B (extend home market)	Strategy C (sell overseas)
Financial				
Available cash	2	3 (1)	4 (2)	4 (2)
High stocks	3	2 (1)	4 (1)	4 (1)
Physical				
Modern machines	5	5 (0)	3 (2)	3 (2)
Distribution network	0	1 (1)	5 (5)	5 (5)
Human				
Skilled engineers	5	5 (0)	1 (4)	2 (3)
Marketing expertise	0	2 (2)	5 (5)	5 (5)
Other				
Reputation for quality	5	5 (0)	5 (0)	5 (0)
Overseas contacts	0	0 (0)	0 (0)	4 (4)
Degree of mismatch		(5)	(19)	(22)

(a) This would be produced from a strength and weakness analysis (see section 4.5 of Chapter 4).
(b) From previous resource analysis 0 = major weaknesses, 5 = major strength.
(c) 0 = unimportant, 5 = critical to success of strategy.

The resource requirements of alternative future strategies should be laid out indicating the key for each strategy. For example, an extension of the home market would be critically dependent on marketing and distribution expertise together with the availability of cash to fund increased stocks. The resource analysis of the company should then be matched with the resource requirement for possible strategic options. In the example it is clear that the company's resources are specifically geared towards the current product/market strategy and may represent a constraint to any change.

There is a danger that resource deployment analysis will simply result in organisations choosing strategies which most closely fit the configuration of their present resources. It should be remembered that the real benefit of such an analysis should be the identification of those necessary changes in resources which are implied by any strategy. This relates to resource planning which needs to take place during strategy implementation and will be discussed in Chapter 9. For example, in Table 8.1 both strategies B and C will require quite significant changes in resources.

3. In Chapters 4 and 6 it was stressed that if an organisation's competitive position is to be sustained it will normally require a consistent theme – a generic strategy – to be supported by the resource base of the organisation (its value chain). In particular, the *linkages* which exist between value activities within the value chain and with the value chains of suppliers, channels and customers are likely to be an important source of competitive advantage. Therefore in screening specific strategies it is useful to assess how far any new strategy would add strength to the linkages which already exist, or develop needs for linkages that competitors cannot match.

8.2.3 Decision trees

Although decision trees[4] have been widely used in operational decision making, their use in strategy formulation has not, in general, received a great deal of attention. A typical strategic decision tree is illustrated in Figure 8.2. It can be seen that the end-point of the tree is a number of discrete development opportunities, as in Chapter 6. However, the difference lies in the way in which these options are screened for evaluation. Whereas previous methods have assumed that all options have equal merit (in the first instance), the decision tree approach ranks options by the process of progressively eliminating others. This elimination process is achieved by identifying a few key elements or criteria which future developments are intended to incorporate such as growth, investment and diversification. For example, in Figure 8.2 choosing growth as an important aspect of future strategies would automatically rank options 1–4 more highly than 5–8. At the second step the need for low investment strategies would rank options 3 and 4 above 1 and 2, and so on. Decision trees combine the identification of options with a simultaneous ranking of those options.

Perhaps the greatest limitation of decision tree analysis is that the choice at each branch on the tree can tend to be simplistic. For example, answering yes or no to diversification does not allow for the wide variety of alternatives which might exist between these two extremes (see Chapter 6). Nevertheless, as a starting point for evaluation, decision trees can often provide a useful framework.

Although the discussion of decision trees has been confined to that of a screening technique, readers should note that decision trees can also be used to evaluate specific aspects of strategic decisions. Historically, most emphasis has been placed on the

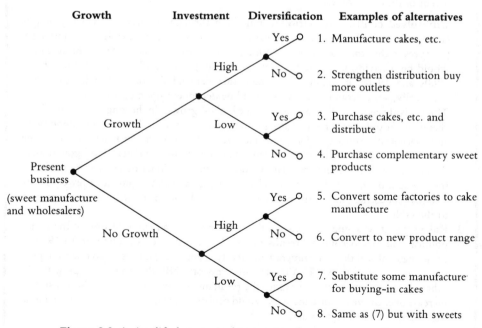

Figure 8.2 A simplified strategic decision tree for a sweet manufacturer.

assessment of the pay-off or profitability of alternative strategic decisions such as investment programmes or major R&D exercises. Such an analysis usually relies on forecasts of the profitability of various outcomes or performance levels being achieved. For example, probabilities must be assigned to the successful launch of a new product, the degree of market share gained, or the level of sales. It is not intended to discuss this particular use of decision trees here but to remind readers that the use of any evaluation technique at a strategic level is always limited by the difficulties of forecasting the factors which are used in the analysis. This is sometimes forgotten when using neat techniques like decision trees.

ILLUSTRATION 8.3

One use of scenario-building
Shell UK

By taking a conceptual or qualitative approach to planning, management can base its decision on a series of possible future outcomes, rather than on centrally set forecasts.

Scenario-building has been used on several occasions by Shell UK Ltd. where it has had to take into account societal and political analyses, as well as economic and technical analyses of the environment, and how these could influence long range planning.

In 1980 Shell used scenario-building to examine possible trends in the growth of the UK GNP and to use this information to link up what might be the likely demand for oil in the event of these outcomes.

1. **Unresolved conflicts scenario**. A 'muddling through' scenario in which policy is largely determined on the basis of expedient compromise in response to short term pressures, rather than tackling the country's underlying problems. Since the economy would be behaving in much the same way through the 1980s as it did through the 1960s and 1970s, it might be assumed that demand for oil would increase only marginally, since economic growth would be dependent upon oil revenues.

2. **The revival scenario**. This would give the highest growth in the long term. It implies a change in attitude and a restructuring of industry away from the older, declining fields and concentrating on areas of growth. The eventual upturn after restructuring has taken place may vary in its time scale depending upon the consistency of government direction, but in any event the trend would be similar. Under this scenario, it is likely there would be increased energy efficiency with greater development of fewer energy intensive industries, and so the demand for oil would not increase in direct proportion to the GNP.

3. **Rake's progress scenario**. This would be the result of an extrapolation of the social, political and macroeconomic trends for the UK for the years leading up to 1980. It could materialise if the government persistently changes its policies so no one strategy is given enough time to work. Although in terms of GNP, this scenario represents the other extreme to the revival scenario, the resultant energy demand may show a similar increase over the years since industry would probably remain energy intensive and hold less energy-efficient equipment.

Source: P. W. Beck, 'Corporate planning in an uncertain future', *Long Range Planning*, **15**(4), 1982.

8.2.4 Scenarios

Scoring methods screen options against a specific list of items from the strategic analysis; decision trees achieve the same outcome by eliminating options through progressively introducing additional criteria to be satisfied. A third approach to screening is that of *scenario planning*[5] which attempts to match specific options with a range of possible future situations (or scenarios). In other words, screening is used to categorise strategies as well as to eliminate some which do not fit any scenario. It is a particularly valuable approach where the future is uncertain and the organisation needs to be ready to respond to a range of different eventualities. The approach is essentially qualitative and is used as a means of addressing some of the less well structured or uncertain aspects of evaluation. It is often used to forecast the likely impact of possible environmental changes as Illustration 8.3 shows in the case of Shell UK Ltd. Although scenarios are usually qualitative they are, nonetheless, detailed. They should identify the key elements which could influence company performance such as competitive, economic, technical, social or political forces. The type of scenario used will differ depending on the level within an organisation. For example, in a multinational organisation like Shell the highest levels of management will be most interested in 'global scenarios' – worldwide developments – whilst the focus becomes narrower for the purposes of specialised divisions, functions or business sectors. Some aspects of global scenarios may, nonetheless, be relevant to more localised decision making – for example, developments in the Middle East will inevitably have an influence on the local energy situation.

Scenarios are essentially a qualitative forecast of events but (unlike traditional forecasting) based on the belief that the future is very difficult to measure and control.

The critical issue in scenario planning is that the organisation is clear on how it would respond to each scenario. This is usually formalised in terms of a set of *contingency plans* to meet the various scenarios. In other words, different strategic options would be implemented in each scenario. Equally important is the organisation's ability to monitor the onset (or otherwise) of a particular scenario in time to implement appropriate strategies.

8.3 ANALYSING RETURN

An assessment of the returns likely to accrue from specific options is a key measure of the *acceptability* of an option. However, there are different ways in which the returns can be reviewed requiring different approaches to the analysis of return. This section looks at two different assessments:

1. *Profitability* analyses which are important where financial return is regarded of central importance – the situation which prevails in most commercial organisations.
2. *Cost/benefit* analysis where the returns are often less tangible as occurs in many public service organisations where strategies are more likely to be justified in terms of improving provision rather than financial return.

8.3.1 Profitability analyses

Profitability is a most important measure of financial acceptability.[6] For profitability measures to be useful they must relate back to a sensible basis for comparison. In strategic evaluation the most useful measures are those which relate anticipated earnings to the amount of capital needed to generate those earnings.

A useful evaluative measure is the anticipated *return on capital employed* x years after a new strategy is implemented (e.g. the new strategy will result in a return on capital of

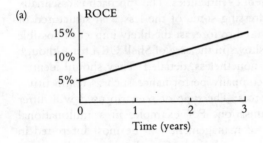

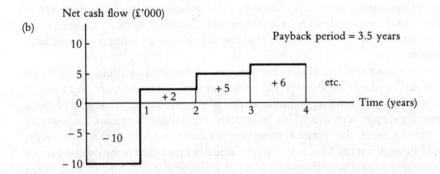

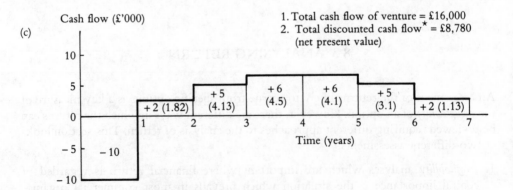

*Using a discounting rate of 10%.
Figures in brackets are discounted by 10% annually.

Figure 8.3 Some useful measures of profitability for strategic evaluation. (a) Return on capital employment. (b) Payback period. (c) Discounted cash flow (DCF).

20% by 1992) – see Figure 8.3(a). Care must be taken to establish whether this measure is to be applied to the whole company or simply to the extra profit related to the extra capital required for a particular strategy. The former is more relevant to a company undergoing slow strategic changes whilst the latter would normally be applied to large investment programmes.

When new strategies involve significant sums of capital investment then there are better measures of the relationship between capital expenditure and earnings. One such measure is that of *payback* which assesses the period of time required to pay back the invested capital.

In Figure 8.3(b) the payback period can be most easily established by estimating the *net cash flow* of the project or strategy in each of the periods ahead. A typical investment would follow the pattern in the figure. The payback period is calculated by finding the time at which the cumulative net cash flow becomes zero – in the example about three and a half years. The judgement is then whether this is regarded as an adequate outcome and if the company is prepared to wait that long for a return. This will clearly vary from one industry to another. In capital intensive industries, major investments normally have to be justified over a minimum of five years. In contrast, in fast moving consumer goods and services, payback is usually required more quickly. Major public sector ventures such as bridge building may well be assessed on a payback period of up to sixty years.

Discounted cash flow (DCF) analysis is perhaps the most widely used investment appraisal technique and is essentially an extension of the payback period type. Once the net cash flows have been assessed for each of the preceding years (see Figure 8.3(c)) they are discounted progressively to reflect the fact the funds generated early are of more real value than those in later periods (years). In the example, the discounting rate is 10% which reflects the value placed on money tied up in the venture. So the projected net cash flow of £2,000 in year 2 is discounted to £1,820 and so on. The net present value (NPV) of the venture is then calculated by adding all the discounted annual cash flows over the anticipated life of the project. DCF analysis is particularly useful for comparing the financial merits of two or more strategies which have very different patterns of expenditure and return. Most computer spreadsheet packages have an NPV function available for DCF calculations. Readers are referred to the references for a fuller discussion of these financial analysis techniques.

8.3.2 Cost/benefit analysis

In many situations the analysis of profit is too narrow an interpretation of return, particularly where intangible benefits are an important consideration. This is often the case, for example, in projects such as the siting of an airport or a power station.

Cost/benefit analysis[7] attempts to put a money value on all the costs and benefits of a strategic option – including these intangibles. Although this monetary representation of intangible costs and benefits can prove difficult in some cases this is not always the case. Figure 8.4 is an example of the expected costs and benefits of a particular strategy and the basis on which the intangibles could be quantified. It can be seen that the basis of quantification needs to be justified carefully and is likely to be subject to disagreement from different interested parties. For example, the value put on the loss of amenity (the public garden) could be argued to be far greater than the proposed basis of

A local authority was considering whether to construct a new town centre car park to be built on a public gardens.
  The main **costs** and **benefits** were identified as:

Costs	**Bases of quantification**
1. Acquiring site	Already owned, market value known
2. Construction costs	Tenders obtained
3. Loss of amenity (gardens)	Known usage of gardens and notional entry charge (if privately owned)
4. Increased total transport costs	Differential between public and private (car) travel
Benefits	
1. Revenue	Demand and price forecasts
2. Reduced congestion in streets	Incremental increase in consumer spending due to easier access

Figure 8.4 Cost/benefit analysis: an example.

assessment if the general character of the town centre is 'spoilt' by replacing the gardens with a car park.

One of the greatest difficulties of cost/benefit analysis is deciding on the boundaries of the analysis. For example, in Figure 8.4 the increased attraction of shoppers to the town centre will undoubtedly result in a diversion of spending from neighbouring areas rather than being an overall increase. Interestingly enough, it was this latter argument which was used by many Labour controlled local authorities against the introduction of Enterprise Zones in the early 1980s. These were areas where small businesses were given favourable treatment in terms of low rents, less red-tape, etc. It was argued that rather than encouraging new start-ups and the growth of existing businesses the main impact of Enterprise Zones was to relocate businesses from one area to a neighbouring Enterprise Zone.

Despite these difficulties with cost/benefit analysis it is an approach which is valuable if its limitations are understood. Its major benefit is in forcing people to be explicit about the variety of factors which should influence strategic choice. So even if people disagree on the value which should be assigned to particular costs or benefits, at least they are able to argue their case on common ground and decision makers are able to compare the merits of the various arguments. A detailed cost/benefit analysis would proceed to assign weightings to the various items in Figure 8.4 in order to reflect their relative importance to the decision in hand.

8.4 ANALYSING RISK

The likely return from a particular strategy is an important measure of the acceptability of that strategy. However, there is another, different, measure of acceptability against which strategic options might need to be assessed. This is the *risk* which the organisation faces in pursuing that strategy. This section outlines how this risk can be assessed as part of an evaluation of specific options.

8.4.1 Financial ratio projections

One of the simplest analyses is the projection of certain key financial ratios[8] which give a broad measure of the risk which the organisation would be taking by pursuing various strategies. At the broadest level an assessment of how the *capital structure* of the company would change by pursuing different options is a good general measure of risk. For example, options which would require the extension of long term loans will increase the gearing of the company and increase its financial risk. The collapse of Laker Airways in 1982 was a reminder of the dangers of funding capital investment exclusively through long term loans (in the case of Laker, to the tune of £150m) particularly if market demand does not develop as forecasted. The level of financial risk created by funding a proposed strategy from long term loans can be tested out by examining the likelihood of the company reaching the *breakeven point* (see below) and the consequences of falling short of that volume of business whilst interest on loans continues to be paid. In this respect there is a clear link between the assessment of risk and the feasibility of alternative strategies.

It should not be assumed that these analyses of financial risk are entirely a matter for the private sector. The 1980s proved to be an extremely difficult period for many of the big-city local authorities in the UK as they struggled to cope with a financial structure which was a legacy of the late 1960s and 1970s.

At a more detailed level a consideration of the likely impact on an organisation's *liquidity* is important in assessing options. For example, a small retailer eager to grow quickly may be tempted to fund the required shopfitting costs by delaying payments to suppliers and increasing bank overdraft. This reduced liquidity increases the financial risk of the business. The extent to which this increased risk threatens survival depends on the likelihood of either creditors or the bank demanding payments from the company.

8.4.2 Sensitivity analysis

Sensitivity analysis[9] is a useful technique for incorporating the assessment of risk during strategy evaluation. Its use has grown with the availability of computer spreadsheet packages which are ideally suited to this type of analysis.

The principles behind this approach are very straightforward. The technique allows each of the important assumptions underlying a particular option to be questioned and changed. In particular it seeks to test how sensitive the predicted performance or outcome (e.g. profit) is to each of these assumptions. For example, the key assumptions underlying a strategy might be that market demand will grow by 5% p.a. or that the company will stay strike-free, or that certain expensive machines will operate at 90% loading. Sensitivity analysis asks what would be the effect on performance (in this case profitability) if, for example, market demand grew at only 1% or as much as 10% − Would either of these extremes alter the decision to pursue that particular strategy? A similar process might be repeated for the other key assumptions. This process helps management develop a clearer picture of the risks of making certain strategic decisions and the degree of confidence it might have in a given decision. Illustration 8.4 shows how sensitivity analysis can be used in strategy evaluation.

8.4.3 Decision matrices [10]

There are many circumstances where specific aspects of strategic choice can be reduced to simple choices between a number of clearly defined courses of action. This is often the case when choosing between different development methods for a particular strategy. For example, an organisation which has decided to expand its operations by developing a new geographical market may be faced with three different methods of achieving this: by building new premises; buying and converting existing premises or leasing a purpose-built building (see Figure 8.5). Supposing there was some uncertainty about the likely level of demand in the new market particularly in relation to obtaining one major contract; if the contract is won, demand is likely to be 20,000 units p.a., otherwise a demand of 10,000 units p.a. is anticipated.

Having analysed the costs of these various options the likely impact on unit production costs in each case was estimated as shown in Figure 8.5(a). In deciding which option to choose it is necessary (before any detailed analysis) to be clear on which type of decision rule would be used to weigh these options against each other.

ILLUSTRATION 8.4

Sensitivity analysis is a useful technique for assessing the extent to which the success of a preferred strategy is dependent on the key assumptions which underlie that strategy.

In 1987 the Dunsmore Chemical Company was a single product company trading in a mature and relatively stable market. It was intended to use this established situation as a cash cow to generate funds for a new venture with a related product. Estimates had shown that the company would need to generate some £4m cash (at 1987 values) between 1988 and 1993 for this new venture to be possible.

Although the expected performance of the company was for a cash flow of £9.5m over that period (the *base case*), management was concerned to assess the likely impact of three key factors:

(a) Possible increases in *production costs* (manpower, overheads, and materials) which might be as much as 3% p.a. in real terms.
(b) *Capacity fill* which might be reduced by as much as 25% due to ageing plant and uncertain labour relations.
(c) *Price levels* which might be affected by the threatened entry of a new major competitor. This could squeeze prices by as much as 3% p.a. in real terms.

It was decided to use sensitivity analysis to assess the possible impact of each of these factors on the company's ability to generate £4m. The results are shown in the graphs.

From this analysis the management concluded that its target of £4m would be achieved with *capacity utilisation* as low as 60% which was certainly going to be achieved. Increased production costs of 3% p.a. would still allow the company to achieve the £4m target over the period. In contrast, *price* squeezes of 3% p.a. would result in a shortfall of £2m.

The management concluded from this analysis that the key factor which should affect their thinking on this matter was the likely impact of new competition and the extent to which they could protect price levels if such competition emerged. They therefore developed an aggressive marketing strategy to deter potential entrants.

For example, in Figure 8.5 there are four different rules which could be applied:

1. The *optimistic* decision rule would choose the best of the best outcomes for each option. In this case the best outcome (i.e. lowest cost) for each option are £35, £33 and £40 respectively so purchase and refit is chosen as the best of these three outcomes, since at £33 it represents the lowest possible cost situation.

2. The *pessimistic* decision rule would take the entirely opposite view. In this case the best of the worst outcomes for each option is chosen. In the example the worst outcomes for each option are £58, £56, and £50 respectively – hence the option of leasing would be chosen on this basis, since if demand proved to be only 10,000 units this option would have the lowest cost.

3. The *regret decision* rule would favour options which minimise the lost opportunity which might occur by choosing a particular option. So, in the example, if 'purchase and refit' was pursued and sales turned out to be only 10,000 units then the wrong decision would have been made since leasing would have produced a lower cost – so the regret

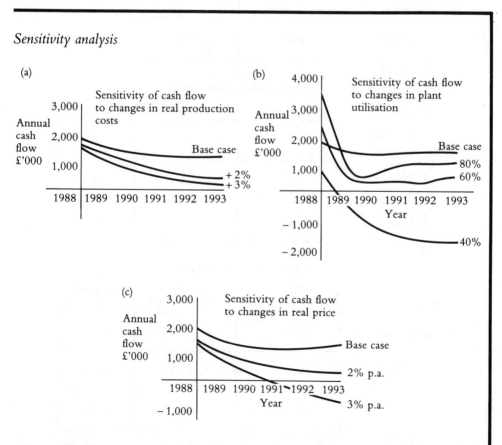

Sensitivity analysis

Source: The Dunsmore example is from the authors. The calculations for the senstivity test utilise computer programs employed in the Doman Case Study by P.H. Jones (Sheffield City Polytechnic).

with this choice would be £6 per unit (i.e. £56 – £50). Similarly, if leasing had been chosen and sales turned out to be 20,000 the regret would be £7 per unit since option 2 would have been a cheaper alternative by that amount (i.e. £40 – £33). Figure 8.5(b) shows the regret table for each combination of option/outcome. The regret rule would give preference to 'purchase and refit' since this minimises the possible lost opportunity or regret.

4. The *expected value* rule introduces an important new dimension – namely the *probability* that each outcome (demand) would occur. This can then be used to weight the outcomes for each option and, then, compare the options on this basis. Figure 8.5(c)

Annual sales volume (units)

Option	10,000	20,000
1. Build new premises	£58	£35
2. Purchase and refit	£56	£33
3. Lease	£50	£40

(a)

Annual sales volume (units)

Option	10,000	20,000	Maximum regret
1. Build new premises	£8	£2	£8
2. Purchase and refit	£6	£0	£6
3. Lease	£0	£7	£7

(b)

Annual sales volume (units)

Option	10,000 (probability = 0.7)	20,000 (probability = 0.3)	Weighted average cost
1. Build new premises	£58 × 0.7	£35 × 0.3	£51.10
2. Purchase and refit	£56 × 0.7	£33 × 0.3	£49.10
3. Lease	£50 × 0.7	£40 × 0.3	£47.00

(c)

Figure 8.5 Decision matrices: an example. (a) Unit cost table for the options. (b) Regret table for the options. (c) Unit costs weighted by the probability of each outcome.

shows how this process would be undertaken in a case where it was felt that the higher demand of 20,000 was only 30% certain. It can be seen that in these circumstances the leasing option would be preferred, since it has the lowest weighted average cost.

Although decision matrices are helpful in analysing some aspects of strategic choice (as in the example) they clearly need to be tempered by other considerations which would not be directly included in this simplified analysis. In the example it may be that one reason for leasing the available premises is to deny a major competitor the opportunity of setting up quickly in that location.

8.4.4 Simulation modelling

In the 1960s there was great enthusiasm for the possibilities which global strategic models[11] could bring to policy evaluation. Models of this kind attempt to measure and predict all the complex relationships which shape a company's future. For example, a model might include all the relevant environmental factors and the way they affect company performance, together with internal factors such as cost structure, deployment of assets and so on. In other words, strategic models attempt to encompass all the factors considered by the separate analyses discussed in this chapter into one quantitative simulation model of the company and its environment. It should be no surprise that such global models have been virtually impossible to build. Nevertheless, the principle of *simulation modelling* is a useful one in strategy evaluation in those aspects which lend themselves to this quantitative view.

Financial models are often used to assess strategic options. *Risk analysis*[12] is a technique which seeks to assess the overall degree of uncertainty in a particular option by (mathematically) combining the uncertainties in each of the elements of the option. For example, the likelihood of a particular profit projection is governed by the uncertainties surrounding costs, prices and volume forecasts. Although risk analysis is theoretically much neater than sensitivity analysis (see above) it is less widely used. The main reason for this is that sensitivity analysis often more clearly depicts the strategic importance of this assessment of uncertainty. In other words it is a better technique for communicating the key messages to decision makers.

One of the limitations on the use of strategic modelling is the need for large amounts of high quality data concerning the relationship between environmental factors and company performance. In this respect the recent work of the Strategic Planning Institute (SPI) using the Profit Impact of Market Strategy (PIMS data base)[13] has been interesting (see Chapter 7). Research at SPI has tried to build a number of quantitative causal models (multiple regression) which explain how companies' performance have been influenced by up to two dozen different factors.

8.4.5 Heuristic models

Many of the techniques applied to management decision making attempt to find the best or optimum solution to a problem or situation. In strategy evaluation this is invariably very difficult due to the complexities of the situation and the high levels of uncertainty involved. It has also been acknowledged in Section 8.2 that many strategic decisions are concerned with finding a satisfactory option rather than the 'best' option.

Heuristic models[14] are a means of identifying satisfactory 'solutions' in a systematic way. Perhaps the simplest forms of heuristic model are the 'rules of thumb' which managers use continuously in their day-to-day decision making and which create a central part of management intuition and judgement. Some examples might be:

'Always run the plant at 90% capacity fill.'
'Have five times the number of sales leads as the order book.'
'One doctor can cope with a 2,500 patient roll.'
'Reorder when stock gets down to 200 units.'

Readers should note the strong link to discussion elsewhere in the book (particularly Chapter 2) concerning the importance of the 'recipe' in guiding the actions of managers and also the dangers of sticking blindly to the historical recipe.

Where the situation is more complex – when there are many options available to an organisation and many different requirements to be fulfilled, a more detailed approach will be needed. This requires all of the decision criteria to be listed (e.g. 'a satisfactory option must provide 5% p.a. revenue growth, labour productivity gains of 2% p.a., must avoid plant closures in Yorkshire, must etc. ...'). The various options are *searched* until one is found which satisfies all the criteria. This is not necessarily the best option. Indeed, the search can be continued to provide a shortlist of options which fit the criteria and in that sense could be used for screening. With the advent of cheap and powerful computers, heuristic modelling is becoming useful as an evaluation technique since the search process can be undertaken quickly even when many criteria need to be met and several hundred options exist.

8.4.6 Stakeholder reactions

There is some danger that the assessment of risk will be regarded as a totally dispassionate, objective analysis. In practice the assessment of the *political risk* inherent in various strategies can be an important deciding factor between those strategies. For example, a strategy of market development might require the cutting out of middlemen (such as wholesalers) hence running the risk of a backlash which could jeopardise the success of the strategy.

A new strategy might require a substantial issue of new shares which might be unacceptable to certain powerful groups of shareholders since it dilutes their voting power. Plans to merge with other companies or to trade with new countries might be unacceptable to unions, government or other customers. Clearly in the public sector an understanding of these softer measures of risk is invariably important during strategy evaluation. It would be unwise to proceed with options which are likely to be permanently undermined by the political activity of either consumers or other organised groups. The key judgement is how long-lived these reactions are likely to be.

Often the most important issue is the likely reaction of competitors to particular strategic changes. Therefore, *game theory*[15] should, in principle, have some use as an evaluation technique. However, the difficulties of coping with the complexity of the strategic situation have limited the use of game theory to largely qualitative applications. Perhaps the biggest difficulty with using game theory lies in the assumption that the strategic competitive behaviour of companies can be predicted by using simple rules. Readers should refer to the references for a fuller discussion of this technique.

8.5 ANALYSING FEASIBILITY

The previous two sections have largely been concerned with the acceptability of strategic options. This section looks at ways of assessing the feasibility of options although it should be remembered that many approaches actually combine a parallel assessment of both of these criteria.

8.5.1 Funds flow analysis

The assessment of financial feasibility would normally be an important part of any strategy evaluation. A simple and valuable piece of analysis is a *funds flow forecast*[16] which seeks to identify the funds which would be required for any strategy and the likely sources of those funds. For example, in Figure 8.6 the evaluation of a proposed strategy (X) would proceed by the following steps:

1. An assessment of the capital investment needed (e.g. new buildings, machines or vehicles) – £13.25m.
2. A forecast of the cumulative profits earned over the period 1988–1990. 'Funds from operations' of £15m are calculated from an estimate of future profits plus the adding back of any non-fund items such as depreciation, and represents the real flow of funds into the company forecasted for that period.
3. An estimate of the necessary increases in working capital required by the strategy

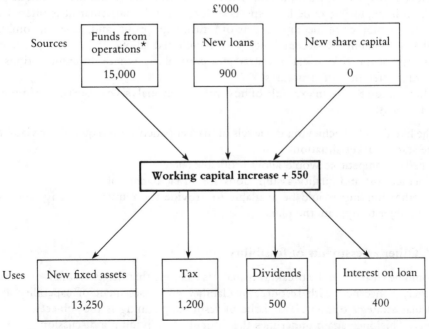

*Funds from operations = Profits corrected for non-fund items such as depreciation.

Figure 8.6 A funds flow forecast for strategy X (1988–1990), £'000.

can be made by the separate consideration of each element of working capital (stock increases, increased creditors, etc.) or by using a simple *pro rata* adjustment related to the forecasted level of increase in sales revenue. For example, if the present revenue of £30m requires a working capital level £10m then a forecasted increase in sales revenue to £31.65m would account for the anticipated increase in working capital of £0.55m. This type of *pro rata* adjustment would only be valid when looking at future strategies which are similar in nature to the present company activities.

4. *Tax* liability and expected dividend payments can be estimated (in relation to the anticipated profitability). In this case £1.2m and £0.5m respectively.
5. The calculation so far leaves a shortfall in funds of £0.5m. The forecast is then finalised by looking at alternative ways of funding the shortfall and this is where the critical appraisal of financial feasibility occurs. In Figure 8.6 this shortfall is to be funded by an additional short term loan of £0.9m (which in its turn will incur interest payments of £0.4m over the three year period assuming simple interest at 14.8% p.a.).

It should be remembered that funds flow analysis is a forecasting technique and is subject to the difficulties and errors of any method of forecasting. Such an analysis should quickly highlight whether the proposed strategy is likely to be feasible in financial terms and could normally be programmed onto a microcomputer should the model be repeatedly required during evaluation.

8.5.2 Breakeven analysis

Breakeven analysis[17] is a simple and widely used linear programming technique which is helpful in exploring some key aspects of feasibility. In particular, it is often used to assess the feasibility of meeting targets of return (e.g. profit) and, as such, combines a parallel assessment of acceptability. As mentioned above, this also provides an assessment of the risk in various strategies particularly where different options have markedly different cost structures.

   Illustration 8.5. is an example of how breakeven analysis can be used to investigate such issues as:

● The likelihood of achieving the levels of market penetration required for viability (in the static market situation).
● Whether competitors would allow profitable entry.
● Whether cost and quality assumptions are, in fact, achievable.
● Whether funding would be available to provide the required capacity and skilled manpower to operate the plant.

8.5.3 Other assessments of feasibility

It should be clear from the breakeven analysis example that the assessment of feasibility is largely concerned with resource availability and assessment of capability against particular strategy options. This issue of resource planning is the subject of the next chapter. This once again underlines the difficulty of dividing a discussion of strategic choice from that of strategic implementation.

   Assessing feasibility is an important part of evaluation but, by necessity, requires a detailed consideration of the resource implications of implementation including the planning of when resources will be needed.

In the previous chapter it was also argued that a key determinant in choosing strategies should be their 'cultural fit' with the organisation. This will be of central concern in discussing the implementation of strategies within the realities of an organisation's structures, people and systems (Chapters 10 and 11). So, in the same way as with resource planning, these factors are an important consideration in choosing strategies as well as when attempting to make chosen strategies work in practice.

ILLUSTRATION 8.5

Using breakeven analysis to examine strategic options

A manufacturing company was considering the launch of a new consumer durable product into a market when most products were sold to wholesalers who supplied the retail trade. The total market was worth about £4.4m (at manufacturer's prices) – about 630,000 units. The market leader had about 30% market share in a competitive market where retailers were increasing their buying power. The company wished to evaluate the relative merits of a high price/high quality product sold to wholesalers (strategy A) or an own-brand product sold directly to retailers (strategy B). The table below summarises the market and cost structure for the market leader and these alternative strategies. The important conclusion is that the company would require about 22% and 13% market share respectively for strategies A and B to break even.

Market and cost structure	Market leader	Strategy A	Strategy B
Price to retailer	£10	£12	£8
Margin to wholesaler	30%	30%	–
Wholesaler buys at	£7	£8.40	–
Variable costs/unit			
raw material	£2.50	£2.90	£2.50
marketing/selling	£0.50	£0.60	£0.20
distribution	£0.20	£0.20	£0.20
others	£0.30	£0.30	£0.20
total	£3.50	£4.00	£3.10
contribution/unit	£3.50	£4.40	£4.90
Fixed cost	£500,000	£600,000	£400,000
breakeven point (units)	£500,000	£600,000	£400,000
	3.50	4.40	4.90
	= 142,857	= 136,363	= 81,633
Market size	630,000	630,000	630,000
Breakeven point (market share)	22.6%	21.6%	13%
Actual share	30%	0	0

Source: Authors.

8.6 SELECTION OF STRATEGIES

The discussions in Chapters 7 and 8 have been concerned with how evaluation of strategic options can be undertaken both in terms of the general suitability of particular types of strategy and also the merits of specific strategic options. However, it is important for readers to recognise that these evaluations do not by themselves determine which strategies should be *selected* for implementation. Readers are reminded of the discussions in Chapter 2 about the process of strategy development. There are three ways in which strategies are commonly selected.

8.6.1 Selection against objectives

This is a widespread view[18] of how a rational choice of future strategies should occur. This method uses the organisation's objectives, quantified where possible, as direct yardsticks by which options are assessed. Evaluation methods are therefore central to the decision making process and are expected to provide quantified answers regarding the relative merits of various options and to indicate the right course of action. In practice, however, even where this rational selection process occurs, it is very often the case that objectives need to be adjusted as the evaluation proceeds and become what is often called 'post-rationalised'. The objectives, therefore, fit the strategy and vice versa. In general it is a sound discipline to assess the extent to which strategic options might fit specified objectives of the organisation provided it is also recognised that there are likely to be other ways in which strategies will be selected.

8.6.2 Referral to a higher authority

A common way in which the selection of strategies occurs is by referring the matter to a higher authority as mentioned in Chapter 2. Those managers responsible for evaluation may not have the authority to give the go-ahead to the 'solution'. Equally, those senior managers who must decide on strategy may not have participated in the evaluation of options. This is a very important observation which should have a strong influence on how the results of evaluation are conveyed to senior management. In particular, it is unlikely that senior managers will have the time or inclination to unravel all the detailed ramifications of an evaluation. They are more concerned with using their judgement of the situation on the available facts and also seeing how different strategies will fit the overall mission of the company. Thus the evaluation process is best seen as a means of raising the level of debate which occurs amongst senior managers when they are using judgement on the selection of strategy.

In large diversified organisations (including the public services) there will be different types of evaluation occurring at the centre than in the divisions, subsidiary companies or (in public services) the various service departments. The board of a holding company, for example, might look at their businesses using product portfolio analysis, and the issue of a balanced portfolio might be at least as important a selection criterion as the more specific business criteria of one of the businesses. At the same time the management of the different businesses will be evaluating their alternative strategies to convince their corporate masters that they should be given more resources to try out some new ideas.

8.6.3 Outside agencies

Sometimes within organisations there are disagreements on strategy between parties who have similar power within the company. This may be between management and unions, or between two different managers. In these circumstances it is not unusual for an outside agency, such as a consultant, to evaluate the situation for the company. Often this process of evaluation is described as objective and rational by virtue of the consultant's detachment from the situation. In practice, of course, consultants are aware of the political reasons for their involvement. To a large extent their role may be one of arbitrator and the evaluation must reflect those circumstances. In multinational ventures, particularly where government is involved, it is likely that consultants will be employed to assess the merits of the various strategies or at least to act in an advisory role to the decision makers – for example in the case of the Channel Tunnel bids in 1986.

8.7 SUMMARY

Strategy evaluation has often been presented as an exact science – a way of deciding what organisations should do. In fact, the analytical methods discussed in Chapters 7 and 8 are only useful as a *source of information* to makers of strategic decisions. It has been seen that the contribution which various techniques make to improving the quality of strategic decision making will differ quite considerably. Some methods of analysis are valuable because they are eye-openers – they help managers to see the logic or rationale behind strategies rather than assessing those strategies in detail. Other methods are more detailed and are useful ways of understanding how suitable, acceptable or feasible a specific strategy might be.

However, even the most thorough strategy evaluation cannot possibly anticipate all the detailed problems and pitfalls which might be encountered in the implementation of a strategic change. So it is necessary to recognise that strategic decisions will be refined or even reversed as part of their implementation which is discussed in the final part of the book.

REFERENCES

1. J. Argenti, *Practical Corporate Planning*, Allen & Unwin, 1980, describes an approach to corporate planning which is essentially focused around the idea of gap analysis.

2. A discussion of the opportunity analysis matrix can be found in F. F. Neubaurer and N. B. Solomon, 'A managerial approach to environmental assessment', *Long Range Planning*, **10**(2), 1977; and G. Johnson, 'The strategic workshop', *Management Today*, Oct., 1980. This extension of the technique is called 'strategy mapping' by G. Johnson.

3. C. Hofer and D. Schendel, *Strategy Formulation: Analytical concepts*, pp. 36–9, West, 1978,

discusses the resource deployment matrix as a method of historical resource analysis. We have extended this idea into an assessment of the future (i.e. evaluation).

4. Decision trees are discussed in many books on management science and operational research. For example: P. G. Moore and H. Thomas, *The Anatomy of Decisions*, chapters 4 and 6, Penguin, 1976, R. D. Harris and M. J. Maggard, *Computer Models in Operations Management* (2nd edn), Harper & Row, 1977 – Exercise 4 (p. 55) describes a computer package called *Decide* which uses a decision tree.

5. The following references provide useful discussions of scenarios: P. W. Beck, '*Corporate planning for an uncertain future*', *Long Range Planning*, **15**(4), 1982; J. H. Grant and W. R. King, 'Strategy formulation: analytical and normative models', in D. E. Schendel and C. W. Hofer (eds), *Strategic Management*, p. 111, Little Brown, 1979; G. Steiner, *Strategic Planning*, p. 235, Free Press, 1979.

6. Most textbooks on financial management will include sections relating to the techniques discussed in the text. We would recommend J. M. Samuels and F. M. Wilkes, *Management of Company Finance* (3rd edn), pp. 172, 217, 218, Nelson, 1980.

7. A. Rowe, R. Mason and K. Dickel, *Strategic Management and Business Policy: A methodological approach* (2nd edn), chapter 9, Addison-Wesley, 1985.
Cost/benefit analysis is also included as a computer model in: A. Rowe, R. Mason, K. Dickel and P. Westcott., *Computer Models for Strategic Management* Addison-Wesley, 1987. E. J. Mirsham, *Cost/Benefit Analysis* (3rd edn), Allen & Unwin, 1980.

8. See, for example, reference 6, Chapters 10 and 12. Rowe *et al.* (reference 7) has some useful computer routines for ratio analysis.

9. B. Taylor and J. R. Sparkes (*Corporate Strategy and Planning*, pp. 48–52, Heinemann, 1977) discuss the use of sensitivity and risk analysis as do Samuels and Wilkes (reference 6, p. 233) as methods of incorporating uncertainty into strategic evaluation. Computer spreadsheet packages are ideally suited for simple sensitivity analysis.

10. S. Cooke and N. Slack, *Making Management Decisions*, chapter 7, Prentice Hall, 1984.

11. The use of corporate simulation models is discussed by J. H. Grant and W. R. King (reference 5, p. 109). For computer based strategic models see Rowe *et al.* (reference 7).

12. A long-standing article on risk analysis is D. B. Hertz, 'Risk analysis in capital investment', *Harvard Business Review*, Winter, 1964.

13. For details of the PIMS studies see Chapter 7.

14. See Cooke and Slack (reference 10) and Rowe, Mason and Dickel (reference 7)

15. The application of game theory is discussed in a number of texts. For example: J. H. Grant and W. R. King (reference 5, p. 113, P. Kotler (reference 12, p. 622), M. E. Porter, *Competitive Strategy*, pp. 88–107, Free Press, 1980.

16. Most books on financial management will include a section on funds flow analysis. For example, See J. M. Samuels and F. M. Wilkes (reference 6, pp. 280–3). Also Rowe *et al.* (reference 7) for a computer model.

17. Breakeven analysis is discussed in J. Sizer, *An Insight into Management Accounting* (2nd edn), Pitman, 1979.

18. For example: J. Argenti (reference 1), and D. Hussey, *Corporate Planning: Theory and practice* (2nd edn), Pergamon, 1982.

Recommended key readings

- An extensive discussion of approaches to strategy evaluation is to be found in C. W. Hofer and D. Schendel, *Strategy Formulation: Analytical concepts*, West, 1978. Also S. Tilles, 'How to evaluate corporate strategy', *Harvard Business Review*, July/Aug., 1963, is still worth referring to.

- Readers should be familiar with the financial evaluation techniques discussed in the chapter. If they are not they should read relevant chapters of a financial management text. For example: J. M. Samuels and F. M. Wilkes, *Management of Company Finance* (3rd edn), Nelson, 1980, or L. J. Gitman, *Principles of Managerial Finance*, Harper & Row, 1976.

- S. Cooke and N. Slack, *Making Management Decisions*, Prentice Hall, 1984, is a useful text on decision making techniques.

- A. Rowe, R. Mason, K. Dickel and P. Westcott, *Computer Models for Strategic Management*, Addison-Wesley, 1987, provides some useful computer routines.

Part IV

STRATEGY IMPLEMENTATION

Strategic analysis and choice are of little value to an organisation unless the proposals are capable of being implemented. Strategic change does not take place simply because it is considered to be desirable; it takes place if it can be made to work. Part IV deals with the vital problems of implementing strategy and with the planning of that implementation. Chapter 1 made it clear that one of the major characteristics of strategic decisions is that they are likely to give rise to important changes in the resources of an organisation. Chapter 4 explained that such resources do not simply mean physical materials, plant and finances but also include the people in the organisation and the systems used to manage those people. So when thinking about how strategic change affects the resources of an organisation it is necessary to think about all these sorts of resource.

- Chapter 9 is concerned with planning how resources will have to be reallocated given strategic change. It does this at two levels: at the corporate level where the problem is the allocation of resources between different parts of the organisation (e.g. between different businesses in a conglomerate); and at the operating unit (or business) level where the problem is the provision and allocation of resources between departments, functions or projects, such as the phasing in of production, the addition or deletion of new products, the raising of finance or the retraining of part of the workforce. Strategic changes usually involve and affect many resource areas: they may be implemented on a day-to-day basis through the operating functions of the organisation, but they need to be thought through as a whole to see if they form a coherent package. In Chapter 9 the approach is not to regard the implementation of strategy through resource management as a matter of functional planning but to look at the overall strategic planning of resources.
- A major resource of any organisation is the people who work for it. How they are to be managed is obviously important: it is also clear that changes in strategy are likely to give rise to the need to reorganise how people are managed. The last two chapters of the book examine this problem. Chapter 10 concentrates on how people are to be organised in terms of who will be responsible for what: it is therefore concerned with structural questions – What shape should the organisation take? At what level should different sorts of decision be taken? The chapter also considers the conditions under which certain organisational forms might be more or less appropriate.
- Chapter 11 examines more specifically how strategic change might be managed through the people and systems of the organisation. Here the problems and

mechanisms of strategic change are considered in terms of systems of control and regulation available to management; and also in terms of cultural and political systems.

Throughout Part IV it is important to remember the distinction between the planning of implementation and actually carrying out the tasks of implementation. As the three chapters proceed they move progressively from planning to the often problematic realities of implementation.

Chapter 9

PLANNING AND ALLOCATING RESOURCES

9.1 INTRODUCTION

The successful implementation of strategic change will invariably require some degree of change in the organisation's resource profile. The careful planning of these resource changes is therefore extremely important. The discussions in Chapter 4 (resource analysis) highlighted the fact that the specific resource issues which need to be considered differ with the level in the organisation at which the analysis is focused. This is equally true when detailed resource planning needs to be undertaken.

Resource planning usually entails two levels of consideration. First, the broader issues of how resources should be allocated between the various functions, departments, divisions or separate businesses. This analysis should be aided by the analysis of the balance of an organisation's resources referred to in Chapters 4 and 7. Second, the more detailed considerations of how resources should be deployed within any one part of the organisation to best achieve the strategies. This is concerned with the operational aspects of resource planning and is supported by the detailed assessment of strategic capability discussed in Chapter 4 – in particular the value chain analysis. The chapter concludes with some practical advice on how organisations might develop resource allocation plans in a systematic way.

It is also important to emphasise again that in thinking through how strategy will be put into effect, detailed thought is in fact being given to the feasibility of its implementation. As such, the planning of resource allocation is part of the evaluation of strategy. There is no sense in proceeding with the implementation of a strategy if, in planning how it should be done, it becomes clear it is unrealistic. Indeed, given the often generalised nature of strategic decision making as it occurs in reality, it may be that really detailed consideration of a strategic course of action does not actually take place until the planning of implementation begins. Managers should then realise that they are not simply planning how something is to be done but also whether it is possible or sensible to do it.

9.2 RESOURCE PLANNING AT THE CORPORATE LEVEL

At the corporate level in an organisation resource planning is mainly concerned with the allocation of resources between the various parts of the organisation, whether those

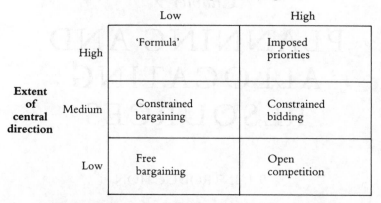

Figure 9.1 Resource allocation at the corporate level.

be the business functions (marketing, finance, etc.), operating divisions or geographical areas (e.g. in a multinational) or service departments (e.g. in public services). Clearly, in large organisations this could consist of several layers or stages of resource allocation. This section looks at how these broader issues of allocation might be tackled in order to support the implementation of strategies and Figure 9.1 illustrates some commonly occurring approaches. It can be seen that the two factors which are of most importance in determining the general approach to allocation are:

1. The *degree of change* required in the resource base if strategic change is to be achieved successfully. This could be the extent to which the aggregate level of resources might need to change (e.g. growth or decline) or where significant shifts are required between resource areas within a largely unchanged overall resource.
2. The extent of *central direction* of the allocation process. Whether detailed allocations are dictated from the corporate level or are in response to the detailed plans and aspirations of the various units of the organisation.

To illustrate these general approaches to resource allocation the following three situations will be discussed:

1. Few changes in overall resources or in the deployment of resources.
2. Growth in the overall resource base.
3. Decline in the overall resource base or significant reallocations within a static resource base.

In each case the contrasting approaches of centralised or decentralised 'control' of resource planning will be considered.

9.2.1 Few resource changes

If the aggregate resources of an organisation and the way in which they are deployed is unlikely to change significantly with new strategies then resource allocation tends to proceed along largely historical lines. In some circumstances this could mean allocating resources by an agreed 'formula'. For example, the advertising budget might be 5% of sales, or in the public services revenue might be allocated in a per capita payment (e.g. doctors' patients). Often there is some room for bargaining around this historical position – for example in redefining the formula or the way in which resources are measured (when resource sharing or central overhead charges are involved). Zero-based budgeting[1] (discussed later in the chapter) could be a means of building some fluidity into the resource planning process and avoiding some of the worst aspects of formula allocations which can be a particular problem where historically based formula allocations reflect the relative political strength[2] of different groups rather than their resource needs.

9.2.2 Allocations during growth

During growth resources can often be reallocated in relative terms without any particular area of the organisation suffering a reduction in resources – simply by directing new resources selectively across the organisation. Some organisations will establish these priority areas centrally and impose the resource allocations from the centre. At the other extreme some companies adopt an openly competitive attitude towards the various parts of the business. Quite often the centre of the organisation operates as an *investment bank*[3] from which divisions or functions must bid for resources in an openly competitive way. This mechanism is quite common where new investment funds are being allocated. Clearly, the criteria for judging bids must relate to the chosen strategies of the organisation and the resource profile needed to underpin them. Perhaps it is not surprising that most organisations during growth would tend to follow a middle path between these two approaches. This would be described as *constrained bidding* where the various parts of the organisation are able to bid for additional resources but within defined constraints. One of the political skills needed for managers within the units is to understand the extent to which these constraints can be challenged and adjusted as seen in Illustration 9.1.

9.2.3 Allocating resources in static or declining situations

The example of the computer company (Illustration 9.1) shows some of the resource allocation problems in an organisation experiencing major growth. Many of the same issues apply in static or declining situations but there are important differences. In particular, resource reallocation will require some areas to reduce in absolute terms to maintain other areas and/or to support new developments. There are differing approaches to these (often difficult) reallocation problems. In some organisations the reallocation is simply imposed centrally – for example as with some plant closures. In other circumstances the reallocation may be achieved in an openly competitive way – for example a freeze may be imposed on all resource replacement by units, particularly employees may not be automatically replaced as they leave. Instead, as vacancies arise they are made subject to open competition and go to those units with the most pressing case. The most common situation is between these two approaches, in other words *constrained bidding* for resources, but in this case for resources which may be diverted from other areas. This is often achieved by earmarking a proportion of the total organisational resources for reallocation to new ventures.

ILLUSTRATION 9.1

American Computers (UK)

An American computer manufacturer operating worldwide through a range of subsidiaries developed its own approach to resource allocations during rapid growth.

During the 1980s the American Computers (UK) company was committed to following the 'natural' growth in the market (as high as 50% p.a. in the early part of the decade) in order to maintain its worldwide market position. This required very substantial efforts in terms of hardware developments (particularly personal computers) and the redirection of the business into a service orientated philosophy rather than an old style hardware manufacturer. Not surprisingly the company experienced considerable difficulties in following such a rapidly changing business situation and had some difficult resource planning decisions to make at the corporate level. Specifically the following allocation issues had to be resolved:

1. It was soon clear that a 'fair shares for all' policy between subsidiaries would be impractical and undesirable. The company followed a policy of internal competition for investment resources largely based in the previous year's performance against target. But this policy was only pursued within limits. For example, the most successful subsidiaries were only permitted to increase their resource base (particularly people) up to an agreed target 'head count'. What happened in practice was that the more successful subsidiaries would always achieve sales beyond their target (based on head count) and use this as a source of pressure to lift their head count target in the next round of allocations.

2. Difficult decisions had to be made at the parent company on how much resource to 'cream off' for new product development which was done centrally. Clearly, in such a fast-moving market R&D could not be neglected but the constant pressure from subsidiaries for more operational resources to support current activities made these investment decisions quite difficult.

3. At the area level (e.g. Europe) there was rivalry between the various subsidiaries to be 'top dog' in their area. Although this was an understandable result of the internal competition for new resources there was also a recognition amongst the more astute managers that, sometime in the future, operations within the area could well be rationalised (as had already occurred in mature multinational industries like motor cars) and a strong position *vis-à-vis* other subsidiaries was needed once that time arrived.

4. At the subsidiary level there were different problems of allocation. During the middle part of the decade one of the major issues was the need to build up strength in the supporting functions such as software support, marketing, and technical support from a situation where sales had been the one dominant function. Indeed it required some con- siderable skill to ensure that these functions got more than their proportional share of new resources in recognition of their weaker starting point.

Equally there was a major shift in selling effort from the traditional mainframe and minicomputers towards personal computers which required the use of independent sales outlets rather than direct selling. This meant the diversion of some of the sales budget to establish a new selling offshoot to deal with these intermediaries.

Source: Authors.

Many companies and public service organisations in the UK experienced the difficulties of reallocating resources during the 1980s.[4] Some of the ways in which this was achieved illustrate these general points:

- Often reductions were achieved by amalgamating related areas or activities. Although resulting resource savings were often explained by 'cutting out overlap' or 'economies of scale', usually neither of these were as important as the new opportunities which arose to prioritise within the new unit rather than the more difficult task of favouring one unit against another. For example, within a hospital two related specialisms may be merged under the same consultant.
- Paradoxically, another common solution was through the creation of new units outside the normal structure. This is particularly appropriate where the unit clearly supports the defined strategy. The unit was resourced by the marginal paring back of all other areas (hence maintaining 'equality of treatment'). Once established, the new unit (if successful) was often the subject of some considerable rivalry and competition from the more established units even to the extent of wishing to devote some of their scarce resources to help the unit develop. This competitive process often determined in which area of activity the new unit was reassimilated into the mainstream. By this obtuse process resource reallocation occurred – often to a substantial degree.
- Of course there were some circumstances where resource allocation was achieved by a more overt and less subtle process – by simply closing down one part of the organisation and some organisations received wide press coverage (e.g. the coal industry).

9.2.4 Resource sharing/overlap

One of the particularly difficult aspects of resource allocation at the corporate level is the extent to which overlap, sharing or duplication of resources should occur between the various parts of the organisation. This arises in many different ways such as the extent to which services (e.g. secretarial) should be shared between departments to grander issues like whether two divisions should share their production capacity or have a common salesforce. Issues of this type are very closely tied to the structure and systems of the organisation and will be discussed in the next chapters.

9.3 RESOURCE PLANNING AT THE OPERATIONAL LEVEL

In the discussion of resource analysis (Chapter 4) the idea of the *value chain* was introduced as a means of analysing the variety of ways in which an organisation's capabilities relate to the strategies being pursued. It was emphasised that an organisation needs to understand which particular value activities most contribute to the success of the organisation's strategies – for example through cost advantage or differentiation from competitors (or in the public services of cost efficiency or quality of service).

Clearly, during the implementation of new strategies these same issues are of central importance in the resource planning which needs to occur:

- Resource planning must address resource requirements throughout the value chain – including linkages between resources and with the value chains of suppliers, channels or customers.
- The planning must establish which value activities are of greatest importance to successful implementation of the selected strategies and ensure that these are given special care and attention.

In order to ensure that these issues are given proper attention in the resource planning at operational level it is useful to ask a few questions which are of central importance in resource planning (see Figure 9.2). These questions will now be given some brief discussion before considering how they will be applied to the various activities of an organisation's value chain.

9.3.1 Central questions in resource planning

RESOURCE IDENTIFICATION
The most basic requirement is the identification of what resources are required to carry out the strategy. Effective planning of resources must depend on the extent to which the planner is clear about resource needs. The danger is that resource requirements will be overlooked or that it will be assumed that the resource needs of the past will cope with the strategies of the future. The powerful influence of recipes[5] on the views and practices of managers has already been pointed out: it is likely that both at an individual level and at a corporate or even industry level, managers manage very much on the basis of past experience. There is the danger that new strategies will be considered in the context of old expectations or existing bases of operating rather than in terms of what is required in the future. Illustration 9.2 shows how one such company – Sinclair – built on the undisputed innovative skills of its founder, faltered at several stages of its development because it did not adequately consider the resource implications of its own developments.

In general value chain analysis should help establish which value activities are of crucial importance in maintaining the organisation's competitive position. These are the areas where particular care and attention needs to be paid to resource planning.

FIT WITH EXISTING RESOURCES
Assuming the resources required to implement the desired strategy are identified, then it is possible to move to the next stage, which begins to clarify just how problematic

---

1. Exactly what resources will a strategy require for its implementation?
   (**Resource identification**)

2. To what extent do these required resources build on or are a change from existing resources?
   (**Fit with existing resources**)

3. Can the required resources be integrated with each other?
   (**Fit between required resources**)

Figure 9.2 Central questions in operational resource planning.

implementation is likely to be. Strategic change may well entail important changes of resources. Since major resource changes will inevitably raise problems both of operational logistics and probably of conflict within an organisation, it is important to be clear on the extent to which existing resources can cope, will need to be changed or added to, or perhaps will need to be replaced altogether. The likelihood is that some will be adequate and some will become redundant.

Chapter 4 emphasised that the strategic capability of an organisation is not only determined by the intrinsic strength of its resources but also by the way the resources

---

ILLUSTRATION 9.2

Sinclair Research

Clive Sinclair would have liked to see his companies launching his latest inventions, but during the 1970s and 1980s he ran into a succession of problems in managing resources.

As founder, chairman and chief executive of Sinclair Radionics in the 1970s, Clive Sinclair found himself faced with trying to exploit his talent for invention without becoming embroiled in the problems of managing an enterprise. His undoubted skill was his eye for a market opening but he consistently failed to maintain the momentum of a series of inventions.

Sinclair launched his pocket calculator in 1973, soon followed by a digital 'black watch'. However, both soon came under severe market pressure from the Far East leaving him short of finance for his subsequent developments. The first project to suffer was the pocket-sized television which was delayed and launched against severe competition in the mid 1980s. Although financial resources were the outward symptom of the company's difficulties, Sinclair realised that his major shortcoming was the company's lack of management expertise. The company never developed the mass consumer marketing skills which were needed to give the stability it required. Indeed, in the early 1980s, he decided to establish the company as Sinclair Research, undertaking only research and invention and subcontracting production and marketing to other companies. So Timex Corporation manufactured the ZX81, Spectrum and QL microcomputers which he introduced between 1981 and 1984. W. H. Smith undertook much of the marketing (which had previously been done directly, creating severe difficulties for Sinclair and complaints about delays from customers).

Following the mid 1980s recession in the home computer market, Sinclair sold their computing interests to Amstrad – a company which had developed and prospered in microelectronic equipment supply as a result of their marketing expertise. Sir Clive's comment on the deal was:

> We had a choice, we could have sold some of the company to raise money to stay in the existing business but then we wouldn't have had enough to develop the new technologies [waferscale] ... So far as I was concerned [the microcomputers] were well developed, mature products. My principal interest was in the future and we wanted to keep the new technologies within the company. It leaves me to get on with my next generation of computers without the burden of the other products. In particular we don't have to consider any degree of compatibility.

Sources: *Management Today*, March 1981, *QL World*, November 1986.

are deployed and controlled. These same considerations are important when assessing the fit of new resources with old. For example, a company may choose to manufacture and market a new product range through a new division or even a new company to avoid problems of conflict with existing operations. So the planning of resources also leads into structural considerations and issues of managing change which will be discussed more fully in the next two chapters. An assessment of this fit with existing resources begins to establish the extent to which implementation is likely to require major changes within the organisation or is achievable by an adjustment of the current resource base. It also leads to a consideration of the current resources which the organisation possesses. New strategies may require a reconfiguration of the value chain and previously perceived strengths of the organisation may not really be strengths at all.

FIT BETWEEN REQUIRED RESOURCES

One of the critical ingredients of successful strategies is the way in which the linkages between the important value activities and with the value chains of suppliers, channels or customers are planned in order to give the organisation a genuinely distinctive capability. For example, Burtons and Next[6] were successful in the 1980s through a

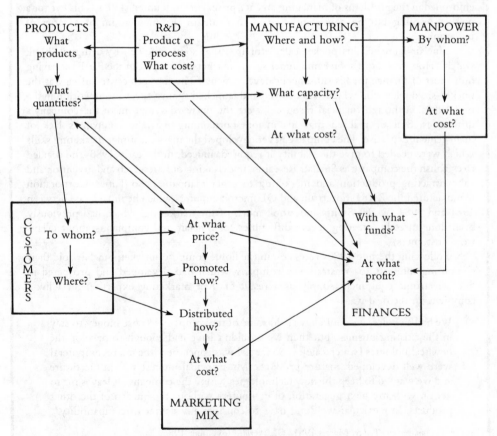

Figure 9.3 Some implications for resource integration in a product launch.

strategy of product/market differentiation *but* this was sustained by careful resource planning through the value chain. The procurement of merchandise, the hiring of shop staff, the shop design and layout were just as important as the product range, pricing and promotion strategies. The fit between these various resources was critical to their success. Figure 9.3 shows some of the ways in which resource interaction occurs in a new product launch.

The remainder of the discussion in this section will be devoted to the resource planning which might be needed in each of the primary activities of an organisation's value chain as new strategies are implemented. Within each activity these three central questions of overall requirements, fit with existing resources and fit between resources will be considered. The implications are summarised in Table 9.1.

9.3.2 Inbound logistics

The planning of resources is not confined to the internal resources of the organisation. In many cases the distinctive strength of a company may arise from the skilful planning of the resource inputs to the organisation and the linkages which exist with the value chains of suppliers.[7] Some important questions might be:

1. *What sources of supply* are available for new or changed products? Where are the locations of such supplies and what sort of suppliers are they? Are the sources able to provide regular and reliable delivery?

2. *To what extent should there be a spread of supply?* There may be advantages such as high levels of service and continuity of supply in establishing a long term relationship with a limited number of suppliers. This has to be set against the possibility that the organisation may become so linked to that supplier that new ideas from other suppliers are overlooked or more competitive prices ignored.

3. *Cost of supplies* is likely to be a major problem for new product initiatives. In its early stages of growth the sales volume may be too low to achieve benefits of low costs through bulk buying. How are costs to be reduced?

4. What are the financial requirements of the proposed strategy in terms of *current and capital expenditure?* To examine this sensibly it may require an exercise in both cash and capital budgeting (discussed later in the chapter) since the timing of financial support is of key importance. The identification of these requirements leads on to considerations of the way in which such finance is to be obtained.

5. What *sources of product and process technology changes*[8] will be used? Will technological developments be in-house or through technology transfer? Will the company own exclusive rights to the technology (e.g. patents or licence agreement)?

6. *What should be the R&D focus?* Should the firm concentrate on product development or process development and at what time should the emphasis switch? Product development will be of crucial importance during the development stage of a product lifecycle; and process development and cost reduction as maturity approaches. But when should a company switch its R&D focus from one to the other? Too early and it

Table 9.1 Some resource implications of strategic change.

Resource planning issue	The value chain				
	Inbound logistics	Operations	Outbound logistics	Marketing and sales	Services
Overall resource requirement	Sources of supply Cost of supply Capital required Source of technology	Production capacity Location of plants Manpower levels/skills	Transport Stocking Channels	Marketing mix (product, price, place, promotion) Subsidies	Product information Technical back-up Customer returns Maintenance Ancillary products
Fit with existing resources	Suitability of supplies Technology transfer Financial structure Working capital	Convert or new build Replace plant Training Manpower reductions/recruitment	Type of transport Choice of operators Storage and handling Ordering systems	In-house skills Outlets Agents Franchisees Role of salesforce Merchandising	In-house provisions Service agents
Fit between resources	Make or buy Stocking policy	Make or buy Plant flexibility Manning/demanning Team development	Stocking Lead times Transport costs	Compatibility of costs and price production volumes	Cost of services

runs the risk of a competitor developing significant product advantages: too late and it runs the risk of an uncompetitive cost position.

7. *Is the R&D capability compatible* with the other operational areas of the organisation? Is R&D effort being put behind a project that can be marketed, financed and produced effectively, for example?

8. *Is there sufficient support from other areas* of the operation? One of the major reasons for the failure of R&D activity is the lack of resources due to current business pressures or problems of short term profitability.

9. *To what extent are existing suppliers suitable?* The decision to change a supplier is important: for example, a new model of a product may call for a component which could be made more cheaply by a different supplier; but a company may still be very reliant on their existing supplier for other components or for spares for existing models and, as such, would wish to retain their goodwill.

10. The *make or buy* issue is important. To what extent is it advantageous to own sources of supply as distinct from buying them from elsewhere? This closely relates to the issue of vertical integration, and its advantages and disadvantages of integration have already been covered in Chapter 6.

11. To what extent is the *image or reputation of a supplier* important to other aspects of the business? A new product could benefit (or suffer) considerably in the market if customers know of the use of a component manufactured by a particularly well known supplier.

12. Is the project to be financed, over time from *internal resources?*[9] There are indications that management prefer this to be the case, if possible, and particularly in small firms. If this is impossible or not seen as sensible, then where are funds to be obtained? There may be a need for further equity capital for example. Is this to be raised through a new share issue or by raising further equity from existing shareholders through a rights issue? Alternatively or in addition, *loan capital* may be more attractive. If so, from where is this to be obtained and on what basis? In the public sector will grant–aid be available and appropriate? To what extent might third parties be willing to partly finance the venture?

13. How is an increase in *working capital* to be financed? There are two likely sources: tightening up the operation to provide increased profit margins through increased productivity, decreased wastage rates or credit control for example; or negotiating an increase in overdraft facility with the bank.

14. An examination of *sourcing of funds* may give rise to a need for change in the financial structure of the organisation. When the company's profits are growing a high level of debt may be advantageous since it increases earnings per share and retained earnings; but when profits are declining, high debt worsens the situation, both for earnings per share and retained earnings. Since the ability of a firm to generate funds for growth is likely to depend largely on the confidence of shareholders and the funds available for reinvestment from retained earnings, decisions on *levels of debt* become of critical importance.

15. A company that decides to raise capital by issuing new shares may also have its problems: there may be further dilution of control, particularly for a private company or the share price may be such that it would be more sensible to achieve an increase in share price before an issue of shares; there may even be fears that a failure to sell the shares might affect confidence in the company.

16. In terms of both fixed and current assets, what policies will guide the *asset management* of the company? For example, what levels of cash are to be held? If the levels are too high then questions will be asked both by shareholders and potential buyers as to why the company is not using or distributing the cash.

17. Another important aspect of the management of assets is the *deployment of funds* within the enterprise. If funds are to be allocated to one division for a product development strategy, are there other divisions for which funds are not to be made available or curtailed?

9.3.3 Operations[10]

There are many questions which might need to be addressed in planning the resources within the organisation's operations.

1. What level of *production capacity* is desirable? At least three levels can be considered. 'Demand matching' entails attempting to match levels of demand with levels of production and is therefore likely to involve high costs through short production runs. 'Operation smoothing' involves producing to average demand, building up stocks in low demand periods, and drawing off these in high demand periods. 'Subcontracting' entails producing at a minimum level and buying in the remainder.

2. *Where should plant be located*? Influences on this might include the proximity of markets, the cost of transport and access to supplies, and the cost, availability and skills of labour or the extent to which there are government incentives to move to an area. So too may economies of scale: for example, a choice between a large, single site with the benefit of economies of scale, or several smaller sites nearer to local markets or raw materials.

3. *What should be the timing of investment in plant*? Whilst demand may rise smoothly, costs of investment do not; they take place in a stepwise fashion resulting in periods of costly excess capacity: so the timing of investment becomes important. Choices on timing are problematic. Whether to be first with new plant and run the risk that later competitors will invest in improved plant; or to invest above levels of demand and accept overcapacity as the price of moving down the *experience curve* faster; or to introduce new plant later and run the risk of higher unit cost because of uncompetitive plant or being unable to meet demand.

4. *What skills are required*[11] to implement a course of action? These skills may be at a managerial or operative level. For example, a decision to move to a capital intensive, automated plant will need quite different skills from a labour intensive plant.

5. Associated with this may be the actual size of the *manpower requirement* of the organisation. In the case of a switch to automated plant, for example, the total numbers of staff may be reduced but the numbers required in specific skills increased.

6. The *identification of training needs* is important. Which individuals need what sort of experience to develop general management and operating abilities.

7. In terms of changes in manning levels, how are numbers to be increased or reduced? In the case of reductions, will this be through *natural wastage, redundancy or redeployment*. Will skills that are needed be met from within the organisation or by recruitment?

8. What will be the *financial implications* of an extensive redundancy programme? In the short term, redundancy payments can reach such high levels that they may mean the difference between relatively healthy overall profits and a loss.

9. Increasing emphasis is being placed on *team development* for managers and staff that are capable of working together productively. Has sufficient consideration been given to the teams of managers or staff needed to implement strategic change?

10. Given a change in production process, is it more sensible to *convert existing plant or build new plant*? There may be arguments in favour of each. Conversion may be less costly in terms of capital investment but mean that the down-time of plant during conversion is high. New plant may be more expensive to build but provide more efficient production on completion.

11. *Should the company make or buy the products*? If it makes or if it buys, to what extent should it do so? The issue is whether or not a company is well advised to tie up its funds in manufacturing when it could be investing in something else – more extensive marketing operations for example.

12. *Is the production resource flexible enough*? As companies follow paths of increasing replacement of capital equipment for labour there is the danger that expensive plant will need to be utilised to the full; if this plant is not flexible enough to handle different product ranges or variants then the only way full utilisation can be achieved is by seeking extra volume of sales, usually at low margins resulting in lower profits.

9.3.4 Outbound logistics

For many organisations success or failure can hinge on the way in which the shipments of goods to customers or outlets is handled. This may be a substantial element of cost for some companies and/or provide an important means of differentiating an organisation from its competitors (e.g. through speed of delivery). In service organisations many of the issues are equally important – particularly the order processing systems. Some key areas are:

1. The *transport and stocking requirements* need careful assessment – particularly issues of centralisation or geographical dispersal. Centralisation may be cheaper but reduce the speed of delivery to customers.

2. The *type of transport* is also a crucial decision – especially for international operators. Other important decisions concern the choice of specific operators and whether they have experience in handling the types of product concerned (e.g. frozen or delicate goods).

3. The *ordering systems* may be important. In public services the equivalent would be the

extent to which the organisation's systems encourage or discourage usage of the service for example in a library. This is a major strategic problem in many public services.

4. *Storage and handling facilities* may also be of central importance with particular types of product. For example, toxic substances, fresh foodstuffs etc.

5. The choice of *distribution channels* will determine the speed and quality of delivery.

9.3.5 Marketing and sales [12]

Issues concerning the market are of major importance in strategy formulation in both private and public organisations. Many of these broader issues concerning the choice of markets, the competitive position and strategy have been discussed in previous chapters. However, ultimately the success of the product/market strategy is dependent

---

ILLUSTRATION 9.3

Allocation of council houses

In most areas of the UK demand for council houses outstrips the local authority's available supply. Allocation procedures have to be developed which reflect the various national and local housing policies – usually with some difficulty.

Allocation of a scarce resource is always a difficult problem – even more so when the resource is central to life and human dignity and the allocation process is the subject of continual public debate. This is the position which the housing departments of local authorities find themselves in.

A major factor contributing to their difficulties is the conflict which can exist between the various (mandatory) obligations which the authorities have to the different groups which they serve. The 1980 *Housing Act* required local authorities to publish a summary of the rules for determining priority between applicants for housing.

This required authorities to consider:

1. *Who* is allowed to go on a housing waiting list at all.
2. How *selection* from the list occurs.
3. How *emergencies* and special need applicants are dealt with.

Most authorities used 'points' schemes either by individual applicant or by specified group. Even so there were several variations on the theme. Some used *date order* schemes, with or without bypass provision, whilst some allowed allocation on 'merit' to play a considerable part in their priority scheme. Some used a complex mixture of all these.

In all cases it proved necessary and desirable to leave some degree of discretion and flexibility without allowing the system to degenerate into a predominantly 'special pleadings' system. Indeed, if the local authorities were to fulfil some of their mandatory obligations (e.g. under the *Housing/Homeless Persons Act* of 1977) they had to use the rules flexibly to allow for 'bypass' of these special cases.

The management of many other public services had to cope with similar resource allocation problems (e.g. hospital waiting lists, student places in higher education, places in homes for the elderly).

Source: *Housing and Planning Review*, September 1985.

on detailed and astute planning of the organisation's marketing activities. In the public services these issues are equally relevant – although the term 'marketing' tends not to be used, the need to plan services around the genuine needs of users is of great strategic importance. For example, Illustration 9.3 shows how difficult decisions have to be made when demand for a public resource (housing) outweighs supply.

Some of the questions which need to be addressed are:

1. *Product planning*. What range of products/services will be offered, on what quality levels and to whom?

2. *Pricing*. What price levels are appropriate to balance the financial needs of the organisation and the attractiveness to potential consumers. Will customer *subsidies* be appropriate and available?

3. Will *agents or franchisees* be used?

4. *Selling and promotion*. What will be the role of the salesforce? Will merchandising activities be crucial? Will joint promotional activities (e.g. with outlets) be appropriate?

5. Choice of *collaborators*. Even where the general marketing strategy looks fine the specific choices of individual outlets, franchises, etc., is a major on performance. Will the chosen individuals/companies enhance your performance/competitive advantage? Will they prove an important link in the value chain?

6. Can the marketing requirements be met in terms of levels of *production*, at the *required quality and cost* so as to market the product successfully and make it sufficiently profitable to be financially acceptable?

9.3.6 Services

Many organisations neglect the services which they provide in support of their products and in doing so weaken the overall value of their products in the eyes of the potential consumers. Important areas are often:

1. Good quality *information* about products/services.
2. *Technical back-up*.
3. Good systems for *handling customer returns*.
4. A well organised *maintenance network* (e.g. for consumer durables).
5. Availability of *ancillary products* (e.g. computer or video software can be crucial as shown in Illustration 9.4).

There is a feeling in many organisations that these items simply add cost (which they do) without appreciating that they also add significant value to the product. As such they are likely to be important activities within the *value chain*.

9.3.7 Key resources in implementing generic strategies

A useful way of bringing this section together is by returning to the concept of generic strategies. *Differentiation* and *cost leadership* are basic strategic choices facing an organisation: the extent to which either can be put into practice will depend on the extent to which the organisation has, or can configure, the set of resources and skills required for the generic strategy it chooses to follow.

ILLUSTRATION 9.4

Philips and the compact disc

In assessing the ability of a company to pursue a new strategy, care needs to be taken not to overlook critically important resources outside the direct control of the company.

Although it was widely acknowledged that the Philips video cassette system (video 2000) was technically superior to the Japanese VHS system, the product failed to make much impact on the market in the early 1980s. Indeed, it represented the most conspicuous product failure of the company for some years. The product failed partly because it was beaten to the market and partly because of the erroneous judgement that users would have little interest in hiring commercially produced videos (mainly films). They had, therefore, launched the hardware with no 'software' back-up. After four expensive years they were forced to bring out their own VHS machine, using Japanese technology.

This experience was very influential in shaping the company's parallel efforts in the audio market, particularly in relation to compact disc machines. The technical know-how of Philips was 'offered' to the Japanese electronics giants and Sony took the bait. The two companies agreed to develop the compact disc to a common standard. Ultimately the whole industry fell into line with that standard.

This experience illustrates the importance of two key resources which were partially outside the company's control. First, the ability to impose an industry technical standard/system, and second, the availability of related products (in this case suitable 'software', i.e. films on video).

Source: *Management Today*, January 1986.

A cost leadership strategy will require an emphasis on cost efficient plant and processes, with an ability to renew investment to maintain advantage in these areas. It is also likely that particular attention will be paid to achieving simplicity of operating processes and low cost distribution systems. An organisation following a strategy of diversification, on the other hand, is likely to require different sorts of skills and resources. In particular there will be a need for strengths in marketing, research and creativity with an emphasis on product development and engineering and strong links into the value systems throughout its distribution channel.

One of the problems that organisations face is coping with the realities of resource requirements of these sorts. In particular, problems can occur for diverse organisations seeking to pursue different generic strategies or focus strategies for different products. This will require specific configurations of resources for specific markets or market segments, and is likely to be difficult for an organisation with plant, labour and management held in common across products and services.

9.4 PREPARING RESOURCE PLANS

So far this chapter has dealt with some of the underlying principles behind the planning of resources at both a corporate and operational level and discussed some of the detailed resource issues which need to be resolved during implementation. This final section is concerned with the process of resource planning and considers some ways in which resource plans can be prepared.

9.4.1 Priorities and key tasks

Organisations need to be clear about their priorities and the key tasks which they should undertake to ensure the successful implementation of new strategies. This also provides the basis for the management and control of new strategies (which will be discussed in the next two chapters). Key tasks and priorities are different from each other. The term 'key tasks' refers to those tasks on which the strategic change is fundamentally dependent for its success. This may be the creation of a new value activity or the development of new linkages within the value chain or with the value chain of suppliers, channels or customers.

Priorities, on the other hand, are more to do with timing: they are the actions that need to be tackled to get the project underway: so the design and commissioning of plant or ensuring that financial resources are available might be priorities in this sense. The identification of priorities and key tasks also provides a basis for the allocation of responsibilities. Who is to be responsible for each of the key areas? Where key areas interlink, who is responsible for co-ordination? It is also worthwhile to be explicit about what is not so important. What are the things that should or can be left until later or, more likely, which of the different priorities being advocated are to be followed up and which are not?

9.4.2 The plan of action

A plan is the output of the series of questions raised so far in this chapter. It sets out what resources need to be obtained and which disposed of. This may well be in the form of a budget, but might also be usefully expressed as a sequence of actions or a timetable in a written plan. For example, an organisation introducing a new product line would need a plan of action to co-ordinate the various aspects of its resource planning. For example, on-the-job production line retraining cannot begin until a production facility exists. Until the company has examined in detail the timing of development, installation, commissioning and completion of plant, it is not possible to examine fully the flow of funds required to finance the venture. Until it knows at what rate production is to be geared, it cannot take a sensible view about the extent of the product launch; that in turn means that it will not have a clear idea of expected revenue flow, so again it cannot think sensibly about the requirement for funds.

The circularity of the problem is quite usual in developing a plan of action and raises the question of where to start – with a market forecast, an available level of funds, a production level constraint or what? The answer is that it may not matter too much where the starting point is since the plan will have to be reworked and readjusted several times. A useful guideline is to enter the problem through what appears to be the major change area. So an organisation planning new strategies of growth may well start with an assessment of market opportunity. Someone starting a new business may well begin with a realistic assessment of how much capital they might have available. Many public services have been compelled to replan their resources to achieve particular levels of cost savings.

A plan of action should also provide the basis for understanding the impact of changes in the sequencing of activities. What would be the effect of a delay in one part of the programme on the rest of the programme? Are some areas of activity less sensitive to delays or change than others? It might be found that delays in the installation of plant do not have major impacts on the retraining programme or even on the recruitment and activity of the marketing team since both are fairly flexible. However, such a delay may have very serious marketing consequences if it means that the launch is delayed giving the competition time to react. The plan of action will also provide a means of monitoring and controlling the development of the project. It helps identify points in the programme at which certain key stages should be completed for example.

9.4.3 The recognition and testing of key assumptions

All plans are based on assumptions. They may be assumptions about resource availability, the capacity of the organisation to adapt existing resources or co-ordinate the resource requirements of a new strategy. Assumptions may also be to do with the environment; that a market will grow, that funds can be raised or that suppliers will deliver on time. The questions raised so far in this chapter help identify the main assumptions upon which a plan is based and these assumptions should be made explicit as part of the planning process.

The danger is that when a plan is drawn up the assumptions built into it take on the appearance of fact and become unquestioned. This means that the vulnerable areas of the plan are disguised and reasons for shortfalls or failures may not be recognised. If assumptions are made explicit the plan can be used as a model to help both in the evaluation of strategy and also in the investigation of alternative means of implementation of strategy. Different assumptions about market conditions, price acceptability, competitive action, cost levels and so on, can be tested out to see how vulnerable plans of action are to different assumptions. So, too, can different assumptions about timing be tested out: the effect that delays in a construction programme would have on capital requirements, for example. A common way of carrying out this sort of sensitivity analysis is to build 'best', 'worst' and 'most likely' assumptions into budgets, models or a breakeven analysis to see what the implications are. The 'best' view would be a budget based on an optimistic set of assumptions, the 'worst' on a pessimistic set, and the 'most likely' on what might be, for example, a consensus view of most reasonable assumptions. The resulting plans can be examined to see the implications of the differing assumptions.

9.4.4 Financial planning and budgeting[13]

Financial planning is concerned with translating the resource implications of decisions or possible decisions into financial statements of one sort or another. This is most commonly done through the various types of budget that managers use. Budgets have many uses and perform different roles in organisations. The concern here is with budgets as plans and as models.

A budget may take the form of a consolidated statement of the resource position required to achieve a set of objectives or put into effect a strategy. To achieve such a statement it is necessary to identify and think through the required resource position of the organisation. A budget expresses these in a monthly or yearly form, perhaps split down by departments in the organisation. As such it represents a plan of action stated in resource terms for an organisation. The process of budgeting also involves the thinking through of the resource implications of action and so has a useful role to play in forecasting the impact of decisions on the resources of an organisation or part of an organisation. For example, the planned launch of a new product might mean increased demands on the R&D department. It is likely that the department would then undertake a budgeting exercise to forecast the resource implications for themselves and may, as a result, come up with requests for additional resources.

Whether at an organisational or departmental level, a budget is in effect a model of required resources. A model can be examined, tested and adjusted to see the implications of change in assumptions about the future or changes in the progress that might be achieved in a project. Can the resources needed be sensibly co-ordinated or are there incompatibilities? Especially useful is the facility to examine the implication of changes in expected performance, or a failure to meet required target deadlines and thus identify key tasks and priorities within the plan. This can be easily achieved if the budget is set up on a computer spreadsheet package.

There are different types of budget. [14] It is always risky to say exactly which types are most needed for resource planning, but the following might typically be used.

1. *Capital budgeting* is concerned with generating a statement of the flow of funds related to a particular project or decision. A company may decide to invest in new plant or acquire a new business. A capital budgeting exercise might well seek to determine: (a) what the outflow and inflow of funds associated with that project will be; (b) what the implications of different means of financing the project would be (for example, how an acquisition financed by increased loan capital would differ from one financed by increased equity capital); or (c) some assessment of how worthwhile the project is through some measure of return of investment (discussed in Chapter 8).

2. *Revenue budgets* show the expected outcome of decisions in terms of changes in stocks, cash, debtors and creditors. Underlying such an exercise would be decisions on expenditure and the management of working capital: it might be that the exercise would examine different policies on cash, stock or creditor management.

3. *Departmental budgets* may be important if strategic changes are likely to affect parts of the business differently. As mentioned earlier, a decision to adopt a more aggressive product development programme might well mean a much larger allocation of resources to departments such as R&D and a cut-back in others.

4. *Consolidated budgets* and projected profit and loss accounts may well be useful in projecting, perhaps over a period of years, implications of decisions on an organisation's overall performance. For example, a new venture might reduce a company's overall profits for many years before its benefits at an organisational level are apparent. This may, in turn, highlight as a key task the need to convince shareholders of the wisdom of the venture and the need for patience.

One of the very real difficulties experienced in budgeting is the extent to which the process actually helps the reallocation of resources to fit future strategies. This is because the budgeting process is usually tied into the power structure in the organisation as mentioned in Chapter 5. The types of reallocation which may be necessary at both the corporate and operational level may well prove extremely difficult due to historical vested interests. This has been shown to be particularly problematic in public service organisations where spending is justified against 'need' rather than income and often subject to approval through a democratic, political process. The outcome is often the strong remaining strong even where there is agreement to a changing strategy.

In order to address these budgeting difficulties some organisations have attempted to adopt a *zero-based budgeting*[15] approach where the historical size of the various budgets is given no weight in establishing the future deployment of resources (see Illustration 9.5). On the whole this process has been unsuccessful unless tempered with some short term pragmatism. The most effective use of zero-based budgeting usually provides a 'safeguard' whereby any individual budget will not vary by more than an

---

ILLUSTRATION 9.5

Zero-based budgeting (ZBB)

Although zero-based budgeting arose in the US private sector (Kodak), its greatest potential may be for public service organisations.

Zero-based budgeting is an approach which requires managers to propose and justify their (departmental) budgets in relation to cost/benefit and alternative uses of that resource. The existence of a budget in the previous year is not an acceptable argument in this case. The UK government through its Financial Management Initiative (FMI) was keen to emphasise value-for-money – a concept sadly lacking in traditional public sector budgeting. This can be somewhat difficult to define in areas of indirect spending (say a computer services unit). For these reasons value-for-money is usually divided into three subsidiary concepts of:

Economy (minimising inputs whilst achieving objectives).
Efficiency (productivity).
Effectiveness (achieving targets).

The FMI therefore placed great emphasis on defining objectives; deciding how to measure them and evolving performance indicators. Both the National Audit Office in central government and the Audit Commission for local government now devote a high proportion of their time to value-for-money audits. ZBB is ideally suited to form part of both the planning and control systems in this drive for better cost/benefit.

Despite the technical difficulties of setting up ZBB, its virtues compare favourably with the old style budgeting/planning in local authorities. There the medium term budgets are projections of annual budgets which in turn are entirely based on measuring *inputs* with scant regard to the output of each department or service. Perhaps the most regrettable weakness of traditional budgets is that they pay no regard to alternative ways in which resources could be used and, as such, many valuable developments are passed by as the budgeting juggernaut rolls on.

Source: *Management Today*, July 1986.

agreed percentage from the previous year (this is the 'constrained bidding' or 'constrained bargaining' referred to in Figure 9.1). There are often good practical reasons for this. For example, the redeployment of resources from one area to another may be achievable, and even universally supported, if the pace of change does not lead to an unmanageable period of transition. In the public sector it is quite common to signal a commitment to redeploying resources (particularly people) by 'red circling' individuals within the organisation. That individual is not redeployed, but once they leave then the post is automatically redeployed. The critical issue is the extent to which future strategies can wait for redeployment to occur.

9.4.5 Network analysis[16]

Network analysis, also known as *critical path analysis,* was developed for the purposes of military planning during the Second World War and has been adapted for management use since. It is a technique for planning projects by breaking them down into their component activities and showing these activities and their interrelationships in the form of a network. By considering the times and resources required to complete each of the activities it is possible to locate the critical path of activities which determines the minimum time for the project. The network can also be used for scheduling materials and other resources and for examining the impact of changes in one subarea of the project on others. The technique is particularly relevant to projects which have a reasonably definite start and finish.

It has been used very effectively in new product or service launches, construction of plant, acquisitions and mergers, relocation and R&D projects all the sorts of activity relevant to strategy implementation. Figure 9.4 is an outline network analysis diagram for the launch of a new car. In fact, the analysis would probably be a great deal more detailed, but as an example it can be seen how this sort of analysis can help in resource planning.

- It demands the breakdown of the programme of implementation into its constituent parts by resource area.
- It helps identify priorities because it identifies activities upon which others depend. For example, the network identifies that pilot-building cannot take place before the development of tooling: and since the runout of the old model is not scheduled to start before the pilot-build, and may well need to be fitted into the selling and promotional calendar, it places an emphasis on the priority of tooling that might not have been obvious at the outset.
- A network represents a plan of action. It enables the analyst to examine the implications of changes in the plan or deviations from the plan. He can ask questions and follow through the implications on the whole programme of development of tooling, engineering design, or the pilot-build programme taking a longer, or shorter, time than expected. So a network is of particular value in thinking through the timing implications of a plan.

The network itself may be drawn up at several levels. The sort shown in Figure 9.4 may be fine as a generalisation of a plan of action: however, there would need to be much more detailed planning at a departmental level for example. There might be subnetworks for marketing and production or, indeed, a much more detailed overall network.

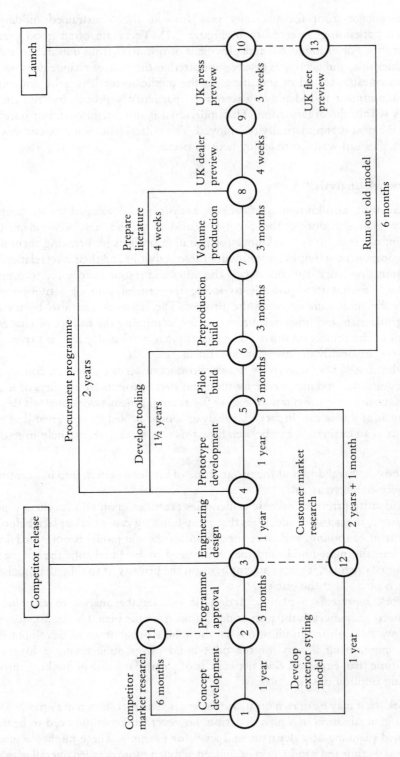

Figure 9.4 A network analysis for the launch of a new car.

A common alternative or addition to a network is some form of departmental or project plan which details activities within the network, sets target dates for completion, and allocates clear responsibilities for completion of specific tasks.

There are a number of developments of network analysis methods which readers may find of interest. 'Programme evaluation review technique' (PERT) allows uncertainty about the times of each activity in the network to be taken into account. For example, in Figure 9.4, steps 4 to 6 would be so dependent on the outcome of the market research that, in reality, it may be difficult to make a precise estimate of the time needed for these activities. PERT would be a useful refinement in such circumstances.

Network analysis can be very valuable in establishing the sequence in which tasks need to be planned. A good network should also assist in drawing up a time schedule (i.e. the precise time when each task should start and finish). However, there are other techniques which can also be helpful in scheduling tasks such as Gantt charts or route planning. The operations management literature is very helpful in this area of resource planning and should be consulted by readers who have a particular interest.

One specific approach to task scheduling which has received considerable attention and proved to be of strategic importance to many manufacturing companies is 'just-in-time',[17] as shown in Illustration 9.6. This technique has revolutionised the way in which some companies plan the acquisition of resources with the resultant reduction in costs and, at least in the short run, the potential of gaining competitive advantage on that basis.

ILLUSTRATION 9.6

Just-in-time

A simple and commonsense approach to resource planning, just-in-time has had to await the computer revolution to become a practical tool.

Just-in-time is a simple philosophy according to which every stage in the manufacturing operation from receipt of materials to assembly and despatch occurs *precisely* when it is needed – not before and never later. In effect, split-second timing is applied throughout the process, allowing a factory to work at the desired level of production with no idle stocks. An exceptional level of control is needed to ensure that there are no reject parts to be replaced, no shortages, and, equally important, no surpluses. Although it is not a computer technique as such, it would be impossible to implement without a computer.

The motto of just-in-time is 'if you don't need it now don't make/buy it now'. Its attractions are greatest in industries with a wide product range which have to contend with volatile demand and constant changes in specification – fittingly the computer industry itself falls squarely into this category. Xerox is one of the leaders in using just-in-time *and* in the supply of software and consultancy to other users. At one Xerox copier plant the technique reduced manufacturing unit costs by 50%. More typically, costs can be cut by 20% to 40%, stocks by as much as 70% and productivity increased by 40%. Other advantages can be the freeing of floor space.

Within the UK the IBM plant at Greenock is a big user of just-in-time techniques. Between 1982 and 1985 output from the factory increased fourfold while the payroll only increased by 15%.

Source: *Management Today*, September 1986.

9.5 SUMMARY

By looking at the resource planning process this chapter has started to provide material by which readers can think through how strategies can be put into effect.

It has been seen that resource planning needs to occur at two general levels within most organisations. First, there are the broad issues of resource allocation between different divisions, service departments, functions or businesses within an organisation. This has been referred to as resource planning at the *corporate level* where the focus is one of deciding how resources should be allocated in order to provide an appropriate balance to pursue the overall organisation's strategies. A variety of methods are used to allocate resources at this level depending on the degree of change envisaged in the resource base and the extent to which priorities will be dictated centrally.

Second, the success of a strategy is dependent on a detailed consideration of the resources required at the *operational level*. The organisation's value chain is a useful framework for identifying the resource requirements of any strategy.

Whereas the people of an organisation are a critical resource which will determine the success or failure of strategic change their influence on strategic implementation is more pervasive than that. Successful implementation also depends on the organisation, motivation and control of people. The next two chapters look at these very important aspects of implementation.

REFERENCES

1. A useful article on zero-based budgeting is by D. Wise in *Management Today*, July, 1986.

2. J. Pfeffer, *Power in Organisations*, pp. 101–106, Pitman, 1981, outlines the important links between resource allocations and processes of power.

3. For example, T. Peters and R. Waterman, *In Search of Excellence*, Harper & Row, 1982, explains how an investment bank was operated in 3M's company.

4. P. Dainty, 'How to manage retreat', *Management Today*, Nov., 1985.

5. The notion of the recipe as proposed by J-C. Spender, 'Strategy making in business', PhD thesis, University of Manchester, is to do with the 'received wisdom' in an industry and expressed in terms of how an organisation should be operated. In this sense the recipe is likely to encapsulate views about which resource requirements are particularly important. Also see, P. H. Grinyer and J-C. Spender, 'Recipes, crises, and adaptation in mature businesses, *International Studies of Management and Organisation*, **IX**(3): 113, 1979.

6. See article on Next, *The Guardian*, 25 March, 1985.

7. Supplies strategy, important though it is, is not extensively discussed in the literature. However, there is some useful discussion of the area in a chapter by D. F. Cooper called 'Corporate planning and purchasing strategy' in D. H. Farmer and B. Taylor (eds), *Corporate Planning and Procurement*, Heinemann, 1975. D. H. Farmer also discusses supplies strategy in *Insights in Procurement and Materials Management*, Institute of Purchasing and Supply.

8. R. E. Burridge, *Product Innovation and Development*, Business Books, 1977, widely covers this

field. Readers may also refer to G. Randall, 'Managing new products', *BIM Management Survey Report*, No. 47, 1980, which is a survey of activity and problems in the area, as is W. P. Sommers, 'Improving corporate performance through better management of innovation', *Outlook*, Fall/Winter, 1981.

9. A sound general discussion of financial strategy and planning can be found in Chapter 5 of John Sizer, *An Insight into Management Accounting* (2nd edn), Pitman, 1979. More detailed discussion of financial management as it relates to financial strategy is to be found in books on managerial finance: for example, J. F. Weston and E. F. Brigham, *Managerial Finance*, Dryden, 1978 or L. J. Gitman, *Principles of Managerial Finance*, Harper & Row, 1976.

10. Many of the resource planning issues relating to operations are discussed in: R. Wild, *Production and Operations Management: Principles and techniques* (3rd edn), Holt, Rinehart & Winston, and T. Hill, *Production/Operations Management*, Prentice Hall, 1983.

11. G. McBeath, *Organisation and Manpower Planning* (2nd edn), Business Books, 1969, is still one of the most thorough treatments of manpower planning in relation to strategic change.

12. The discussion of marketing strategy in P. Kotler, *Marketing Management* (4th edn), Prentice Hall, 1980, is useful at this level.

13. As a general introduction to budgets and budgetary control see John Sizer, *An Insight into Management Accounting* (2nd edn), Pitman, 1979.

14. Readers who are not familiar with these techniques should read any good book on management finance. For example, see L. J. Gitman, *Principles of Managerial Finance*, Harper & Row, 1976, or J. M. Samuels and F. M. Wilkes, *Management of Company Finance*, Nelson, 1980.

15. See reference 2.

16. Network analysis is explained in almost any text on management science or operations management. So, for example, readers could refer to R. Wild (reference 10, chapter 13), or K. Howard, *Quantitative Analyses for Planning Decisions*, McDonald & Evans, 1975, or P. G. Moore, *Basic Operational Research* (2nd edn), chapter 2, Pitman, 1976.

17. Just-in-time is explained in T. Hill, *Manufacturing Strategy*, Open University Press, 1985.

Recommended key readings

- Chapters 11, 12 and 13 of *Strategic Planning* (Free Press/Collier Macmillan, 1979) by G. A. Steiner provides a useful guide to the translation of strategic plans into functional and operational management, as does R. G. Murdick, R. H. Eckhouse, R. C. Moor and T. W. Zimmerer, *Business Policy: A framework for analysis*, Grid Inc., 1976.

- As a guide to the sort of financial planning necessary: L. J. Gitman, *Principles of Managerial Finance*, Harper & Row, 1976, or J. M. Samuels and F. M. Wilkes, *Management of Company Finance*, Nelson, 1980.

- For an explanation of the techniques of network planning: R. Wild, *Production and Operations Management* (3rd edn), Holt, Rinehart & Winston, 1984.

Chapter 10

ORGANISATION STRUCTURE

10.1 INTRODUCTION

One of the most important resources of an organisation is its people; so how they are organised is crucial to the effectiveness of strategy. The last chapter dealt with how resourcing aspects of implementation might be planned. The next two chapters are primarily concerned with how its implementation is effected through the people in the organisation.

Traditional views about regulation through organisation can be traced back to early twentieth-century management 'scientists' and beyond.[1] Typically such views hold that: (1) There is an optimum number of subordinates that an executive can control, so this dictates what the span of control should be in an organisation. For instance, it is sometimes argued that no manager should have more than about six direct subordinates. (2) Everyone should have one boss only with clear lines of reporting; so the flow of instructions and reporting goes up and down the organisation. (3) There should be a clear delineation of who is responsible for what; jobs should be compartmentalised, usually functionally, so that individuals and groups can develop high degrees of specialist skills. (4) There should be clear rules and procedures to govern people's behaviour in the organisation.

These views are commensurate with a view of strategy making which is essentially top-down: strategy is formed at the top and the rest of the organisation is seen as a means of implementation: organisation design becomes a means of top down control. Such principles of control are known as bureaucratic or mechanistic.[2] As was seen in Chapter 2, however, the idea that strategy is formulated in a top-down way is questionable, and the extension of this, that mechanistic structures are necessarily appropriate, is therefore also questionable.

This chapter and Chapter 11 consider organisational design and control in the context of the strategic management of organisations. It is accepted that there is a need for the regulation of the implementation of strategy: but this needs to take account of many influences. For example, what are the sorts of problem that the organisation faces in constructing strategy? Is it in a highly complex or changing environment or a fairly stable environment? How diverse is the organisation; for example, the needs of a multinational company are different from a small local firm? To what extent is the organisation reliant on simple or complex technologies? How answerable are the top executives to external influences; for example, is the organisation a public body, perhaps answerable to a government minister; is it a privately owned firm; or perhaps a charity or a co-operative? All these different influences must have a bearing on the way the organisation needs to be designed. It is not possible to have a simple set of rules which can prescribe organisational structures and systems.[3] This chapter examines the structure of organisations in two ways. First, it reviews the basic structural forms that exist. Second, the chapter considers what is likely to influence the sort of structure appropriate to an organisation.

10.2 STRUCTURAL TYPES

Managers asked to describe their organisations usually respond by drawing an organisation chart, in an attempt to map out its structure. These sorts of structure are like skeletons: they define the general shape and facilitate or constrain certain sorts of activity; but they are incomplete in themselves without the 'flesh' that is dealt with later in this chapter and the next. It is also worth noting that the categories used here, although common, are not always employed. For example, in some texts[4] a separate category of 'holding company' is omitted: it is included here because it is still in common usage, particularly in the UK. Other writers[5] split down the general category of 'multidivisional' into subcategories. However, what follows does provide a basic description of structural types.

10.2.1 The simple structure

A simple structure could really be thought of as no formal structure at all. It is the type of organisation common in many very small businesses. There is likely to be an owner who undertakes most of the responsibilities of management, perhaps with a partner or an assistant. However, there is little division of management responsibility and probably little clear definition of who is responsible for what if there is more than one person involved. The operation is then run by the personal control and contact of an individual.

The main problem here is that the organisation can only operate effectively up to a certain size of operation beyond which it becomes too cumbersome for one person to control. What this size is will depend on the nature of the business: an insurance broker may personally handle a very large turnover, whereas a similarly sized business (in terms of turnover) manufacturing and selling goods, may be much more diverse in its operations and therefore more difficult to control personally.

10.2.2 The functional structure

A functional structure is based on the primary tasks that have to be carried out such as production, finance and accounting, marketing and personnel. Figure 10.1 represents a typical organisation chart for such a business. This structure is typically found in smaller companies or those with narrow, rather than diverse, product ranges. However, within a multidivisional structure, the divisions themselves are likely to be split up into functional management areas. For example, a local authority is structured into departments (which in many respects are similar to the idea of divisions) but within these there is likely to be a functional structure.

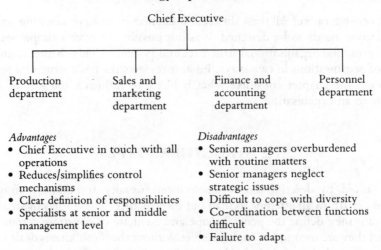

Figure 10.1 A basic functional structure.

The functional structure has some advantages.[6] If the operation is not too large it enables the chief executive to keep directly in touch with the operations and it is likely to reduce problems of management control because the natural flow of information is vertical and lines of communication short. It also means that there are likely to be specialists in senior and middle management positions which, it is argued, improves the quality of the management of the functions. In functional structures, job roles are likely to be clearly understood and easy to define because they are based on the tasks that the organisation has to carry out.

There are some disadvantages too, particularly as organisations become larger or more diverse in their interests. Senior managers may become overconcerned and overburdened with routine matters, neglecting the strategic concerns which face the organisation. If the organisation's interests have become diversified then the functional structure may not cope easily with the different competitive environments in which it is operating. Suppose, for example, a one-product company operating in one market develops a new product for a different market. Not only are the managers faced with understanding the demands of different markets, they may also have to cope internally with different technologies of production for the new products. A result may be that such organisations fail to adapt to changing competitive situations. It may be difficult for the organisation to deal with these differences by continuing to manage on a functional, task-based structure since the environment and technology are no longer of the same kind. A further problem which often arises is where co-operation between functions is required, such as the planning of new products, which may need the co-ordination of marketing, production and the finance and accountancy functions. If this has to be done by referring problems continually up vertical lines of authority for decisions then co-operation may become a difficulty. Advantages and disadvantages of functional structures are summarised in Figure 10.1.

10.2.3 The multidivisional structure

The main characteristic of a multidivisional structure is that it is subdivided into units which are responsible for defined market, service or product areas of the enterprise. These divisions may be formed on the basis of products, as for example in Figure 10.2: there are, however, other bases for divisionalisation such as geographical areas, or the processes of the enterprise. For example, a vertically integrated company might have manufacturing, wholesaling and retail divisions. Illustration 10.1 shows how Bass plc has within it different bases of divisionalisation; some are product/market based, others based on processes such as marketing and production; others geographic, and there are still other parts of the business which are part owned with other companies.

The most popular structure now adopted in industrial companies is the multi-divisional structure. In 1960 just one-third of major manufacturing companies had a divisional structure. By the end of that decade over two-thirds had such a structure. This dramatic change coincided with a major programme of diversification by these firms, many of which were involved in extensive acquisition programmes at that time. Divisionalisation has then been a response to the need to manage diversity.[7]

This structural form has come about as an attempt to overcome the sorts of problems that functional structures have in such circumstances. The main advantage of the multidivisional structure is that each division is able to concentrate on the problems and opportunities of its particular business environment. For example, it would be difficult to make a functional structure work across the diversity of interests for a company such as Bass (see Illustration 10.1). The product markets in which it operates are so different that it would be impractical to bring the tasks together in a single body. It makes more sense to split up the company according to the different product markets or operations and then ensure that the needs of each division are met by tailoring the operations within the division to the particular business needs. The result can be quite a

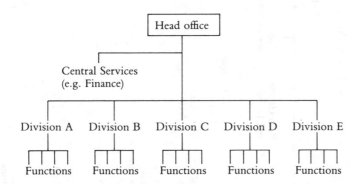

Advantages
- Concentration on business area (e.g. product market)
- Facilitates measurement of unit performance
- Ease of addition and divestment of units
- Facilitates senior management's attention to strategy
- Encourages general manage-ment development

Disadvantages
- Possible confusion over locus of responsibility (centralisation/ decentralisation confusion)
- Conflict betrween divisions
- Basis of intertrading
- Costly
- Divisions grow too large
- Complexity of co-ordination if too many divisions

Figure 10.2 A multidivisional structure.

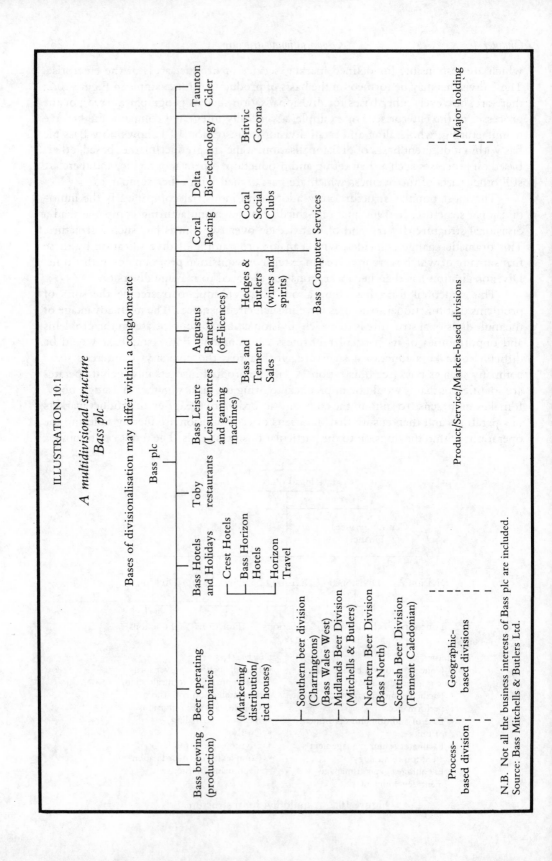

ILLUSTRATION 10.1

A multidivisional structure
Bass plc

Bases of divisionalisation may differ within a conglomerate

N.B. Not all the business interests of Bass plc are included.
Source: Bass Mitchells & Butlers Ltd.

complex organisation; for example, a company may decide that it needs a number of levels of divisions in order to break up business activities sensibly. Figure 10.3 shows this. The company might be broken into a first level of divisions based on broad product markets: for example in Reed International in the 1970s one was DIY, another magazines and newspapers, another the production of paper and board and so on. Within each of these first level divisions, the businesses may again be split up. In the case of Reed International they were split into named business units – Crown, Polycell and so on. Indeed, within these business units there might be further divisions; for example, Crown was divided into a paints division, a wallcoverings division, a merchant division for distribution, and a retail operation. At some level in the organisation a division will then be split into functionally based departments dealing with the specialist tasks of that business.

This raises another problem. Which functions are to be included at what level of divisionalisation; and which functions are properly placed within the corporate head office rather than within any one of the divisions? For example, within Figure 10.3 where should a function such as financial planning be placed. Presumably this is required both at a corporate level and at some level within an operating business; but should this be at level one, two or three for example? Similarly, at which level should personnel policy be decided or pay bargaining take place? Where should technology development best occur, or property decisions be made. There is no best way in which such functions can be placed within an organisation. It is a matter of deciding on the most sensible design for the organisation in structural terms and also at what level decisions need to be made.

Certain advantages arise from divisional structures. For example, because each division addresses itself to one business area it is possible to measure the performance of that division as a business unit. It becomes clear if it is performing up to expectations or below par. So the company as a whole is able to measure more easily its performance in diverse areas of activity. Moreover, because these activities are set up as separate operating units, they are easier to divest if necessary: an example here is the way in which British Telecom and the letter post services of the Post Office were separated in

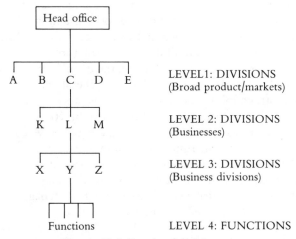

Figure 10.3 Levels of divisions.

the early 1980s to facilitate the privatisation of British Telecom in 1985. Divisionalisation also facilitates the passing of profit and general management responsibility down
the line. This can have two benefits: first it means that the senior management in the
parent company is more able to concentrate on strategic matters, and second it helps to
develop general management ability at a lower level.

There are, however, disadvantages and difficulties with the multidivisional structure. One is to do with this issue of devolution of responsibility. To what extent should
responsibility be passed to the divisions? It may be accepted by all, for example, that
operating responsibility to meet profit objectives or deadlines for new product launches
should be devolved. But who decides on strategic objectives? Who decides if new
product development should take place at all and in what areas? Who decides on levels
of expenditure or borrowing? What about the responsibility for acquisition programmes? If immediate action is required to counter a major competitive attack and that
action could mean short or even long term reversals, at what level is the decision to be
made? These are problems of decentralisation which are returned to again in Section
10.3.

Another problem is conflict between the divisions for the resources of the parent
organisation. On what basis should financial resources be allocated? How will the
management of one division react if, despite meeting their budgets, some other
division, deemed to have greater growth prospects, is favoured more? Yet further
problems occur if there is intertrading between the divisions; how should transfer
prices be fixed and what should the trading relationships be? The same sorts of problem
occur if the divisions, based on different product markets, use common plant. Who
controls it, who has first call on it, on what basis are the costs of raw material allocated?
So problems of operation and control are often far from straightforward in a
multidivisional firm. These issues of control will be dealt with more fully in Chapter
11.

Another disadvantage often cited is that divisional structures are costly because
they replicate management functions in each division and, with the addition of a central
head office staff, this leads to high overheads. This argument is only valid if the cost of.
the overhead is greater than the cost of inefficiency that could result from an
inappropriate structure: it is a matter of management judgement. Inefficiency may also
arise because the divisions, themselves, become too big and cumbersome and 'suffer
from all the problems of oversized functional structures'.[8] Figure 10.2 summarises the
advantages and disadvantages of a multidivisional structure.

There has been some research work done on the financial performance of different
structural forms.[9] This appears to show that, in general, multidivisional structures
out-perform other structural types. However, this does require some important
qualifications. Divisionalised firms perform better than functional firms on measures of
growth than they do on measures of rate of return; the gap between measures of return
on investment and equity are marginal when compared to measures of growth in
earnings and sales. But since divisionalisation tends to occur when firms expand and
diversify, it might be expected that firms with divisional structures should show higher
growth figures. It appears that firms which are content to manage though a functional
structure perform virtually as well on measures of return as those which opt for
divisionalisation. Indeed, it has been argued that companies emphasising high growth
best achieve this by divisionalisation and fairly informal management styles, whilst

those emphasising profit performance may well be more advised to look for a more functional structure with specialist senior managers and more formal management styles.[10]

10.2.4 The holding company structure

In its most extreme form a holding company is really an investment company. It may simply consist of shareholdings in a variety of individual, unconnected, business operations over which it exercises little or no control. However, the term is also applied to an enterprise which, itself, operates a portfolio of virtually autonomous business units. Although part of a parent company, these business units operate independently and probably retain their original company names. The role that the parent company takes may be limited to decisions about the buying and selling of such companies with very little involvement in their strategy. The logic behind such a structure is one of two kinds. It may be that the holding company is simply a portfolio of interests (or investments): arguably, this is the situation as far as Lonrho or BTR is concerned. A holding company may also come about in the interests of the member companies: for example, Norcros was established in 1956 as a sort of club of independent companies which could offset their independent profits against others' losses.[11]

An example of a holding company structure is given in Figure 10.4. The business interests of the parent company are likely to be varied, some of them may be wholly owned and some not, and there may be many business units within the group. To a large extent, the business units retain their own identity and perhaps their own individual structures. Central corporate staff and services may be very limited. The essential differentiating feature for a holding company is, then, the extent of the autonomy of the business units, particularly over strategic decisions.

The advantages a holding company can offer are based on the idea that the constituent businesses will operate to their best potential if left alone. It has been argued that as business environments become more turbulent, because greater decentralisation

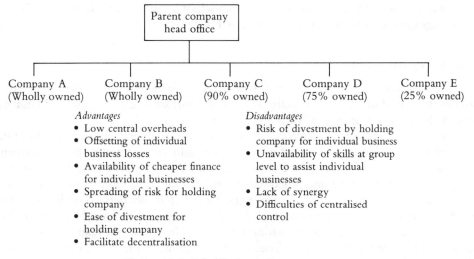

Figure 10.4 A holding company structure.

of strategic decision making is required, holding company structures facilitate the situation to a greater extent than formal divisionalisation. However, Channon's study[12] of the UK service industry sector in the 1970s found that on all measures of performance the holding company structure performed worse in this sector than other structures: this led him to argue that there was a need for more central direction and control than holding companies could exercise. The two views are, of course, not incompatible. It could be argued that the business environment is now a great deal more turbulent than it was in the 1960s and 1970s and that companies, particularly where they are faced with complex businesses to operate and such turbulent environments, cannot effectively exercise tight central control. It is an issue returned to shortly in discussing the advantages and disadvantages of decentralisation.

There are other organisational advantages and disadvantages of holding company structures. For example they do not have to carry the burden of a high central overhead since the head office staff of the parent is likely to be small. However, the business units can benefit from their membership of the group in such ways as the offsetting of profits against others' losses, the benefits of cheaper finance for investment from the parent company and, arguably, in bad times, from the protection of the group. The holding company itself may also claim benefits such as the spreading of risk across many business ventures and the ease of divestment of individual companies. On the other hand, the businesses may run the risk of being sold off to make room for businesses that can perform better. There simply may not be the skills at the centre to provide help since the aim is to keep the centre as slim as possible. Perhaps the greatest weakness of this structure is, however, the risk of lack of internal strategic cohesion and duplication of effort between business units. It is one thing to say that business units operate better if they are given the profit responsibility to do so on their own: but in a large, perhaps multinational, operation there may be very considerable pay-offs from having some sort of overall 'logic' to the activities – some sort of horizontal integration[13] in the group. It may also be that the different parts of the corporation are difficult to control at times when the centre would wish for such control. For example, in 1986 when BTR tried unsuccessfully to acquire Pilkington, their case was not helped by one of their subsidiaries announcing redundancies in Manchester just before Christmas! These advantages and disadvantages are summarised in Figure 10.4.

10.2.5 The matrix structure

A matrix structure is a combination of structures. It usually takes the form of product and geographical divisions or functional and divisional structures operating in tandem. Figure 10.5 gives examples of such a structure.

Matrix structures most often come about because an operation is involved in two distinct types of operation, both of which require substantial amounts of management emphasis so that 'pure' divisional structures would be inappropriate. For example, suppose a company increasingly extends its operations on a multinational scale and develops new product interests. It may regard geographically defined divisions as the operating units for the purposes of local marketing and product divisions as responsible for the central worldwide co-ordination of product development, manufacturing and distribution to the geographical divisions. Or a group with a number of product divisions may argue that there is no benefit (and perhaps disadvantages) in having all functions in all divisions. It may make sense to have centrally organised selling (with a company-wide salesforce) and manufacturing operations (particularly if different divisions are common manufacturing plants) with product development and marketing planning lodged in product divisions.

It is not necessarily the case that a matrix structure as such will result if there are two distinct types of operation in multinational firms. There are other ways of dealing with this situation which are discussed in Section 10.2.6. Also, matrix structures do not

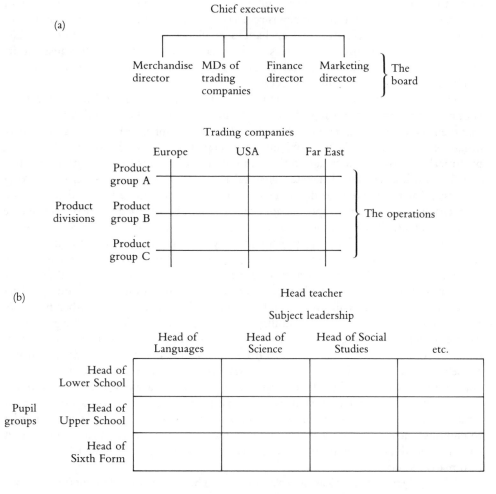

Advantages
- Quality of decision-making where interests conflict
- Direct contact replaces bureaucracy
- Increases managerial motivation
- Development of managers through increased involvement in decisions

Disadvantages
- Length of time to take decisions
- Unclear job and task responsibilities
- Unclear cost and profit responsibilities
- High degrees of conflict
- Dilution of priorities
- 'Creeping bureaucracy'

Figure 10.5 Two examples of matrix structures. (a) In a multinational organisation. (b) In schools.

only arise in large, highly complex organisations, they are sometimes used in quite small, apparently straightforward organisations but which have distinct types of operation or interest in them. For example, matrix structures exist in university departments and schools: one arm of the matrix might be responsible for academic, subject-based work and the other for administration and programming.

The benefits claimed for matrix structures [14] are several. It is argued that quality of decision making is improved in situations where there is a risk of one vital interest of the enterprise (e.g. the interests of a geographical area) dominating considerations of a problem at the expense of other vital interests (e.g. worldwide co-ordination of manufacturing). Formal bureaucracy is replaced by direct contact between individuals; the structure encourages informal exchanges of views across responsibilities. Linked with this, it is supposed to increase both managerial motivation because of its participative nature and managerial development because of the extent to which all levels of management become involved in activities.

However, many of these claims may not be borne out in reality. Matrix structures appear to have some very real problems associated with them. Peters and Waterman say that their 'favourite candidate for the wrong kind of complex response ... is the matrix organisation structure'. [15] The problems are several. There is a high risk of a 'dilution of priorities' whereby the message to those in the organisation is that everything matters equally and deserves equal debate. The end result can be a sort of decision making paralysis. The time taken for decisions to be made may be much longer than in more 'conventional' structures simply because the structure is designed to encourage debate between potentially competing interest groups. It can be clear who is responsible for what; whilst the idea of joint responsibility may conceptually be laudable, it can give rise to problems. What happens, for example, in a multinational operation when the division responsible for Africa wants to reformulate a product and the central functions of manufacturing and worldwide marketing co-ordination insist on product uniformity? Who is actually responsible for marketing? This raises another problem. Exactly where does profit responsibility lie? The African division could argue that it cannot be held profit accountable if it does not control its own products. On the other hand, the central functions are not profit responsible because they are not responsible for selling and distribution. In fact, organisations with matrix structures may have to cope with a good deal of conflict because of the lack of clarity of role definition and responsibility. In such circumstances, a key issue in the effective working of matrix structures is the need for one arm of the matrix to be acknowledged as leading in order to minimise the risk of paralysis through bureaucratic procedures or sheer confusion. A summary of advantages and disadvantages is provided in Figure 10.5 which also shows two matrix structures.

These, then, are the basic structural forms. They each provide benefits and may give rise to problems and the choice between them is not straightforward. Illustration 10.2 shows how, even for a small company, this may be so.

10.2.6 Intermediate structures and structural variations

There exists a whole range of 'shades of grey' between types of structure. These may arise for a number of reasons. It may be that there are problems of change from one sort of structure to another: for example, a wholesale move from a functional structure to a

ILLUSTRATION 10.2

West Midlands Engineering Limited*

Choice of organisational structure for a small engineering firm was not a straightforward matter and depended on the strategy they chose to follow.

West Midlands Engineering was an electrical engineering firm with a turnover of around £5 million. Originally a manufacturer of switching devices for electrical distribution, it had gradually moved into the building of switchboards, into which it had built its own switching devices. There were, then, two sides to the business; switchboard building and component manufacturing. In the 1980s two major changes occurred in its markets. First, overseas imports of switching devices, based on microelectronics rather than mechanical engineering, began to replace Midland's product base. Second, 'panel builders' entered the market; they saw their business as building switchboards, incorporating whichever components met specifications at the lowest cost. The result was that Midlands was squeezed at both ends of its business; overseas supplies of components began to erode their components business; and panel builders began to undercut their prices and reduce their share of the switchboard market.

West Midlands had always been privately owned, run by engineers, and functionally organised. The Managing Director had reporting to him a Commercial Director responsible for manufacturing, engineering, design and the drawing office functions; the Sales Director was responsible for two fields salesforces – one for switchboards and one for components – and the tendering and order processing functions in the sales office; and a company secretary was responsible for the financial and personnel functions. However, in 1987 a new Managing Director took over the firm and began to consider structural changes. Whilst he accepted that the functional structure had the merits of simplicity, he was also considering divisionalising the operation or even moving it to a holding company structure. A divisionalised operation would allow the business to split out component manufacturing and sales from switchboard manufacturing and sales. The main benefit here was the isolation of costs and contributions from the two sides of the business which hitherto had become confused and clouded just where profits and losses were coming from. Moreover, it would have the benefit of separating personnel, who still saw the business as a component manufacturer, from those who believed the future lay in the manufacture of switchboards, and who wished to have a freer hand in the components they could install in those boards. The difficulty was just what functions should be allocated to each division and how they could be separated out when manufacturing for both took place on the same premises.

A holding company structure also had additional potential benefits. In the first place it was possible that the components side of the business might benefit from some sort of joint activity with an overseas component manufacturer. Such joint venture arrangements would be made the more simple if the component business was, quite literally, a separate business, so that Midlands could act as a holding company, perhaps with a 100% shareholding in the switchboard business and a majority shareholding in the components business. Such an arrangement, arguably, would also facilitate the problem of transfer pricing and purchasing of components for the switchboard side of the business. There would be no quibbles about the sourcing of components since the two companies would be quite separate.

* West Midlands Engineering is a pseudonym for an existing business.
Source: Authors.

divisional structure may be difficult and very disruptive; some form of intermediate structure may make sense which might eventually evolve into a divisional structure. A company faced with this problem might find that problems arise with a functional structure as new products/markets compete for resources. Initially these conflicts might be resolved by pushing the decision upwards until a sufficiently senior executive makes the decision. When too many conflicts need to be resolved in this way new rules, guidelines and procedures may be developed to advise people on how resources are to be shared between products. The next step may be to formalise these procedures in the planning process by, for example, allocating a budget to the new product/markets. Up to this stage the problem has been dealt with by manipulating methods of control and operation rather than by structural changes. As the new products/markets become more important and create competition for resources it may be necessary to create interdepartmental liaison roles. For example, marketing priorities may not be clear within the production function, so some sort of committee may be set up with representatives from both departments or a temporary taskforce set up to advise on priorities. The next stage may be to create either permanent teams of co-ordinators or special co-ordinating jobs (the product manager is a good example). The last step which may prove necessary to maintain the functional structure is the creation of departments with the sole function of co-ordination: centralised planning departments for example. Ultimately, as the diversity increases, the organisation may be forced to divisionalise since the costs of maintaining the functional structure will be unacceptably high or the administrative difficulties might become too great.

There are also some common intermediate structural answers to such problems. It might be more appropriate to describe the structure of some companies as *functional with subsidiaries*. [16] Their main business, which employs by far the majority of employees could be a straightforward functional structure; the more peripheral business interests could be the divisions. The converse of this is the company which is divisionalised except for certain key functions which remain at the centre and have responsibilities across all the divisions. Channon [17] calls this a 'critical function' structure and found it quite common in insurance companies where investment departments often remain a central function. In many divisionalised retail operations, too, there are central functions responsible for cross-divisional property dealings and, increasingly, for control of information systems.

Another intermediate structure often arises when there are development activities outside the responsibility of any one function or division, say a major capital project or new product development. Here it might make sense to set up a temporary full-time project team drawn from different functions or divisions. Peters and Waterman suggest that so-called excellent companies, characterised by their ability to continually change to meet the needs of the changing environment, are characterised by the extensive use of such *project teams* and *taskforces*. [18] They maintain a basic form of organisation which is simple, lean and easy to understand; they may change the precise configuration of that fairly regularly but its basic form remains the same. However, around that form, in order to respond to the different challenges they face, and to innovate and experiment, they set up ad hoc teams for short or longer periods of time. In 3M, project teams with quite small numbers grow up around new ideas regularly; some die out fairly quickly, but it is possible that others will develop, together with their project into new business ventures or even separate divisions.

Henry Mintzberg suggests that there is a new form of structure developing in those companies that face really complex and dynamic environments, especially where those companies are young, highly technical in their business base, and with many highly specialist roles for managers and staff to perform. This is the 'adhocracy'.[19] These are organisations which have very little formal structure at all. They are groupings of specialists who work together through a process of mutual adjustment and professional understanding and training. There will be very few bureaucratic procedures – few job descriptions, or hierarchies, for example. It may be that the outsider observer has difficulty in seeing who is responsible for what, or indeed who is superior to whom. Such organisations do, of course, depend on high degrees of mutual respect and tolerance if they are to survive efficiently.

Another way of coping with the need for organisational change without fundamentally affecting what already exists, is to 'externalise' the change by moving the responsibility for it to outside the enterprise. There are many examples of this. In the 1980s Conservative controlled councils in the UK began to offer what were traditional local authority operations, such as refuse collection, to private companies rather than maintain the operational side of the service within their own structure. *Franchising* is another means of structuring externally. Here the functions of marketing services, some elements of finance and accounting and perhaps manufacturing, are retained within the franchise operation whilst the local selling and cash collection may be dealt with by franchisees.

The disaggregation of organisations may, however, go much further than this. Some corporations, faced with the high cost of production in the western economies, are developing into 'vertically disaggregated' companies or *dynamic networks*. These companies essentially rely on other companies for manufacturing and many other business functions. Illustration 10.3 gives an example. The argument runs that, as western industrial society becomes more orientated towards high technology production and service industries, the production of commodity goods can be more cheaply done elsewhere. Such companies, therefore, seek to take advantage of low cost foreign labour and foreign technology by reducing their reliance on their own fixed capital, and looking for markets which they can develop by buying-in products or services. In effect, parts of the value chain are externalised and the organisation structure takes the form of a tight, small central headquarters around which functions of the enterprise operate and are controlled. It may be that virtually all those functions are performed by other companies. There may be overseas suppliers, and home-based distributors or marketing agencies, together with external accountancy services, designers and so on. There are advantages, and disadvantages, in such an arrangement. Such companies may be more agile and fast-moving in exploiting markets. They certainly need less capital to do so and are likely to carry lower overheads; and in having the flexibility to source from anywhere their product costs are likely to be low too. On the other hand, the extent to which they can exercise control over production must be reduced, they are vulnerable to suppliers entering their own markets, are entirely reliant on the continuity of supply from companies outside their control, and they do, of course, demand a totally different sort of management skill to run the operation. It may be that such organisations can only operate on small scales unless the type of business permits the breaking up and contracting out of services: for example, companies within the publishing industry are moving rapidly towards disaggregated operations in editing,

---

ILLUSTRATION 10.3

Disaggregation and Galoob Toys, Inc.

Could disaggregated structures become more popular as costs of production and management rise in western economies?

Business Week reported on the organisation structure adopted by Galoob Toys; a type of structure which, until the 1980s, was most uncommon but which has shown signs of becoming less so.

Lewis Galoob Toys, Inc. is obviously a successful company. It sold $58 million worth of its sword-wielding Golden Girls 'action figures' and other trendy toys last year – ten times the 1981 total. Its stock, issued in 1984 at 10, has soared as high as 15 and now sells for 13½. Yet by traditional standards of structure, strategy, and management practice, Galoob is hardly a company at all ...

A mere 115 employees run the entire operation. Independent inventors and entertainment companies dream up most of Galoob's products, while outside specialists do most of the design and engineering. Galoob farms out manufacturing and packaging to a dozen or so contractors in Hong Kong, and they, in turn, pass on the most labour-intensive work to factories in China. When the toys land in the US, they're distributed by commissioned manufacturers' representatives. Galoob doesn't even collect its accounts. It sells its receivables to Commercial Credit Corp., a factoring company that also sets Galoob's credit policy. In short, says Executive Vice President Robert Galoob, 'our business is one of relationships'. Galoob and his brother, David, the company's president, spend their time making all the pieces of the toy company fit together, with their phones, facsimile machines, and telexes working overtime.

Source: 'And now, the post-industrial corporation', *Business Week*, 3 March 1986.

---

production and distribution. If such structures are to develop, it also probably means that businesses will have to be broken down into small operating units to avoid extremely unwieldy networks of operations.

10.2.7 Structural types in multinational companies[20]

The growth in size and the importance of multinational businesses warrants some special mention of the structural implications for them. Since multinational activity usually involves some form of divisionalisation the discussion will also usefully point out that any one divisional type may have several variations. The most basic form of structure for a multinational is the retention of the home structure and the management of whatever overseas subsidiaries exist through direct contact between the manager of the subsidiary and the chief executive or some other manager in the parent company. In effect, there are no changes to the overall structure. This is most common in single-product companies or where the overseas interests are relatively minor, so it cannot be described as typical.

One of the most common forms of multinational structure is the *international division*. Here the home-based structure may be retained at first – whether functional or divisional – but the overseas interests managed through a special international division. In turn it is possible that within an overall international division there will be other geographic divisions each reporting to a home-based head office. The international subsidiaries may draw in the products of the home company or, if large enough, may manufacture for themselves.

Such structures tend to work best where there is a wide geographical spread but quite closely related products. They tend to emphasise local responsibility rather than central control and so may be particularly useful where local knowledge or close relationships with national governments are important. The logical extension of this structure is that geographically-based divisions or companies evolve which are part of a multinational whole, but operate essentially independently by country. In these companies virtually all the management functions are nationally based. In such circumstances the control of the parent company is likely to be dependent on some form of planning and reporting system and perhaps the ultimate veto over national strategies; but the extent of control is likely to be low. However, there is one simple mechanism of control: since the national businesses are, for operational purposes, not dependent on the parent company, they can be disposed of relatively easily.

There has been a move away from the international divisional structure to what has become known as a *global product* or integrated structure.[21] Here the multinational is split into product group divisions which are then managed on an international basis. The logic of such an approach is that it should promote cost efficiency (particularly of production) on an international basis and provide enhanced transfer of resources (particularly technology) between geographical regions. There is also a tendency for companies to move to global structures as foreign product diversity increases and as foreign sales, as a percentage of total company sales, increase.[22] There should also be better strategic planning on an international basis through the centralised product focus. In these organisations control over, for example, manufacturing may well be co-ordinated internationally. The network of plants, each one in a separate country, may be making parts of cars, for example, which are assembled in yet another country: this manufacturing network may be supported by an international research and development network. Clearly in such circumstances a key requirement is planning mechanisms to co-ordinate the various operations, and it is in these organisations that the planning and control systems are likely to be most sophisticated. It is argued that such structures are beneficial where there is a diversity of products, a reliance on high technology and a relatively low need to distinguish between different geographical areas. However, research has shown that these benefits do not always occur.[23] Although cost efficiency is improved it does not appear that technology transfer is necessarily enhanced: technology transfer seems to be better achieved through geographic divisions than in a global product structure. Also, whilst the structure is well suited to promoting defensive or consolidation strategies, it does not seem to meet the expected benefits of heightened strategic planning and is not suited to the promotion of aggressive or expansion strategies. These difficulties may be accounted for in part by the almost inevitable separation of senior management of the global division from local problems; they are mainly concerned with central co-ordination and this reduces the sensitivity to local needs, particularly in terms of marketing needs and competitive activity. The tendency to move to global product structures is probably associated with attempts to rationalise the increasing diversity and problems of control within international divisional structures. Such rationalisation has often taken place through some sort of portfolio planning which has tended to emphasise concentration on a more limited product range.

Matrix structures are also common in multinational organisations. Most typically the matrix is based on a head office responsibility for product and manufacturing planning and geographical divisions for local administration, including selling and distribution. The argument for a matrix structure is that a multinational is just not suited to an hierarchical structure; decisions are better made through a 'contractual' arrangement between central co-ordinators and local management. It certainly appears that the structure is better at promoting technology transfer, for example, but this has to be set against the costs of co-ordination and conflicts discussed in Section 10.2.5. It can provide greater flexibility in terms of geographical responsiveness in the global product structure whilst coping with a greater diversity of products and providing closer corporate control than geographic structures. However, the problems of matrix structures as previously discussed hold for multinationals too, and in at least one major electrical company decision making became so cumbersome in the late 1970s that managers openly campaigned for a shift to an alternative structure.

Doz[24] has argued that there is evolving a multi-focal strategy in some organisations in which there is no predetermined decision to follow a geographical route or a global product route. Rather, the extent to which the firm is integrated and controlled will depend on local market circumstances, as does the necessity to switch priorities and emphasis from one area of the world to another. In such circumstances it is not possible to predetermine a structure which can exist over time and be relevant to operations in all parts of the world. There is more likely to evolve the sort of adhocracy previously described in which there is a strong reliance on informal communication between top management on a global basis. Such top managers cannot expect to control the whole enterprise by formal systems but are, rather, dependent on establishing control mechanisms to access and analyse key data, establish clear over-arching strategies which can be pursued by carefully selective management and, themselves, be prepared to resolve conflicts of interests where they arise.

Davison and Haspselagh's[25] research in 180 USA-based companies in 1980 showed that the most common structure (in 32% of the companies) was the global

Table 10.1 Advantages and disadvantages of different multinational business structures.

	Geographic divisions	Global product divisions	Matrix
Diversity of products	L	H	H
High technology	L	H	H
Close corporate control	L	H	H
Close government relations	H	L	M
Resource allocation: priorities			
Product	L	H	M
Geographic	H	L	M
Functional	L	M	H
Relation cost	L	M	H

H = High   M = Medium   L = Low
Adapted from J. Hutchinson, 'Evolving organizational firms', *Columbia Journal of World Business*, XL:51, 1976.

product structure followed by the international divisional structure. This differs from the findings of Stopford and Wells[26] in the late 1960s when 52% of the multinationals they researched had international divisions and 18.5% global product structures.

Table 10.1 summarises some of the advantages and disadvantages of geographic, global product and matrix structures for multinational businesses.

10.3 CENTRALISATION AND DECENTRALISATION

When planning the implementation of strategy in organisational terms, structure is important because it creates what has previously been described as 'the skeleton' which facilitates – and sometimes limits – the activities that need to occur. However, it is a mistake to think it is enough to design an organisation in terms of the 'bones' of a structure. One divisional structure may be much the same as another in name and the sort of organisation chart that may be used to describe it: but that does not in itself help with some other vital aspects of organisational design. One of these other aspects is what sorts of decision should be taken at each level in the organisation, and how this affects the ability to implement (and decide) strategy. This concerns issues of centralisation and decentralisation.

It is important to be clear what is meant by decentralisation: it is to do with the extent to which power of decision making is devolved in an organisation. This raises the question: 'Power over what?' Does it mean power to take decisions on operational issues – the scheduling of production or the hiring of executives, for example – or the power to take decisions about the strategic direction of the firm – to diversify or consolidate, for example. Decentralisation may mean either, which is one of the reasons why there has been confusion over the use of the term: managers and consultants have too often assumed that decentralisation of strategic and operational decisions necessarily go hand in hand, when they need not. For example, there is very considerable decentralisation of operation decisions in a company such as Unilever. A product marketing group in one of Unilever's subsidiaries would make decisions about substantial amounts of advertising expenditure and significant amounts of capital expenditure. But these decisions would be taken within the context of a strategic framework for the subsidiary approved by Unilever itself. It would be highly unlikely, for example, that Walls Meat or Lever Brothers could take a decision to move outside their existing product market scope without the approval and active involvement of Unilever, who might well decide that such a new venture would be better lodged in some other subsidiary. On the other hand, it is quite possible that a business unit within a company such as Lonrho might take decisions about such a move much more independently and even have the facility to raise funds to do it from outside the parent group. In the case of the Unilever subsidiary, *operational decentralisation* is high and *strategic decentralisation* more restricted: in the case of the Lonrho subsidiary both operating and strategic decentralisation are high. This distinction is important because there are indications that performance characteristics of firms may be influenced by the nature of decentralisation.

It is argued that decentralisation allows and encourages rapid managerial response to local or product specific problems. For example, if sales or profits drop in a particular market it is not necessary to refer the matter along hierarchical chains of decision making; a decision can be made by the manager responsible for that market. However, the speed of response may well depend on how well defined are the responsibilities for strategic and operational decisions at different levels of management. For example, if the decision is to do with a local distribution problem, then the local manager will probably have the authority to deal with it. But suppose the problem has important strategic implications: perhaps a product requires major redesign and its reformulation requires major funding; local management may not have this authority, and the decision may have to be referred to more senior levels in head office. Unless the company is clear as to what sort of decision making is to be decentralised and what is to remain centralised, delays and ineffectual decisions may result. In some organisations inefficiencies may arise precisely because of the failure to decentralise operational decisions: for example criticisms of the services provided by the public sector services in the UK frequently stem from the centralised nature of decision making which often results from the pressures of public accountability through statutory bodies or ministerial channels.

Perhaps the most powerful reason for strategic decentralisation is that it is necessary and beneficial when the complexity faced at the top of the organisation is too great to be handled by senior management alone. Take the extreme example of a multinational operation with interests as diverse, dynamic and complex as microelectronics, oil exploration and communications technology. It is not conceivable that all strategic decisions could be made at the most senior level. They would certainly be decentralised to strategic business units such as divisions. Some of the reasons for decentralisation are shown in Illustration 10.4 which gives the arguments which led to different organisations increasing levels of decentralisation.

There are, of course, arguments for centralisation. Co-ordination of activities may be facilitated by centralisation. Senior management know what is going on in all parts of the organisation if decision making is routed through them so there is less need for complex control systems. Centralisation of major strategic decisions could be important because it is only at the most senior level that an overall perspective of strategic implications can be appreciated so as to decide the overall aims and core strategies of the *whole* organisation and allocate funds between competing claims. Another argument for centralisation is that it provides for speedier decision making. It is apparently the opposite claim to the first argument in favour of decentralisation. Yet this may not be such a contradiction if the distinction between strategic and operational decentralisation is remembered. Decentralisation speeds up strategic management only if there is effective devolution of power to take strategic decisions and they do not need to be referred up and down management hierarchies for agreement. However, this may not occur for many reasons. For examples, effective strategic decentralisation would involve the authority to allocate funds to major projects: yet the sums of money required for major projects may be in excess of those under the control of the business unit concerned. In such an event the decision has to go to the parent group for funds where it will be competing with other business units. Here is the responsibility for making strategic proposals rather than decisions that has been devolved, and the authority to take the decisions has been centralised. The danger is that the process of proposal, discussion and agreement or rejection is institutionalised into a lengthy formal process which slows down strategic responses.

ILLUSTRATION 10.4

Reasons for decentralisation

Three quite different organisations – ICI, the BBC and Walsall Borough Council – moved to more decentralised structures in the 1980s.

ICI

John Harvey Jones, Chairman of ICI in the early 1980s, explained his advocacy of decentralisation as follows:

> Organisations have a centralising tendency – a creeping centralisation. How the hell can I know whether the guy in India should be changing his product, or whether somebody in Argentina should be changing his technology. People don't like centralisation because it uses people as machines... While we've set businesses free to pursue their own objectives, the controls have actually got more rigid. We only manage on a small number of parameters but they are pretty ruthless ... there's nothing easier than to stand on the bridge shouting instructions. But absolutely nothing happens unless people believe that what you're doing is right. What I want is a federation of freemen working together of their own free will for a socially decent common cause. (*Guardian*, 5 March 1987)

The BBC

Early in 1987 Michael Checkland was appointed Director General of the BBC. In March the *Financial Times* reported that his plans included:

> Much greater devolution of management ... to liberate more money for programme-making ... accompanied by a strong centre prepared to set and maintain standards, devise strategy and allocate resources.

> Making departmental heads responsible and accountable for all but the most major decisions in place of the hallowed BBC tradition of referring tricky decisions ever upwards in the organisation. The referral system, Mr Checkland says, apart from obvious failures in the past 'may be a substitute for saying no oneself'. (*Financial Times*, 24 March 1987)

Walsall Borough Council

In the 1980s Walsall Council, in common with some other local authorities, introduced 'neighbourhood offices' which administered council affairs at neighbourhood level. The reasons for the introduction can be traced back to the Labour Party local manifesto of 1980; they were explained by Brian Powell, the leader of the Council in 1981, as follows:

> We saw that people should be continually involved in decision making about themselves, their neighbours and their town. The barriers and alienation between the people and the council were to be broken down permanently. Council officials were to become of the people and for the people, working towards a common aim and purpose. Residents are to have creative permanent input into local government. Decentralising and creating a dialogue between residents and one part of the council will: (a) break down the remoteness, (b) spread knowledge of how the local system can work and be controlled by the community, (c) increase the confidence of people in their own abilities to make decisions (and accept responsibility for the outcome of those decisions).

Figure 10.6 summarises some of the benefits and difficulties (and problems) of both centralised and decentralised organisational structures. Peters and Waterman have argued that a characteristic of the best performing organisations is that they are simultaneously able to retain central control whilst maximising the degree of flexibility, innovation and contribution from lower levels. These organisations have 'simultaneous loose–tight properties' of structure and control[27]. The means whereby this might be done are not strictly matters of structure but rather matters of management style and corporate culture and are discussed in the next chapter.

The issue of decentralisation is an important one, not least because the extent of decentralisation seems to affect company performance according to the overall aims and strategy of those companies. Horovitz and Thietart[28] found that companies that successfully achieved high growth tend to be more decentralised than those emphasising profits; however, they also found that high performing companies, whether on measures of growth or profits, tend to retain fairly high degrees of central control on matters of general strategic direction of the company.

There is no absolute 'right' or 'wrong' about the extent of decentralisation. What matters is not so much whether an organisation is centralised or decentralised but the extent to which the design of the organisation is internally consistent.[29] John Child has shown how, within the aircraft industry, companies operating in the same environment

	Benefits	**Difficulties/problems**
Centralisation	• Ability to achieve and control consistent strategy • Co-ordination of activities • Simpler control systems Allocation of resources facilitated • Speedier strategic decision making	• Failure to achieve response to local conditions • Difficulties in developing general managment capabilities • Cumbersome and costly central overheads
Decentralisation	Operational • Rapid response to specific or local problems • Improved motivation/ commitment Strategic • When environmental or decision making complexity too great to dealt with at apex of the organisation	• Definition of split of operational and strategic responsibilities • Failure to devolve *power* of decision making: resulting in: • Lengthy referral processes and delayed decisions • Frustrated management • Complicated control procedures

Figure 10.6 Some benefits and difficulties of centralisation and decentralisation.

had varying levels of performance which could be explained in terms of the extent to which the various aspects of their organisational structure were compatible. Of the four airlines he discusses, two performed better than the others and were competitors. However, their structures were quite different. One was divisionalised, relatively decentralised (at least for operational decisions) and formalised in terms of its control and planning, which was on a long time horizon basis. The other successful airline was not divisionalised, operated on much shorter time horizons, remained centralised with top managers meeting regularly to take the major decisions speedily. The point is that both organisations, though structured differently, operated a structure which was internally consistent and enabled them to handle the environment they faced effect-ively. The poorer performing airlines, on the other hand, had inconsistent structures. For example, though nominally decentralised they severely restricted authority for decision making, failed to monitor the project performance of divisions, and had cumbersome decision making procedures. They were then unable to respond as effectively to their trading environment.

It should be clear by now that there is an important distinction between decentralisation and divisionalisation: yet the two terms are often used synonymously both by managers and management writers. The distinction is made clear by the Unilever example. Unilever is a divisionalised operation; certainly it has decentralised operating decisions but it has retained a large element of central control over strategic decisions. Compare this to an advanced electronics company, for example, which could well be small and perhaps functionally organised yet where considerable strategic power may be decentralised to specialists. Whilst divisionalisation may make decentral-isation easier, the two do not necessarily go hand in hand.

10.4 INFLUENCES ON ORGANISATIONAL DESIGN[30]

Why are organisations designed the way they are? Why are some organisations likely to have functional structures and others divisional structures? Why are some centralised and other decentralised? And what influences other aspects of organisational decision? This part of the chapter summarises some of the influences on organisational design and refers readers to further work in the area. Figure 10.7 provides a summary of the discussion.

In considering organisation design it is not enough to think about structural forms (functional, divisional, matrix) alone. It has already been seen that the extent of centralisation and decentralisation is important. Similarly, the management style of the organisation is important; this will be discussed further in Chapter 11 (Section 11.3.4), but suffice it to say here that the extent to which the organisation is *bureaucratic* (or *mechanistic*) or more informal (or *organic*) is an important aspect of organisational design.[31] So too is the extent to which parts of the organisation are specialised in their tasks and roles; Lawrence and Lorsch[32] referred to this as *differentiation* within organisations and also pointed out that the extent of mechanisms of integration, necessary to co-ordinate specialist activities, is likely to be an important aspect of organisation design. In considering influences on the design of organisations it is, therefore, important to consider more than purely structural forms.

10.4.1 The influence of strategy

Chandler[33] showed that a change in strategy is likely to result in structural changes although the actual processes of change may well be problematic. A change in strategy

		Structural form							Style	
		Functional	Divisional	Matrix	Centralised	Decentralised	Specialisation/differentiation	Integration	Mechanistic	Organic
Strategies	Cost leadership					★		★		
	Differentiation				★		★			★
	Limited product/markets	★			★					
	Market development	★						★		
	Vertical integration						★	★		
	Diversification		★		★		★	★		
Technology	Separate technical processes			★						
	Integrated technical processes	★								
	Mass production				★			★		
	Non-standardised production					★				★
	Complex technology				?	?	★	★		★
	Level of innovation						★	★		★
Type of organisation	Size of organisation			★		★	★	★		
	External accountability				★			★	★	
	'Defenders'	★			★		★		★	
	'Prospectors'			★		★		★		★
Environment	Simple/stable				★					
	Dynamic				?	?		★		★
	Complex			★		★	★		?	?
	Competitive				?	?		★		
	Hostile				★					
	Multinational			★		★				

★|Likely effect of influence
? Likely to raise as key issue

Figure 10.7 Influences on organisational design.

is likely to give rise to administrative problems because the existing organisational structure is not adapted to cope with the new strategy. There may be resistance to change which gives rise to the sorts of intermediate structure discussed earlier in the chapter. Nonetheless, different strategic developments generally tend to give rise to different forms of organisation.

Chandler found in his historical studies that firms with limited product markets and fairly simple operations tended to adopt functional structures and be fairly centralised. The early development of such businesses tended to be through market development which allowed for the retention of functional structures but increased the need for integration through centralised control systems. He found that, typically, the next step in strategic development was vertical integration and this gave rise to the need for increasing specialisation to deal with balancing the flow of goods between different operations in the organisation. This need gave rise to specialist service functions in the centre. Further strategic development tended to take place through product diversification and this tended to give rise to division structures and lead towards more decentralised structures and greater needs for specialisation and integration of operations.

The extent to which diversity of operations tends to lead to decentralisation is a phenomenon not limited only to commercial operations. There have been signs in the public sector of the breaking up of centralised control into more autonomous units where speed of response and coping with diversity is important. Some local authorities have devolved the administration of housing policy and social affairs to 'neighbourhood offices' in an attempt to speed up response to community needs (see Illustration 10.4).

Different generic strategies will also require different forms of organisational design. The organisation following a cost leadership strategy will need to find means of ensuring a cost efficient operation with an emphasis on cost control; whereas the organisation following a differentiation strategy will need higher degrees of creativity and, probably, a rapid response to problems and opportunities. The likelihood is that the cost leadership strategy will require a more mechanistic system of control with clear job responsibilities, frequent and detailed reports on organisational efficiency and cost, and a clear delineation of responsibility for budgets and expenditure. The structure for an organisation following a differentiation strategy, on the other hand, might need to be more organic in nature, with looser controls, a greater encouragement of informality and creativity within a more decentralised structure, but with a good deal of co-ordination between its various functions. The emphasis is likely to be more on groups of managers relating to problems and opportunities rather than to individual managers or departments being concerned with specific job functions.

It should be clear from this that those organisations that seek to follow focus strategies in which they aim to achieve both cost leadership and differentiation for a particular market segment are likely to find some conflicts in terms of organisational design, as will the organisation that seeks to follow differentiation and cost leadership strategies for different parts of its business or product range.

10.4.2 The influence of production process and technology

There are different ways in which product and technology influence structure. When products are manufactured by a sequence of separate, technical processes, companies may choose to forego the possible economies of continuous production and create separate divisions to deal with each process of manufacture as a means of developing the highest quality of product. Conversely, where there is a highly integrated process, divisionalisation is more difficult simply because the process is difficult to subdivide. Similarly, assembly and component manufacture, which are quite different in nature, allow components to be manufactured in separate divisions or subcontracted to other companies, as in the motor industry.

In terms of decentralisation, there is much evidence to show that the production process influences the ways in which, and the levels at which, decisions are taken. As long ago as 1965 Woodward's[34] research showed that there are links between the types of production process and the nature of management. Mass production systems require the standardisation of process and result in greater direction and control by senior managers: in short, there is a tendency towards centralisation. Firms with a less standardised manufacturing process are more likely to have more decentralised and informal decision making processes. However, Woodward's findings have subsequently come under critical scrutiny. In particular, it has been argued that the claim that standardised production systems result in formalised and centralised control is really only true within the production side of the company: other departments and the company as a whole may not be organised in the same way.

The last decade has seen an accelerating complexity in the technology used in organisations. The implications for the structures are considerable. It would appear that the more sophisticated and complex the technology of an organisation the more elaborate the structure becomes for a number of reasons. First, it is likely that a good deal of responsibility and power is likely to devolve to those specialists concerned with the technology itself. This means that the need for liaison between such specialists and the operating core of the business increases, and that the need for liaison between such specialists and the operating core of the business increases, giving rise to an increase in integrating and co-ordinating mechanisms such as committees, joint working groups, project teams and so on.

More sophisticated technology can give rise to increases in centralisation or of decentralisation. For example, the advent of more sophisticated information technology may mean that it is possible for the central core of the organisation to cope with far more complex problems than hitherto; in retailing, the ability to record sales by electronic scanning in the store has provided retailers with greatly enhanced knowledge of rates of sales and stock turn by product. This has facilitated much tighter central decision making on range planning and store layout. Rapid transfer of information and computerised systems of control also allow companies like Galoob (see Illustration 10.3) to contract out services yet retain central control over operations. On the other hand, the same technology might also allow decentralisation of support systems in organisations. For example, the functioning of the neighbourhood offices mentioned above is dependent on local officers being able to communicate rapidly with central departments in order to obtain up-to-date information to provide a basis for localised decision making.

Finally, the extent to which the organisation is required to be innovative in its approach to development of new services or products is likely to affect the extent to which experts have to be drawn from different disciplines, perhaps for short periods of time. Here we have a requirement for more organic approaches to organisation and, in the extreme, a pull towards adhocracies.

10.4.3 The influence of organisational type

Other influences on organisational design stem from the size, accountability and culture of organisations. It is inconceivable that all aspects of a large and diverse corporation could be organised except by splitting the tasks of management. The larger the corporations, therefore, the more there is likelihood of divisionalisation, a need for specialisation and differentiation,[35] and in turn a need for increased co-ordination (or integration). The large corporation is also likely to move towards some form of decentralisation although other circumstances, which will be mentioned below, may counter to this tendency.

The nature of an organisation's accountability will also affect organisational design. This is well illustrated by nationalised industries and other public sector bodies. Where government involvement is high, the issue of public accountability becomes an important influence; it is likely to give rise to a centralised structure of decision making where both power and accountability are in the hands of an easily identifiable team or individual at the centre. Higher levels of decentralisation would disperse authority more widely and make public accountability more difficult – or at least more difficult to demonstrate to the public. However, the price that has often been paid for this ease of public accountability has been an inability to respond quickly to market and other environmental changes and has often resulted in unwieldy systems of bureaucratic information and control in order to maintain this centralised structure.

In commercial enterprises where there is pronounced dependency on some external body such as a parent company or a powerful shareholder group, the same sort of result comes about.[36] There is a tendency towards centralisation of decision making and, because external standards of performance are imposed, a more mechanistic style of management. Owner control may also be an important influence on structure. For example, many companies which are owner-controlled retain a high degree of centralisation, even when they grow quite large, as the influence of the owner-manager continues.

The importance of organisation culture has already been discussed in Chapters 2 and 5, and reference made to the 'cultural web'. Organisational structures over time come to reflect and support the organisational recipes that persist and the power structures associated with them. This is well illustrated by the work of Miles and Snow.[37]

The *defender* organisation tends to specialise rather than diversify in terms of strategy. Structurally it is likely to be functional, permitting an emphasis on specialisation at most managerial levels and emphasising efficiency. The functional structure is likely to be mechanistic in management style with an emphasis on keeping costs down by minimising cross-functional or cross-task training. Moreover, there will be a high degree of influence on decisions from the functions concerned with the maintenance of efficiency such as finance and production.

The *prospector*, on the other hand, seeks actively for new opportunities so as to be first in the market. Here there is likely to be much less emphasis on control and efficiency and more on innovation. Strategically, there will be a greater diversity of interests and the pursuit of more perhaps with project teams to develop opportunities, and there may well be a tendency to decentralise and minimise top-down control. The style of management will be organic, encouraging flair and risk taking, and there may be complex systems of co-ordination with, for example, specialist co-ordinating roles. Influence and power is likely to be lodged primarily in development areas of the business, such as marketing and R&D.

10.4.4 The influence of environmental forces

The idea, introduced in Chapter 3, that environmental complexity and dynamism affect organisation design is now discussed. (Readers need to remember that 'dynamic' means the amount of change going on in the environment; and that 'complexity' is to do with the amount of information an organisation needs to deal with, or the range of inputs it is necessary to absorb, in decision making.) The main point is that dynamic or complex environments increase uncertainty in decision making. An organisation can be thought of as a means of facilitating the processing of information or inputs for decision making purposes, so the form that the organisation takes is important as a means of handling uncertainty. Mintzberg[38] argues that the form of organisations is likely to differ in important respects according to these different environmental conditions – these differences are summarised in Figure 10.8.

In an environment which is essentially simple, organisations gear themselves to operational efficiency. Not faced with high degrees of change, they can standardise their ways of operating, for example in terms of production, and in their modes of management. Management styles tend to be mechanistic[39] or bureaucratic and there is fairly centralised management. Mintzberg calls this type of organisation *centralised bureaucratic*. They are exemplified by some mass production companies or raw material

	Stable	Dynamic
Complex	Decentralised bureaucratic e.g. hospitals	Decentralised organic e.g. advanced electronics
Simple	Centralised bureaucratic e.g. mass production	Centralised organic e.g. retailing or Decentralised bureaucratic

Figure 10.8 Environmental influences on organisational structure. (Adapted from H. Mintzberg, *The Structure of Organizations: A synthesis of the research*, p.268, Prentice Hall. Reprinted by permission of the publisher.)

producers which, historically at least, faced fairly simple, stable environments. The danger, of course, for such organisations is that their environments cease to be benign and place them under threat which they find difficult to handle.

Increasing complexity is handled by devolving decision responsibility to special-ists. This means that organisation in complex environments tend to be more decent-ralised at least for operational purposes. Hospitals and universities are good examples of those that traditionally have been in fairly stable or predictable environments but of a complex nature. They are *decentralised bureaucratic* organisations. The ongoing operational tasks – the operations management of a hospital, for example – are done in a standard way, often with a highly bureaucratic management style. The complexity of some of the aspects of the patient care are then devolved to the specialist skills of the physicians, surgeons, psychiatrists and so on.

In dynamic conditions the need is to increase the extent to which managers are capable of sensing what is going on around them, identifying change and responding to it. It is unlikely that bureaucratic styles of management will encourage such behaviour, so as the environment becomes more dynamic a more organic style is likely.[40] This is not to say that such organisations necessarily devolve authority for major decisions to lower management. In a simple but dynamic environment it may make sense to retain fairly centralised strategic decision making as a means of ensuring speed in important matters, whilst removing bureaucratic procedures, lengthy referral processes, extensive departmentalisation and layers of management. Mintzberg calls this type of organis-ation *centralised organic*. However, this may not be the only response to dynamic conditions. In situations of high levels of competition – which require rapid response and change – it has been noted[41] that organisations may decentralise decision making but ensure that overall control at a strategic level is monitored and planned through systematic, more formal, systems. In such competitive environments a key organis-ational issue is likely to be centralisation versus decentralisation. The answer is likely to depend on the circumstance of competition and the size of the organisation. It would be difficult to centralise all strategic decisions in a conglomerate with a very wide diversity of business interests; here there needs to be some degree of decentralisation, pre-sumably at least to the business unit level. The structure will also be dependent on the nature and degree of the competition and the sorts of decision that need to be taken: for example, the greater the degree of competitive hostility, the more the organisation will centralise, and also flatten the levels in the organisation so as to speed up the response to competitive pressures. Indeed, it has been suggested that in extremely hostile circum-stances organisations are likely, if only temporarily, to revert to 'simple structures, becoming dependent for strategic discussions on a dominant leader'.[42] On the other hand, supposing a necessary response to competitive pressures is the continual innovation of change – perhaps in the fashion industry, or pop record industry – then it is more likely that a much more organic system of management with a good deal of decentralisation is likely to be necessary.

What then happens where the environment is both complex and dynamic? These are the conditions in which Mintzberg suggests that *decentralised organic* organis-ations may be found. Some of the firms operating at the frontiers of scientific development are in these conditions. Their environment is changing so fast that they need the speed and flexibility that organic styles of management provide; and the level of complexity is such that they must devolve responsibility and authority to specialists.

It is here that real decentralisation of authority – operational and often strategic – to units within the organisation takes place. These units may be divisions or they may be specialist departments, but it is they that must respond to the change that is occurring so fast around them.

10.5 COPING WITH THE PROBLEM OF ORGANISATIONAL DESIGN

Choice of organisational design may not be at all straightforward. There can often be conflicting influences on structure so, as with strategic choice, there are likely to be several possible structural designs and many influences on which of them is to be adopted. A common problem of the 1970s and 1980s has been the conflict between the influences of an increasingly turbulent environment and traditional technology. There are companies in which mass production core technologies had a major influence on the structure and nature of the organisation. Such a company would very likely be fairly centralised and bureaucratic in its mode of operation. However, faced with a dynamic environment the company may well have attempted to diversify away from its core technology. This strategic decision might argue for divisionalisation and increased decentralisation at least of operational decision making, whilst the nature of the environment and the need for innovation might demand more organic styles of management. Yet the business may still be highly dependent on the traditional core technology and managers perhaps unwilling to decentralise authority. In such circumstances the structural choice is not straightforward; there are different influences pulling in different directions. Illustration 10.5 shows how one organisation changed its organisation structure given different pressures and influences.

Given conflicting influences on organisational design, how is it sensible to set about dealing with the problem? There is no formula for doing this, no 'right answer'. It is again a question of analysis and in the end, judgement. However, it might be useful to ask these questions:

● What are the influences inside and outside the organisation which affect how it should be structured? The influences discussed in this chapter should provide a basis for this.
● From these, which are the critical influences (that is, those that will either affect performance more than the others or those that simply override all others)? Readers might consider that from the example above, the critical influence on the mass producer has become the increasingly dynamic nature of the environment; if the company does not cope with this, then its performance will continue to deteriorate.
● Given the identification of these critical influences, it may be that some clear structural implications emerge, or it could be that there are options. If there are options then it is sensible to consider the advantages and disadvantages of each in the context of the strategy that the organisation wishes to follow.
● The final point is too often overlooked. No matter how elegant a structure is, the most important point is that it has to be workable. How will the structure be put into effect? If divisionalisation of a holding company is recommended then exactly

what is going to happen to the chairmen of the many virtually autonomous businesses that are to be rationalised into a few divisions? Who is to report to whom in this new organisation? Where will decisions of what sort be taken? If substantial decentralisation is to take place in the divisions, will more senior management accept it and will more junior management be able to handle it? Part of the evaluation of structural alternatives just as for strategic alternatives is to consider feasibility.

ILLUSTRATION 10.5

Nipont

As the circumstances it faced changed, Nipont changed its organisational structure to divisional and then back to functional.

In the years following the Second World War, up to the 1970s, Nipont grew to become Japan's largest manufacturer of synthetic textiles, operating from twelve plants in the centre of Japan. Over the years, the company had found opportunities for its business interests to grow over a whole range of related products in the fields of fibres, plastics and chemicals. Despite this spread of activity, Nipont had retained its original functional organisational structure.

By 1970, however, it was clear that if growth was to continue, the company would need to take initiatives in several fields of activity at the same time in order to cope with the rapid changes that were occurring on all fronts of its business. For this reason, product divisions were created which allowed managers to become attuned to the particular needs of their product base so they could best manage the growth that was taking place. Because of the specialisation that occurred in each product area, there was also a need for decision making to be decentralised to each division.

In the mid 1970s, Japan was subjected to a series of economic shocks; oil price rises, the forced revaluation of the yen, a worldwide shortage of commodities, inflation and then recession. Nipont, in common with the rest of Japanese industry, was faced with rapidly rising material and labour costs and decreasing demand. This resulted in intensified price competition and reduced demand which led to the deterioration of Nipont's financial operations.

In order to restore profitability and to cope with a more uncertain future, the company decided to revert to a more centralised and functional structure which increased top management's control and afforded a more unified perspective of the company's activities as it struggled through a difficult period. Consequently, each functional element of the three product divisions was regrouped into a new common functional division. The new manufacturing division, for example, was composed of the combined production elements of the previous three product divisions. This 'combined force' was able to concentrate on optimising short run costs throughout the company, and thus help it to respond more effectively to increasing price competition and factor cost pressures.

Nipont has therefore used the type of organisational structure most suited to its needs at the time – the product-based divisionalised structure helped the company to reinvest and expand in several areas at the same time within existing product fields. But, given a more hostile environment and the need for an emphasis on cost reduction and efficiency, a functional and centralised structure was reintroduced.

Source: Lex Donaldson, 'Regaining control at Nipont', *Journal of General Management*, Summer, 1979.

10.6 SUMMARY

This chapter has concentrated on structural implications or organisational design. It has been argued that strategic implementation is effected through the people in the organisation, and that of key importance is the way in which those people are organised. To help readers understand how this might be accomplished, the chapter has reviewed the various forms of structure in common use, together with their advantages and disadvantages. It then examined the sorts of influence from within the organisation and from outside that may affect structure. The chapter concluded by discussing how consideration of the most appropriate structure might take place.

However, this chapter has only touched on a second, equally vital aspect of organisation: how the people within the structure are to be managed. It is this issue that is turned to in the next chapter.

REFERENCES

1. Some of the early writings on organisation are brought together in a volume of readings edited by Derek Pugh, called *Organisation Theory* published by Penguin (1984). It includes papers by Fayol and Taylor, the proponents of 'scientific management'.

2. There is further discussion of the definitions of different management styles, including mechanistic and organic styles, in chapter 11. However, the terms originate from the work of T. Burns and G. Stalker reported in *The Management of Innovation*, Tavistock, 1968.

3. Perhaps the most extensive study of the way in which different organisational structures are adapted to different strategic and environmental influences was carried out in the series of studies which has become known as the 'Aston Studies', and has promoted the idea of a contingency theory of organisation. There are a number of papers written on this particularly towards the end of the 1960s, for example see D. S. Pugh, D. J. Hickson, C. R. Hinings and C. Turner, 'The context of organisation structures', *Administrative Science Quarterly*, pp. 91–114, 1969.

4. For example, R. Rumelt does not include the category 'holding company' in his book on American industry, *Strategy, Structure and Economic Performance*, Harvard Press, 1974.

5. P. Grinyer and J-C. Spender, *Turnaround: Managerial recipes for strategic success*, Associated Business Press, 1978, use subcategories of the term 'multidivisional' which they describe as 'diversified majors' and passive or acquisitive conglomerates. These are terms we return to later in the chapter to differentiate between the nature of different multidivisional organis- ation. Also see P. H. Grinyer and J-C. Spender, 'Recipes, crises and adaptation in mature businesses', *International Studies of Management and Organisation*, **IX**(3): 113, 1979.

6. A good summary of the advantages and disadvantages of different structures is given in an article by M. Davis in 'Current experiments in management structure' in *Reviewing the Management Structure*, BIM, 1972. Readers may also care to refer to the discussion of the problems of functional structures in *In Search of Excellence* by Peters and Waterman (Harper & Row, 1982), and by Henry Mintzberg in *The Structuring of Organizations* (Prentice Hall, 1979).

7. The view of divisionalisation as a response to increasing diversity was put forward by A. D. Chandler in *Strategy and Structure*, MIT Press in 1962. It is supported by other writers, for example, Derek Channon in *The Strategy and Structure of British Enterprise*, Macmillan, 1973.

8. This quotation is taken from page 314 of *In Search of Excellence* (see reference 6).

9. The books which most thoroughly examine the relationship between basic organisational structures and performance are based on data of the 1960s and 1970s; see R. Rumelt, *Strategy, Structure and Economic Performance*, Harvard University Press, 1974; and Derek Channon, *The Service Industries Strategy, Structure and Financial Performance*, Macmillan, 1978.

10. See J. H. Horovitz and R. A. Thietart, 'Strategy, management design and firm performance', *Strategic Management Journal*, **3**, 1982, and J. Child, 'Managerial and organisational factors associated with company performance. Part II: A contingency analysis', *Journal of Management Studies*, **12** (1), 1975.

11. The early development of Norcros is described in a case study by Nigel Campbell, available from the Case Clearing House.

12. See reference 9.

13. The benefits of horizontal integration are discussed in Michael Porter, *Competitive Advantage*, Free Press/Collier Macmillan, 1985.

14. The benefits and problems of matrix structures are discussed more fully in K. Knight, 'Matrix organisation: a review', *Journal of Management Studies*, May, 1976.

15. This quotation is taken from page 306 of *In Search of Excellence* (see reference 6).

16. 'Functional with subsidiaries' is a term used by R. Rumelt (see reference 4).

17. D. F. Channon uses the description 'critical function' structure in his study of structure and performance in the UK service industry (see reference 9).

18. Peters and Waterman have found the extensive use of project teams and taskforces in the excellent companies which they reported on (see reference 6).

19. For a discussion of 'adhocracy' see Henry Mintzberg, *The Structuring of Organizations*, Prentice Hall, 1979.

20. For a more extensive treatment of the structure of multinational companies see: M. Z. Brooke and H. L. Remmers, *The Strategy of Multinational Enterprise*, chapter 2, Pitman, 1978, and Y. Doz, *Strategic Management in Multinational Companies*, Pergamon Press, 1986.

21. 'Integrated structures' is a term used by Doz (see reference 20).

22. J. M. Stopford and L. T. Wells, *Managing the Multinational Enterprise*, Longman, 1972, found this tendency. However, it should be noted that their findings are based on 1968 data.

23. These findings are from research published by W. H. Davidson and P. C. Haspeslagh, 'Shaping a global product organisation', *Harvard Business Review*, July/Aug., 1982.

24. See reference 20.

25. See reference 23.

26. See reference 22.

27. 'Loose–tight' is an expression used by Peters and Waterman (reference 6) and explored in more detail in Section 11.6 of Chapter 11 of this book.

28. See reference 10.

29. Both P. N. Khandwalla, 'Viable and effective organisational design of firms', *Academy of Management Journal*, Sept., 1973; and J. Child, *Organisation: A guide to problems and practice*, Harper & Row, 1977, have found this relationship between the consistency of an organisation's structure and its performance.

30. Overall, the most thorough treatment of influences on organisational design is the volume by Henry Mintzberg (see reference 19) which is also summarised in '*Structure in Fives: Designing effective organizations*' by the same author (Prentice Hall, 1983).

31. See reference 2.

32. See P. Lawrence and J. Lorsch, *Organisation and Environment*, Irwin, 1969.

33. A. Chandler, *Strategy and Structure*, MIT Press, 1962, began a whole series of investigations into the relationship between strategy and structure. It is a fine study of the historical development of American industry but, in drawing conclusions about organisations in the 1980s, it should be remembered that the period being studied was the 1940s and 1950s – a time when the influences on business were somewhat different from the 1980s.

34. See J. Woodward, *Industrial Organisation: Theory and practice*, Oxford University Press, 1965.

35. A major study highlighting this is that of P. Lawrence and J. Lorsch (see reference 32). Similar findings are, however, reported by D. Pugh *et al.* as a result of their research programme which has become known as the Aston Studies (see, for example, 'Dimensions of organisation structure', *Administrative Science Quarterly*, 1968). P. N. Khandwalla discusses relationships of size and structural characteristics in *The Design of Organisations*, Harcourt Brace, 1977.

36. This has been found to be the case in several studies: Mintzberg, *The Structuring of Organisations*, pp. 288–91, Prentice Hall, 1979; D. Pugh *et al.*, 'The context of organisation structures', *Administrative Science Quarterly*, pp. 91–114, 1969, and B. C. Beimann, 'On the dimensions of bureaucratic structure: an empirical reappraisal', *Administrative Science Quarterly*, pp. 462–76, 1973.

37. The work and findings of R. E. Miles and C. C. Snow, Organisational Strategy, Structure and Process (McGraw-Hill: 1978), have been discussed earlier in Chapters 2 and 5 and readers should refer to this discussion for a more detailed explanation of their organisational types.

38. See reference 19.

39. Mechanistic management is a term used by T. Burns and G. M. Stalker (see reference 2) to describe a management system which is fairly regulated and prescribed. Managers are likely to have clearly defined job roles with specified reporting relationships and a clear idea about who takes decisions about what sorts of things.

40. Again it is T. Burns and G. M. Stalker (see reference 2) that use this term. Organic styles of management are much less formal with less clearly defined job roles, responsibilities and reporting relationships. There may, then, be a good deal more conflict and apparent confusion, but the likelihood is that managers will be more likely to be aware and sensitive to changes outside their immediate day-to-day jobs.

41. This association between high levels of competition and decentralisation combined with formalisation is supported empirically by studies by C. Perrow in 'The bureaucratic paradox:

the efficient organisation centralises in order to decentralise', *Organisational Dynamics*, Spring, 1977.

42. This point is made by Mintzberg and Waters in 'The mind of the strategist(s)' in S. Srivasta (ed.), *The Executive Mind*, Jossey Bass, 1983.

Recommended key readings

- A clear exposition of the different basic organisational structures together with a summary of a good deal of research on structure is in chapters 2–4 of *Strategy Implementation: Structure, systems and process*, by J. R. Galbraith and R. K. Kazanzian, West, 1986.

- A good summary of the influences on organisational design is to be found in Henry Mintzberg, *Structure in Fives: Designing effective organisations*, Prentice Hall, 1983.

- For a useful insight into the organisational workings of multinationals see Yves Doz, *Strategic Management in Multinational Companies*, Pergamon Press, 1986.

Chapter 11
PEOPLE AND SYSTEMS

11.1 INTRODUCTION

Implementation of strategic change requires the identification of the key tasks needed to effect that change as discussed in Chapter 9, and a proper consideration of the organisational structure and design to facilitate those changes, as discussed in Chapter 10. However, the success with which the key tasks are actually performed, and strategic change occurs, is dependent on the way in which the people within and around an organisation are managed and controlled. The way in which the different systems of control in the organisation may be employed to implement strategy is the subject of this chapter.

Strategic changes can take place over long periods of time and give rise to considerable differences in the way an organisation operates. As a result the process of implementing strategic change generates a great deal of uncertainty within the organisation which, in turn, triggers off political and social activity as groups and individuals try to cope with the consequences of change. Mumford and Pettigrew[1] have shown how this uncertainty 'cascades' down through the organisation triggering off more uncertainty as a consequence. This process is demonstrated in Illustration 11.1. Faced with such uncertainty groups and individuals in the organisation tend to seek to reduce that uncertainty and; as was seen in Chapter 2, they are likely to do this by relying the more on organisational systems, routines and rituals with which they are familiar. Managing strategic change is, therefore, problematic.

Broadly speaking there are two ways in which this problem of achieving change can be coped with. The first is to do with the employment of systems of control and regulation to ensure that the tasks of implementation are clear, that their execution is monitored, that individuals and groups have the capabilities to implement change, and that they are rewarded for so doing. However, interaction between groups and individuals is also important on a social basis. It is therefore important for those trying to implement change to understand and work within the social, political and cultural systems (discussed in Chapters 2 and 5) that regulate organisational behaviour, and can give rise to the resistance to strategy change, but which can also be employed to help achieve successful strategic change.

Figure 11.1 is a framework demonstrating how the implementation of strategic plans might be undertaken through difference systems that exist in organisations. It will be used as the structure for this chapter and is now briefly reviewed. It suggests that the implementation of strategic change can be considered under four broad

ILLUSTRATION 11.1

Cascade of uncertainty

The rapid development of microcomputer technology during the late 1970s caused a considerable amount of political activity at one university.

For many years the provision of computer facilities had been an important strategic issue for universities due to their high cost and their importance to teaching and research. Up until the late 1970s a mainframe computer provided the only source of computing. However, by 1978 microcomputers had reached a level of development where senior management in one university had to consider whether they should begin to make use of this new technology. Being a recent innovation, most of the microcomputers did not have a proven track record, leaving senior management uncertain as to whether they needed microcomputers at all and if they did need them, which system would be most appropriate.

At departmental level there was uncertainty as to the outcome of senior management's deliberations, triggering off political activity amongst groups. The computer services department, who operated the university's main frame computer, pressed for its upgrading, realising that the widespread introduction of microcomputers would erode their power. Their main weapon was their expertise, and as senior management was lacking in this area, the computer services department were able to get representatives onto the committee advising on computer provision. The other tack of their argument was that there would be government funding for the upgrading of the main frame computer resulting in an improved facility with no direct cost to the university.

The other groups involved in the political activity were the user departments. They faced the uncertainty brought about by the seemingly impregnable position held by the computer services department and the fear that the decision to upgrade the mainframe would be pushed through quickly. The user departments (who preferred microcomputers) attempted to delay the decision to allow departmental members to improve their knowledge of computer systems and so enable them to challenge the computer services' arguments. They also tried to discredit the quality of service provided by the main frame computer, suggesting that departmental microcomputers would provide the type of service the users required. The various user departments also formed alliances in order to create a more powerful lobbying force within the university's formal decision making structure.

The user departments' response (the pursuit of greater computing knowledge and a justification for departmentally based microcomputers) in its turn led to uncertainty for the individual members of the departments who responded in differing ways. Those who were familiar with computers realised the opportunity to enhance their own position within the department, while others, who were previously uninterested in the role of computers in teaching, saw the need to gain such knowledge quickly. The course leaders encouraged the use of microcomputers as a means of enhancing the image of their particular course. However, a minority responded by suggesting that microcomputers were a 'passing fad', and sought to emphasise the traditional role of the teacher.

The response of senior management to this political activity was to permit the purchase of a limited number of microcomputers, partly as a result of the users' arguments, but also because not buying them may have jeopardised the university's claim for a large sum of money from the government to upgrade the mainframe computer. To some extent this could be regarded as a 'side payment' to allow the main decision to proceed.

Source: Authors.

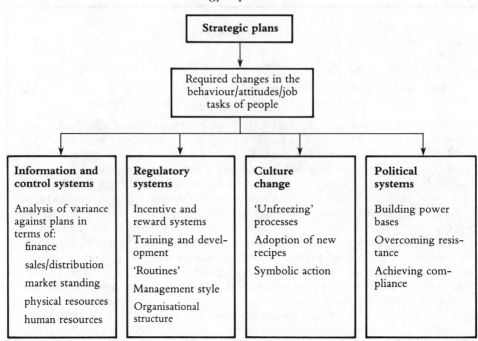

Figure 11.1 Strategy implementation: the influence of organisational systems.

headings (although, as will be explained later, these should certainly not be conceived as entirely distinct from each other).

First strategic change requires that the sorts of key task identified through the planning processes discussed in Chapter 9 are implemented. It is therefore important that there are mechanisms to ensure that people in the organisation follow the plans and procedures necessary. This chapter deals with how this might be achieved under four headings: 'control and information systems', 'regulatory systems', 'culture change' and 'political systems'.

1. *Control and information systems.* Control and monitoring systems, usually quantitative in nature, can be employed to provide information to establish if a course of action is being followed or desired results achieved.

2. *Regulatory systems.* There are procedures that can be followed to regulate or guide behaviour: they could include training to ensure people have the capabilities to implement strategy; systems of incentives and rewards to encourage compliance with required change; the changing of organisational routines and work systems to modify established ways of operating; the management style of the organisation; and, as already discussed in Chapter 10, the changing of organisational structure.

These are ways in which managers seek to ensure that the plans necessary for the implementation of strategic change are complied with. However, such action does not necessarily mean that groups or individuals in the organisation will accept the need for change or feel happy about it: in other words such action might achieve compliance without identification or internalisation of the need for change.[2]

3. *Culture change.* The successful management of strategic change is most likely to be achieved if the uncertainty and resistance discussed at the beginning of the chapter can be avoided or overcome. Ideally, this requires that the need for change be accepted by those involved in making it work; that they identify with the change or really believe it necessary. This is likely to mean that the existing recipe has to be changed and that its constraining cultural influences minimized.

The problem is, then, one of culture change. This will be discussed in this chapter in terms of means of achieving *recipe change* by which is meant that people in the organisation actually change the ways in which they perceive their organisational world. Some of the mechanisms relevant to this process are discussed in this chapter including means of 'unfreezing' the status quo, challenging recipes and changing power structures. *Symbolic action* as an influence on culture change will also be considered.

4. *Political systems and strategic change.* It is also recognised that all of this activity goes on in a political context. Therefore how strategic change might be managed through political systems is also discussed at the end of the chapter. Here the concern is with the way in which individuals and groups, in their interaction, can achieve conditions to exercise the power to implement strategic change.

Finally, the chapter concludes with a discussion of how all these systems – the more formal control systems, the regulatory systems, the cultural and political systems, might combine in so-called excellent organisations to provide a system of relatively continual change so as to avoid the dangers of strategic drift noted in Chapter 2.

11.2 CONTROL AND INFORMATION SYSTEMS[3]

The successful implementation of strategic change may involve steering the organisation into areas where there is little previous experience. Even strategies of consolidation which were discussed in Chapters 6 and 7 may require modified production systems, changed incentive schemes, or relocation of salespeople. When the organisation becomes involved in the real problems of implementing strategic change managers therefore need some means of identifying how implementation is proceeding and the extent of variance from the plan.

Figure 11.2 sets out some of the bases of analysis for providing data for control and strategy implementation. Essentially these build on many of the sorts of analysis discussed previously. For example:

- Different means of financial analysis (similar to those shown in Chapter 4) can be used to measure the extent of variances from financial plans.
- Market analysis may well take a form similar to that outlined in Chapter 3 in trying to establish the extent to which strategic plans are achieving improved competitive standing, for example by monitoring the changes in demand in the market and changes in market share achieved.
- Sales and distribution analysis can monitor the extent to which sales budgets or distribution levels planned are being achieved.
- Physical resource analysis concerns itself with the plant and materials of the

Type of analysis	Used to control
1. *Financial analysis*	
Ratio analysis	Elements of profitability
Variance analysis	Cost or revenue
Cash budgeting	Cash flow
Capital budgeting	Investment
2. *Market analysis*	
Demand analysis ⎫	
Market share analysis ⎭	Competitive standing
3. *Sales and distribution analysis*	
Sales budgets	Sales effectiveness and efficiency
Distribution analysis	Distribution effectiveness
4. *Physicial resource analysis*	
Capacity fill	Plant utilisation
Yield	Materials utilisation
Product inspection	Quality
5. *Human resource analysis*	
Work measurement ⎫	
Output measurement ⎭	Productivity
Labour turnover	Workforce stability
Needs assessment	Skills capability

Figure 11.2 Some analyses for controlling strategy implementation.

organisation and, again, may take form in some of the measures discussed in Chapter 4.

● Human resource analysis examines the productivity and stability of the workforce and the capabilities of those concerned with the implementation of strategy to put it into effect.

Many of the bases of control outlined here are therefore also bases of strategic analysis. As was pointed out in Chapter 1, the control and information systems used as means of implementing strategy are also means of analysing strategic performance. This serves as another reminder that the process of strategic management is continual and cannot be thought of simply as a step by step process.

Certainly organisations without some such systems of monitoring the implementation of strategy will find major difficulties in achieving strategic change. However, the introduction of such measurements is not in itself sufficient to ensure successful implementation of strategy. Rather, it is important to consider carefully how such information and control systems should be designed to aid the implementation of strategy and help ensure useful feedback for further analytical and planning purposes. The following guidelines, also summarised in Figure 11.3, are designed to identify some of the key issues in achieving this.

1. *Distinguish between various levels of control.* Anthony[4] has suggested that control needs to take place at three levels which he calls the strategic, management, and operational levels. Implementation of new strategies requires control at all these levels, each of which will have a quite different purpose and require different information. For example, a venture into new overseas markets would require controlling at a strategic level through an overall budget, at the management level by monitoring expenditures

1.	Distinguish levels of control e.g. strategic control/management control/operational control

1. Distinguish levels of control e.g. strategic control/management control/operational control

2. Identify responsibility centres
   revenue centres
   cost centres
   profit centres
   investment centres

3. Identify key factors and collect relevant information to control them

4. Allow diversity of control
   e.g. avoid temptation to have universal standards such as sales volume

5. Use a sensible time period
   e.g. where investment is involved use a realistic measure of pay-back period

6. Avoid misleading measurement
   e.g. the use of surrogate measures can be misleading

7. Avoid purely 'negative' monitoring
   e.g. only identifying performance below plan

Figure 11.3 Guidelines for the effective control of strategy.

and motivating employees, and also at the operational level by ensuring that routine tasks are properly performed. If strategy implementation is to be successful the control systems need to take these different levels into account. Operational control will normally require more detailed information and should be dealt with by line managers. In contrast, strategic control may consist of a few global measures monitored by senior management.

2. *Create responsibility centres.* The complexity of strategic change usually requires the subdivision of control within a company. These smaller units can be regarded as responsibility centres.[5] They are identifiable parts of the whole organisation and are responsible for a certain aspect of the business; their performance is measured and controlled accordingly. There are a number of bases on which this responsibility can be apportioned as shown in Table 11.1. The limited devolution of responsibility

Table 11.1 Different types of responsibility centre.

Type	*Examples*	*Control exerted over*	*Typical controls*
1. Revenue	Sales department	Income	Sales targets
2. Cost centre (a) Standard cost centres (b) Discretionary expense centres	Production dept. (manufacturing) R&D Administrative dept.	Cost of labour, materials, services, etc. Total expenditure	Detailed budgeting, Standard product costing Budget
3. Profit centres	Internal services (e.g. design) Product or market division subsidiary company	Profit	P&L accounts
4. Investment centres	Subsidiary company	Return on capital	Complete financial accounts

represented by revenue or cost centres has the advantage that senior management are more able to control the political activity between groups; but the disadvantage that the degree of motivation which the control system provides to individuals or groups may be quite limited. In contrast, the creation of profit or investment centres may provide motivation to perform but create political tensions within the company which may be difficult to control.

3. *Select key factors and collect relevant information.* It is crucial to identify those aspects which are critically important to the success or failure of the strategy. These should have been identified during resource planning (Chapter 9). It is then necessary to ensure that information relevant to those key factors is made available and known to be the measures of performance which are most significant. There are often cases where companies recognise the need to be selective but either do not identify or fail to monitor performance in those areas. For example, an organisation may become obsessed with a single measure of performance like volume of output or sales without assessing how this fits the overall objective of the company. This can be a severe constraint when new strategies are introduced which do not neatly fit this yardstick. A company wishing to introduce a low volume, high profit product into its traditional range of high volume, low profit lines would have great difficulties if they continued to measure the performance of the sales staff entirely by volume.

4. *Allow diversity in control.* The previous example also illustrates the danger of assuming that all an organisation's activities can be controlled by an all-embracing system of control. Not only is this not achievable in practice, but is not desirable when attempting to control strategic implementation. The facts that strategic decisions are long term and made in conditions of uncertainty are themselves sufficient for requiring the more liberal application of control.

   The continued evolution of new strategies requires this diversity of control. The most obvious example is the lack of profitability of new products during their early days. Chapter 7 explained the importance of a balanced portfolio of products or activities. The profitability of cash cows and stars would not be expected to be the same since the strategic purpose of those two groups of products is different. Their contribution to the company may have to be measured and controlled differently.

5. *Avoid misleading measurements.* Control relies heavily on measurement, but many aspects of strategy are difficult to measure quantitatively. This can lead to situations where the pressure to produce quantitative measures distorts the process of control and, in some cases, leads to poor performance. The police force has a problem in this respect as the assessment of how well law and order is being maintained is very difficult. In the absence of any precise measures there is a tendency to develop surrogate measures, i.e. those things which are measurable. In the case of the police, surrogate measures might be the number of arrests, convictions, or proportion of cases solved. A police force which had extremely good relations with its local community might score badly by these measures.

6. *Beware of 'negative' monitoring.* There is, the danger that systems will be concerned with purely negative monitoring of performance,[6] for example only with highlighting variances which are below plan. The result can be that departments and individuals become over-concerned with minimising the risk of such negative variances. This can

ILLUSTRATION 11.2

Control systems in two integrated multinational corporations

Systems of control and information play important parts in achieving integration
worldwide in IBM and between the various subsidiaries of Ford Europe.

IBM

One way in which the management at the centre of IBM can evaluate progress and
determine priorities for its subsidiaries is through its planning and accounting processes.
Planning in IBM is a two way process. Corporate headquarters may set targets and plans
for local subsidiaries: however, local subsidiaries can also put forward their plans to the
centre and, if not approved, could appeal to the Corporate Managing Committee, which
comprises the top three IBM executives. For each subsidiary, plans include financial and
operating statements on strategy which are used consistently throughout the group to
measure performance of subsidiaries. Thirteen different elements of performance are
monitored against plan by corporate staff; and volume and manpower measures are reviewed regularly by a Corporate Managing Committee. Corporate staff also report to this
committee on any substantial deviations on any of the other measures. Since high and low
parameters are set within the budget for performance, any deviations by subsidiaries
outside these are also subject to more detailed studies by staff functions. The same measures
in the plan are also likely to be used for any bases of incentive policy for managers of
subsidiaries.

Ford of Europe

In the 1960s Ford of Europe operated in a far less integrated way than it does in the 1980s.
Sales subsidiaries, for example, bought cars from national manufacturing companies at
'export prices' set by the manufacturing companies. Since the centre measured the
performance of subsidiaries in terms of net profit, these subsidiaries were primarily
concerned to maximise their performance with the risk that they might not be benefiting
the corporation as a whole; for example, they might promote products on which they
made the greatest margins and thus lead to an imbalance of production throughout Europe.
A different means of accounting was introduced in an attempt to integrate and track
profitability on a European wide basis. This allowed for the identification of the
contribution made by sales of specific models by country, thus providing information to
managers of subsidiaries as to the extent to which they were contributing to the performance of Ford Europe as a whole, and the means of measuring the contribution of sales
subsidiaries themselves. A Ford manager explained it as follows:

> Our accounting system now allocates a share of the corporate [Ford of Europe]
> operating profits to the various national subsidiaries. This is accompanied by an
> annual business plan for each company. Before this accounting allocation system
> was implemented the managing directors of the sales companies had no idea of
> the overall profitability of what they were doing. Now the impact of their actions
> on corporate profits can be measured and they are evaluated on what they
> generate for the corporation as a whole. This plays an important role in shifting
> the focus of our sales companies from that of internal agents to that of real
> businesses, run by general managers, and playing their part in the whole
> corporation.

Source: Y. Doz, *Strategic Management in Multinational Companies*, Pergamon Press, 1986.

lead to a situation in which risks are avoided or attempts are made to transfer the blame for poor performance onto other departments or individuals. It is important that it is understood that monitoring systems are there to ensure that everyone knows how performance against plan is being achieved and that they highlight excellent perform- ance as well as negative performance. One of the implications here is that the agreement of objectives against which performance is to be measured usually benefits from a participation in setting those objectives rather than them being prescribed by top management alone. In this way it is more likely that the objectives will be 'owned' by those responsible for achieving them and, in turn, that they will regard them as useful measures against which to monitor their own performance, rather than seen as the heavy hand of top management.

Systems of control are particularly important in complex organisations to ensure that the various parts of such organisations are integrated sufficiently to implement corporate strategy. Illustration 11.2 shows how the implementation of integrated multinational strategies at IBM and Ford Europe depends heavily on such systems.

11.3 REGULATORY SYSTEMS

Information is not the only basis of control open to organisations. There exist other means by which a change in the behaviour of those who must implement strategy might be attempted. These vary from fairly formalised organisational systems – such as training and reward systems or changes in work practices – to the management style adopted in the organisation.

11.3.1 Reward systems

Reward systems[7] are an important means of achieving compliance with planned strategic change. They can be considered in terms of monetary reward systems such as graded pay schemes, bonuses, profit sharing schemes; and productivity schemes and also non-monetary reward systems such as promotion and increased status. It is also important to remember that reward systems have both positive and negative impacts. The failure to achieve rewards, or the withdrawal of rewards may be perceived as 'punishment'. In addition, the nature of the rewards needs to be carefully considered in terms of the objectives to be achieved; for example, if long term growth of profits is the aim then rewards based on short term achievement of sales targets are not likely to be helpful. This section considers how reward systems might affect the behaviour of people and therefore be important in the management of strategic change. It does this by considering some of the key issues that are likely to arise in implementing strategic plans and how reward systems might relate to these issues. Since the particular issues that will be important are likely to vary by context the reader should bear in mind that there is no one correct way of designing reward systems; the 'package' of rewards needs to be designed for the circumstances faced by the organisation, and the groups and individuals within it.

1. *Short versus long run perspectives.* As has already been indicated, the nature of rewards

needs to vary according to the time horizons of the plans to be implemented. In general, the shorter the time horizons, the more important it is that any incentives such as bonuses should be based on clear quantitative measures of performance relating to the short term. On the other hand, the longer the time horizons, the more likely it is that more qualitative measures may be appropriate upon which to base incentives unless quantitative measures can be made relevant to long term performance; for example, some companies have recently begun to give bonuses or share options based on the rise of real earnings per share over a number of years (see Illustration 11.3). A common problem is that organisations expect managers to devote effort and attention to long term problems when rewards are mainly tailored to short term performance. It is unrealistic to suppose that managers will jeopardise the achievement of short run goals in the long term interest of the organisation, particularly when their remuneration is based on the attainment of such short term goals. This needs to be considered carefully given the growing use of bonus incentive schemes: in the UK in 1986 63% of larger firms had bonus incentive schemes and on average 25% of executive recommendation in these firms was in this form. The corresponding figures in 1981 were 24% and 11% respectively.[8]

2. *Risk aversion and risk taking.* Salter[9] suggests that the organisation that wishes to encourage greater risk taking amongst its managers is likely to find that more qualitative measures of performance upon which to base bonus awards or share options are likely to be beneficial. Quantitative measures of performance may result in minimising behaviour to avoid failure rather than risk taking behaviour to achieve results even greater than expectation. However, it is equally important that executives expected to take risks are provided both with salaries and incentives commensurate with the business and personal risks likely to be involved.

3. *Profits versus volume/size.* Researchers have observed that organisations under managerial control (as opposed to those with marked sharehold influence) tend to follow strategies of growth and the achievement of size sometimes at the expense of profit performance.[10] There is also evidence that chief executives in managerially controlled organisations tend to be remunerated on the basis of size and scale of operations, whereas those in organisations with dominant sharehold influences are more likely to be rewarded in terms of profit performance.[11] Those concerned with designing reward systems should bear in mind that there may exist expectations about the bases of reward systems rooted in the ownership and control structures of the firm; those in managerially dominated firms may expect to be rewarded in terms of scale of operations, whereas those in which shareholders play a more dominant part may expect to be rewarded in terms of profit performance. For the change agent, perhaps trying to move the organisation towards a greater profit focus in a managerially dominated firm, the implication is that the package of rewards to achieve such ends will have to be especially sharply focused towards the achievement of profit objectives.

4. *Rewards for individuals.* An important issue is to consider how reward systems can or should reflect individuals' *capabilities*, direction and degree of *effort* and *job satisfaction*. The Human Relations Movement of the 1930s[12] saw job performance as primarily related to job satisfaction. Others[13] have seen rewards and payment as a major stimulus to effort and emphasis has been placed on payment by results (e.g. piecework, sales

Table 11.2 Types of reward system.

Type of reward	Factor being rewarded or stimulated		
	Capability	*Effort*	*Satisfaction*
Monetary	Graded job/pay system Bonuses (e.g. for qualifications)	Piecework Productivity schemes Profit-sharing	Differentials important
Non-monetary	Promotion (dependent on qualifications)	Promotion Dismissal	Promotion More autonomy Bigger budget Status symbols (car, office, carpet, etc.)

commission, etc.). In other organisations rewards tend to reflect capability, e.g. where skilled workers are paid more than unskilled workers. It is important to bear in mind that reward systems which are geared to only one aspect, such as effort, can have a negative effect on people's performance in other ways. For example, the satisfaction and compliance of a departmental manager may be undermined by a productivity scheme (effort related reward system) which results in his operatives earning higher wages than himself. Table 11.2 illustrates the range of reward systems commonly available and which of the aspects discussed here each reward system is designed to deal with. For example, graded pay systems are designed to reward capabilities, even to the extent in some organisations of giving increments of pay to those who possess certain qualifications irrespective of job performance. In contrast, non-monetary rewards such as cars or size or location of offices, are often a method of improving job satisfaction.

5. *Individual or group rewards.* Rewarding individuals for effort and performance can prove difficult unless the organisational structure and the systems of control allow an individual's performance to be isolated from the efforts of others. From a strategic point of view, therefore, it may be an important consideration as to whether reward systems should seek to influence the behaviour of individuals or groups. A manufacturer of quality silver plated tea sets,[14] in an attempt to move from a craft based operation to a light engineering operation, found problems as a result of its payment schemes. The existing piece-rate scheme had been effective whilst the craftsmen had control of the whole process and took personal pride in product quality: but when it was applied to the new production process, quality dropped significantly. The company found it necessary to phase out piecework payment and move to a factory bonus scheme rewarding consistent quality of output for the factory as a whole.

Organisations choosing to introduce incentive schemes for managers face similar problems in deciding whether the scheme should be based on the performance of each individual manager or on the management team as a whole.[15] Table 11.3 summarises some of the pros and cons of each system. This list is useful in choosing reward systems since it helps in matching the conditions described in the table with the type of strategic change being undertaken. For example, individual incentive schemes are clearly more appropriate for strategies which are independent of other company activities and where performance can be easily measured. In contrast, a group incentive would be better where a high level of overlap exists between activities, or where many (perhaps

Table 11.3 Managerial rewards – individual and group incentives.

Aspects to be considered	Schemes based on individual performance	Schemes based on group performance
Managerial contribution to company performance	(a) Appropriate where individual's contribution is relatively independent	(a) Appropriate where individuals' contributions are relatively interdependent
	(b) Appropriate where performance standards are relatively variable, i.e. some managers at much higher standard than others	(b) Appropriate where performance standards are relatively uniform
Type of behaviour	Encourages entrepreneurial, self-reliant or creative types of behaviour	Encourages greater co-operation, co-ordination and team management
Flexibility of scheme	Scheme can be negotiated individually, or can be uniform	Scheme can be negotiated individually, but is more likely to be standard or uniform
Administration	Administrative requirements relatively great	Administrative requirements relatively slight
Discrimination	Relatively easy to achieve high discrimination between different levels of performance	Discrimination can be achieved between different groups or teams, but not so easily between individuals

Source: Angela M. Bowey, ed., *Handbook of Salary and Wage Systems*, 2nd edn, p.254, Gower, 1982.

specialist) managers are involved, or where performance is difficult to assign to individuals.

6. *Business unit versus corporate perspective.* Care has to be taken to balance the corporate interest against the business unit interests. For example, a distributor of cars moved to a geographically based divisionalised structure and at the same time introduced divisional profit targets upon which bonus schemes were based. Prior to these changes the garages in different parts of the country had informally accommodated each other's needs by transferring cars at short notice to meet customer requirements. After the changes, such transfers became much less common as managers were wary of releasing, and so missing sales.

The greater the independence of the units from the centre or from each other, the more it is likely that unit-based reward systems are sensible. Similarly the more removed the individual manager or group within the unit is from influencing corporate performance, the more sensible it is to have unit-based reward systems. However, real problems occur in the case of divisional or unit-based general managers and directors. Such managers typically have dual influences; both on their unit performance and in contributing to the corporate well being. Considerable care has to be given to a sensible balance of rewards which are likely to focus attention on the areas of greatest concern or priority and minimise the risk of negative influence either at unit level or at corporate level.

These are some of the key issues which need to be considered in designing reward systems. It is increasingly being realised that there is no one best way of designing such systems to achieve strategic change. More organisations are moving towards a mixed

Table 11.4 A weighted–factor approach used to reward achievement of strategic goals.

SBU* category	Factor	Weight
High growth	Return on assets	10%
	Cash flow	0%
	Strategic funds programs	45%
	Market share increase	45%
		100%
Medium growth	Return on assets	25%
	Cash flow	25%
	Strategic funds programs	25%
	Market share increase	25%
		100%
Low growth	Return on assets	50%
	Cash flow	50%
	Strategic funds programs	0%
	Market share increase	0%
		100%

*SBU = Strategic business unit.
From P.J. Stonich, *Implementing Strategy*, p.136, Ballinger, 1982.

basis of remuneration depending on the strategic requirements of the organisation. Table 11.4 gives an example of such an approach, showing how different performance measures might vary according to different growth objectives for different business units within a corporation. The measures of performance are all the same but the weight given to the mix of remuneration depends on the strategic circumstances of the organisation. Illustration 11.3 also serves to show how a mixed system of remuneration was put into effect.

In summary, the design of reward systems is a key element in creating a climate for strategic change. The need is to decide what the most important issues are for the reward system to deal with. Figure 11.4 is a checklist of some of these issues and summarises the discussion above.

---

1. Which aspects of the strategy will rewards be most concerned with? e.g.
   - Profits or volume
   - Risk or stability
   - Short versus long time horizons
   - Quality

2. Should reward systems focus on groups or individuals?

3. Should reward systems focus on the business unit or the corporation?

4. Should the systems reward effort or capability?

5. Should rewards be mainly monetary, promotion or status?

6. What sanctions and punishments, if any, are needed?

7. Is there a sensible balance between types of reward systems to achieve strategic objectives?

8. Are political consequences of reward systems likely to help or hinder strategic change?

Figure 11.4 Reward systems and strategic change: a checklist.

ILLUSTRATION 11.3

Executive reward systems in Burtons

The performance related reward package introduced in Burtons in 1987 was, according to its Chief Executive, Ralph Halpern, designed to create a culture of enterprise, crucial to the success of the British economy.

Ralph Halpern was, in 1986, the highest paid chief executive in the UK with a remuneration package in excess of £1 million in salary and performance related payments. His view was that there was a need for high incentives for executives who achieved success. However, these reward systems should also both relate to the managers' own area of responsibility and encourage the manager to look at the business from the point of view of the shareholder.

At the Annual General Meeting in 1987 Halpern introduced a reward package for senior executives including himself, which offered performance related share options worth up to eight times annual remuneration. The *Financial Times* reported that:

> The proposed Burtons scheme will enable managers to exercise options worth four times their remuneration if the company's real earnings per share growth exceeds 30% within a five year period. A further four times remuneration will be on offer if the company's cumulative earnings per share growth put it in the top 25 companies in the FT/SE 100 share index. Even if these goals are achieved, the exercise of the options can be restricted if the manager fails to achieve the goals set for him personally... Although the work of staff executives is more difficult to quantify, at Burton, they too are given individual tasks to achieve. The Personnel Director, for example, might be set the task of reaching an agreement which rationalises the company's pay scales by a specific date. The Financial Director might be set the task of introducing a new accounting system. If these goals are achieved on time, the managers would receive their incentive payments, provided the group as a whole achieved its own target.

Halpern's view was that such a scheme would not only be beneficial for the executives but for the corporation and the shareholders.

> When you have a choice between working for a large company or a small company, in the old days you'd say I would rather work in a large company because it's safer. When takeovers came along, those days of security went. Now on one in a large company is safe from a predator unless he performs. We have replaced the attitude of I work for this company for loyalty and a gold watch, to I work for this company so I can improve my standard of living and because they reward results.

Source: *Financial Times*, 20 January 1987.

11.3.2 Training and development

One of the most difficult aspects of implementing strategic change is ensuring that the employees are able to undertake the key tasks which that change requires. During strategic change the nature of people's jobs might change, with the result that their *capability* in their new role or their *identification* with the required changes may be in

question. Either of these problems will reduce the possibilities of successful implementation of strategy.

Strategic change in organisations is likely to require that individuals cope with a
good deal more uncertainty and ambiguity[16] than when faced with operational change
only. A new work practice may raise problems enough in trying to get people familiar
with new techniques, and it can raise problems of resistance to change because they do
not identify with such change. Strategic change, however, is the more difficult because
the emphasis is more likely to be on getting people to accept new ways of thinking
about their roles – for example new attitudes to customer service, or a greater level of
risk taking. These are not matters capable of being dealt with by providing people with
information or skills training alone. Rather they need individuals to adopt both new
operational skills and to cope with and help resolve situations of uncertainty. As
explained in Chapter 2, the extent to which new ways of doing things will be accepted
may be particularly low in organisations where there is a long established recipe and
cultural web: whilst programmes of training and development can help manage such
change, they probably also need to be considered together with the means of culture
change discussed later in the chapter.

A precursor to the design of training and development programmes is a reassessment of the roles and responsibilities of people within the organisation. A proper
understanding of the capabilities of people to operate in different ways is essential to
implement change. This underlines the need for an analysis of an organisation's human
resources as discussed in Chapter 4. Approaches to training and development[17] will
then vary according to the extent of changes and the capabilities of individuals and
groups identified in the assessment. Figure 11.5[18] not only provides a checklist of
training aims and methods but also suggests that the greater the degree of strategic

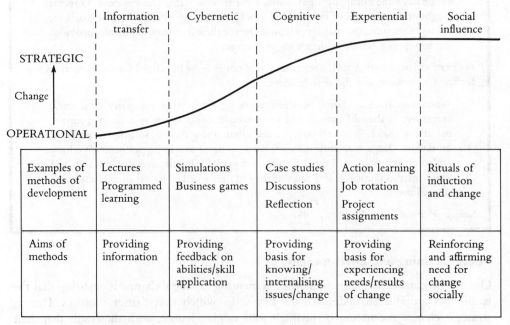

Figure 11.5 Methods of training and development for managing strategic change.

change, the more likely it is that methods of training and development will be needed suited to providing bases for understanding and internalising change and experiencing the results of change. Such aims are unlikely to be achieved through programmed learning techniques, but more likely to be achieved through group discussion work and, particularly, on the job, practical and project based experience related to the changes. Some corporations wisely regard such development, not merely as a matter of training, but as a matter of career planning; they ensure that managers gain a breadth of experience needed at higher levels for managing change during their careers by undertaking jobs and experiencing situations in different parts of the corporation. Certainly in Japanese companies the development of such a breadth of experience is seen as essential to the development of management.[19]

11.3.3 Organisational routines

There is another major influence which will regulate behaviour within the organisation. Nelson and Winter refer to 'routines' as: 'a general term for all regular and predictable behavioural patterns of firms ... from well specified technical routines for producing things, through procedures for hiring and firing, ordering new inventory, or stepping up production of items in high demand, to policies regarding investment, R&D or advertising, and business strategies about product diversification and overseas investment'.[20] In many respects these routines are the institutionalised 'ways we do things around here' which tend to persist over time and guide how people do their jobs. It may, of course, be that an organisation which becomes especially good at carrying out its operations in particular ways achieves real competitive advantage in so doing and therefore searches for strategies which best utilise such advantages[21] – although here there is a need to beware of the chances of strategic drift discussed in Chapter 2.

Certainly the power of such routines is clear enough when they are required to be changed in order to accommodate some new strategy. As one manager explained about the implications of a strategic change in his organisation: 'It's like turning an oil tanker; you may know that you want to go somewhere else but the systems keep grinding on and you can't turn the ship'. The result is that attempts to change strategy may fail because its implementation tries to be accommodated within existing routines. The logic of the strategy may be to change the routines but these are in fact what define the organisational work patterns for perhaps thousands of individuals. Managers often make the mistake of assuming that because they have specified a strategy which requires operational changes in work practices, and even identified to more junior management what such changes are, that the changes will necessarily take place. They may well find that the reasons which emerge as to why such changes should be delayed or cannot occur, are to do with the persistent influence of long standing routines. Just as it was argued earlier with regard to control systems, there is a need to identify the priority areas for changes in such routines. It is then important that senior management, responsible for the strategic changes, take personal responsibility for ensuring such changes in routines occur. A few examples make the point:

● Buyers in a major retailer had always 'bought long' to obtain the greatest discounts: a new managing director wanted a more responsive, fashion orientated operation and insisted in cutting buying lead times by half.

- The new chief executive of an engineering firm, appointed to turn round the business, found an unacceptably high level of stock, particularly in small items. These were kept in 'bins' in the stock room. He ordered that the bins be replaced with smaller ones and the size of the stock room reduced.
- The new personnel director of a firm trying to diversify away from its traditional base in heavy chemicals noticed that recruitment practices were biased towards chemical engineers. He reduced the space available in application forms to do with past career and qualifications and requested that applicants write about possible future company strategy. He also changed the journals in which advertisements were placed and involved more outsiders in the interviewing procedures.

11.3.4 Management style

The management style of an organisation is, in the end, an expression of the nature and characteristics of the managers, those they manage, the tasks in the organisation and the organisational culture.[22] These have been discussed elsewhere in the book (particularly Chapters 2 and 5). Management style is, however, also to do with how the different systems of control and regulation are put into effect and this is likely to differ between organisations. Chapter 10 began by explaining that, traditionally, organisations were conceived of rather as machines with clear structures and mechanisms for working. This has become known as a bureaucratic or mechanistic approach to organisation.[23] It is not, however, the only way in which organisations may work. It may well make sense for organisations to be less mechanistic, 'more organic', in some circumstances than in others. Figure 11.6 contrasts mechanistic and organic systems of organisation. Organic systems assume that the ability and efficiency with which individuals work together is not so much reliant upon formal standardisation of work patterns or job

Mechanistic	Organic
1. Specialised differentiation and definition of tasks in the organisation	1. Contributive nature of special knowledge to the total concerns of the organisation
2. Hierarchical supervision and reconciliation of problems	2. Redefinition of tasks and responsibilities through interaction with others
3. Precise definition of job responsibilities, methods, rights and obligations	3. Commitment to the organisation beyond any technical/precise definition; such commitment more valued than loyalty
4. (Perceived) location of superior knowledge at the top of the hierarchy	4. Network structure of control, authority and communication
5. Vertical interaction of individuals between subordinate and superior	5. Omniscience not imputed to senior executives; knowledge located anywhere in the organisation and this location may become centre of authority for given issue
6. Insistence on loyalty to organisation and obedience to superiors	
7. More prestige attached to job (and local) than to more general knowledge, experience and skills	6. Lateral rather than vertical direction of communication
	7. Communication consists of information and advice rather than instructions and decisions

Figure 11.6 Characteristics of mechanistic and organic systems in organisations.

descriptions as on the commitment of the individuals to organisation-wide concerns and the organisation's ethos. The result are more fluid systems of management in which it may be more difficult to determine exactly who reports to whom or precisely what job is done by any one individual. Such systems are characterised by their informality and their loose, rather than tight, definition of work practices.

Again, just as there is no right or wrong about levels of centralisation in organisations, there is no absolute right or wrong as to whether an organisation should sensibly be organic or mechanistic, or something in between. The point is that in different circumstances, different systems of organisation are more, or less, sensible. This was made clear in discussing different influences on organisational structure in Chapter 10. For example, for the organisation facing very stable environmental conditions and with established work practices it may make sense to exercise control through mechanistic systems. This would, however, be inappropriate for an organisation in a rapidly changing environment where more organic systems of management control would be more appropriate.

In implementing strategic change it is important that all of these aspects of regulation are considered and a sensible mix of actions instituted to achieve desired change. Illustration 11.4 shows how Nabisco UK utilised incentive and reward schemes, training and development, and changes in systems of communication to promote organisational change in the mid 1980s.

11.4 ACHIEVING CULTURE CHANGE

Managing strategic change is, in the end, to do with achieving a change in the culture of the organisation;[24] that is, a change in the recipe and the aspects of the cultural web that preserve and reinforce that recipe. It is unrealistic to suppose that strategic change can be implemented if the current beliefs and assumptions and ways of doing things remain the same. This section examines some of the processes important in recipe change: and goes on to discuss why changes in the symbols of organisational life can be important.

Recipe change is essentially to do with cognitive change – changing the way in which members of the organisation make sense of their organisational world and its environment. Broadly, two stages can be discerned in the process of cognitive change. The first is the process of 'unfreezing' or breaking down the beliefs and assumptions which currently exist. Second is the process of reformulation – the assertion and adoption of new sets of beliefs:[25] in effect the acceptance of a new recipe. This is discussed below and summarised in Figure 11.7.

11.4.1 The unfreezing process

Unfreezing the existing recipe might be achieved in a number of ways.

1. As was seen in Chapter 2, there is likely to be the need for some form of organisational *trigger* which signals the need for change. Typically, this is a downturn in performance or market share, or perhaps a threatened takeover. Such triggers may, of course, be deliberately manipulated by management on occasions to create a climate in which change may occur more readily.

ILLUSTRATION 11.4

Managing change at Nabisco

The need for both strategic and culture change in Nabisco UK was aided by
planned changes in systems of control and regulation in the company.

In the 1980s Nabisco UK was formed as a result of the US parent's merger of Nabisco
Brands, which included Walkers Crisps, and Associated Biscuits which itself included
businesses such as Jacobs, Huntley & Palmers, Smiths and Peak Frean. One of the
problems faced by the top management was therefore to integrate quite different
businesses and also implement a major rationalisation programme to reduce employees
from some 19,000 to 13,500. Much depended on the implementation of a personnel
strategy for change.
The changes introduced included:

● A reorganisation of the personnel function itself so that personnel managers on sites
  reported to senior operating managers rather than more senior personnel managers.
  Personnel directors within divisions became redundant and the central personnel
  function limited to just four managers.
● On amalgamation of the different businesses there had existed seven separate
  approaches to grading and a variety of reward structures. None of the systems of
  reward were related to performance. A new grading structure was introduced with
  eight grades each with wide salary bands to allow lateral development of managers,
  flexibility in recruitment and, most important, reward for performance. Overall salaries
  and benefits moved the company from a relatively low base of remuneration to a 'high
  paying company'.
● The new remuneration package was accompanied by a performance appraisal system
  which quite clearly signalled that salary progression would depend on merit and
  performance alone. For the first time salaries and appraisal were linked.
● The performance appraisal system also provided a basis for an annual management audit
  in which training needs were identified together with management gaps to be filled
  internally or externally. To cope with the training needs of individuals and the gaps
  identified in the firm, movement between divisions began to occur, a graduate
  recruitment scheme was introduced and a general management programme designed
  and implemented in cooperation with the Manchester Business School.
● All this was accompanied by improved communication systems including the
  adaptation of the group newspaper to accommodate the local needs of business units,
  the development of skills training for briefing systems for line managers, and quarterly
  meetings of the top fifty senior managers or the chief executive for a review of the
  business.

Source: 'Nabisco's winning strategy', *Personnel Management*, May 1987.

2. *Challenge and exposure* of the current recipe is likely to be required. The mechanisms
   by which such challenge may occur can be varied. It may be as formalised as a
   deliberate planning procedure, or as informal as management meetings which begin
   to question ways of operating. It may also be that such challenge takes on a more
   symbolic dimension: for example, Schein[26] tells of a new chief executive who, on
   taking over his job in a transport company, ordered that the liveries of all the

---

Recipe change through:

- **Unfreezing processes**
  The need for a *trigger*
  Challenging/exposing the recipe
  Reconfiguring *power structures*
  Involving *outsiders*

- **Adopting a new recipe**
  Showing through *deeds*
  Enhancing or diminishing *status*
  Participation and *partial implementation*

- **Symbolic activity**

Figure 11.7 Achieving culture change.

vehicles be removed and vehicles painted plain white. Despite initial objections, the new chief executive insisted and when managers then asked how they should repaint the vehicles, his answer was to ask them to make proposals. In effect he was asking them to rethink what the business was about without the preconceptions rooted in its history.

3. It is likely that there will be a need for the reconfiguration of *power structures* in the organisation. This may well go hand in hand with the legitimising of dissent from those in the organisation who are questioning the existing ways of operating. In order to effect this reconfiguration of power it is likely that the momentum for change will need *powerful advocacy* within the organisation, typically from the chief executive, a powerful member of the board or an influential outsider. It is not unusual in such circumstances to find that a new chief executive is appointed to take on the change agency role.[27]

4. Major change is often accompanied by the intervention of an *outsider*, perhaps in the form of a new chief executive, senior executive, or perhaps a consultant. An outsider is not defined here as someone necessarily physically from outside the company, though this is quite likely to be the case, but rather as someone with little or no commitment to the existing recipe[28] who can therefore more easily perceive its limitations. Moreover, the role of the outsider may be very specific in terms of reformulating the strategy itself. It is not suggested that outsiders necessarily 'invent' totally new solutions, rather that they may import or borrow from their previous experience relevant new approaches. In effect, the outsider applies his or her past experience to new situations.[29]

11.4.2 The adoption of a new recipe

A new view of the organisational strategy, perhaps brought by an outsider, is in itself no guarantee that members of that organisation will accept such views and beliefs and change their ways of perceiving the organisation. Nor does unfreezing the current recipe mean that new beliefs and approaches will be accepted. Indeed, the unfreezing and reformulation process may be seen by management as destructive in taking apart that which already exists.[30] At such times the organisation is likely to go through a period of turbulence in which there is a likelihood that it will revert to old ways of operating. There needs to be means, therefore, by which new ideas gain the confidence of management and other stakeholders. There are a number of ways in which this may occur:

1. There is evidence to suggest that the most powerful mechanism for the adoption of new strategy is by *showing through deeds*[31] the effectiveness of new strategies. Concrete performance improvement or real, visible signs of change are much more powerful than analytical arguments about the need for change.
2. The acceptance of new strategies is likely to be linked to the extent to which such change enhances or diminishes *status*. For example, it is quite common for a new chief executive to remove all or part of the old board. Not only may this have the effect of removing resistance to change and signifying the intent of change, but also it may mean that more junior managers are provided with opportunities for advancement, and this will increase the likelihood of their accepting change.
3. Acceptance of such change may also be assisted through managers' *participation* in discussions to do with the change and its *partial implementation*, perhaps in some test market activity or in the formulation and implementation of trials to examine the feasibility of new strategies. This is one reason why the use of project teams and taskforces which come together to introduce new strategies may be a useful means of implementing strategic change.[32]
4. Finally *symbolic activity* may play an important role in achieving the acceptance of recipe change. For example, organisational and personnel changes which symbolise the irreversibility of change may be very powerful: the replacement of a board by a new chief executive is a common signalling of such permanence of change. However, there are other ways in which symbolic activity can be a powerful means of achieving and cementing culture change, and this is now discussed.

11.4.3 Symbolic action and strategic change[33]

Four years before *In Search of Excellence* was published, Tom Peters argued that managers needed to understand better that 'the mundane tools that involve the creation and manipulation of symbols over time have impact to the extent that they reshape beliefs and expectations'.[34] The point he was making was that managers need to understand that for change to be meaningful to individuals in the organisation, that meaning must be apparent in their day to day experience in the organisation: and the day to day 'reality' of organisations is represented by the many mundane aspects of organisational life that come to take on symbolic significance. These include the sorts of story that people tell, the rituals that take place, the status symbols such as cars or sizes of office, and the type of language used. They also include the very systems discussed elsewhere in this chapter and the last; the sorts of reward, information and control system that people become accustomed to; the 'ways of doing things around here' that have been termed organisational routines; and the organisational structures that represent reporting relationships and often status. In addition, the budgeting and planning systems discussed in Chapter 9 come to take on symbolic significance in so far as they come to represent to individuals the reality of day-to-day organisational life. As previously explained, these culture devices preserve and legitimise the recipe: they are part of the cultural web which represents the reality of the organisation to its members.

Changing them, or employing them to signify or emphasise change can be a very powerful mechanism for change. For example:

1. *Organisational rituals* are both important means of regulating behaviour within organisations and also, potentially, for changing behaviour and challenging and changing recipes. Trice and Beyer[35] argue that there exist six different types of rite (or ritual) which organisations typically employ to cement or change existing modes of behaviour and organisational assumptions: these are shown in Table 11.5, the last column of which has been added to give some examples of how such rituals are used for the purposes of promoting or consolidating recipe and culture change.

Table 11.5 Types of rite (ritual) and their roles in culture change.

Types of rite	Social consequences	Role in promoting/ consolidating culture change	Examples
Rites of passage	Facilitate transition of people into social roles and statuses that are new for them	Consolidate ways people carry out social roles Promote new ways of social interaction	Induction of new recruits
Rites of degradation	Dissolve social identities and their attendant power	Provide public acknow-ledgements that problems exist Defend group boundaries by redefining who belongs and who does not Reaffirm social importance and value of role involved	Firing and replacing top executive
Rites of enhance-ment	Enhance social identities and their attendance power	Spread good news about the organisation Provide public recognition of individuals for their accomplishments and motivate others to similar efforts Emphasise social value of performance of social roles	Award ceremonies at company conferences
Rites of renewal	Refurbish social structures and improve the ways they function	Reassure members that something is being done about problems Focus attention on some problems and away from others Legitimate systems of power and authority	Problem-centred/project taskforces Appointment of consultants on specified projects
Rites of integration	Encourage and revive shared feelings that bind people together and keep them committed to a social system	Permit venting of emotion and temporary loosening of various norms Reassert and reaffirm, by contrast, moral rughtness of usual norms	Office Christmas parties
Rites of conflict reduction	Reduce conflict and aggression	Re-establish equilibrium in disturbed social relations Compartmentalise conflict and its disruptive effects	Internal appeal systems Union–management committees

Adapted from H.M. Trice and J.M. Beyer, 'Using six organizational rites to change culture', in R.H. Kilman *et al.* (eds), *Gaining Control of the Corporate Culture*, pp.374–5, Jossey Bass, 1985.

2. Formal *control mechanisms* may also take on symbolic significance and be important in promoting change; a computerised stock control system which may have the apparent aim of minimising stocks, may also be used in a retailing operation to challenge managers assumptions about what can and cannot sell in a shop. Rates of depreciation, apparently an accountancy measure, also encapsulate whole sets of assumptions about degrees and rates of change, so changing them may challenge expectations of change. Targets set for managers may demand that they think outside their current horizons and invent new ways of approaching old problems.

3. Organisational *stories* (or *myths*) can also be an important vehicle for stimulating change, because they communicate in ways readily understood the 'vision of the organisation's mission or role'.[36] The importance of quality in Mars is enshrined in the story of Forrest Mars throwing Mars bars at his managers on finding just one miswrapped in a store.[37] One company faced with significant resistance to change found acceptance accelerated rapidly when the word spread that one of the long serving senior executives had 'been converted' to the new approaches being introduced. In another, stories about the 'irreverent' behaviour of a new chief executive towards a long established family-dominated board spread through the company before he had made any formalised changes.

4. More generalised *symbols of change* can also be important. The flowery kipper ties and long hair of Sir John Harvey-Jones of ICI were not just eccentricity: they also signified the presence and significance of an identified leader at the top of a major company which hitherto had seen somewhat anonymous chief executives. Moreover the personal letters received by ICI managers, or the fact that Harvey-Jones would go out of his way to support – and be seen to support – the attempts by divisions to implement change, quickly demonstrated the changed expectations at the top of the company. In a university business school a new director, instead of merely trying to explain the need for a greater orientation towards research for the staff, moved his study and computer terminal to a position adjacent to the lobby: there he was visible to staff as they entered each morning doing his own research. Symbols of change might include relocation of offices, changes in furnishings and decor, changes in logo or house style, changes in the clothes people wear and so on.

5. The sorts of *structural change* discussed in Chapter 10 are also of symbolic significance. The replacement of a board of directors, the amalgamation of divisions or the splitting of a division into smaller parts, the change from functional to divisional structure are not merely structural changes; they also signify changes in the expectations of those making such changes.

11.5 MANAGING STRATEGIC CHANGE THROUGH POLITICAL SYSTEMS

One of the themes running through this book is that management should be seen not only as an analytical and planning activity, but as a political process. It is therefore important to consider how strategic change might be implemented from a political perspective. Managers need to realise that analysis and planning may themselves take on political dimensions. A new marketing director of one company commissioned market research on customer perceptions of service and found the results were highly critical. The director found that the presentation of the findings to the board gave rise, not to analytical debate, but to systematic 'rubbishing' of the research report. As he later stated, he failed to realise that it was 'not so much an analytical statement, as a statement of political threat.'

11.5.1 Power and the management of strategic change

Chapter 5 showed the importance of understanding the political systems of the organisation. Having established this understanding there is also a need to plan the implementation of strategy within this political context. The approach developed here draws on the content of Chapter 5 and also some of what has been discussed in this chapter to provide a framework for considering such political activity: Table 11.6 summarises some of the political mechanisms in organisations.[38] These include the manipulation of *organisational resources*, the relationship with powerful groupings, or *élites*, activity with regard to *subsystems* in the organisation, and *symbolic activity*. All of these may be used to: (a) build a power base, (b) overcome resistance, and (c) achieve compliance.

1. The control and manipulation or organisational *resources* was shown in Chapter 5 to

Table 11.6 Political mechanisms in organisations.

Activity areas	Mechanisms				Key problems
	Resources	*Elites*	*Subsystems*	*Symbolic*	
Building the power base	Control of resources Acquisition of/identification with expertise Acquisition of additional resources	Sponsorship by an élite Association with an élite	Alliance building Team building	Building on legitimation	Time required for building Perceived duality of ideals Perceived as threat by existing élites
Overcoming resistance	Withdrawal of resources Use of 'counter intelligence' information	Breakdown of division of élites Association with change agent Association with respected outsider	Foster momentum for change Sponsorchip/ reward of change agents	Attack or remove legitimation Foster confusion conflict and questioning	Striking from too low a power base Potentially destructive: need for rapid rebuilding
Achieve compliance	Giving resources	Removal of resistant élites Need for visible 'change hero'	Partial implementation and participation Implantation of 'disciples' Support for 'young Turks'	Applause/ reward Reassurance Symbolic confirmation	Converting the body of the organisation Slipping back

be a source of power. For example, acquiring additional resources or being identified with important resource areas or areas of expertise, and the ability to withdraw or allocate resources, can be valuable in overcoming resistance or persuading others to accept change: and the careful use of information or news to counter that being used to justify opposition to change may be important.

2. How existing powerful groupings (or *élites*) in the organisation are handled is likely to be of crucial importance. Association with an existing élite, or support by that élite, can help build a power base. Similarly, association with a change agent who is respected or seen to be successful can help a manager overcome resistance to change. It has already been seen in this chapter that the breaking down or, indeed, dismantling of such élites is also a powerful means of overcoming resistance and signalling change.

3. Similarly how the *subsystems* of organisations are handled will be important. Building up alliances and a network of contacts and sympathisers, even though they may not be powerful themselves, may later be important in overcoming the resistance from more powerful groups. Certainly the building of a team of individuals, perhaps within a manager's own department, but strongly supportive of the activities and beliefs of that manager will be helpful. The danger here is that existing élites may regard the building of a strong team around a manager as a threat to their own power which needs to be minimised. Resistance to change is unlikely to be overcome by attempting to convert the whole organisation to an acceptance of change: it is, however, likely that there are parts of the organisation more sympathetic to that change than others. It is these the change agent will work on to develop that momentum. Moreover, if that group can visibly be rewarded for such enhanced momentum, that is likely to speed the process of overcoming resistance. The danger, however, is that change will be seen as a short term hiccup, that strategic change will be temporary and will slip back into former patterns of behaviour.

The main vehicles for implementing change are therefore to do with communicating and consolidating its acceptance throughout the organisation. Whilst it is important that the more senior levels in the organisation, and particularly the chief executive, are visibly seen to be associated and committed to the change implemented, it is also vital that processes are underway which achieve compliance throughout the organisation. The management of change throughout the subsystems of the organisation might begin within the phase of overcoming resistance; for example, it may be that the change agent has set up committees or projects with representatives throughout the organisation testing out the feasibility of certain changes. In such circumstances these individuals are likely to become not only identified with and party to the changes but also involved in the partial implementation of those changes: it may be that they go back into their functional operations as disciples of change.

4. Finally, as has been seen, the conscious employment of *symbolic mechanisms* of change is likely to be useful. From a political point of view this may take several forms. First, the manager needs to realise that these symbols act to preserve and reinforce the recipe: so, to build power, the manager may consciously seek to identify with such symbols – to work within the committee structures, become identified with the organisational rituals or stories that exist and so on. Conversely, in breaking resistance to change, removing challenging or changing rituals and symbols may be very powerful – means

of achieving the questioning of what is taken for granted. Third, symbolic activity can be used for consolidating change: by concentrating attention or 'applause' and rewards on those who most accept change, its wider adoption is more likely; and there may be means of confirming through symbolic devices such as new structures, titles, and systems of control that the change is to be regarded as important and not reversible.

11.5.2 Problems with managing political systems

The management of change through political mechanisms, though likely to be necessary, is a difficult, and potentially hazardous task. Table 11.6 summarises some of the problems. The problem in building a power base is that the manager may have to become so identified with existing power groupings that he or she either actually comes to accept their views or is perceived by others to have done so, thus losing support amongst potential supporters of change. Building a power base is a delicate path to tread.

In overcoming resistance the major problem may simply be the lack of power to be able to undertake such activity: attempting to overcome resistance from a lower power base is almost bound to be doomed to failure. There is also a second major danger: that is that in the breaking down of the status quo, the inevitably destructive process in the organisation is so fundamental, and will take so long, that the organisation cannot recover from it. If the process is to be gone through, then its replacement by some new configuration of beliefs and the implementation of new strategy is vital and needs to be speedy. And, as already identified, in implementing change the main problem is likely to be carrying the body of the organisation with the change. It is one thing to change the commitment of a few senior executives at the top of an organisation; it is quite another to convert the body of the organisation to an acceptance of significant change. Individuals are quite likely to regard change as temporary: something which they need to comply with until the next one comes along.

11.6 ACHIEVING EXCELLENCE THROUGH PEOPLE AND SYSTEMS

It has been seen that over time organisations are likely to get out of line with the forces at work and requirements of their own environments: this is the phenomenon of strategic drift. Researchers who have examined so-called excellent companies[39] argue that the reason for such excellence is that these organisations are able to avoid such drift, are better able to maintain an alignment with the requirements of their environment more or less continually. How is this possible?

Managers do not reinvent their organisational world every time they face a new situation. They have to employ some set of assumptions or guiding principles to make sense of that world – what is referred to in this book as a recipe. However, if the recipe is necessary so that managers can operate effectively, it is also dangerous, as has been seen, because it is likely to create the sort of drift that the organisation must avoid. There is, therefore, a need for the maintenance of a system of beliefs, but at the same time the ability to challenge and change that system of beliefs. 'Excellent' organisations appear to have the ability to do this simultaneously; they are what Peters and Waterman call 'simultaneous *loose–tight*' organisations,[40] and how they manage through the organisational systems can be used to draw together much of what has been covered in this chapter.

These are organisations which have a 'clear culture'. That is, members of the organisation clearly identify with what that organisation is about. However, within such an organisation there is also the facility to readily challenge assumptions and current ways of operating. Managers in these organisations seek to encapsulate core, underlying strategies into over-arching goals and expectations which form a coherent philosophy for that organisation; they have a clear mission which is owned throughout the organisation. Further, it is likely to be reflected and sustained in the everyday language and working practices of the organisation. It is not just a set of ideas but rather permeates the organisation. Peters and Waterman provide the example of Walt Disney Productions. Here the mission is one of providing happiness through entertainment but it is translated into a set of values and messages which are at one and the same time simple to understand but which require total commitment and intensive training to carry out. Customers are 'guests' who form an audience; employees are 'cast members' and the personnel department is 'casting'; when the employees work with the public they are 'on stage'; total commitment and intensive training is required to carry this through. The point is that the strategy is not shrouded in obscure detail of objectives and plans. These may exist in the organisation but their manifestation is in the everyday lives of those who work at Disney.

Such organisations are also likely to demonstrate other 'loose–tight' properties. The mechanisms for analysis planning and the systems of control in such organisations will be highly developed; there may be centralised decision making and control systems which allow very fast response to change; it is usual in such organisations to be able to get decisions made quickly from the top. However, in addition to this, there is likely to be the facility for the challenging of taken-for-granted assumptions. This may take many different forms: it may be achieved through the organic management systems that exist, giving rise to high degrees of informality between levels of management; it may be that the organisation has a high level of internal competition within it and an expectation, built up over time, that managers will question and challenge each other; it is likely that in such organisations the onus will be on experimentation rather than just doing your job. In such organisations the emphasis will be on systems and structures that encourage the exchange and challenging of ideas across groups and between levels of management, and minimise the extent to which powerful groups can isolate themselves from others or force their views and ways of doing things upon others.

These systems which lead to the ability to challenge and question are likely to be supported in a number of ways. There may be visible 'change heroes' within the organisation, role models with whom employees can identify a successful ability to maintain change. In some organisations this may well be the chief executive, but not necessarily so. Structures are likely to be flat with the minimum degree of enforced hierarchy and the ready ability to cut across functions and job roles. It is likely that, in addition to any formal structures, there will be taskforce or project groupings around particular issues.

Senior managers in such organisations are likely to adopt a 'hands on' approach to management. They may be strategists but they are also involved in the organisation, continually prompting the sort of change and innovation that they, themselves, expect to see coming up from below. They will also appreciate the importance of symbolic support of change. For example, the adoption of modes of behaviour in line with such challenging and questioning is reinforced through visible reward; the rituals and stories evident in the organisation are to do with change rather than history; there is an avoidance of emphasising formal systems to maintain the status quo: rather, the emphasis is on systems which underline the need for change or continual questioning. For example, reward systems, accountancy measures, stock control systems and so on, may actually be used to challenge current management thinking about what can be achieved and how. Illustration 11.5 gives an example of one senior executive who sought to operate in some of these ways.

ILLUSTRATION 11.5

Hands-on leadership in Wrekin District Council

A local authority chief executive seeks, through his personal style, to put management excellence into practice.

Since the publication of Peters and Waterman's *In Search of Excellence*, many chief executives have tried to implement the principles outlined in the book. Central to these is the role of the chief executive in creating a culture of participation, energy, change and closeness to the customer through 'hands on' involvement in the management of the organisation.

Roger Paine became chief executive of Wrekin District Council in 1980. The *Local Government Chronicle* reported on his background and approach to management as follows:

In Telford's new-town atmosphere of constant change and rapid industrial development, Mr Paine has achieved major structural changes. An important element to him is effective communication. In six years he has never sent a written memorandum to any of his chief officers. And they are instructed not to do so to him, because he believes that face to face communication is essential. This is not across an expanse of mahogany either: the small desk in his office is pushed into a corner where no one can be on the other side. And if this seems a novel idea – his predecessor had no desk at all!

He also likes to meet all new employees, and does this by attending the first day of each Corporation Induction Course to talk to new recruits about corporate values and what is expected of them. Mr Paine tries to be as accessible to the public as time will permit, and has found ways of doing this which sustain an impact on both staff and public while keeping control of his time. At intervals during the year he picks at random complaints received from members of the public and visits the complainant personally to discuss the problem and arrange necessary action. Anyone calling in at the main reception desk of the council buildings first thing of a Monday morning is likely to be answered by the chief executive himself: Mr Paine sits there for half an hour every week to receive all enquiries. He learns a lot that way, as well as demonstrating an interest in the Council's everyday work.

Source: *Local Government Chronicle*, 22 August 1986.

In these organisations the aim is to overcome many of the problems of strategy formulation seen in Chapter 2. The aims are to speed up the triggering of the perceived need for change, the lag that can exist between individuals spotting the need for change

---

Clear mission/corporate values

- Owned throughout the organisation
- Relevant to the market

'Loose–tight' systems

- Analysis/planning/control *but*
- Informality/organic management
- Internal competition
- Challenging/questioning approach
- Experimentation

Supported by

- Top management visibility
- 'Change heroes'
- Absence of political élites
- Flat, integrative structures
- Taskforces, project teams
- Symbolic communication

Figure 11.8 Managing change in 'excellent' organisations.

and their response in an organisational sense; and second, to ensure that the response to change is not so dictated by 'managerial experience' that the maintenance of existing strategy becomes inevitable. Figure 11.8 summarises some of the mechanisms discussed here by which this may be achieved.

11.7 SUMMARY

The implementation of strategy involves both the planning of resources and the management of the people in the organisation. Chapter 9 dealt with the planning aspects of strategy implementation. Chapters 10 and 11 have dealt with some of the ways in which people involved in implementing strategy might be managed through the structural and systems design of organisations. This chapter, in particular, has highlighted the need to consider how systems of control and regulation, and the cultural and political systems of organisations are important in terms of achieving strategic change. The chapter has also served to remind readers of the integrated nature of the strategic management problem: in considering how organisational systems might contribute to – or constrain – the implementation of strategy, and by putting into effect systems of control managers are also involved in activities of resource analysis, the analysis of cultural and political systems, in the examination of the feasibility of strategies and in the planning of strategy implementation.

REFERENCES

1. E. Mumford and A. Pettigrew, *Implementing Strategic Decisions*, Longman, 1975, is a report on the research into the introduction of large scale computer systems in four large organisations. The process of implementation was monitored over a period of two to five years.

2. For a fuller discussion of the notion of 'compliance' see A. Etzioni, *A Comparative Analysis of Complex Organisations*, Free Press, 1961.

3. Useful references on control systems are R. N. Anthony and J. Dearden, *Management Control Systems: Text and cases* (3rd edn), Irwin, 1976, and the section on the control process in chapter 7 of L. G. Hrebiniak and W. F. Joyce, *Implementing Strategy*, Collier Macmillan, 1984.

4. See reference 3.

5. Responsibility centres are a useful means of dividing control systems. They have been discussed by many authors, for example: Anthony and Dearden (reference 3) and R. F. Vancil, 'What kind of management control do you need?', *Harvard Business Review*, March, 1973.

6. The dangers of negative monitoring are discussed by L. G. Hrebiniak and W. F. Joyce (reference 3, pp. 200–201).

7. A useful review of research on the relationship between rewards and strategy can be found in J. R. Galbraith and R. K. Kazanjian, *Strategy Implementation: Structure, systems and process*, West, 1986.

8. See 'Now cash is clean again', *Financial Times*, Tuesday, 20 January 1987.

9. See M. S. Salter, 'Tailor incentive compensation to strategy', *Harvard Business Review*, Mar./Apr., 1973.

10. A number of researchers have pointed out that managerially controlled firms tend to follow a growth and size objective in business organisations; for example see R. Marris and A. Wood, *The Corporate Economy*, Macmillan, 1971; and W. S. Baumol, *Business Behaviour, Value and Growth*, Harcourt, Brace and World Inc., 1967.

11. For discussion of the relationship between ownership and managerial compensation see L. R. Gomez-Mejia, H. Tosi and T. Hinkin, 'Managerial control, performance and executive compensation', *Academy of Management Journal*, **30**(1): 51–70, 1987.

12. F. J. Roethlisberger and W. J. Dickson, *Management and the Worker*, John Wiley, 1964, is an interesting book written by two of the Hawthorn researchers of the 1930s. Pages 517–35 describe how cash incentives are not the prime motivation to perform well.

13. Payment by results is discussed in most texts on rewards, personnel management, and often operations management. A useful discussion can be found in G. H. Webb, 'Payment by results systems' in A. M. Bowey (ed.), *Handbook of Salary and Wage Systems*, Gower, 1975.

14. This example is taken from the case study on 'Executive Holloware' by Kevan Scholes available from the Case Clearing House of Great Britain.

15. This issue of group versus individual rewards for managers is discussed by M. White, 'Incentive bonus schemes for managers' (in Bowey (ed.), see reference 13).

16. J. R. Galbraith and D. A. Nathanson explain more fully a number of research findings in the link between 'tolerance for ambiguity' and performance in *Strategy Implementation: The role of structure and process*, pp. 86–7, West, 1978.

17. For a review of different methods of management development see A. Huczynski, *Encyclopedia of Management Development Methods*, Gower, 1983.

18. Figure 11.5 is based loosely on a paper by J. Burgoyne and R. Stewart, 'Implicit learning theories determinants of the effects of management development programmes', *Personnel Review*, 6(2): 5–14, 1977.

19. Chapter 2 of *Theory Z: How American business can meet the Japanese challenge*, W. Ouchi, Addison-Wesley, 1981, explains how such an attitude towards the development of individuals contrasts with many American and UK companies where specialisation is all-important. Ouchi cites this as an important reason for the success of Japanese companies.

20. See R. R. Nelson and S. G. Winter, *An Evolutionary Theory of Economic Change*, p. 14, Harvard University Press, 1982.

21. S. A. Lippman and R. P. Rumelt, 'Uncertain imitability: an analysis of inter-firm differences in efficiency under competition', *Bell Journal of Economics*, 13 (2): 418–38, 1982.

22. Charles Handy's *Understanding Organizations* (Penguin, 1976) is a useful book to be referred to in order to understand components of management style more fully.

23. The terms 'organic' and 'mechanistic' systems of management were introduced by T. Burns and G. M. Stalker in *The Management of Innovation*, Tavistock, 1961.

24. Readers who would like to refresh their memory about the use of the term culture in this book should refer back to Chapter 2 (Section 2.4).

25. The idea of unfreezing and reformulation in achieving change is not new. Kurt Lewin (*Field Theory in Social Science*, Tavistock, 1952) and Edgar Schein ('Personal change through interpersonal relationships' in W. G. Bennis, D. E. Berlow, E. H. Schein and F. L. Steel, *Interpersonal Dynamics*, pp. 237–67, Dorsey, 1973) developed models of change processes upon which this discussion is based.

26. This example is taken from Edgar Schein, *Organisational Culture and Leadership*, Jossey Bass, 1985. Chapter 12 includes a number of examples of culture change mechanisms.

27. The role of a new chief executive in promoting strategic change is noted by both P. H. Grinyer and J-C. Spender in 'Recipes, crises and adaptation in mature businesses', *International Studies of Management and Organisation*, 9: 113–23, 1979, and also by Stuart Slatter in *Corporate Recovery*, Penguin, 1984.

28. Edgar Schein (reference 26) refers to members of the organisation who are not wedded to the recipe as 'hybrids'.

29. The notion that the outsider, in effect, applies his old experience (or old recipe to the new situation) is proposed by Grinyer and Spender (reference 27) and supported by Gerry Johnson in *Strategic Change and the Management Process*, Basil Blackwell, 1987.

30. The term 'destructive processes' is used by N. W. Biggart in describing the processes of change that he observed in the US Post Office, described in 'Creative–destructive processes of organisational change: the case of the Post Office', *Administrative Science Quarterly*, 24: 410–26, 1977.

31. The importance of 'showing through deeds' the effectiveness of change in order to consolidate that change is argued by V. Sathe in *Culture and Related Corporate Realities*, Irwin, 1985.

32. The usefulness of project teams and taskforces is particularly emphasised as a means of partial implementation by Peters and Waterman in *In Search of Excellence*, Harper & Row, 1982.

33. The importance of symbolic activity in managing change is referred to by a number of writers; for example, see N. W. Biggart (reference 30), D. M. Boje, D. B. Fedor and W. M. Rowland ('Myth making: a qualitative step in OD interventions, *Journal of Applied Behavioural Science*, **18**(3): 17–28, 1982) and Tom Peters, 'Symbols, patterns and settings: an optimistic case for getting things done', *Organisational Dynamics*, pp. 3–22, Autumn, 1978.

34. This is a quotation from page 11 of Tom Peter's paper (reference 33).

35. See H. M. Trice and J. M. Beyer, 'Using six organisational rites to change culture', in R. H. Kilman (ed.), *Gaining control of the Corporate Culture*, pp. 374–5, Jossey Bass, 1985.

36. See A.L. Wilkins, 'Organisation stories as symbols which control the organisation', in L. R. Pondy, P. J. Frost, G. Morgan and T. C. Dandridge (eds), *Organisational Symbolism*, p. 85, JAI Press, 1983.

37. This story is told by Tom Peters and N. Austin in *A Passion for Excellence*, pp. 278–81, Collins, 1985.

38. This discussion is based on observations of the role of political activities in organisations by, in particular, Henry Mintzberg in *Power in and around Organisations*, Prentice Hall, 1983, and Jeffrey Pfeffer in *Power in Organisations*, Pitman, 1981.

39. See T. Peters and R. Waterman, *In Search of Excellence*, Harper & Row, 1982; R. M. Kanter, *The Change Masters*, Unwin/Counterpoint, 1985; T. Peters and M. Austin (reference 37); and J.B. Quinn, *Strategies for Change*, Irwin, 1980.

40. The term 'loose–tight' is taken from *In Search of Excellence* (reference 39), p. 318.

Recommended key readings

- The fullest discussion of control systems remains that in the writings of R. N. Anthony. Particularly: *Planning and Control Systems: A framework for analysis*, Harvard Graduate School of Business, 1965, and R. N. Anthony and J. Dearden, *Management Control Systems: Text and cases*, Irwin, 1976.

- For further discussion of reward systems and their links with strategy see chapters 5 and 6 of *Strategy Implementation: Structure, systems and process* by J. R. Galbraith and R. K. Kazanjian, West, 1986.

- For illustrations and explanations of strategic change through cultural and political processes see *Strategic Change and the Management Process* by Gerry Johnson, Basil Blackwell, 1987.

- There have been a number of books published on 'excellence' in organisations. For example, T. Peters and R. Waterman, *In Search of Excellence* (Harper & Row, 1982), T. Peters and N. Austin, *A Passion for Excellence* (Collins, 1984) and M. Kanter, *The Change Masters* (Unwin, 1985).

CONCLUSION

By necessity, textbooks need to be structured and written in a way which allows the reader to systematically develop an understanding of the subject. However, there are dangers in this since the reader may gain an insight into the 'building blocks' which make up the subject but fail to appreciate its 'wholeness'. This is a particular concern with the study of corporate strategy since the essence of the subject is that of 'wholeness' rather than intensive study of the parts.

The point was made at the beginning of the book that the adopted focuses of analysis, choice and implementation may not take the form of a step-by-step process in practice. They are likely to be interrelated and, indeed, it is likely that the emphasis placed upon each will differ according to the organisation and its circumstances.

The simplest way to understand this is by looking at some of the examples which have been discussed in various parts of the book. The purpose of doing so is to show that corporate strategy in all organisations is concerned with managing strategic change but that this process may be achieved in different ways.

- In a large conglomerate or divisionalised company, those employed at the centre or head office may be primarily concerned with *analysis*, trying to understand the company's position, its balance of activities, and the opportunities which exist, perhaps through a corporate planning department. In contrast managers in each division may spend most of their time on *resource planning* and implementing new strategies.
- In a multinational company the corporate management may be absorbed in aspects of *company structure*. For example, whether the company strategy will be more effective if lines of responsibility are shifted from global product divisions to international divisions.
- In contrast, the owner of a small fast growing company may be mainly worried about obtaining the *resources* to capitalise on the opportunities which have been opened up. At a later stage as growth slows the search for new *strategic options* may dominate the strategic thinking in the company.
- Many industrial companies need to spend large sums of money on capital equipment and therefore pay a great deal of attention to the *analysis* and *evaluation* of capital expenditure projects. Retailing companies, however, may have little money tied up in fixed assets (properties can, after all, be sold) and may develop new strategies by a series of small incremental steps where the company learns through *implementation* of ideas.
- In public sector organisations there may be a special need to understand the *political environment* within which decisions are made and implemented.

● In Japan the process of *strategic evaluation* is much more overtly political in the sense that acceptability of proposed changes tends to be tested out much more fully during evaluation than tends to be the case in Europe and North America.

In all of these situations the development of strategy will depend on the development of an understanding of the strategic position (strategic analysis), choosing between possible options (strategic choice) and planning and executing the strategy (strategy implementation). But where the process begins and what the focus of attention is, is likely to change over time, or depend on the position in the organisation from which corporate strategy is viewed.

There is, of course, a danger associated with these differences in emphasis or focus. The danger is that an organisation, or a manager, may come to see strategy in too limited a way, that some of the 'building blocks' will be emphasised at the expense of the 'wholeness' of the problem. A theme throughout this book has been that strategic decision making will depend on the interaction of many management issues and activities, but that above all it is necessary for management to be sensitive to, and develop an understanding of, the overall nature of strategic problems. It is common for managers to fail to do this. They become so familiar with their own functions, or the particular way they have been used to approaching problems, that they find it difficult to conceive of wider issues. Communication on matters of strategic importance is often difficult between different levels of management or between different functions for example. Managers cannot be expected to conceive of problems or opportunities in strategic terms unless they are familiar with concepts and practices of strategic management wider than their own particular experience. The view expressed in this book is that the sort of flexibility, sensitivity and imagination required of managers today at all levels in an organisation can be enhanced by their 'exploring corporate strategy'.

INDEX